CALIFORNIA GREENIN'

**Princeton Studies in American Politics:
Historical, International, and Comparative Perspectives**
Ira Katznelson, Eric Schickler, Martin Shefter,
and Theda Skocpol, series editors

A list of titles in this series appears at the back of the book.

California Greenin'

How the
Golden State
Became an
Environmental
Leader

David Vogel

PRINCETON UNIVERSITY PRESS

PRINCETON AND OXFORD

Copyright © 2018 by Princeton University Press

Published by Princeton University Press,
41 William Street, Princeton, New Jersey 08540

In the United Kingdom: Princeton University Press,
6 Oxford Street, Woodstock, Oxfordshire OX20 1TR

press.princeton.edu

Jacket image courtesy of Lantern Press

All Rights Reserved

ISBN 978-0-691-17955-1
Library of Congress Control Number: 2017959788

British Library Cataloging-in-Publication Data is available

This book has been composed in Adobe Text Pro and Gotham

Printed on acid-free paper. ∞

Printed in the United States of America

10 9 8 7 6 5 4 3 2 1

To
Maximilien and Alexandre Girerd,
the future of California

CONTENTS

Preface   ix

1   Introduction   1

2   Gold Mining: Wealth Creation and
     Environmental Devastation   22

3   Protecting the Land   48

4   Protecting California's Coast   84

5   Managing Water Resources   115

6   Protecting Air Quality   154

7   Energy Efficiency and Climate Change   189

8   California's Regulatory Leadership:
     Broader Implications   231

     Notes   245
     Index   267

PREFACE

While writing *Trading Up: Consumer and Environmental Regulation in a Global Economy* (1995), I found myself looking for a geographic designation to contrast with the "Delaware effect," which has been used to symbolize a regulatory "race to the bottom." After learning how California's stringent regulation of automotive emissions had strengthened those of Germany, its major European trading partner, I chose the term "California effect" to describe how trade liberalization could lead to regulatory "trading up." In a subsequent book, *The Politics of Precaution: Regulating Health, Safety and Environmental Risk in Europe and the United States* (2012), I describe and explain why many European regulations have become more stringent than those in the United States. But this volume also notes an important exception: many of the risk regulations adopted by California more closely resemble those of the European Union than those of the American government.

In those two books I wrote about California's relative regulatory stringency and even identified the idea of "trading up" with the name of the state. But I had yet to ask an important question: *Why* were many of California's regulatory standards so stringent in the first place? Why was the "California effect" named after California? It was precisely to answer this question that I wrote this book.

In writing this book, I have learned several things. First, in spite of having lived in this state since 1973, I realized how little I knew about the history of its environmental policies or indeed its history in general. I was struck by how much has been written about every dimension of the state's environment, including its mountains, trees, lakes, valleys, rivers, coast, bays, and delta. There are also extensive literatures on gold mining and oil drilling; Yosemite and other national parks; California's water management policies; its regulation of automotive emissions; environmental issues in Los Angeles, Santa Barbara, and the San Francisco Bay; and the state's more recent policy initiatives to promote energy efficiency and reduce greenhouse gas emissions. This is in addition to several historical studies of California—most notably the magisterial multivolume history of California by the late Kevin Starr—as well as biographies of key individuals in the state's history such as John Muir, Gifford Pinchot, Frederick Olmsted, and Pat Brown and the informative research of Ann Carlson, Barry Rabe, and Roger Karapin. My work owes an enormous debt to this rich and fascinating literature, which has taught me much and which I have tried to synthesize into a broader narrative.

Second, while my interest in environmental policy had previously primarily been that of a scholar, in writing this book I developed a much stronger appreciation for the importance of environmental protection. I have always been broadly sympathetic to the goals of environmental regulation, but now I came to recognize the critical role such regulation has played in making California and the San Francisco Bay Area such an attractive place for my family and I to live and work. I owe a debt to all those whose efforts during the last 150 years have made it possible for California to remain such a "Golden State." I am pleased to be able to recognize their accomplishments— while also acknowledging their shortcomings.

Richard Walker, now retired from the Department of Geography at the University of California at Berkeley has written extensively on environmental policy in California, and I have been educated by his writings and benefited from his constructive comments on my research. Graham Wilson, Dan Esty, and Chris Ansell were kind enough to read the book in its manuscript form, and Ben Cashore extensively annotated each of the book's chapters. Roger Karapin and Lucas Davis reviewed and commented on the chapter on energy efficiency and climate change. I owe a special thanks to my good friend and former colleague Bob Kagan, who carefully and critically read through the entire manuscript, writing literally hundreds of marginal comments, notes, questions, and suggestions. Their editorial advice, along with that of the two readers for Princeton University Press, has made this a much better book than I could have written by myself. Needless to say, its shortcomings remain my own.

My research assistant, Gaby Goldstein, a doctoral student in the School of Public Health at the University of California, Berkeley, has closely worked with me on this project for the last two and a half years, reviewing, commenting, and correcting numerous drafts and tracking down references. Jae Park provided much-appreciated assistance on manuscript preparation, and Molly Roy and Rob McCaleb prepared the book's maps. Sarah Vogelsong did an outstanding job editing the final manuscript. Finally, I am also grateful for the early and continuing support of Eric Crahan, my editor at Princeton University Press, for this project.

Earlier versions of this research were presented at a colloquium organized by Aseem Prakash at the University of Washington's Center for Environmental Politics, a seminar organized by Ben Cashore at the Yale School of Forestry and Environmental Studies, a panel at the 2015 annual meeting of the American Political Science Association, a seminar organized by Bruce Cain at Stanford University, a conference on corporate sustainability supported by the Borchard Foundation, a workshop organized by Jack Citrin at the Institute for Government Studies at UC Berkeley, and the Oliver Williamson Institutional seminar of the Business and Public Policy Group at the Haas School of Business.

Primary financial support for this project came from the Haas School of Business, which graciously continued to fund my work after I officially retired in June 2015. I also received financial assistance from the Institute for Government Studies at UC Berkeley.

I am pleased to express my appreciation to my daughter and son-in law, Barbara and Michel Girerd, who have marked each recent birthday and holiday by presenting me with yet another obscure but very useful book on California's environment.

This book is dedicated to my twin native Californian grandsons, Max and Alex Girerd, in the hope that the state will remain as beautiful for them when they grow up as it was when they were born. My greatest debt is to my wife, Virginia, whose patience, encouragement, and advice have helped us both survive the writing and endless rewriting of another book.

Oakland, California
September 2017

CALIFORNIA GREENIN'

1

Introduction

The Golden State

The name *California* and its nickname "The Golden State" evoke a distinctive and unusually beautiful natural environment. As Josef Chytry has noted, "No land has been more often associated with the evocative term 'Paradise' than California."[1] The state's most striking attribute may well be its weather, which is arguably the best in the United States. California's geographic boundaries encompass North America's only Mediterranean climate, characterized by winter rain and dry summers. Winters are relatively mild in the coastal areas where most of its population lives, while Southern California has sunshine throughout the year. Most Americans imagine that those who live in California are happier because of the state's benign climate.[2] They believe, as the 1965 hit by the Mamas and Papas declared, "I'd be safe and warm / If I was in L. A. / California dreamin' / On such a winter's day."

The state has an unusually long and beautiful coastline—the longest of any state in the continental United States. The northern two-thirds of this 1,100-mile border on the Pacific Ocean contain much spectacular scenery, while the southern portion features miles of sand beaches. William Reilly has called this coast the "greatest" of the state's abundant natural treasures. "One has only to stand at the continent's western edge, confronting the Pacific Ocean from the California coast," he writes, "to understand the fascination so many people have for this memorable meeting place of land and water."[3]

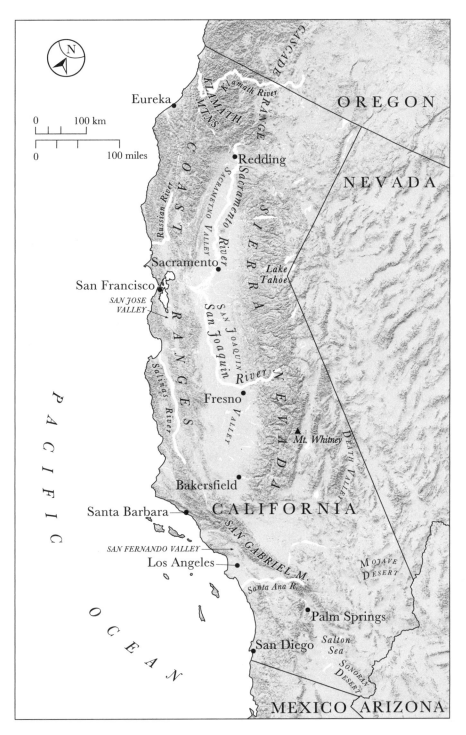

MAP 1. The Geography of California

Inland, the state's forests along the western slopes of the Sierra Nevada contain the sequoias, and those in the northern and central coastal regions are home to the redwoods. These "Big Trees," which are only found in California, are not only the largest and oldest trees in the United States but the largest and oldest living species on the planet. To Kevin Starr, they are "among the natural wonders of the world . . . cathedrals of nature: cool, silent, the products of a profound historicity."[4]

These examples do not exhaust the attractiveness of the state's geography, which also includes San Francisco Bay; the unusual granite formations, rivers, and lakes of the Sierra Nevada Mountains, which form virtually the whole eastern boundary of the state; and the deserts of Southern California. California also contains both the highest (Mount Whitney) and lowest (Death Valley) elevations in the continental United States, as well as more national parks than any other state. For more than 150 years, Yosemite Valley has been one of the best-known and most widely visited scenic attractions in the United States. Not surprisingly, California's beauty and unique geography are two of the primary draws that bring residents and tourists to the state.[5]

Besides its beauty, the "Golden State" nickname also has a second association. According to some accounts, California's name was coined by the Spanish explorer Juan Cabrillo, who derived it from a sixteenth-century Spanish chivalric novel that described the legend of Califia, queen of a "mythical and wondrous land of riches." Upon arriving in what is now California, Cabrillo believed that he had found the physical source of this legend. The name stuck. Ever since, Gerald Nash observes, California "has been a symbol of wealth and abundance."[6]

Throughout its history, California's natural resources have been an important economic asset, with the state benefiting from its mountains of gold and silver, rapidly flowing rivers, thick forests, deposits of oil, and fertile agricultural lands. While its economy has since diversified, California remains the nation's largest agricultural producer and its third-largest oil producer.[7] It has been the nation's most populated state since 1962 and has had the largest gross domestic product (GDP) of any state since 1971. Were California a country, its economy would now be the sixth largest in the world, with its GDP surpassed only by China, Japan, Germany, the United Kingdom, and the United States.

This book describes and explains the long history of California's efforts to protect its unusually attractive but also highly fragile environment. It examines the politics and economics underlying several of the state's most important environmental policy initiatives, beginning with the protection of Yosemite during the Civil War and continuing through the state's ambitious efforts to address the risks of climate change. It then draws upon these policies to explain why this particular state has consistently led the United States in adopting new environmental regulations and why being "greener" has become a central part of California's political identity. Finally, this book highlights the role that states have played and continue to play in making environmental policy in the American federal system—an important and timely subject.

A History of Environmental Policy Innovation

Other states in the United States contain many attractive natural features as well as abundant natural resources. But California is distinctive in one important respect. No other state has enacted so many innovative, comprehensive, and stringent environmental regulations over such a long period of time. Compared to all other states as well as the federal government, California has been a national leader in regulatory policymaking on issues ranging from forestry management, scenic land protection, air pollution, and coastal zone management to energy efficiency and global climate change. Its distinctive geography, high degree of citizen mobilization, business support for many environmental measures, and steadily growing administrative capacity have produced a continuous stream of environmental policy innovations in multiple areas over a long period of time. Consider the following examples, each of which are discussed and explained in the pages that follow:

- In 1864, only fourteen years after California became a state, Yosemite Valley and an adjacent grove of sequoias became the first publicly protected wilderness areas in the United States.
- In 1884, a federal court in northern California issued the nation's first important pro-environmental judicial ruling when it banned the dumping of gold mining debris into the rivers flowing into the Sacramento Valley.
- In 1885, California became one of the first states to regulate logging and promote reforestation, acting in advance of the federal government.
- By 1890, three of the nation's four national parks were located in California.
- In 1947, California enacted the first state air pollution control statute.

- From the 1940s through the 1960s, Los Angeles led all other cities and states as well as the federal government in its research and enforcement efforts to fight air pollution.[8]
- In 1964, California issued the nation's (and the world's) first emissions standards for pollutants from motor vehicles.
- In 1967, California became the only state permitted by the federal government to enact its own automotive emissions regulations.
- In 1969, California established the nation's first coastal protection agency in order to protect the San Francisco Bay.
- In 1976, California's Coastal Commission established the nation's most comprehensive regulations for coastal planning and land use controls.
- In 1977, California adopted the nation's first energy efficiency standards for appliances.
- In 1979, California adopted the first state energy-efficient building code.
- In 1982, California became the first state to introduce "decoupling," which incentivized utilities to meet the state's energy needs through efficiency and conservation measures rather than by building new power plants.
- In 2002, California enacted the world's first restrictions on tailpipe emissions of greenhouse gases. That same year, it adopted the nation's most stringent and comprehensive renewable energy mandate, which has been progressively strengthened. Under current targets, utilities will be required to generate 33 percent of their energy from renewable sources by 2020 and 50 percent by 2030.
- In 2006, California passed the most ambitious climate change legislation ever enacted in North America. The Global Warming Solutions Act required California to reduce its greenhouse gas (GHG) emissions to 1990 levels by 2020—a goal that the state was on target to meet in 2017. Legislation enacted in 2016 extended and strengthened this mandate, requiring GHG emissions to decline 40 percent below their 1990 levels by 2030.

Challenges and Accomplishments

All governments frequently confront the tension between economic development and population growth on one hand and the need to protect the environment on the other. The mobilization of political and regulatory responses to environmental degradation is always difficult and often occurs too late. California has faced and continues to face economic and environmental challenges in protecting its coasts, rivers, valleys, and forests; managing its limited water resources; protecting its air quality; and achieving its climate change goals. In doing so, the state has accepted certain trade-offs: its environmental regulations are an important reason why Californians pay significantly more for gasoline and have among the nation's highest residential and commercial energy rates. Land use and other environmental controls have raised the costs of doing business in the state, increased housing costs, and reduced its share of manufacturing investment and employment.

Reasonable people can and do disagree as to whether California has struck the appropriate policy balance between protection of its environment and growth of its economy and whether in particular cases it has protected its environment too strictly or not strictly enough. Not all of the state's environmental regulations have been either sensible or practicable. Many have been adopted after considerable delay and in some cases only after irreversible harm to the state's natural environment has occurred. Additional regulations are undoubtedly needed. But given the substantial and continuing challenges that it has faced, California's long-standing efforts to protect the quality of its natural environment are noteworthy. Overall, it has done a better job than most states—and certainly the United States as a whole—in balancing the ongoing challenges of integrating economic development and environmental protection. With a population of more than 39 million and a GDP of $2.46 trillion, California remains in both dimensions of beauty and wealth a "golden state."

This book describes what is in many respects a remarkable success story. It demonstrates how a state government has been able to overcome substantial obstacles and enact a wide range of regulations that have made measurable—though admittedly uneven—progress in protecting its environment and improving the quality of life of its residents. Although California has often seemed on the verge of ecological (as well as economic) catastrophe, it has proven remarkably resilient. The state's ability to remain the most important source of environmental policy innovation in the United States over so many decades and across such a diverse range of policy areas is a significant accomplishment. It is worth understanding why and how this particular state came to play such an important leadership role in this area, as well as the broader policy implications of such leadership.

Federalism and the "California Effect"

One key implication of California's leadership on environmental action has to do with the environmental policy role of states in the nation. The United States is a federal system in which states play important roles in shaping policy. This is certainly so in the area of environmental policy. In 1932, Supreme Court Justice Louis Brandeis wrote: "It is one of the happiest incidents of the federal system that a single courageous state may, if its citizens choose, serve as a laboratory; and try novel social and economic experiments without risk to the rest of the country."[9] No state in the United States has exercised its discretion over environmental regulation as extensively as California. In this area, it has been the nation's most "courageous" state and its most important and influential policy "laboratory."

Nor has any state had as much impact on the environmental regulations of the federal government as well as on other states. This pattern of state policy leadership and diffusion has come to be labeled the "California effect."[10] Consistently at the cutting edge of most environmental policy innovations in the United States, California, in the words of Wendy Leavitt, "casts a long shadow across the U.S."[11]

The state's protection of Yosemite in 1864 served as the inspiration for the creation of the nation's first official national park, Yellowstone National Park, in 1872, as well as for the establishment of the Adirondack Forest Preserve in 1883. After other states were given the option of adopting automotive emissions standards set either by the California Air Resources Board or by the federal Environmental Protection Agency (EPA), thirteen states plus the District of Columbia, which account for one-third of all cars sold in the United States, chose California standards. Nine other states follow California's zero-emissions vehicle mandates. The size of California's market, when added to that of those states that have adopted its emissions standards, has given California regulators important leverage over American automobile production. As Barry Rabe has said, "As California goes, at least in air pollution, so goes the nation."[12]

Several of California's most innovative vehicle pollution regulations were subsequently adopted by the federal government, including the requirement that cars be equipped with two-way catalytic converters and use unleaded gasoline. Since the mid 1960s, federal standards for health-related pollutants from motor vehicles have often tracked those of California. Most recently, California's pioneering tailpipe greenhouse gas emissions standards became the basis for rules issued by the Obama administration. According to former EPA administrator William Reilly, "Had California never introduced its groundbreaking clean-cars standards in 2002, we would never be where we are today as a nation—cruising toward 43.5 mpg and growing healthy markets for hybrid vehicles, plug-in hybrids, clean diesels, electric and other innovative technologies."[13] The federal government also followed California's lead by issuing energy efficiency standards for appliances, with other states and many national appliance firms following suit. In the important policy area of global climate change, states have become the most important initiators of regulatory policy in the United States. The state that has played the most active and influential role in addressing the risks of global climate change is California.

Californians have also played national leadership roles in promoting environmental protection. From the later decades of the nineteenth century through the beginning of the twentieth, John Muir was the nation's most prominent advocate of nature protection. Stephen Mather, Horace Albright, and William Kent were instrumental in the 1916 creation of the national park system. More recently, Democratic California congressman Henry Waxman (1975–2015) was an influential supporter of federal environmental legislation, while California governor Arnold Schwarzenegger (2003–2009) was a prominent international advocate of using public policy to address the risks of global climate change.

Following the 2016 election of President Donald Trump, California governor Jerry Brown (2009–present) emerged as a leading defender of environmental "states' rights" in opposition to the deregulatory initiatives of the Trump administration.[14] To the extent that stringent environmental policies are now more likely to come from states rather than the federal government, states such as California represent the future of environmental policy innovation in the United States.

What happens in California also has a global impact. During the 1980s, the relative stringency of California's vehicle emissions standards was an important reason why Germany chose to support the adoption of similar standards by the European Economic Community.[15] Not only was the United States a major export market for German cars, but half of all German car sales in the United States were to California. More recently, according to Mario Molina, a Nobel Prize–winning scientist from Mexico, "the rest of the global economy is looking to California, as one of the world's largest economies, to take the lead" in addressing the risks of global climate change.[16] The state has come to play an increasingly active international role, cooperating with national and local governments throughout the world to reduce and mitigate the effects of greenhouse gas emissions, efforts that accelerated following the withdrawal of the United States from the Paris global climate change agreement in 2017. Understanding California's long-standing efforts and achievements in protecting its own environment and exercising both national and global regulatory leadership is thus both important and timely.

Environmental Threats

California's geography and its environmental policies are closely connected. An important key to California's long-standing regulatory leadership has been the continuous threats faced by its beautiful and abundant but also highly vulnerable and fragile natural environment. As James Parsons argues, "The regional consciousness of Californians, remarkably strong for so restless and rootless a population, has its origins in the common problems and interests imposed by geography."[17] Here, I note a few of the most significant environmental threats that have spurred regulatory action in the Golden State.

Hydraulic Mining. Notwithstanding the iconic image of the "forty-niner" panning for gold flakes in a clear mountain stream, gold mining in California may well have been the most environmentally destructive natural resource development in nineteenth-century America. Beginning in the 1850s, hydraulic gold mining radically transformed the lower Sierras and the Sacramento Valley. As one contemporary observer put it, California "resembled a princess captured by bandits who cut off her hands to obtain the rings on her fingers."[18] Debris from hydraulic mining filled the rivers that flowed from the Sierras, causing them to overflow their banks, periodically flood the cities of the Sacramento Valley—including the state's capital—and cover large acres of formerly fertile farmlands with toxic sludge.

Redwood Extraction. Between 1890 and 1910, one quarter of all the mature redwoods in California were harvested, and the rate of redwood logging subsequently accelerated. The First World War substantially increased the demand for redwoods, which were extensively used at military bases in the United States and France. The newly formed California Redwood Association also began to aggressively pursue international markets opened up by the construction of the Panama Canal. As one scholar summed it up, "All in all, 1917 was a terrible year to be an old redwood."[19]

Oil Production. During the first decades of the twentieth century, California led the United States in oil production. More than 1,000 oil wells were drilled within the city limits of Los Angeles, and more than 100 offshore wells were dug in Southern California, filling the region's beaches with derricks, drilling piers, fences, and pipes and leaving them fouled by oil spills. It was not uncommon for people to sunbathe surrounded by oil rigs. Both on the beaches and in residential areas, wooden derricks, open oil tanks, and spilled crude oil often caught fire, and there were frequent explosions of natural gas.

Air Pollution. In the 1940s, a haze obscured Catalina Island off the coast of Los Angeles as well as the mountains to the east. It was not uncommon for the smog to engulf the city, causing myriad respiratory ailments in its citizens.[20] The nearly 3 million cars registered in Los Angeles County in 1956 represented "the greatest concentration of motor vehicles in the world."[21] Thanks also to its topography and industrial and population growth, the Los Angeles region soon had the worst air quality in the United States. During the 1970s, Los Angeles averaged 125 Stage 1 smog alerts per year—more than any other American city.

Coastal Oil Spills. In 1969, the largest offshore oil spill in the United States up to that date occurred off the coast of Santa Barbara. By the time the leak from the well was finally sealed, it had deposited between 2 and 3 million gallons of oil in the Santa Barbara Channel. The spill impacted 800 square miles of ocean and coated more than thirty-five miles of coastline with deposits of oil up to six inches thick.

Coastal Degradation. While California's state constitution legally guarantees public access to the coast, during the 1960s only one-fifth of that area was available for public use.[22] By 1960, nearly a third of the San Francisco Bay had disappeared as a result of land reclamation, with the rate of infill also accelerating.

Energy and Climate Change. In 1972, a government report predicted that unless California was able to reverse its current trajectory of increasing energy consumption, utilities would need to construct an additional 130 new power plants by 2002, with their emissions expected to adversely affect the state's air quality and their construction to threaten the state's scenic areas, including its coast. A 2004 report provided a quantitative estimate of how California would be threatened by global climate change. Specifically, a rise in summer temperatures would increase the risks of forest fires, while warmer winters would reduce the size and density of the snowpack in the Sierras, endangering the state's water supply. California would also experience rising sea levels along its Pacific shore.

Key Policy Decisions

The above examples of environmental degradation are not unique to California, especially prior to the 1970s. Before that time, oil development often led to a deterioration of environmental quality both in urban areas and along the country's coastlines. As bays and rivers became highly polluted, cities also experienced deteriorating air quality or expanded by filling in their bays. Much of the coast along the southern and eastern borders of the United States became publicly inaccessible, and substantial deforestation occurred in many states. Global warming also adversely affects other states. However, it does not necessarily follow that because a state's environment has been threatened, it will choose to strengthen its environmental regulations. Certainly, many states have responded to such challenges differently.

In California, things could just as easily have not turned out so well: the state could have readily become a "paradise lost."[23] At many critical junctures, policymakers in California could have made different policy decisions. The debris flowing from the foothills of the Sierras could have continued unchecked until all the gold was exhausted. Many more of the redwoods could have been cut down for lumber. The air in Southern California could have continued to deteriorate, and its beaches could have continued to be used for oil drilling. Public access to and use of the coast could have been increasingly restricted, coastal oil drilling could have continued to expand, and the San Francisco Bay could have been steadily filled in. Likewise, the state could have met its increasing demands for energy by continuing to build more fossil fuel power plants.

None of these outcomes occurred, however, because at several key points, California enacted public policies that halted, slowed down, or reversed much of the environmental deterioration that had taken place or threatened to take place. *California's attractive geography gave it the potential to be a desirable state in which to live, invest, work, and vacation. But without effective government regulation, that potential would have been squandered.* What distinguishes California, then, is not that its current environmental quality is necessarily better than that of any other state. Rather, its distinction—and achievement—lies in its ability to maintain a relatively, and in some respects remarkably, beautiful natural environment in the face of the magnitude of the threats posed to it—threats rooted in the state's distinctive geography and exacerbated by its continuous and often-rapid economic and population growth.

Explaining California's "Greening"

How can we account for California's "greening"? The state's unique geography has played an important role in shaping both the threats the state has faced and how it has responded to them. Had California contained fewer valuable natural resources, its environment would have been less threatened. Had California's environment been less beautiful, there might have been less public and business support for defending it against such threats. But geography does not by itself create public policies.

This book demonstrates the importance of three interconnected political, economic, and institutional factors that have shaped the state's policy responses to the threats and opportunities created by its geography: (1) citizen mobilization, (2) business support for critical environmental policy initiatives, and (3) the state's regulatory capacity. These factors' relative roles in shaping particular regulatory policies have varied, but collectively they help us understand why California's environmental policies have long been so distinctive.

CITIZEN MOBILIZATION

For a critical number of residents, living in California has been associated with the expectation of being able to enjoy, experience, or benefit from the consumption of a wide range of (public) environmental goods. This in turn has helped create an influential political constituency that has supported environmental regulation. Such values and interests have deep historical roots. The formation of the Sierra Club in 1892 by a group of academics, professionals, and businessmen from the San Francisco Bay Area gave expression to a distinctively California relationship to the outdoors, one that reflected "a deep California hope: that a regional heritage could be defined and protected," as well as enjoyed.[24]

In this context, it is important to appreciate the political importance of the highly visible threats to California's environment that have emerged throughout the state's history. This visibility has made it easier for citizens to become mobilized. Californians could actually witness the destruction and defacement of the ancient groves of sequoias and redwoods, the destructive impact of the debris-filled rivers flowing from the Sierras, the deterioration of air quality in the Los Angeles Basin and other urban areas, the oil rigs on the beaches of Southern California, the devastation of the oil spill in Santa Barbara, the loss of public access to California's coast, and the filling in of the San Francisco Bay.

An important reason for the broad political support that many of the state's environmental policy initiatives have enjoyed has been the benefit many Californians have received from those initiatives. Environmental regulations have made a material difference in the quality of life of Californians: they can visit the state's beaches, engage in nature recreation, enjoy the coastal views of the ocean, and, perhaps most importantly, breathe cleaner air. None of those public goods would have been as available without extensive government regulation.

The phrase "not in my backyard," or NIMBY, has been typically used to describe the narrow self-interest of local residents opposed to developments that adversely affect their particular neighborhood. But looked at more broadly, such a concept can help illuminate the extent of public support for environmental regulation in California. Historically, the state's citizens have focused on protecting environmental amenities that, for them, have been located in their "backyards."

The intensity and extent of grassroots support for environmental protection in California may be related to the fact that many of California's cities are located close to the state's unique natural wonders.[25] This in turn has given many of the state's urban residents a sense of "ownership" toward them: they are part of their (public) property. Richard Walker writes:

> The unity of country and city is evident in the San Francisco Bay Area. People here have commonly been immersed in the city *and* in love with the country, notably Yosemite, Lake Tahoe and Big Sur. . . . The most cherished environments of the Bay Area have often been ones nearest the city, because they have been the most accessible, the most visible, and the most threatened. These are sainted venues like Muir Woods, Napa Valley and Point Reyes.[26]

Much the same is true of Southern California. The region's warm and sunny weather, along with its beaches and ocean views, is a major part of the attraction of living there. This has given its residents a strong material interest in protecting its air quality as well as opposing oil drilling offshore and on its beaches. After all, what is the point of living in Southern California if you have to breathe unhealthy air or are unable to enjoy its beaches, sunshine, and ocean views?

Historically, much environmental activism in California has been rooted in local geographic threats. For example, coastal oil drilling was opposed by those from Southern California, smog was originally seen as a problem only for those in Los Angeles, and the protection of the sequoias in the Sierras and the redwoods along the coast primarily engaged those who lived in the San Francisco Bay Area. But in the late 1960s and early 1970s, the "backyard" of Californians became defined more broadly: rather than "not in my city" or "not in my region," their opposition to environmental threats came to mean "not in my state."

This broader geographic perspective, or emergence of a "green" state political identity and culture, is clearly reflected in three events: the broad statewide opposition to the proposed federal preemption of automobile emissions standards in 1967; the 1972 backing for coastal protection by voters in both northern and Southern California; and, more recently, widespread public support for state policies to address the threats posed by global climate change to the state's forests, coast, and water supply.

Another important change has marked citizen mobilization in California. During the nineteenth and early twentieth centuries, much environmental activism was elite driven. The memberships of the Sierra Club, Sempervirens Club, and Save-the-Redwoods League were relatively small and dominated by professionals and businessmen. But over time efforts to protect the state's environment began to mobilize larger numbers of citizens. The campaigns to improve air quality in Los Angeles, protect the San Francisco Bay, and ensure public access to the Pacific coast during the middle decades of the twentieth century were largely grassroots affairs. More recently, the growth in the number, size, and influence of environmental organizations in California has played a critical role in the enactment of state policies to promote energy efficiency and reduce greenhouse gas emissions.

BUSINESS SUPPORT

Had a unified business community opposed the regulatory policies supported by citizens and civic groups in California, far fewer of them would have been enacted. But the politics of environmental protection in California have typically been characterized by a lack of business unity. The interests of business have frequently been divided, with some firms and industries supporting more stringent standards and others opposing them. Significantly, the more politically influential firms or industries have had a financial stake in placing California on a "greener" growth trajectory.

Throughout its history, numerous important business interests in California have supported stronger environmental protections. These include the railroads that wanted to protect the sequoias in the Sierras in order to profit by bringing more tourists to California, the farmers in the Sacramento

Valley whose property was being damaged by the debris from gold mining, the shoreline real estate developers who wanted to keep oil companies off the beaches and out of offshore waters in Southern California in order to make the coast a more attractive place to live and visit, and the real estate and other business interests in Los Angeles that feared that the city's worsening air quality would threaten the region's economic growth.

More recently, firms and investors in California's large and influential clean technology sector have backed many of the state's climate change initiatives. The state's renewable energy sector was largely created by state regulatory requirements and then became an active advocate for expanding them. Policies to promote the sale of electric cars to help meet the state's climate change goals have been backed not only by car manufacturing firms based in California such as Tesla, but also by the state's utilities, which are eager for new sources of revenue from electric vehicle charging stations.

Baptist–Bootlegger Coalitions. The division of business interests over environmental issues has made possible the formation of alliances called *Baptist–bootlegger coalitions*—with "Baptist" referring to civic or environmental organizations and "bootleggers" to members of the business community with green policy preferences.[27] These parties have often cooperated to challenge business firms and industries advocating weaker environmental regulations. For example, during the 1940s and 1950s, both citizen groups and the Los Angeles Chamber of Commerce supported controls on automotive emissions, which were in turn opposed by the Detroit-based car manufacturers. In 2010, the state's clean technology firms cooperated with environmental organizations to defeat the efforts of oil companies to roll back the state's GHG emissions reduction goals. In sum, an important reason why California has been able to adopt and maintain so many relatively stringent, comprehensive, and innovative environmental regulations is *that many of these policies have created both public/collective goods and private/pecuniary benefits.* As will become clear throughout this book, Baptist–bootlegger alliances in California have been both frequent and influential.

REGULATORY CAPACITY

A third component of the state's long record of environmental policy leadership has been the growth in its regulatory capacity and the quality of its public administration. Starting in the Progressive Era, California began to give regulatory authority to a wide array of professionally managed, quasi-independent boards and commissions. These bodies include the Fish and

Game Commission (established in 1909, although preceded by the Board of Fish Commissioners in 1870, the first wildlife conservation agency in the country), the Public Utilities Commission (established in 1911 as the Railroad Commission), the California State Parks and Recreation Commission (established in 1927 as the State Park Commission), the California State Lands Commission (established in 1938), the Water Resources Control Board (established in 1967, although preceded by the State Water Pollution Control Board established by the Dickey Water Pollution Act of 1949), the Bay Conservation and Development Commission (established in 1965 and the nation's oldest coastal zone agency), the California Air Resources Board (CARB; established in 1967), the Coastal Commission (established in 1972), and the California Energy Commission (CEC; established in 1974), along with several regional air and water boards and commissions.

These regulatory institutions, whose number and scope have grown over time, have enabled California to develop its own regulatory expertise and administrative capacity independent of the federal government. The most important of these has been the CARB, which during its fifty years has developed into what Carlson calls "one of the most sophisticated and well-regarded environmental agencies in the world."[28] With the largest staff and budget of any state environmental regulatory body, the CARB is second in size and influence only to the federal EPA. In light of its impressive record in improving the state's air quality, in 2006 the state legislature gave the CARB sweeping authority to administer the state's wide-ranging efforts to reduce greenhouse gas emissions. The CARB was also the regulatory agency that played a critical role in documenting and exposing the Volkswagen "dieselgate" scandal in 2015.[29]

Taken together, the measurable and often visible accomplishments of the state's regulations and regulatory institutions have created and sustained a political tradition that has placed a high value on regulatory policy innovation. Being a national environmental leader has become part of the state's political identity.

Other Explanations

These three factors—citizen mobilization, business support, and the state's regulatory capacity—are what I consider to be the primary drivers of California's "greening." But other factors too may have played a role in this process. Here I examine several other possible drivers.

California's physical distance from Washington, DC, may well have contributed to the state's history of regulatory independence on environmental matters. But it is important to recognize that geographic distance from the nation's capital could just as easily have led California in the opposite direction of supporting weaker environmental regulations, as some other western states and Alaska have done.

Similarly, the state's relative geographic isolation—its western border is the Pacific Ocean and its eastern the high Sierra Nevada mountain range—may have played a role in its policy trajectory. Unlike many other states, most notably in the Northeast and the Midwest, much of California's air and water pollution both originates in and remains within the state. This geographic autonomy has made it possible for the state to internalize both the costs and the benefits of many of its pollution control policies.

What about the importance of California's wealth or the size of its GDP? California's pattern of environmental policy innovation long predates its relatively recent emergence as a "rich" state. Moreover, California ranks fifteenth among American states in per capita income. In addition, Texas, Florida, and Illinois are among the five states with the largest GDPs—and none have played leadership roles in environmental protection.

Nonetheless, there are three important ways in which the relative size of California's economy has had an impact on its environmental policies. The first has to do with the capacity of its public administration. California has benefited from important economies of scale in the management of regulatory agencies such as the CARB or the California Energy Commission. States with smaller GDPs may well have found it more difficult to develop and support regulatory bodies with sufficient scientific and technical expertise to craft so many of their own regulations (though this would not explain why other large rich states have not done so). Second, the relatively large size of California's market has given the state considerable economic leverage, increasing both the willingness and the ability of national and global firms to make products that meet California's distinctive regulatory standards. Third, both the large size of the state's economy and its relative attractiveness as a place to invest have given the state a certain amount of economic independence, making California less vulnerable to industrial flight in response to excessive regulatory burdens.

Another plausible explanation for California's distinctive environmental policies has to do with partisan politics. In recent years, California has certainly become the "bluest" of states. The 2016 elections marked the seventh consecutive time the state's electoral votes went to a Democratic presidential candidate. California last elected a Republican senator in 1994, and in 2017, thirty-seven of the state's fifty-three members of the House of Representatives were Democrats, as was the state's two-term governor and two-thirds of its legislature. With the exception of Governor Arnold Schwarzenegger, no Republican has been elected to any of California's eight statewide offices since 2006. California is now one of only six states in which Democrats control both the governorship and both houses of the state legislature. In light of the increase in partisan polarization over environmental regulation in general, and climate change in particular, it would certainly be plausible to ascribe California's "green" policy preferences to the electoral strength of the Democratic Party and the electoral weakness of the Republican Party within the state.

That, however, would be reading the present into the past. Notably, the state's most important global climate change policies were enacted with the strong backing of Republican governor Arnold Schwarzenegger (2003–2011). Republican governor Ronald Reagan (1967–1975) signed the legislation establishing the California Air Resources Board, the Bay Conservation and Development Commission, and the California Energy Commission, as well as the California Environmental Quality Act. The 1988 California Clean Air Act was signed into law by Republican governor George Deukmejian, while the Coastal Commission's authority was expanded during the administration of Republican governor Pete Wilson (1991–1999). The state's 1967 campaign to persuade Congress to allow California to have its own automotive emissions standards was backed by its entire congressional delegation, including its two Republican senators, Thomas Kuchel and George Murphy. Looking further back, the state's first air pollution control statute was signed by Republican governor Earl Warren (1943–1953).

Nor has California always been such a solidly Democratic state. With the exception of the 1964 election, Republican presidential candidates carried the state from 1952 to 1988. Of the state's nine governors since 1953, five have been Republicans. Through the 1980s Southern California was largely a conservative Republican Party stronghold. Yet this did not prevent its citizens from opposing local oil drilling, backing stronger controls on automotive emissions, and voting for the 1972 California Coastal Initiative.

In sum, California's history of environmental policy innovation owes at least as much to a Republican Party that has included politicians and voters who have supported environmental regulation as it does to the recent electoral strength of Democrats within the state. More recently, the relative political weakness of the Republican Party in California compared to its electoral strength at the national level has increased the divergence in environmental policymaking between Sacramento and Washington. However, in 2017, eight Republican members of the state legislature supported the extension of cap-and-trade.

A Lighter Shade of Green

However, the depiction of California as a "green" state needs balance. It is important to note that California's environmental performance has also had important shortcomings, which also need to be explained. Two of the most significant involve motor vehicles and water management. Both are linked to the interaction of public policy and geography.

First, because of both its land use patterns, which have promoted suburban sprawl—especially in Southern California—and the extensive construction of freeways throughout the state, motor vehicles have always been and remain a significant source of harmful air pollutants in California. This has been especially true in Los Angeles, the topography of which has exacerbated its air pollution levels. Notwithstanding the state's considerable progress in reducing vehicular emissions, six of the seven American cities with the worst air quality are in California.[30] Steady increases in the numbers of personal and commercial vehicles owned and miles driven represent a major challenge to the state's ability to maintain its air quality and achieve its long-term goal of reducing greenhouse gas emissions. Californians may care about their environment, but they also need and want to drive their cars. Currently, the state has more than 18 million registered vehicles, double the number in Texas or New York, and Californians are driving more than 332 billion miles a year.[31]

California finds itself on a treadmill. The more it grows economically, the greater the challenges it faces in protecting its fragile environment. A larger GDP means more cars and trucks, which exacerbate the state's levels of air pollution, as well as produce more congestion. Most critically, the more rapidly the state grows, the more difficulty it will face meeting its ambitious long-term greenhouse gas reduction goals.

The most effective way California could better protect its environmental quality and the quality of life of many of its residents while simultaneously reducing its carbon footprint would be to grow more slowly. This, however, would be a political nonstarter, a reality that reveals an important limit to the state's embrace of environmentalism. Californians value both economic growth and environmental quality. Compared to the federal government and many other states, California may be *relatively* "green," but both its economy and the lifestyle of its citizens are far from "sustainable."

California's second major environmental shortcoming has to do with the state's water management. In this case, geography has not been kind to California. Because the state receives no precipitation for most of the year and most of this precipitation falls in the northern part of the state—while most of its population resides in the south—California must store and transport significant quantities of water. Consequently, no state has so extensively transformed—and often disfigured—its natural watersheds. The construction of 1,400 dams and 1,300 reservoirs has led to the damming of virtually all of the state's formerly free-flowing rivers, the inundation of valleys throughout the state, and the draining of several lakes. These actions have also led to the shrinkage of the Sacramento–San Joaquin Delta, which is responsible for two-thirds of the state's water supplies, as well as damages to its marine life.

While this extensive hydraulic management system made possible the state's urban growth along its coasts, promoted flood control, and allowed greater irrigation of farmlands, its overextension permitted the expansion of agriculture into parts of the state that are essentially deserts. Few states have used water as prodigiously or as inefficiently as California, especially for agriculture. The demand for water in California appears inexhaustible: the more that is made available, the more that is used, and the more that is used, the more that is demanded. At the same time, global warming threatens the state's water supplies.

When it comes to water management, the three broad factors that have shaped the state's other environmental regulations have remained influential but have had the opposite policy impact to those seen elsewhere. Historically, Californians have strongly supported the expansion of the state's water management initiatives, consistently voting for bond issues to finance them at both the local and state levels. Until relatively recently, there had been little public interest in protecting the interior rivers and valleys where much of the state's hydraulic infrastructure has been constructed. On this issue, business interests have been unified: both agricultural and urban businesses have all wanted more abundant water. Alliances between citizens and business interests have thus weakened rather than strengthened environmental protection. Finally, it is precisely the expansion of the public sector's administrative capacity that has made possible the development and management of the state's extensive water management infrastructure.

Both these examples illustrate the important trade-offs that California has faced and the often-uneven progress it has made in protecting its environmental quality. They also offer important insights into some of the constraints governments face in protecting the environment.

The Scope of the Book

This book presents a selective rather than comprehensive history of environmental policy in California, omitting many important policy areas ranging from chemical regulation to the regulation of stationary sources of air pollution and giving many of the state's environmental accomplishments and shortcomings less attention than they deserve. Rather, its aim is to provide a sweeping historical overview of several of the most critical environmental challenges California has faced and explain why and how it has responded to them.

The following six chapters each explore a different dimension of the state's history of regulatory policy innovation. They focus, roughly chronologically, on the environmental impacts of gold mining, the protection of forests and other scenic areas, coastal protection, the management of water resources, automobile emissions, and energy efficiency and global climate change. The concluding chapter reviews the key themes of the book and explores some of its broader implications, including the geographic roots of environmental activism, the role of business in environmental policymaking, and the economic and political constraints faced by regulators. It also discusses the increasingly important role states are playing in environmental protection in the United States and shows how California has economically benefited from its environmental policy leadership.

2

Gold Mining

WEALTH CREATION AND ENVIRONMENTAL DEVASTATION

The discovery of gold in the Sierra foothills in 1848 literally created the state of California. But the geography of those foothills and the valley into which their rivers flowed also made gold mining one of the most environmentally destructive natural resource activities in nineteenth-century America. It sharply divided the business interests of northern California, leading to a prolonged and bitter battle between mining companies and farmers in the Sacramento Valley. This conflict was finally resolved by a federal court decision in 1884 that banned hydraulic mining—the first important environmental ruling issued by a federal court. This decision was issued in San Francisco by a California judge, illustrating the important role played by the state in the history of pollution control in the United States.

This chapter, which begins by exploring California's early history, demonstrates the critical role played by both geography and public policy in shaping the state's early economic development, the environmental impacts of that development, and the state's efforts to address those impacts. It underlines the critical policy importance of divisions within the business community, without which it is unlikely that hydraulic mining would have been forced to end when it did. It also describes the modest beginning of the development of the state's administrative capacity with the establishment of the Office of the State Engineer and the hiring of a skilled staff of engineers

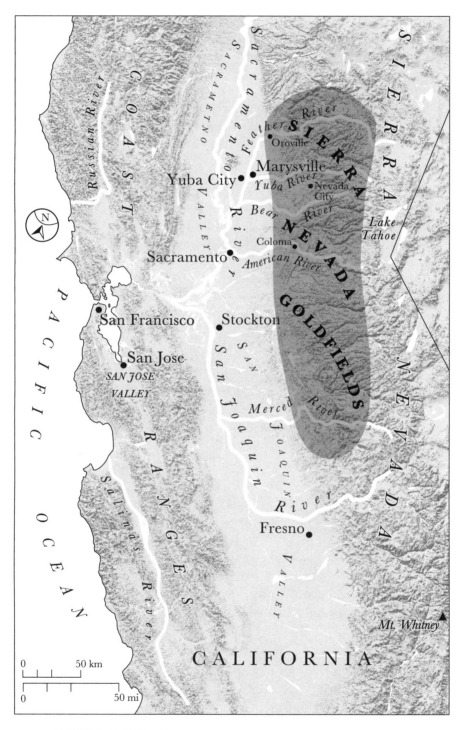

MAP 2. Gold Mining in California

to examine the state's water problems. Finally, this chapter introduces the critical importance of the management of water resources to California's economy and its environment—a topic that will be further explored in chapter 5, which describes the extensive hydraulic management system that came to be constructed and managed by the public sector.

However, on one dimension, the story told in this chapter is distinctive. While both hydraulic mining and its banning had important environmental impacts, conservationists were not engaged in this decades-long battle, which was essentially fought over competing property rights. Rather, as the next chapter will discuss, during the nineteenth century, they were primarily interested in protecting Yosemite and the sequoias in the Sierras.

Early History

California's geography, which features extensive forests, abundant wildlife and fish, a long coastline, and numerous inland waterways, historically enabled the region to sustain an unusually large Native American population. Prior to Western settlement, it is estimated that approximately 350,000 Native Americans lived in what is now the state of California.[1] This figure represents an estimated 13 percent of North America's native population and a population density greater than that in any region north of Mexico.[2]

Access to water was critical to the viability of the state's Native American population—a pattern of dependence on water resources that has continued to the present. Native American villages tended to be located on the banks of watersheds. Prior to Western settlement, northern California's principal rivers, the Sacramento and the San Joaquin, flowed uninterrupted into valleys, marshes, bays, and ultimately the ocean. The state's Central Valley, located between the Sierra Nevada Mountains and the coastal mountain ranges, included numerous rivers, lakes, and marshlands that were in existence all year round, and fish, game, and waterfowl were abundant.[3] Throughout the state, some 23 million acres of dense forests grew alongside the rivers, streams, and wetlands. The forests were home to tens of thousands of game animals, including rabbits, bears, elks, antelopes, small deer, and bighorn sheep, as well as several varieties of edible plants. Inland rivers and lakes, several of which were then larger than Lake Tahoe, also contained large quantities of rainbow trout and king salmon, while sea mammals such as whales, dolphins, seals, sea lions, and sea otters, as well as shellfish, flourished along California's long Pacific coast.

EUROPEANS ARRIVE

The region's abundant natural resources impressed its first Western visitors. When Francis Drake's global expedition landed in California in 1579, a member of the team reported finding "a goodly country, and fruitful soyle, stored with many blessings fit for the use of man: infinite was the company of many large and fat Deere, which we saw by the thousands."[4] Otto von Kotzebue, who visited the Sacramento Delta in 1824, recalled, "There was such a superfluity of game that even those of us who had never been sportsmen before, when once they took the gun in their hands they became as eager as the rest."[5]

However, within the Spanish Empire, California was a backwater. Indeed, the only reason the Spanish crown sent expeditions north from Mexico to settle there during the mid-1700s was because it feared that England and France had designs on the territory. Otherwise, the Spanish largely ignored their northern possession along the Pacific coast, concentrating their colonizing efforts on exploiting the valuable gold and silver found in Central and South America. As Norris Hundley has noted, "Few, except missionaries, wanted to go to such a forlorn place where nothing even remotely valuable had been found."[6] In 1776, California contained only seventy-two inhabitants of European descent; a half-century later, that number had risen only to 3,000.[7] Virtually the entire European population lived along the coast, mostly in and around largely economically self-sufficient missionary settlements, though after Mexico became independent from Spain in 1821, there was a considerable increase in commercial cattle ranching.

AMERICANS ARRIVE

One of the first American citizens to visit the area that would become California, Captain Robert Shaler, commented favorably on the state's climate—an appraisal that would subsequently be echoed by millions of residents and visitors to the state. He noted that "the climate of California generally is dry and temperate, and remarkably healthy," and that "on the western coast the sky is generally obscured by fogs and haze, but on the opposite side is constantly clear; not a cloud to be seen day or night."[8] During the 1820s, American fur trappers began to arrive in California, and by 1830 the Hudson Bay Company had established a trading post near what is now San Francisco. Attracted by published accounts of a rich yet still unsettled and unexploited land, immigrants began to arrive overland from the United States during the

1830s. In 1841, the Western Immigration Society based in Missouri started to lead organized groups to California to establish permanent settlements. Other groups of American settlers, including the ill-fated Donner Party, followed in their path. But the region's nonnative American population remained small: through 1848, it numbered fewer than 15,000.

California was ceded to the United States in 1848 by the Treaty of Guadalupe Hidalgo following the Mexican War. The interest of the United States in acquiring California was similar to that of the Spanish Empire a century earlier: the United States feared the designs of England and France on this strategically located territory. Otherwise, California was of marginal interest to the United States—certainly compared to the acquisition of Texas, with its fertile agricultural lands and much larger number of American settlers.

The Gold Rush

DISCOVERY AND POPULATION GROWTH

The same year that California was acquired by the United States, an event took place that fundamentally transformed the region economically, politically, and environmentally. Nine days before the Treaty of Guadalupe Hidalgo was signed, but still unknown to its negotiators, gold was discovered by one of the workmen at a sawmill owned by John Sutter at the confluence of the American and Sacramento rivers. *Harper's Weekly* described the find as "perhaps the most significant, if not the most important event of the present century connected with America."[9] Soon, upward of 4,000 men were working the streambed of the American River, washing gravel to obtain flakes and nuggets of gold.

In almost every way possible, the Gold Rush changed California.[10] It was the discovery of gold that enabled the realization of the mythical promises of riches that had given the state its name three centuries earlier. Virtually overnight, McWilliams has noted, "California became a world-famous name, and as a name, California meant gold." Starr adds: "The Gold Rush established for better or worse, the founding patterns, the DNA code of American California," a code that made the state exceptional.[11]

Shortly after the discovery at Sutter's mill, William Sherman, a U.S. Army officer stationed in California, sent a letter to Washington informing the federal government of the existence of large deposits of gold, which he described as "enough to pay the costs of the present war with Mexico a hundred times over."[12] His letter arrived just in time for President James Polk's annual message to Congress. In this speech, the president announced that "the accounts of the abundance of gold in that territory are of such an extraordinary character as would scarcely command belief." He also reported that "nearly the whole of the male population of the country has gone to the gold districts. Ships arriving on the coasts are deserted by their crews and their voyages suspended for a want of sailors."[13]

Polk's message led to a massive migration to California. Within the year, more than 150,000 "forty-niners" had arrived in California from other states, Europe, and Asia. Within two years, the region's nonnative population had increased twenty-fold. This sudden population growth made possible the territory's unusually rapid transition to statehood. In 1850, just two years after the territory had been ceded to the United States by Mexico, California became the nation's thirty-first state.

CALIFORNIA THE STATE

The speed of California's transition not only from a foreign territory to a state but also from being fairly undeveloped to a major center of economic activity and population growth was unique and unprecedented.[14] It had made the transition from territory to statehood faster than any other American state. By virtue of having essentially skipped the territorial phase experienced by every other state added to the union, California had little initial experience of federal rule or authority. This in turn fostered what Carey McWilliams has called "a spirit of independence and a tradition of bold action."[15] The fact that California was the first of eleven western states to be admitted to the union also made the state into a kind of political laboratory for both state and federal policies toward the West, one of the earliest examples of the state's broader policy impact.

What also made California distinctive was its geographical isolation from the settled parts of the United States. Its eastern border was 2,000 miles from the western edge of the frontier. The state was separated from the nearest eastern settlements by both the two highest mountain ranges in the United States and hundreds of miles of desert and rocky wasteland. Thus, as part of the United States, California was as remote from its major population centers and the center of government as it had been under Spanish and Mexican rule. As the historian Theodore Henry Hittell wrote, "Other new states were in substance merely the expansion of the outer boundaries of older states; but California . . . developed as a distinct and for the time being a disconnected organization."[16]

Measured in terms of comfort, money, and time, California prior to the completion of the first transcontinental railroad in 1869 was actually nearer to China and South America than it was to Mississippi. An American president did not visit the state until three decades after California was admitted to the union. Its geographic isolation during its formative decades provided it with an early tradition of independence from the national government—one that would subsequently be reflected in many policy areas, including environmental policy.

Water and Property Rights

THE LEGAL FRAMEWORK

The discovery of gold led California's courts and legislature to develop a new type of water law, one based on the principle of "first in time, first in right."[17] This principle of first possession gave individual miners and subsequently mining companies the same legal claim to any water resources they accessed as they had to the minerals themselves. Both claims were based on the principle of first appropriation, a legal doctrine adopted from Spanish law.

In 1855, the California Supreme Court ruled that "however much the policy of the state, as indicated by her legislation, has conferred the privilege to work the mines, it has equally conferred the right to divert the streams from their natural channel."[18] This principle of water rights was subsequently codified by the California legislature. The doctrine of prior appropriation eventually came to be adopted as water law in all other western states—an early example of California's broader policy impact, albeit one that facilitated the exploitation rather than the protection of natural resources.

California's policies favoring miners' control of water resources were also influenced by earlier legal developments in other states that had moved away from the English common law principles of riparian law, which had both restricted property rights regarding streams and rivers to those who lived along their banks and protected those water rights from injuries caused by upstream users. As part of this shift, Horwitz has argued, "the idea of property underwent a fundamental transformation . . . to a dynamic, instrumental, and more abstract rule of property that emphasized the newly paramount virtues of productive use and enjoyment."[19]

But California went a step further: it allowed any individual (or company) who first came upon any body of water, even if he or she did not own property adjacent to it, to enjoy unrestricted use of it. This enabled the forty-niners to use any water they could find to fill their sluice boxes and subsequently granted hydraulic mining companies unlimited access to the rivers, lakes, and streams of the Sierras. What become known as the "California Doctrine" was later adopted by several other states.[20]

California's courts also assisted the development of gold mining in another important way. They restricted the ability of landowners whose property had been injured by overflows from or breaks in mining company ditches to bring claims for compensation. Judges also made it more difficult for property owners to seek redress for the damages that resulted from poorly constructed dams or reservoirs. In 1858, for example, the California Supreme Court overturned a lower court ruling that had awarded damages to plaintiffs whose land had been flooded by a break in the reservoir of a water company. It held that the construction and safety standards imposed by the lower court "imposed impossibly high burdens on water companies and hydraulic miners."[21]

FEES AND ROYALTIES

At the time of discovery, virtually all of the land on which gold was found belonged to the federal government, which was the primary landowner throughout the western region. With the sudden arrival of more than 150,000 prospectors in California, the federal government faced the challenge of managing these suddenly valuable lands. Officials in Washington initially hoped to maintain the federal government's property rights while at the same time encouraging private mineral development.

However, this task proved impossible. Hundreds of meetings were held throughout the state to oppose any federal control over public lands in California, including the taxation or collection of fees from the miners or mining companies. Although Congress considered several proposals to address the question of land rights in California, such as leasing lands for a fee or selling them off in small parcels, it ultimately took no action, leaving the question of royalty payments to be decided locally. One federal military official told the miners: "This is public land and the gold is the property of the United States; all of you here are trespassers, but as the Government is benefited by your getting out the gold, I do not intend to interfere."[22] In fact, his disavowal of military action was only symbolic, since the federal government lacked a sufficient military presence in California to either evict the miners or demand payments from them.

Between 1849 and 1858, California produced more than $550 million worth of gold. This figure represented one-third of total global gold production and was greater than the entire monetary gold stock of the United States.[23] The issue of whether the government had the right to revenue derived from mining on federal lands was put on hold by the Civil War and did not reemerge until 1865. However, the state's representatives in Congress, who had close ties with the gold mining industry, strongly and effectively opposed government efforts to collect revenues from the gold found on federal lands in California.

In 1866, Congress enacted the Mining Act, which both affirmed that *all* mineral lands in the public domain would be open to exploitation and occupation and confirmed the titles of the miners to any federal lands that they had substantially improved. Six years later, the federal government effectively gave up its right to collect fees from mining on public lands. This policy was subsequently applied to sheep grazing on public lands in the West—another early example of the national impact of a policy that originated in California, though hardly one conducive to responsible land management.

Gold Mining

PLACER MINING

The forty-niners prospected for gold using the labor-intensive technique of panning in the waterbeds of rivers and streams. In this process, they loosened the dirt and gravel of the streambeds and shoveled it into sluices, where it was washed and any gold extracted. These "placer" deposits, which yielded high concentrations of the mineral, had been washed downstream from the mountains over millions of years. However, the unevenness of water flows presented a problem. High water levels in the spring made it difficult for miners to access the gravel beds. Alternatively, during the summer, when stream flows receded, there was insufficient water with which to wash (pan for) the gold. In order to control water flows, groups of miners laboriously built reservoirs, ditches, and dams, but these structures were often poorly constructed and frequently collapsed.

For all the romance surrounding the forty-niners, within a few years virtually all the easily accessible deposits of gold flakes in the region's rivers and streams had been exhausted. In the hillsides above Nevada City, several shafts were sunk clear to the bedrock of the ancient streambed. One miner wrote home: "The whole valley has literally been dug up and washed over and these heavy forest trees have been undermined and actually dug up by the roots."[24] However, most of the laboriously dug shafts in the hillside yielded little or no gold.

In the spring of 1852, a miner named Anthony Chabot was breaking down a gravel bank that contained gold with a pick and then shoveling the gravel into a sluice for washing. It occurred to him that he could greatly speed up his work by tapping into the water in a ditch on the hill above him with a hose made of canvas. The force of the water from the hose would wash more gravel into his sluice, which he could then loosen using hand tools. As gold was much heavier than gravel, once dislodged, it would settle to the bottom of the sluice. In other words, the water itself would do the digging. This technique, originally called ground-sluicing, spread rapidly, since it made it possible for miners to "wash" considerably larger amounts of gravel each day. The following year, a tinsmith developed a tapered nozzle of sheet iron that could be affixed to the canvas hose. This invention enabled a strong, concentrated stream of water to be directed at the gravel, significantly increasing its dislodgement capabilities. Gold mining now became much more productive. It was now possible for one man with proper equipment to collect more gold in a day than a dozen forty-niners could have found in weeks.

HYDRAULIC MINING

The stage was now set for hydraulic mining, a technology that would radically transform both the gold mining industry and California's environment. This technology moved water by ditch, flume, or pressurized pipes into high-pressure water cannons, which weighed almost a ton "and could wash away hillsides, meadows, stands of timber, and even mountains in their entirety."[25] Although hydraulic mining had been used by the Romans, its efficiency and effectiveness were considerably enhanced by the new technologies that were developed and fabricated in the foundries of Marysville and Sacramento.

One innovation, developed in 1861, tripled the amount of water pressure that could be produced. A more important one, introduced in 1870, consisted of an iron monitor, or nozzle, with a six- to ten-inch bore. Labeled the "Little Giant," it released a concentrated stream of water that could tear open a hillside hundreds of feet away. The most powerful of these nozzles required six to eight adults to hold them, and some were so heavy they had to be anchored by steel and iron. The water that flowed from them was, in the words of a contemporary observer, "worried and rumbled and beaten into foam until one might easily believe that it comes out with not merely the force of gravity, but also with a wicked, vicious, unutterable indignation." Before it, huge rocks would "fly like chaff."[26] Robert Kelley describes a typical example of this extraordinary technology:

> A large hydraulic mine was an awesome sight. From a water ditch above the mine, large sheet iron pipes, 11 to 22 inches in diameter, dropped 400 to 500 feet to giant cast-iron nozzles or monitors. . . . Shooting from the monitors in 6 to 8 inch streams, the roaring shafts of water could be turned against an auriferous bank with great effect from a distance of several hundred feet. . . . Gravel, boulders, and dirt melted away before the jet and were carried off in a continual flood. The debris and water then catapulted down the main shaft. . . . At the bottom of the shaft it flowed into an enormous sluice . . . a giant descendent of the device used by the forty-niner.[27]

Mines continually sought to maximize this technology's output. One eight-inch nozzle at a mine in North Bloomfield was capable of discharging 185,000 cubic feet of water an hour, with a speed of 150 feet per second, or over 100 miles per hour. Some large mines employed several high-speed hoses, which were operated throughout the night, illuminated first by oil-burning locomotive headlights and then by electric lights after 1879. Periodically, the water flow was stopped to enable mine workers to extract gold from the sluices into which the water and solid material extracted from the hills and mountains had been deposited.

HYDRAULIC WATER MANAGEMENT

By its very nature, hydraulic mining required a secure, predictable, and abundant supply of water. Indeed, even an efficient mining operation used more than 200 million parts of water to recover one part of gold. As the *San Francisco Bulletin* observed, "Abundance of water is essential to profitable mining."[28] Fortunately for the miners, the Sierra Nevada Mountains receive one of the heaviest snowfalls in the world, averaging ten feet per year. When the snow melted in the spring, great quantities of water flowed into the rivers from the Sierras. However, during other months, water flows were insufficient. Moreover, even when water was readily available, it still had to be collected, stored, and then transported to the mines, many of which were located far from rivers and streams.

This need for water led to the first large engineering project in California: the construction of an elaborate network of dams, reservoirs, canals,

aqueducts, pipes, nozzles, tunnels, and sluices. The substantial capital investments required for hydraulic mining transformed the nature of the mining
industry. Individual prospectors were displaced by large firms capable of making substantial investments, many of which were headquartered outside the
state and often outside the United States. Miners then became employees.

Several corporations specialized in the construction of large ditch systems designed to meet the demand for water by the mining operations of
the northern Sierra Nevada. One such firm, the Eureka Lake and Yuba Canal
Company, created 700 miles of ditches, one of which was 45 miles long. It
also owned dams, reservoirs, and 247 miles of canals. During the winter and
extending into several months of the dry season, this firm supplied nearly
7 million cubic feet of water per day to the mines located along its ditches.
By 1865, the company had acquired its own mining operations, delivering
85 million gallons of water to widely geographically dispersed sites every
twenty-four hours.

Other mining companies developed their own systems for meeting their
considerable water requirements. The North Bloomfield mine built over
150 miles of ditches, dams, and associated reservoirs to supply its large mining operations, which required 100 million gallons of water a day. A mine at
Smartsville constructed over 110 miles of ditches that crossed public lands.
Another mining operation built four reservoirs that supplied water through a
100-mile network of ditches, flumes, and pipes to sixteen hydraulic spraying
machines capable of releasing over 40 million gallons of water per day—three
times the amount then used by the city of San Francisco.[29]

By the mid-1880s, the largest reservoirs in California covered hundreds of
acres and held more than 7 million cubic feet of water. Some privately constructed dams were more than eighty feet high. All told, mining companies
built more than 6,000 miles of canals, pipelines, and ditches to carry water
from the reservoirs where it was collected and stored to the mines where it
was sprayed on the mountains and hillsides. One flume and aqueduct built
in northern California was seventy miles long and took a year to construct.
During the nineteenth century, hydraulic mining was the largest user of
water in the state.

The construction of aqueducts also enabled mining companies to extend
their extraction operations beyond the valleys of the Sierras. To access mineral deposits opposite Oroville, which had remained unexploited because
of the lack of available water, one company constructed a two-mile-long
aqueduct of iron pipes across a canyon 9,000 feet wide and 800 feet deep.
Another mining firm bored a 500-foot tunnel through the crest of a hill

to deliver water to its mining operations. According to a local newspaper, aqueducts and tunnels "enable[d] experienced miners to work to great advantages places that, a few years ago, were deemed relatively worthless." This expansion anticipated the ways in which the construction of dams, reservoirs, and aqueducts would make "worthless" deserts into profitable farmlands in Southern California years later.[30]

Although hydraulic mining required considerable capital investment, it was also highly profitable. By the mid-1880s, mining companies had produced $300 million of gold from $100 million in investments. Virtually all of this gold had been extracted from public lands, but neither the state nor the federal government ever received any royalties for it. On average, California's mines produced $10 million annually, more than any other industry west of the Rocky Mountains.[31] At its peak in the 1880s, the mining industry employed 20,000 workers, and more than 40,000 people lived in the three counties of the northern Sierras where the gold was located. So profitable was hydraulic mining that a mine in Butte County stopped its production only once in twelve years—for the funeral of President James Garfield.

Devastating Environmental Impacts

While mining produced great wealth, it came at a high price. As one contemporary observer put it, "California . . . resembled a princess captured by bandits who cut off her hands to obtain the rings on her fingers."[32] John Muir wrote, "The hills have been cut and scalped and every gorge and gulch and broad valley have been fairly torn to pieces and disemboweled, expressing a fierce and desperate energy hard to understand."[33] Mark Twain described the Sierra foothills as "torn and guttered and disfigured."[34] A survey of the state's natural resources published in 1868 reported:

> It is impossible to conceive of anything more desolate, more literally forbidding, than a region which has been subjected to hydraulic mining. . . . The whole vista is one of extreme desolation and ruin. . . . By no other means does man so completely change the face of nature. . . . Hills melt away and disappear under its influence. . . . The desolation that remains after the ground, thus washed, is abandoned, is remediless and appalling. Water cannons created craters in the Sierra Foothills, hilltops disappeared and whole mountains were washed away.[35]

During the period of hydraulic mining, an estimated 1.5 billion cubic yards of debris were dumped into the tributaries of the Sacramento

River—approximately eight times the amount of earth and stone removed during the construction of the Panama Canal. The debris and silt from mining operations transformed the river environments of the Sierras and the Sacramento Valley, choking the American, Bear, and Yuba river canyons, in some places up to 100 feet deep.[36] As river bottoms became gradually filled with silt, their water levels steadily rose. By the early 1880s, some rivers, like the Bear, had become so filled with sediment and debris that they had essentially disappeared, while others now flowed far away from their original course. The twenty-five feet of hydraulic mining sediment deposited in the Yuba River shifted its flow a mile away from its original course, while in places the river flowed sixty feet higher than it had in pre–Gold Rush days and its riverbed spread to two miles wide.

While mining debris' impact was most obvious upstream, where boulders and gravel filled in riverbeds, its greatest effect was at the bottom of the watersheds. Large quantities of fine sediments called "slickens" flowed from mountain streams and rivers. This fine sand and clay mud material, which remained suspended in the water and thus was able to travel great distances, filled thirty square miles of Suisun Bay—a shallow tidal estuary that is an extension of the San Francisco Bay—reducing its depth to 3.3 feet. In the 113-square-mile San Pablo Bay, another extension of the San Francisco Bay, the water shrunk to a depth of 2.5 feet. The 272 square miles of the San Francisco Bay lost about eight inches of depth. As Matthew Booker has concluded, "No human impact on San Francisco Bay has been more extensive or had more dramatic effect than the washing of sediment into the bay by nineteenth-century gold miners."[37] To this day, large portions of the San Francisco Bay floor contain soil from the Sierras.

FLOODING

Even prior to the advent of hydraulic mining, the raised and sprawling riverbeds of the Yuba, Bear, Feather, Merced, and American rivers regularly flooded the central flatlands of the Sacramento Valley. But by the 1870s, the drainage system of the lower Sacramento Valley contained so much mining debris that it was unable to absorb even normal levels of river volume. As a result, the Sacramento River and its tributaries "became sources of terror and widespread destruction," and "devastating floods became almost annual occurrences."[38]

A particularly severe flood took place in 1881–1882. That winter, it rained for forty consecutive days, depositing more than 100 inches of water in the Sierra Nevada foothills. The Central Valley floodplain filled with more than

ten feet of water, forcing the newly elected governor of California, Leland
Stanford, to travel to his inauguration in Sacramento in a rowboat. While
unusual atmospheric conditions clearly played an important role in what
was one of the greatest floods in California's modern history, the flood's
destructive impact was magnified by the substantial deposits of sediment
that had reduced the carrying capacity of the rivers that flowed into the
valley. At the time the flood struck, the bed of the Sacramento River had in
places been raised by thirteen feet, and its formerly clear and pure waters
had become muddy. Moreover, when the waters receded, they left behind
considerable quantities of mining tailings.

The debris from hydraulic mining also led to the flooding of Marysville,
Sacramento, and other river towns. While urban residents, like many farmers, built miles and miles of levees to protect their lands and buildings, these
structures' construction was very expensive, and they frequently broke or
were overrun. For example, after river bottoms became filled with silt, causing water levels to steadily rise to twenty feet above street level, the city of
Marysville built what was essentially a walled city to protect its residents
from the Yuba and Feather rivers. In 1875, however, the Yuba River overran
Marysville's levees, completely flooding the town. It took several months
for the city's residents to clear its streets of the muck left behind.

LAND DEGRADATION AND OTHER HARMFUL EFFECTS

Hydraulic mining had an especially harmful impact on the 45,000 acres
under cultivation in Sutter County, which is located in the middle of the
Sacramento Valley between the Feather and Sacramento rivers. These farms
grew considerable quantities of wheat and barley and contained more than
30,000 peach, pear, plum, and cherry trees, as well as 160,000 grape vines
that annually produced 26,000 gallons of wine. Once hydraulic mining
began, however, tens of thousands of acres of the most highly productive
farmland were covered by massive amounts of a watery mixture of sand and
gravel, making them into "barren wastelands" on which nothing would grow.
Overall, 39,000 acres of farmland were buried under the debris, while an
additional 14,000 acres were partially damaged.[39]

At the same time, the sediment from the mines created a chemical
mixture that made the water unfit for irrigation, as well as poisonous to
animals. Compounding the deterioration of water quality was the use by
mining companies of mercury. This highly toxic mineral, which was mined
and processed near San Jose, was added to the water in gold mining sluices

because it adhered to gold and thus facilitated its extraction. Producing mercury became the second-largest industry in California after gold mining. In 1874, it is estimated that mining firms used 1.4 million pounds of mercury. While much of it was recovered along with the gold, a significant percentage remained in streams and rivers. Some of it also vaporized, returning to land mixed with rain and snow.

Economically, the increasing costs of levee construction forced local governments to continually raise taxes, which in turn led to a decline in property values. By the mid-1870s, water from the American and Sacramento rivers contained so much silt from upstream mining operations that it was unfit to drink, and city hydrants produced a mixture of mud and water. In addition, the extent to which mining debris clogged the state's waterways appreciably slowed and sometimes completely halted inland shipping between Sacramento and San Francisco. The latter water route was heavily trafficked. It not only linked California's inland cities and farms with San Francisco but also connected California to the East Coast through oceangoing vessels that traveled between New York and Sacramento. The frequent inability of boats to use this water route created considerable hardship for both farmers and urban merchants in the Sacramento Valley.

Mining also damaged California's forests. Not only did the construction and frequent repair of flumes, sluices, and dams consume large amounts of timber, but the reservoirs that supplied the mines with water often submerged whole forests. The clear-cutting of forests to supply the considerable quantities of timber necessary for hydraulic mining also increased soil erosion, increasing the amount of debris that washed into streams.[40]

DESTRUCTION OF THE NATIVE POPULATION

The debris covering the beds of the Sacramento River and its tributaries also destroyed the spawning grounds of millions of Pacific salmon. Prior to the Gold Rush, the Native Americans who lived in the Central Valley had been able to harvest 9 million pounds of salmon, or approximately 650,000 fish, each year. But by the early 1870s, salmon had disappeared from the Feather, Yuba, and American rivers. In 1878, a government report concluded that hydraulic mining debris had destroyed fully half the salmon habitat in the state.[41]

Along with the destruction of forests, the devastation of rivers, the spread of mining debris, the building of reservoirs, and the construction of mining towns, the destruction of the spawning grounds of salmon destroyed much of the physical environment on which many of the state's Native Americans depended for their subsistence.[42] As game were driven from the region by the mining camps or killed for food by the miners and the formerly clear rivers became clogged with mud, it became increasingly difficult for these people to hunt and fish. Thus, the environmental impact of hydraulic mining in California, combined with the role of the Gold Rush in fostering both vigilante and state-authorized violence, contributed to the extraordinarily rapid destruction of the native population of northern California. By 1880, California's Native American population had declined from approximately 350,000 before Western settlement to between 16,000 and 20,000.[43]

AIR QUALITY

Gold mining in California also damaged urban air quality. The technology employed in hydraulic mining led to major investments in iron foundries, which produced the pipes, nozzles, and monitors needed to extract the gold. During the middle decades of the nineteenth century, gold mining–related activity accounted for 40 percent of capital investment in manufacturing and employed more than half of the state's manufacturing workers. The city of Sacramento, located between the coal mines of Contra Costa and the iron ore deposits of the Sierras, became California's second-largest city and one of its largest industrial centers.

In addition to the solid waste that was a byproduct of iron making, Sacramento's factories also emitted large quantities of hydrocarbons, carbon monoxide, methane, sulfur dioxide, and lead. These air pollutants contributed to various respiratory diseases, as well as to increased rates of cancer, making Sacramento one of the unhealthiest places in California during the nineteenth century.[44]

The Political Response

FARMERS ORGANIZE

During the 1860s, the volume of debris produced by hydraulic mining diminished as a prolonged drought curtailed operations. But as the rains returned in the early 1870s, hydraulic mining resumed, causing the river bottoms to fill up with silt and water levels to rise significantly. As a result, more and more farmlands were flooded and destroyed. It was in this context that the first organized protest against hydraulic mining took place. In 1873, a group of farmers filed suit against the Spring Valley Mine. They asked for a permanent injunction against all mining activity and $2,000 in damages as compensation for the destruction of an orchard located six miles down-stream from the mine.

However, the farmers were unsuccessful: the state court denied the damages sought by the plaintiffs on the grounds that there was no way to assign liability to a particular mine, since more than fifty mining companies had dumped debris into the same stream. Moreover, the court concluded that the mines had a powerful property rights claim since they had begun their operations before most of the valley had been farmed. Nonetheless, the lawsuit was historically significant, representing one of the earliest legal challenges to industrial pollution in the United States and signaling a division of business interests over the control of water pollution.[45]

Three years later, in 1876, another farmer turned to the courts for relief, with a slightly different legal strategy. James Keyes, a farmer whose house and 400 acres of farmland in the Bear River Valley had been buried beneath three feet of mud, concluded that if the courts would not allow suits against individual mining companies, then why not sue *all* the mines that were dumping debris into a particular river? Accordingly, he filed a lawsuit asking the Yuba District Court to issue an injunction against all nineteen mines in the region that were dumping debris. As Keyes put it: "I have no objection to the miners digging all the gold they can find. I just don't want them to send the whole hill down upon my ranch and bury me and all I have."[46] Much as the members of the Sierra Club described in the next chapter or the residents of Los Angeles described in chapter 6 would later do, Keyes and his fellow farmers were responding to a local environmental threat that personally affected them—one that was taking place in their "backyard."

Because this legal action threatened not just the named defendants but the entire mining industry, it alarmed the San Francisco business community, whose financial institutions were closely linked to the industry. A number of these companies joined together to form the Hydraulic Miners Association (HMA), becoming the first California business organization to oppose environmental controls. The farmers in turn established the Anti-Debris Association of Sacramento Valley and raised $170,000 in support of their efforts. The latter organization can be legitimately viewed as California's first pro-environmental lobby, even though its goals had nothing to do with environmental protection. The stage was now set for a major political and legal battle between competing business interests over pollution control.

Immediately, however, the HMA faced a stumbling block. As Judge Phil Keyser of the Yuba District Court owned a farm on the Yuba River that had been damaged by mining debris, the mining companies did not want to appear before him. Accordingly, the HMA attempted to move the suit into the federal courts. Two years later, the U.S. Supreme Court decided that the federal government had no jurisdiction and returned the case to the state courts. In 1879, judicial proceedings commenced in the Yuba District Court. There, Judge Keyser heard testimony from Keyes and other farmers about the damages inflicted on their properties by mining debris, while the mining companies countered that the economic benefits of mining outweighed any harm their operations might have caused. Supporting the position of the mines, a San Francisco business publication editorialized: "It is an open question whether the existence of a half dozen villages like the city of Marysville is of as much importance to the State of California and the country as large as the existence of hydraulic mining."[47]

Nevertheless, Keyser ruled in favor of Keyes, basing his decision on the riparian doctrine that the tailings constituted a "nuisance," and issued an injunction prohibiting the mines from depositing debris into the Bear River or its tributaries. His ruling was immediately appealed to the California Supreme Court, which invalidated the injunction on the grounds that even if the activities of each of the defendants contributed to the plaintiff's damages, they could not be sued as a group because they had acted separately. While the mining towns were overjoyed, the farmers were extremely frustrated: they had now been told that they could not sue *either* an individual mine *or* a group of mining companies.

THE STATE LEGISLATURE RESPONDS

While their suit was still tied up in the courts, the farmers turned to the state legislature for aid. Politically, northern California was divided. Many legislators from the agricultural districts of the Central Valley strongly opposed hydraulic mining, while those from the Sierras and San Francisco, which derived much of its wealth from gold mining, were its strongest advocates. For their part, merchants in the cities of the Sacramento Valley were divided: while mining debris physically threated the cities and towns in which they worked and lived, the mining companies were also important customers.

In 1878, the legislature struck a compromise by creating a special committee on mining debris. Its report, which was issued two years later, graphically described a fertile farming countryside that had been laid waste by hydraulic mining.[48] In its accounting, over 70,000 acres of farmland had been either buried by debris or partially destroyed. Total debris was estimated at more than

70 million cubic yards, with some deposits estimated to be as much as 100 feet deep. The report persuasively discredited the claim of the mining companies that they were not responsible for the debris in California's rivers. Even a minority report, written by pro-mining members of the legislature, conceded that a substantial portion of the debris clouding the rivers, altering stream courses, and producing severe flooding came from hydraulic mining operations.

Despite these findings, the legislature overwhelmingly defeated a bill that would have prohibited the dumping of mining debris in rivers. Undoubtedly the legislators were influenced by the minority report's finding that while the annual damage to farmers caused by debris totaled around $2 million, this figure was substantially less than the annual contribution of gold mining to the state's economy. Celebrating the vote, a San Francisco newspaper editorialized: "The miners have a legal right to use the natural channels for the outlet of their sluices, and even if they did not, it would be policy to give them that right, for the State would not afford to do without the $10,000,000 or $12,000,000 obtained from the hydraulic mines annually."[49]

But following a heated debate in Sacramento, the legislature did enact the Drainage Act of 1880. The first pollution control statute enacted in California, this act required the mining companies to build dams under state supervision to catch the debris from their operations. It also created the Office of State Engineer and provided for the hiring of a skilled staff of engineers who would examine the state's water problems. This action marked the beginning of California's administrative efforts to manage the state's water resources. This office subsequently established the state's first public works project, the construction of a comprehensive system of levees and dams that would act as flood controls. It would be financed by a statewide assessment.

However, the Drainage Act proved short-lived. While the city of San Francisco, which sought to protect the growing volume of agricultural exports that were flowing into the city, supported the new regulations, regions unaffected by mining debris protested having to pay for the flood control projects, and there were allegations of corruption in the awarding of contracts. Moreover, many farmers distrusted the construction of brush dams, since when they broke, they increased the amount of mud and gravel that was spilled into the area. The mining companies largely ignored the new restrictions. Only one year after its enactment, the California Supreme Court ruled the Drainage Act invalid. The court held that the management of mining debris was a private rather than a public matter and that the legislature thus lacked the authority to tax everyone in the state for the benefit of a few.

RETURN TO THE COURTS

After the state court's ruling on the Drainage Act, it was clear that the state lacked the expertise or authority to develop or require the implementation of any kind of regulation that might ameliorate the destructive impact of hydraulic mining. Furthermore, the ruling ended any hope of compromise between the miners and the farmers; rather than focusing on debris, the latter were now determined to put an end to hydraulic mining entirely.

In 1882, Edwards Woodruff, a New Yorker who owned farmland in Marysville, brought a lawsuit in the federal circuit court based in San Francisco against the North Bloomfield Mining and Gravel Company, the state's largest hydraulic operation. Supported by the Anti-Debris Association, the suit also named several other mining companies as defendants and asked for a permanent injunction against hydraulic mining. What brought this lawsuit under federal jurisdiction was the plaintiff's claim that the debris discharged by the mines had entered navigable rivers, which the U.S. Supreme Court had found in *Gibbons v. Ogden* (1824) to be under federal jurisdiction.

Woodruff v. North Bloomfield Mining and Gravel Company was assigned to be heard by Judge Lorenzo Sawyer. A distinguished jurist, Sawyer had immigrated to California in 1850 from Wisconsin. In 1863, he was elected to a six-year term as a justice of the Supreme Court of California. In December 1869, President Ulysses S. Grant nominated him to the U.S. Circuit Court for the Ninth Circuit (which subsequently became the U.S. Court of Appeals for the Ninth Circuit), and he was confirmed by the Senate the following year.

The first issue before the court in *Woodruff v. North Bloomfield Mining and Gravel Company* was whether the several mining companies named as defendants could be held jointly liable. In April 1883, Judge Sawyer ruled in favor of the farmers, reasoning that "the final injury is a single one and all defendants cooperate in fact in producing it."[50] He noted that while only some farmers and mining firms had been named in the suit, the case actually involved two entire industries, each of whose associations had financed their respective legal claims. With this obstacle to the issuance of an injunction removed, Judge Sawyer then proceeded to collect evidence. By the end of the case, the special commissioners he had appointed had questioned 200 witnesses and compiled 20,000 pages of testimony. The judge himself personally made several trips along the relevant rivers, to the surrounding farms, and into the mines.

Finally, on January 7, 1884, the judge issued his eagerly awaited decision. Taking more than three hours to read and consisting of more than 225 pages, what became known as the "Sawyer decision" described in detail how mining debris had injured the Sacramento Valley and its residents. In addition to damaging the property of others, the practice of dumping debris from hydraulic mines was found to have severely impaired the navigability of the Sacramento and Feather rivers. With no feasible way of preventing the mining debris from reaching the valley floor or flowing into navigable rivers, Sawyer's decision permanently enjoined the defendants from "discharging or dumping into the Yuba River . . . tailings . . . cobblestones, gravel, sand, and clay debris or refuse matter."[51] This historic ruling ended hydraulic mining in the Sacramento Valley, effectively shutting down the industry that had helped give the Golden State its name. Moreover, as a federal court decision applying federal law, Sawyer's ruling could not be overridden by the California legislature, in which the mining firms enjoyed considerable influence.

It was now the turn of the farmers and urban residents of the Sacramento Valley to celebrate. Fireworks exploded all over the city of Marysville, and taverns filled up with revelers.[52] The large mining operations were forced to shut down, spurring a major economic depression in the northern Sierras as 20,000 miners left the region. For a while, the illegal use of water cannons persisted on isolated hillsides, but thanks to the efforts of the Anti-Debris Association, those mining operations were eventually closed down as well. By 1886, the previously accumulated debris had worked its way through the waterways, and the rivers flowing from the Sierras were clear for the first time in decades.[53] Ironically, the hard mineral sediments that had been dislodged by hydraulic mining and washed downstream by floods would prove useful in the construction of flood control levees to protect delta farmlands.

Like many common law legal decisions of the nineteenth century, especially those involving riparian issues, *Woodruff v. North Bloomfield Mining and Gravel Company* essentially involved competing property rights. It pitted the economic interests of two important California industries, gold mining and farming, against each other. But because the exercise of the former group's property rights had such negative environmental impacts, the Sawyer decision was de facto an environmental decision—one of the earliest and most important such rulings issued by a federal court. For, as Raymond Dasmann has noted, "if gold mining had not been stopped, the gold hunters might well have washed all the soil and loose rock from the Sierra into the Central Valley."[54] The Sawyer decision marked an important departure from the dominant common law jurisprudence in both California and the United States that had held corporations harmless for the damages caused by their "productive" business activity. After the Sawyer decision, the courts recognized, as Ziebarth put it, "the necessity of state-imposed restraint on private industry for the purpose of conservation."[55]

The Sawyer decision's impact extended far beyond the protection of the property of the Sacramento Valley farmers who had brought the suit. It also cleaned up California's northern streams and rivers, making it again possible for fish to thrive; helped protect San Francisco Bay, which had become muddied by mining debris; and made the Sacramento and Feather rivers navigable again. The decision not only ended the flooding of the state's forests by privately constructed reservoirs but significantly benefited residents of the Sierra floodplain by reducing the risks of flooding. Finally, it improved air quality by ending the discharge of mercury into waterways and closing many of the factories that produced the materials for hydraulic mining. In sum, it ended decades of widespread destruction of both private and public property. For the United States in the nineteenth century, this was a highly unusual achievement.

To be sure, the growth of agriculture in California would create a new set of adverse environmental consequences, ironically related to the construction of an extensive hydraulic infrastructure, which would become as important to agriculture as hydraulic mining had been to gold mining. The "embattled farmers" of the Sacramento Valley would subsequently morph into California's agribusinesses, which would play a critical role in the state's environmental transformation—and often destruction—by supporting the construction of an elaborate network of reservoirs, canals, and dams. But in the second half of the nineteenth century, the region's economic transition from gold mining to farming did appear to place northern California on a greener growth trajectory.

In the late nineteenth and early twentieth centuries, many environmental laws, rules, and judicial decisions adversely affected specific industries. They raised these operations' costs and in some cases forced individual facilities or small groups of firms to shut down. But few, if any, environmental decisions in the history of the United States have had such major economic consequences as the Sawyer decision, which effectively ended the industry that had created the state of California and had been its most important source of wealth for more than a third of a century. In one fell swoop, this ruling destroyed hundreds of millions of dollars of private investment, eliminated thousands of jobs, and devastated the economy of the lower Sierra mountain region.

Two factors helped make such an important shift possible. The first was California's geography. Few natural resource developments in the United States during the nineteenth century were as broadly and brutally destructive as hydraulic mining. Nor were any of these operations located so close to major population centers or situated upstream from important commercial activity. The second was the increasing economic importance of agriculture. California's farmers had begun cultivating wheat as early as the 1850s to feed the miners' demand for bread. By 1860, the state was producing 7.5 million bushels of wheat annually, and by 1870, that number had risen to 20 million bushels. As early as 1869, more of California's workers were employed in farming than in mining, and by 1879 agriculture had overtaken mining as the major producer of wealth in California. Thanks to the manufacturing of steam-powered farm equipment in Stockton, wheat cultivation in the Central Valley steadily increased. In 1884, the same year that the Sawyer decision banned hydraulic mining, California led the United States in wheat production, producing more than 57 million bushels in one year and becoming the breadbasket of Europe. In short, *gold mining could be effectively ended because there was a viable economic alternative to it.* Indeed, realizing the potential of that alternative *required* that it be halted.

In effect, the Sawyer decision can be usefully viewed as a kind of judicially mandated industrial policy, one that both reflected and reinforced a new basis for economic growth in California: agriculture. Significantly, the Southern Pacific Railroad, the most politically powerful firm in the state, worked behind the scenes to support the farmers. Its advocacy was due to the increasing importance of agriculture to the state's economy and thus the future revenues of the firm.[56] In short, like many environmental policies, Sawyer disadvantaged some businesses while advantaging others.

Broader Implications

The politics of hydraulic mining demonstrate the importance of divisions within the business community to environmental protection in California. *The key to ending the environmental destructiveness of gold mining was the opposition of those who were economically harmed by it.* This pattern of inter-industry conflict over environmental policy would occur frequently over California's history. However, in one important respect, the conflict over hydraulic mining was unusual. In contrast to virtually all the other environmental policy disputes discussed in this book, the hydraulic mining debate was a purely inter-business battle, with no engagement from citizen groups: that is, there were "bootleggers," but no "Baptists."

What also made this conflict's resolution distinctive was the critical role played by the courts. The bureaucracy that the state established to address the problems of flooding in the Sacramento Valley marked the beginning of California's administrative approach to management of the state's natural environment. This approach would become increasingly important for flood control and subsequently for the reduction of air pollution and the promotion of energy efficiency—each of which required substantial technical expertise. But during the nineteenth century, the state's regulatory capacity was still relatively undeveloped. Hence it was left to the courts to address and resolve this important dispute. Equally importantly, it was a federal court, though one presided over by a California judge and located in California, that ultimately settled the question.

As was true throughout the West, most land in California was owned by the federal government. However, the government took a relatively passive role in its management of this land, allowing gold mining without collecting any revenues and permitting California to establish its own water rights policies. From this perspective, the federal government was complicit in both the frenzied accumulation of wealth and the widespread environmental destruction that characterized gold mining in California. But it was also a federal court that finally ended the destructiveness of hydraulic mining. In a sense, federal policies bracketed the period of gold mining in California.

The conflict over gold mining and the water pollution it produced demonstrates how environmental protection can create private as well as public benefits. The Sawyer decision did impose substantial economic costs, severely disadvantaging mine managers, investors, workers, and local communities in the lower Sierras. Indeed, it was precisely because gold mining was so economically important that it took so many years and so much effort to ban its practice. But in the longer term, the Sawyer decision also *created* substantial wealth by making possible more extensive agricultural production. In the later decades of the nineteenth century, environmental protection was not only compatible with the state's economic growth but actually contributed to it.

Hydraulic mining also demonstrates the critical political and economic role played by the state's distinctive geography. On one hand, California's abundance of gold was critical to its early economic growth. But on the other hand, because of where that gold was located and how it had to be mined, the production of gold adversely affected farmers and urban residents in the Sacramento Valley below the Sierra foothills, in whose "backyard" the debris from gold mining was literally being deposited. Had the lower Sierras where the gold was found been more geographically isolated, and had its mining not so extensively disadvantaged so many property owners, there would have been much less legal and political pressure to end hydraulic gold mining, and its environmental destructiveness would have continued much longer.

Finally, the gold mining conflict demonstrates the critical role of water resources in California. Without access to water—or, more precisely, the development of an extensive infrastructure to store and move water—gold mining would have created much less wealth and ended much earlier. The future growth of California, both in its urban centers along the coast and on its agricultural lands, would be equally dependent on hydraulic management. Much of the same technology that had led to the Sacramento Valley's destruction would now be reconfigured to play an equally important role in the state's growth in the twentieth century—a development that will be explored in chapter 5.

3

Protecting the Land

In addition to gold and fertile land for agriculture, California's geography also contains much scenic beauty. But its attractive natural features, which include Yosemite, the sequoias in the Sierras, and the redwoods along the state's northern coast, have all found themselves under threat at one point or another over the state's history. This chapter explores the effort to protect Yosemite and the sequoias in the Sierras in the nineteenth century and then turns to the more heated conflicts over the fate of the coastal redwoods. As highlighted in the previous chapter, environmental protection in California owes much to divisions within the state's business community. Important business constituencies have had a financial stake in protecting California's natural environment, and their political influence has played a critical role in enacting state and federal policies protecting it. But in contrast to the conflict over hydraulic gold mining—which pitted economic interests against one another—the protection of the state's scenic environment also engaged "Baptists" as well as "bootleggers."

The roots of California's tradition of civic mobilization lie in nature protection. This tradition began with the efforts of a few prominent individuals, including John Muir, Horace Greeley, and Frederick Olmsted, and then became institutionalized in the upper-middle-class Sierra and Sempervirens clubs and the predominantly upper-class Save-the-Redwoods League. Broader grassroots citizen mobilization played a critical role in campaigns to return control of Yosemite to the federal government, expand the size of and increase the funding for state parks, and protect endangered sequoias in the Sierras.

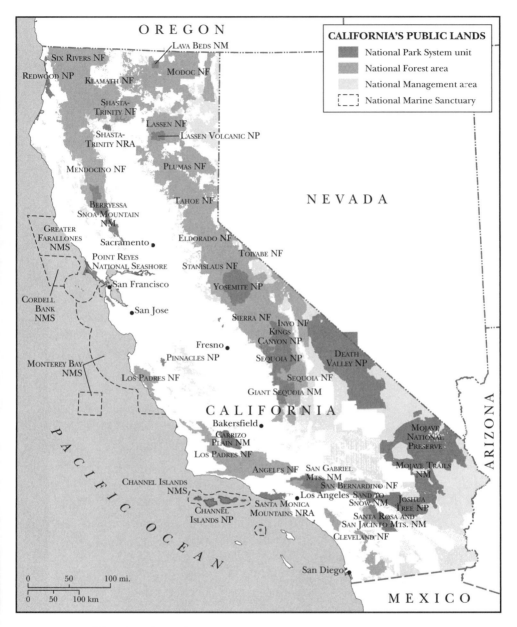

OREGON

LAVA BEDS NM

SIX RIVERS NF

REDWOOD NP   KLAMATH NF   MODOC NF

SHASTA-
TRINITY NF

LASSEN NF
SHASTA-   LASSEN VOLCANIC NP
TRINITY NRA

MENDOCINO NF   PLUMAS NF

NEVADA

TAHOE NF

BERRYESSA
SNOW MOUNTAIN
NM
GREATER   ELDORADO NF
FARALLONES
NMS   Sacramento   TOIYABE NF
POINT REYES
NATIONAL SEASHORE   STANISLAUS NF

San Francisco   YOSEMITE NP
CORDELL
BANK   San Jose
NMS   SIERRA NF
                                 INYO NF
                                 KINGS
                                 CANYON NP
                        Fresno
MONTEREY BAY   PINNACLES NP   SEQUOIA NP   DEATH
NMS   VALLEY NP
        LOS PADRES NF
                                SEQUOIA NF
                         GIANT SEQUOIA NM

CALIFORNIA

                Bakersfield   MOJAVE
                 CARRIZO   NATIONAL
                 PLAIN NM   PRESERVE
        LOS PADRES NF
                                              MOJAVE TRAILS
                        ANGELES NF SAN GABRIEL   NM
                                   MTS. NM
                                    SAN BERNARDINO NF
        CHANNEL ISLANDS   Los Angeles SAND TO
          NMS   SNOW NM   JOSHUA
                         SANTA MONICA   TREE NP
          CHANNEL   MOUNTAINS NRA   SANTA ROSA AND
          ISLANDS NP   SAN JACINTO MTS. NM
                                        CLEVELAND NF

PACIFIC OCEAN

                                        San Diego

0   50   100 mi.
0   50   100 km   MEXICO

ARIZONA

CALIFORNIA'S PUBLIC LANDS

- National Park System unit
- National Forest area
- National Management area
- National Marine Sanctuary

MAP 3. California's Public Lands

The state's administrative capacity to protect California's scenic environment was initially limited, paralleling its inability to regulate hydraulic mining during the mid-nineteenth century. But this capacity subsequently expanded though the establishment of institutions such as the State Board of Agriculture, the State Forestry Commission, and the State Parks Commission.

Yosemite

THE MARIPOSA BATTALION AND THE VALLEY

Yosemite is a deep, glacially carved, virtually enclosed valley in the Sierra Nevada Mountains. Its sheer granite walls, which display a variety of spectacular sculptured forms, rise 3,000 feet from the relatively flat valley floor, and five waterfalls cascade down its cliffs to where the Merced River flows through its trees and meadows. The Yosemite Valley has been inhabited for 3,000 to 4,000 years. While several Native American tribes claimed hunting rights in areas adjacent to it, the largely inaccessible valley was primarily used as a sanctuary by refugees from other tribes. Its occupants were called "Yohe-met'I," meaning in some dialects "they are killers."[1] While located less than 200 miles from San Francisco, the valley was unknown to both Spanish and Mexican settlers, who rarely ventured so far into the steep mountains inland from the coast.

Only weeks after California became a state, violence broke out between gold seekers and Native Americans who lived in the foothills of the Sierras. In January 1851, California governor John McDougall, who was also a gold miner, authorized the creation of the Mariposa Battalion. Comprising 200 men, its mission was to seek out those Native Americans who remained in the Sierra foothills and relocate them to reservations in the Central Valley.

On March 27, 1851, in the course of this mission, the battalion stumbled upon the entrance to the Yosemite Valley and became the first non–Native Americans to look into its chasm. One member of the battalion, a doctor named Lafayette Bunnell, found himself transfixed by the beauty of the narrow valley surrounded by large granite cliffs and the waterfalls that dropped water thousands of feet into the Merced River. "None but those who have visited this most wonderful valley can even imagine the feelings with which I looked upon the view," he wrote. "I found my eyes in tears of emotion."[2]

Bunnell suggested that the battalion give this hitherto "concealed jewel" of the Sierra Nevada Mountains the name "Yo-sem-i-ty," as it was "suggestive, euphonious and . . . by so doing, the name of the tribe of Indians which we met leaving their homes in this valley, perhaps never to return, would be perpetuated."[3] In fact, the Native Americans who had lived in the valley had called it "Ahwahnee," which means "the place of the gaping mouth." The name chosen by Bunnell and his fellow soldiers was actually derived from the Miwok-Paiute word for grizzly bear. But in any event, the battalion had made its mark and put this geographical wonder on the world map.[4]

VISITORS COME TO THE VALLEY

Containing no gold and unsuitable for agriculture, Yosemite quickly became celebrated for its scenery. The valley was difficult to reach, requiring travel from San Francisco or Sacramento by rail, stagecoach, and mule, and once there, accommodations were primitive. Nonetheless, groups of tourists began to visit it. After James Hutchings, a writer and publicist who organized some of these initial excursions, invited the artist Thomas Ayres to accompany him, images of Yosemite were widely reproduced in books and national magazines, making the valley familiar to the broader public. Subsequently, Hutchings brought a photographer to the valley, and his pictures were also widely circulated. Northeastern newspapers and magazines began to feature articles on Yosemite, informing their readers that the "Wild West" contained an unspoiled wilderness that was just waiting for sightseers to explore. These and other promotional efforts helped make Yosemite into a national tourist attraction.

Yosemite also attracted a steady stream of writers and artists from across the United States. Horace Greeley, editor of the *New York Herald Tribune*, visited the valley in 1859 and proclaimed it "the most unique and majestic of nature's marvels," adding that he knew of "no single wonder of nature on earth that can claim superiority over the Yosemite."[5] Another prominent visitor from New York, Central Park designer Frederick Olmsted, described the valley as "the union of the deepest sublimity with the deepest beauty of nature."[6] Ralph Waldo Emerson opined: "This valley is the only place that comes up to the brag about it, and exceeds it."[7] Another visitor, viewing the valley from Inspiration Point, compared it to "the interior of some stupendous roofless cathedral."[8]

Yosemite became an alternative vision of California—a dramatic counterpart to the frenzy of wealth accumulation and despoilation of nature associated with the Gold Rush. It became, in the words of historian Kevin Starr, "a symbol for all that California promised: beauty, grandeur, expansiveness, a sense of power, and a sense . . . of titanic preparation for an assured and magnificent future."[9] Californians, lacking a mythology comparable to the *Mayflower*, made Yosemite a critical part of the newborn state's identity. It became a valuable asset in more ways than one: as scholar John Sears has noted, "In an age when scenery and art were closely identified, Yosemite constituted an unparalleled cultural resource, not only for California but for the entire nation."[10] The valley particularly inspired reformed Protestants from New England, who played a critical role in the promotion of nature protection in California during the second half of the nineteenth century.[11] Thomas Starr King, a minister who had immigrated to San Francisco from Boston and was an important local intellectual leader, preached about Yosemite Valley, describing it as a "sacred place."[12]

Protecting Yosemite

EARLY PROTECTION EFFORTS

Captain Israel Ward Raymond, the California representative of the Central American Steamship Transit Company, became one of the first individuals to push for the valley's protection. Raymond hoped that Yosemite would attract tourists from the East, who would then travel to California on his company's twenty-three ships. However, he worried that loggers and builders would use the trees on the valley's floor for building material and firewood. This would in turn open up Yosemite for livestock grazing and make it less attractive to visitors. On February 20, 1864, he wrote a letter to John Conness, a former gold miner who had recently been appointed to the U.S. Senate by the California legislature.[13]Raymond asked Conness to introduce legislation that would "let the wonders of Yosemite be inalienable forever," deliberately echoing the language of the Declaration of Independence.[14]

Raymond was not the only advocate for the protection of Yosemite. Olmsted, who had been moved by his visit to the valley, also led a group of prominent Californians to Senator Conness's office to urge him to introduce legislation granting custodianship of Yosemite Valley to the state of California.[15] Horace Greeley, after observing the giant sequoias that surrounded the valley, wrote, "If the village of Mariposa, the county or the state of California does not immediately provide for the safety of these trees, I shall deeply deplore [it]." He went on to predict, "I am sure they will be more prized and treasured a thousand years hence."[16]

Senator Conness agreed to introduce legislation to deed to the state of California more than sixty square miles of federal land in the Sierras, to be withdrawn from settlement and preserved for public use and recreation. This land grant included both the Yosemite Valley and the adjacent Mariposa Grove of sequoia redwoods. Commonly referred to as the "Big Trees," this grove of *Sequoiadendron* or *Sequoia giantea* had been named after the battalion that had "discovered" Yosemite. Although states had often received grants of land from the federal government, what made this land transfer both unusual and unprecedented was its purpose, which, as Conness stated on the floor of the Senate, was to preserve it from "devastation and injury."[17]

BUSINESS AND CIVIC SUPPORT

In urging support for his bill, Conness emphasized that Yosemite was "for all public purposes worthless since it was fit for neither mining nor agriculture."[18] The valley's presumed economic "worthlessness" was politically important, as it helped assure Congress that protecting Yosemite would not adversely affect either the state's or the nation's economic development.

However, Senator Conness's statement was not quite correct, as there *were* economic considerations involved in Yosemite's preservation. Most obviously, Raymond's motives for originally suggesting that Conness propose the legislation were pecuniary. Olmsted had predicted that just as the natural scenery of Switzerland had generated a major tourist industry and led to the creation of inns, railroads, and carriage roads, so too would Yosemite "prove an attraction of similar character and a similar source of wealth for the whole community."[19]

Conness's proposal was actively supported by a coalition of road-builders, railroads, and steamship companies. These businesses stood to benefit from the protection of Yosemite, which promised to not only attract more tourists to California but encourage people to settle there. California was fortunate in that early in the state's history its scenic beauty was recognized as an important economic as well as cultural asset. Support for Conness's legislation thus came from both the business community and civic constituencies, producing California's first Baptist–bootlegger alliance in support of environmental protection. But atypically in this case, business interests were not divided.

BUILDING ON NIAGARA FALLS AND CENTRAL PARK

Another important development that influenced the movement to protect Yosemite was the example of Niagara Falls, which had shaped the nation's understanding of what a natural tourist attraction should look like. Early in the nineteenth century, the falls had become the nation's preeminent tourist site, attracting visitors from around the country and the world and playing a prominent role in the mid-century cultural life of the United States. By the time Conness's bill came before Congress, Yosemite was well on its way to acquiring a similarly iconic status. But Niagara Falls also provided another kind of model for Yosemite: it demonstrated how easily the valley could be spoiled if commercial interests were allowed to develop it without obstruction. At this time, unrestricted and uncontrolled commercialization had severely damaged the attractiveness of the American side of the waterfall. Those who wanted to protect Yosemite were determined that the "Shame of Niagara" would not be replicated in what was still an unspoiled western wonder.

It is also likely that the proposal to protect Yosemite was influenced by the earlier planning of Central Park in New York City, which had been carried out by Yosemite Commission member Olmsted. Unlike Central Park, Yosemite was located far from an urban area. But both sites were meant to serve as retreats from the stresses of urban life—as places where the beauty of nature could be freely enjoyed by Americans of all social classes, thereby "advanc[ing] the cause of democratic civilization."[20] In designing Central Park, Olmsted had planted trees around its periphery in order to visually separate it from the buildings of Manhattan. But Yosemite required no such landscaping: its floor was already a natural park, and the high peaks around the valley served to physically isolate it.

FEDERAL ACTION

Conness's legislation attracted little public attention or political debate. Both Congress and the president were preoccupied with more pressing matters. In the same month the bill came before Congress, federal troops were laying siege to Richmond, Virginia, and General William Sherman was marching to the sea through Atlanta. Other legislation that reached President Abraham Lincoln's desk at the same time included additional funding for the U.S. Navy and the repeal of the Fugitive Slave Act of 1850. However, several legislators did view protection of a scenic wilderness in the remote mountains of the far West as a kind of patriotic gesture—one that would help reunite the divided country by promoting pride in the beauty of the American landscape. Lincoln signed the legislation into law in June 1864. Shortly afterward, the California legislature accepted the land grant from the federal government, which included the Mariposa Grove, with the understanding that the Yosemite Valley would be preserved for "public use, resort, and recreation [and] be held inalienable for all time."[21] Starr writes: "Yosemite had been saved. . . . Considering the ravages already wrought upon the California environment by the 1860s, few would have predicted the success of this major act of preservation."[22]

The 1864 statute made Yosemite and Mariposa the nation's first protected wildernesses and first scenic park. It also marked the beginning of wildlife protection in the United States, as the terms of the land grant required California to "provide against the wanton destruction of fish and game found within said park, and against their capture or destruction for the purposes of merchandise or profit."[23] Established only fourteen years after California became a state, Yosemite marked the de facto beginning of the national parks program, with Olmsted's 1865 report to Congress about the park's future becoming a mission statement for the nascent national park movement.[24] Yosemite also influenced the creation of the Adirondack Forest Preserve in New York in 1882 and served as the inspiration for the nation's first official national park, Yellowstone, which was established by Congress the following year.

MUIR IN YOSEMITE

In 1864, James Hutchings, who had helped make the valley known to the broader public, bought a small hotel in order to serve the growing numbers of visitors to Yosemite. To repair and expand its somewhat ramshackle two-story wooden structure and build cottages around it, he needed a sawmill. To construct and operate that mill, he hired John Muir. Born in Dunbar, Scotland, and raised in Wisconsin, where he briefly studied botany at the University of Wisconsin, Muir was an active hiker and wanderer. He arrived in San Francisco in 1868 and shortly afterward visited the Sierras and Yosemite Valley. Muir accepted the sawmill job because it would enable him to earn a living while exploring the Sierras, where he spent six years.

The Yosemite Valley that Muir first witnessed in 1868 was largely unspoiled. Because it contained no gold, it had been spared from the devastation caused by hydraulic gold mining in the lower Sierras. It did, however, contain several hotels in addition to the one owned by Hutchings.[25]

While working at the sawmill, Muir spent his free time exploring the geography, geology, and ecology of the Sierras. He came to admire the wealth and diversity of its flora and fauna and kept a journal to record his impressions. Muir felt a deep spiritual connection to Yosemite and in his journal infused the park with a kind of religious fervor. Camping above the valley during an autumn storm, he wrote: "I spring to my feet crying 'Heavens and earth! Rock is not light, nor heavy, nor transparent, not opaque, but every pore gushes, glows like a thought with immortal life.'"[26] For Muir, biographer Donald Worster wrote, the Yosemite Valley represented a "sense of peaceful refuge . . . a home in nature that had clearly defined boundaries, a wild grandeur that paradoxically shattered and nurtured, a sense of the sublime mixed with a more rustic kind of lived-in beauty."[27]

In 1873, Muir moved to Martinez near the San Francisco Bay and began to write for eastern literary monthlies. His articles, which were based on the notebooks he had kept while in Yosemite, dramatically re-created the feeling of life in the wilderness and made Muir into a literary celebrity and the most nationally recognized voice for "nature" in the nineteenth and early twentieth centuries.[28] Americans who had previously written about their wilderness experiences had typically emphasized their success in meeting nature's challenges, such as killing a wild animal or conquering a rugged mountain peak. By contrast, Muir's writings stressed the "essential kindness" of nature, emphasizing what people and nature had in common.[29] For Muir, the wilderness had both intellectual and spiritual value—a perspective that would shape the American conservation movement and California's imprint on it.

When Muir returned to Yosemite in 1889, however, he was shocked by how poorly his "sacred temple" had been treated. Tunnels had been carved through several of the largest trees, meadows had been converted into hayfields and pastures, and much of the valley was littered with tin cans and garbage. Moreover, the surrounding mountains outside the park had been ravaged by sheep grazing and logging. The thousands of sheep grazing in the Sierras, which Muir described as "hoofed locusts," had destroyed virtually everything at ground level.[30] In short, it had turned out that Yosemite and the mountains surrounding it were economically valuable for something other than nature tourism.

FROM LITERARY MAN TO POLITICAL ACTIVIST

Working closely with Robert Johnson, the editor of *Century Magazine*, where much of his earlier work had been published, Muir now became politically active. In 1889, he and Johnson formulated an ambitious plan for a much larger national park that would surround the sixty square miles deeded to the state of California. This site would be modeled after Yellowstone, which was then the nation's only national park. What made their proposal innovative was the way it combined preservation and recreation. In Johnson and Muir's plan, the watersheds of both the Merced and Tuolumne rivers would be preserved, but they would have different uses: the former would be made more accessible to tourists, while the latter would remain less developed for hiking and camping. Yosemite would thus be "partially tame and partially wild." Its natural beauty would be protected, while the public would be both able and encouraged to visit and enjoy the wilderness.[31] Muir wrote that "everybody needs beauty as well as bread, places to play in and pray in, where nature may heal and give strengthen to body and soul alike."[32] In short, the wilderness needed to be saved both for and from humans.

But now, business interests were divided. Johnson and Muir's plan, which required federal approval, faced strong opposition from local cattlemen, sheepherders, and lumbermen who had financially benefited from their unrestricted access to the lands around Yosemite. Accordingly, Johnson and Muir decided to do an end run around the state's business community and mount a national public campaign. Writing in *Century Magazine*, Muir stated: "All that is perishable is vanishing apace. . . . [W]hen the region shall be stripped of its forests the ruin will be complete."[33] He emphasized that his and Johnson's plan would still enable the area to be visited, but that the mindless destruction of the land surrounding the state park would be halted.

Muir's campaign attracted national attention and received favorable coverage in several eastern newspapers and magazines. California senator George Hearst agreed to back the measure, as did Los Angeles congressman William Vandever. However, the legislation introduced by the latter in the House of Representatives fell short of Muir's goals, as it excluded the Tuolumne River watershed.

Fortunately for Muir, at a key moment in the political process, his plan obtained an important business ally: the Southern Pacific Railroad, the largest and most politically powerful business in California. The Southern Pacific's president, Collis Huntington, instructed the railroad's lobbyists in Washington to quietly support a much larger park than envisioned in the original legislation because he believed it would attract more tourists to California and thus increase the railroad's revenues. The railroad's behind-the-scenes influence proved decisive. Muir later recalled: "Even the soulless Southern Pacific R.R. Co, never counted on for anything good, helped notably in pushing the bill for this park through Congress."[34] The legislation signed into law by President Benjamin Harrison in 1890 created a national park that was five times the size of Vandever's original proposal. Sheep and lumbermen were now banned from the 1,500 square miles of the Sierras that surrounded the Yosemite Valley. An alliance of the nation's most prominent conservationist and the state's most powerful business firm had succeeded in significantly advancing nature protection in California.

THE SIERRA CLUB

This ad hoc but successful political effort to create Yosemite National Park helped inspire the establishment of a permanent organization to preserve the state's scenic wilderness. The initial idea for this organization came from Henry Senger and William Armes, two University of California professors who had been inspired by the Appalachian Mountain Club, which had been formed in 1876 in Boston to protect the Appalachian Mountains—a popular place for northeastern hikers and vacationers. Senger and Armes approached John Muir with the idea of forming a similar organization based in the San Francisco Bay Area to protect the Sierras. Muir agreed, and the organization's first meeting took place on May 2, 1892, at a law office in San Francisco, becoming the nation's second-oldest and California's first conservation organization. Hoping "to do something and make the mountains glad," Muir agreed to become its first president, a position he held until his death in 1914.[35] The club's articles of incorporation stated three purposes: to promote the recreational uses of the mountain regions of the Pacific Coast by making them accessible to the public, to educate the public about the state's natural heritage, and to engage in political activity in order to preserve the forests and other natural features of the Sierra Nevada Mountains. In doing so, the organization's 182 charter members gave, in the words of historian Michael Cohen, "formal expression to a distinctively California relationship to the outdoors," one that reflected "a deep California hope: that a regional heritage could be defined and protected," as well as enjoyed.[36] One of the club's first political campaigns was to defend the nascent 900,000-acre Yosemite National Park from livestock operators.

One-third of the club's charter members were academics, many in the natural sciences. They came from the University of California, established in 1868; Stanford University, founded in 1885; Mills College in Oakland, established in 1852; and the California Academy of Sciences in San Francisco. The remainder of the charter membership was made up of businessmen or lawyers who worked in San Francisco's financial district.[37] The club's distinguished roster included Joseph LeConte, a medical doctor turned geologist who had helped establish the University of California; David Starr Jordan, the founding president of Stanford University; Adolph Sutro, a wealthy businessman and prominent philanthropist who later became mayor of San Francisco; U.S. Senator George Perkins; and California Supreme Court Justice William Beatty.[38]

The Sierra Club's early members were urban residents who valued city life but also believed that frequent exposure to nature enhanced the quality of their lives. The club's formation can be said to represent an upper-middle-class "flowering of ecological stewardship," as well as the beginning of broad support for nature protection among the state's political and business elites.[39] While they lived and worked in cities and suburbs, the club's members had a personal stake in protecting the natural beauty of an area that they considered to be part of their "backyard." In essence, they wanted California to resemble Muir's vision for Yosemite: to be both "partially developed and partially wild."[40]

It is significant that California's first environmental organization was formed in the San Francisco Bay Area. This urban area had a large, relatively affluent, and educated population who also lived relatively close to the Sierras, illustrating the local geographic roots of environmental activism in California. The club's formation marked the beginning of the San Francisco Bay Area's long-standing role as a center of local, regional, and national environmental leadership and activism. Subsequently, the Sierra Club would expand beyond California to play a major role in the national resurgence of environmental activism during the middle of the twentieth century.

The Sierra Club's early activities both emphasized and publicized the spiritual and recreational benefits for city dwellers of spending time in the wilderness—an activity that was personally important to Muir. In July 1901, a hundred members of the organization, including Muir and his family, camped in the Sierras for a month. This outing was a major success and was subsequently repeated each summer. These increasingly popular annual outings significantly aided the recruitment of new members to the club and increased both its appeal and its visibility. Within three years of the first outing, the club's membership had doubled. As one participant put it, "The Sierra Club . . . has come to mean an ideal to us. It means comradeship and chivalry, simplicity and joyousness, and the care-free life of the open. . . . For a little while you have dwelt close to the heart of things."[41]

These outings not only added an important educational and social dimension to the club, but also helped create a political constituency to support its conservation efforts. Too, they reflected the increasing popularity of camping among middle-class Americans during the latter part of the nineteenth century. Just as northeastern urban dwellers were spending their leisure time in the Appalachians, so were San Francisco Bay Area residents engaging in nature tourism in the alpine meadows of the Sierra Nevada.

CAMPAIGN FOR RECESSION

However, Muir was disappointed by the inability of California's Yosemite Commission to adequately protect the Yosemite Valley and the Mariposa Grove, which were located in the middle of the recently created Yosemite National Park. The state's legislature had provided insufficient funds to pay for the expenses of the commissioners and the "guardian" they had hired. As a result, the commission had turned to private sources of funds, granting long-term leases for the building of hotels and the construction of entrance roads, the builders of which then collected tolls. Fences for pasture and hayfields had been allowed to clutter much of the valley floor[42] Accordingly, Muir began a campaign to have the state park transferred back to the federal government, an effort that became known as "recession."

In 1903, Muir and President Theodore Roosevelt spent three days hiking and camping in Yosemite and discussing forest and wilderness conservation. The president regarded Muir as a kindred spirit and reflected on the experience, "This has been the grandest day of my life! One I shall long remember."[43] For his part, Muir used his time with the president to persuade him to support legislation to incorporate the Yosemite Valley and the Mariposa Grove into the surrounding Yosemite National Park.

Both the president and California governor George Pardee, who had joined Roosevelt on his visit to Yosemite along with University of California president Benjamin Wheeler and Columbia University president Nicholas Butler, agreed to back Muir's plan. Muir was delighted: "Sound the loud timbrel and let every Yosemite tree and stream rejoice!" he exulted. "How accomplished a lobbyist I've become."[44] However, Roosevelt's and Pardee's approval weren't the only hurdles: this change in ownership required the approval of the California state legislature and the U.S. Congress as well.

Within California, there was substantial opposition to the land transfer. Several legislators regarded the idea as insulting to the state, as it would imply that the state was incapable of caring for what was now commonly viewed as a "national treasure." The stagecoach companies and the hotels that served the valley feared that they would have less influence over federal park administrators than state ones. Their concerns were well founded, as the latter's supervision of them had been relatively lax. This combination of state pride and local commercial interests defeated the first two state legislative proposals for recession.

At this point, however, the public became politically mobilized. A wide array of state professional and citizen organizations, led by the Sierra Club, mounted a public campaign for recession. They argued that the overlap of state and federal authority over the area was inefficient and had led to frequent administrative disputes. Moreover, they claimed, the federal government had substantially more financial resources than the state and therefore would be better able to protect the entire park from encroachment. Clearly, at this stage in California's history, the federal government was viewed as a better steward of California's natural environment than the state of California. Since recession would also be good for tourism, the California State Board of Trade also supported returning all of Yosemite back to the federal government.

BUSINESS INTERESTS TIP THE SCALES

While a considerable number of local businesses opposed recession, the land transfer proposal also attracted an influential business supporter. Due in large part to the personal relationship that Muir had developed with the powerful financier and railroad magnate Edward H. Harriman of New York, the Southern Pacific Railroad decided to support recession. For Harriman, who had effectively taken control of the railroad in 1901, supporting President Roosevelt and Muir fit neatly into the railroad's business strategy, which mixed land conservation and commerce.[45] The extensiveness of the Southern Pacific rail network meant that Harriman's political reach was nationwide. After Harriman voiced his support for recession, a sudden switch of nine votes in the state legislature enabled the bill to pass in 1905. With gratitude, Muir wrote to Southern Pacific's chief lobbyist: "Many thanks for your Sacramento Yosemite Work."[46]

However, the federal government also had to agree to add the state-owned lands to the surrounding national park. Recession faced strong opposition in Washington, DC, from California's lumbering and grazing interests, who feared (correctly) that federal control would reduce their access to the lands now under state control. Joe Cannon, the powerful Speaker of the House of Representatives, was unenthusiastic about the proposal, as he disliked spending any money, especially for scenery. But the personal intervention of both Harriman and President Roosevelt persuaded Cannon to suspend House rules and let the bill come to a vote. After passing Congress, the legislation was signed into law by Roosevelt in June 1906, becoming one of the president's greatest triumphs.[47] After forty-two years of state control, Yosemite Valley and the Mariposa Grove would now be administered by the Department of Interior's recently created National Park Service. Following the completion of a railroad from Merced in the Central Valley to the park the following year, Yosemite became much more accessible to the general public.

The Giant Sequoias, Ancient Trees

A year after Yosemite was "discovered," A. T. Dowd, a big-game hunter who had been employed by a mining company to procure meat, was tracking down a wounded California grizzly bear[48] when he stumbled upon a grove of gigantic trees in Calaveras County on the western slope of the Sierra Nevada Mountains. News of this discovery, like that of gold, spread quickly both throughout the United States and overseas. These trees, which soon came to be called "sequoias," attracted numerous visitors who were awed by their unusual size, which could be as much as 30 feet wide and 300 feet high. The "giant" Sierra sequoias included five of the ten largest trees in the world. One of them, subsequently named the General Sherman Tree, had a height of 275 feet and a base diameter of 46.5 feet. It was not only the largest tree in the world, but also seen as the world's largest living entity.

Besides their size, what was also noteworthy about the sequoias was their longevity: several appeared to be the most ancient living entities on the planet. Students of the Bible and ancient history enthused that these trees had existed at the time of Moses, King Solomon, Homer, and Alexander the Great. A journalist from the Northeast wrote that the sequoias "began with our Modern Civilization. They were just sprouting when the Star of Bethlehem rose." A correspondent with the London *Times* calculated that one tree had reached maturity "when as yet Adam lived in the Garden of Eden."[49] The oldest tree was found to be more than 3,200 years old, which made it 700 years older than the Parthenon.

California's ancient trees quickly became a source of national pride, with their age seeming to challenge Europe's monopoly on history.[50] For both Americans and Europeans, the sequoias became what Kevin Starr has called "cathedrals of nature: cool, silent, the products of a profound historicity."[51] There was also considerable interest in them from natural scientists working in the growing fields of genetics, botany, soil science, and geology. California's trees, which had been growing in the state for 20 million years and contained a remnant gene pool dating from the Cretaceous period some

125 million years ago, offered these scholars a rich natural laboratory to develop and test their theories about nature.

EARLY PROTECTION EFFORTS

As early as 1852, a resolution had been introduced in the state assembly to make redwood timber the common property of the citizens of California. It failed. Through the 1860s, the only protected trees in the state were those of the Mariposa Grove adjacent to Yosemite. By the 1880s, most of the sequoias in the Sierras were in private hands, and many forests had been logged. One enormous tree could yield 3,000 fence posts, enough to fence in an 8,000-acre ranch while leaving a sufficient number of shingles to cover more than seventy roofs. Because their wood was too brittle to be used for construction, the sequoias were primarily used for fence posts, grape stakes, shingles, patio furniture, and pencils. However, their brittleness caused the wood to shatter when the trees fell, meaning as much as 75 percent of it was wasted.

One stand of giant sequoias in the Converse Basin was completely destroyed. Other trees were defaced by tourists or cut down and shipped around the world to become tourist attractions. Adding to the destruction was the introduction of log flumes in 1889, which opened up previously inaccessible forests to logging. One sawmill was capable of cutting 2 million board feet of sequoias in a single season, and such mills rapidly multiplied. In addition, sheep-grazing companies were burning down forests to make more land available for their flocks. During the 1870s, several hundred sequoias were harvested, though logging crews often ignored the largest trees, as they were too difficult to cut.

Muir's campaign to protect the ancient sequoias of the Sierras began in 1875. In an article published in a Sacramento newspaper entitled "God's First Temples: How Shall We Preserve Our Forests?" he warned that deforestation would allow soil erosion to occur "to a vastly more destructive degree than all the washings from hydraulic mines concerning which we now hear so much."[52] Public awareness of what was happening to these "noble forests" began to grow, as did demands to protect them.[53] Muir petitioned Congress to create a national park to help protect the trees. Legislation to do so was introduced by Congressmen Lewis Payson of Illinois and William Vandever of California. To increase business support for their proposal, the two legislators argued that protecting the forests of the Sierra Nevada would enhance agriculture in the Central Valley by protecting the watersheds that produced the irrigated water needed for summer crops.

A SECOND ALLIANCE BETWEEN MUIR
AND THE SOUTHERN PACIFIC

In addition to the backing of eastern newspapers and national magazines, the campaign to protect the giant sequoias of the Sierras was supported by the Southern Pacific Railroad, which was the largest owner of timber in the United States. The railroad had two reasons for wanting to protect the largest possible acreage of sequoias. First, a mountain watershed in the Sierras would help protect the company's downstream agricultural holdings in the Central Valley. Second, the railroad believed that larger groves of trees would attract more visitors to California and thus increase traffic on the firm's transcontinental line. For this reason, Jared Farmer has observed, during this period "the transcontinental railroads functioned . . . as the greatest advocates of national parks."[54]

In 1890, the same year that Congress created Yosemite National Park, it also created the Sequoia and General Grant (now Kings Canyon) national parks to protect the sequoias of the Sierras. The boundaries of Sequoia National Park were actually drawn up by Daniel Zumwalt, one of the Southern Pacific's Washington lobbyists, who was also an active mountaineer. The three national parks, plus the earlier land grant to California, protected one-third of the Sierras' "Big Trees." The establishment of three national parks in a span of just a few weeks represented a conservation achievement unprecedented in either American or world history.[55] Significantly, three of the nation's first four national parks were located in California.

To supplement Sequoia National Park, which contains the largest grove of sequoias in the country, President Benjamin Harrison in 1893 issued an executive order that placed virtually the entire central and southern Sierra Nevada—more than 4 million acres—in the Sierra Forest Reserve. However, the Calaveras Grove, which had first drawn the world's attention to the trees and had been a major tourist attraction since 1852, remained in private hands. Its owner, seeking to recoup his $100,000 purchase price, planned to log the trees. The announcement of this intention created a national furor. In 1909, a petition signed by nearly 1.5 million people was sent to the White House asking President Theodore Roosevelt to have the federal government purchase the grove. Congress agreed to appropriate the necessary funds and created the Calaveras Big Tree National Forest. These trees eventually became part of Calaveras State Park, the acreage of which was subsequently enhanced by private donations. The next federal acquisition was a forest in Redwood Canyon, which contained one of the finest endangered groves of sequoias still in private hands. In 1940, President Franklin Roosevelt added this area to the Kings Canyon National Park.

In 1952, a state study estimated that about 23,500 of the 35,000 acres that included giant sequoias had never been logged.[56] Approximately 92 percent of the acreage containing sequoias in the Sierra Nevada is now protected, primarily in national parks and forests. This includes an estimated 20,000 trees with a diameter of more than ten feet. All told, national parks cover 2,500 square miles of the Sierras, and they have become a major tourist attraction, visited by 5 million people a year.

Protecting the State's Forests

DEFORESTATION: AN ECONOMIC PROBLEM

The effort to protect California's forests extended beyond the preservation of scenic areas for aesthetic, recreational, or cultural reasons. The forests also constituted an important economic resource. As early as 1869, the State Board of Agriculture had expressed concern about the rate at which the state's formerly abundant timber resources were disappearing. It estimated that one-third of the state's timber had already been cut and predicted that if the current rate of usage continued, within four decades the state's timber supply would be exhausted. A federal official was even more pessimistic, warning in 1872 that "requirements for the State for forest products will be at least ten times greater for the next twenty-two years." An 1878 editorial in the *Sacramento Daily Union* cautioned that at the current rate of logging, "the exhaustion of the forest growth of the Sierra is only a question of some ten years."[57]

Support for halting such widespread timber destruction came from several sources. One was the state's tourist industry, which viewed the state's forests as an important attraction for visitors. A second was commercial consumers of wood, who feared future wood shortages. These included homebuilders who used wood shingles for housing construction, fruit growers who required wooden boxes to harvest and transport their products, and furniture companies. The third and perhaps most important group was those concerned with watershed protection. This was a particularly significant issue in California, where steep slopes and heavy rainfall often produced flooding and soil erosion, which forest destruction exacerbated. Protecting the trees in watersheds also helped ensure supplies of fresh water for both farmers and urban residents.

In 1885, the legislature created the State Forestry Commission to regulate timber cutting and encourage reforestation. California thus became one of the first states to regulate logging and engage in forest conservation efforts.[58] The establishment of this commission represented an important milestone in the development of California's administrative bureaucracy, reflecting the important economic benefits of forest protection.

During the next decade, President Benjamin Harrison responded to pressures from the Southern California business community by creating the San Gabriel Forest Reserve and the San Bernardino National Forest. This largely brush-covered area served as an important watershed for the Los Angeles Basin. Fall wildfires had periodically denuded the hillsides, leading to flooding and mudslides during the winter rainy season and the destruction of valuable farmlands in the basin below. Subsequent presidents, including Grover Cleveland, William McKinley, and Theodore Roosevelt, significantly expanded the state's forest reserves. Importantly, when Congress in 1907 prohibited the president from establishing any additional forest reserves in western states, it explicitly exempted California from the law.[59]

Protecting the Coastal Redwoods

The largest groves of redwoods—technically known as *Sequoia sempervirens* but commonly referred to as "redwoods"—are not in the Sierras but rather grow in a 5- to 47-mile band along the coast of California from Monterey Bay to the Oregon border, a distance of 470 miles. They are the vestigial remnant of a pre–Ice Age forest that once extended through all of North America.[60] In 1850, these forests covered approximately 2 million acres. The enormous size of the trees—with the oldest being 16 or more feet in diameter and 100 to 160 feet tall—is due to their exposure to the moist fog that sweeps in from the Pacific Ocean during the dry summer months and supplements the winter rainfall. Living an average of between 500 to 700 years, a few are documented to be as old as 2,000 years, making them the longest-living organisms on Earth. Fittingly, the name *Sempervirens* means "evergreen" or "everlasting" in Latin.

These trees began to be cut down during the Gold Rush after some frustrated forty-niners turned to lumbering. The rate at which these redwoods were harvested far exceeded that of their "cousins" in the Sierras, partly because their proximity to the coast made them more accessible to loggers. In addition, unlike the sequoias in the Sierras, which were located close to Yosemite Valley, the state's top tourist attraction, and had become national icons, relatively few tourists visited the coastal redwoods during the nineteenth century. Adding to their vulnerability, the coastal redwoods were found in thick forests that seemed to go on forever. In 1882, a botanist with the California Academy of Science described the coastal redwood supply as "so prodigious as to be simply incalculable."[61] Consequently, there was less public interest in protecting them.

But most important was the difference in their commercial value. In contrast to the brittleness of the Sierra sequoias, wood from the coastal redwoods has long been considered one of the most valuable timber species. The California Redwood Association called it a "wonder wood."[62] It was easy to work with; difficult to destroy; more durable than concrete, stucco, or stone; and resistant to water damage. Its uses were endless. They included caskets (advertised for their longevity), sidewalks, gutters, paving blocks, roads, water tanks, and cooling towers, as well as buildings, railway cars, decks, furniture, shingles, bridges, and barns. Because the wood contains a natural preservative that makes it resistant to decay, redwood was also extensively used for railway ties and trestles in California. Not least of its virtues was its flame resistance. Structures built with redwood helped limit the destructiveness of the fire that followed the 1906 San Francisco earthquake.

When it came to the building of California, coastal redwood outranked even gold.[63] The wood was used to help rebuild San Francisco after the 1906 earthquake, as well as to construct homes in the residential communities of the East Bay. It was also ubiquitous in the consumer products found in middle-class California homes. The Arts and Crafts architecture of Berkeley still features houses with redwood panels and shingles. Somewhat ironically, as Jared Farmer writes, "these homes belonged to the back-to-nature bourgeoisie, the same class of people who filled the Sierra Club's membership role and advanced the conservationist cause. For their domiciles, tree enthusiasts desired a simple, local *natural* style that only redwood consumption could provide."[64] By 1900, almost all of the old-growth redwood forests on California's North Coast were owned by lumber companies, and by 1910, one-quarter of the state's redwoods had been logged.

Hydraulic gold mining had raised a critical question: Were the interests of Californians best served by keeping the gold in the ground—and thus stopping the flow of debris into the rivers and protecting the state's agricultural lands—or by continuing to extract the valuable mineral and adding to the flow of debris into the Sacramento Valley? The dual value of the coastal redwoods now posed a similar dilemma: Should the trees be harvested to meet the public's demand for redwood products, or should they be preserved and protected for their recreational and aesthetic values? Put differently: Should they be "consumed" privately or publicly? Were the redwoods more valuable as lumber or as tourist attractions? Fortunately, in this case, compromises were possible: some of the trees could be harvested and others protected.

THE SEMPERVIRENS CLUB

The relatively low value initially placed by the public on the redwoods, along with their much greater commercial value, explains why roughly a half-century elapsed between the initial protection of the sequoias in the Sierras and that of the redwoods along the coast.

Like many environmental initiatives in California, the movement to protect the coastal redwoods began in the San Francisco Bay Area. This region was adjacent to where commercial logging was most extensive, and thus San Franciscans could readily observe the trees' destruction. In addition, the public had become concerned that the removal of the fog-condensing redwoods near the city would adversely affect the region's climate. One prominent biologist warned, "It is my firm conviction that if the redwoods are destroyed, and necessarily will be if not protected by wise action of our government, California will become a desert."[65]

During a May 1901 tour of the Big Basin grove of redwoods located in Santa Cruz County south of San Francisco, twenty-six residents of cities in the central coastal counties formed the state's second environmental organization, which they named the Sempervirens Club, after the coastal redwoods. The club's first goal was to enlist financial support from the state of California to protect an exceptionally magnificent grove of primeval coastal redwoods. Located in the heavily forested Santa Cruz Mountains south of San Francisco, this stand of trees was in immediate danger of being logged. Because these trees were located on private property, to protect them the state would need to purchase the property.

The club's campaign for state funds was supported by a broad coalition of academics, local residents, and others. Academic supporters included Stanford University president David Starr Jordan and two of the university's science professors who were active members of the Sierra Club. The University of California, which wanted to protect the trees in order to establish a forestry school, also jumped onboard. A growing number of local residents who were now hiking, fishing, and camping in the Santa Cruz Mountains joined the campaign as well, as did the 20,000-member California Game and Fish Protective Association—a predominately upper-class sporting organization—and local ministers, the Sierra Club, and several socially prominent women. The city of San Francisco supported the club's bid as a means of safeguarding a potential water supply.

Local industry also came together behind the club, forming the second half of this northern California Baptist–bootlegger conservationist coalition. Several local businessmen who became backers hoped that a state park would attract tourists to Santa Cruz and San Jose. For similar reasons, both the Santa Clara and Santa Cruz boards of trade strongly supported the club's goals, as did the Southern Pacific Railway. The latter had two important motives to support the park's creation. The first was to keep rain falling on the farms of the Santa Clara Valley, where it had extensive holdings (although its hopes for the redwoods' effects on rainfall proved to be misplaced). The second was to increase traffic on its rail line to Santa Cruz, which it planned to extend into the newly created park.

The club coined a memorable motto—"Save the redwoods"—and mobilized its diverse supporters into an effective political coalition. In 1901, after extensive lobbying, the legislature was persuaded to appropriate $250,000 to purchase 3,800 acres in Santa Cruz County. An additional 1,300 acres were then donated by the Big Basin Land and Lumber Company. In 1902, California Redwood Park—since renamed the Big Basin Redwoods State Park—became California's first official state park. In 1906, 4,000 acres of adjacent federal land were added to the site. Speaking at Stanford University shortly after the state park's creation, President Theodore Roosevelt applauded the preservation campaign, stating that "we should not turn into shingles trees which were old when the first Egyptian conqueror penetrated the valley of the Euphrates."[66]

MUIR WOODS

In 1905, after a successful business career in Chicago, William Kent returned to the San Francisco Bay Area where he had grown up. He moved his family to a large tract of land on the shoulder of Mount Tamalpais, which is located just north of San Francisco, abutting San Francisco Bay on its east and the Pacific Ocean on its west. By adding this tract to a plot of land earlier purchased by his father, Kent became the largest landowner in Marin County. Enjoying hiking and camping, he became a member of the Sierra Club. At this time, many of the redwoods in Marin County were being harvested. To protect the remaining trees, Kent, who had fond memories of the redwood groves in which he had spent time as a boy, purchased 611 acres of one of the last uncut stands of old-growth redwoods in the Bay Area. He planned to open up the area to the public by creating a quasi-public park that would be accessible by a scenic railway.

While located just a dozen miles north of San Francisco across the bay in Marin County, this patch of trees had been left untouched because it had been difficult to access. However, after Kent's purchase, a water company in Marin County sought to acquire this 611-acre tract in order to construct a reservoir. Because much of San Francisco had recently burned in the fires following the 1906 earthquake, the city had an urgent need for additional municipal water supplies. As Kent was unwilling to sell his acreage, the company planned to acquire the land through eminent domain. However, Kent believed that what the Marin water company really wanted was not the land, but its valuable timber. The acreage that the water company sought to purchase included a spectacular grove of redwoods, three of which were 300 feet tall, with diameters of 18 feet.

In protest, Kent wrote to Muir decrying "the hideous heedless wickedness of trying to butcher those trees."[67] To avoid the threat of a condemnation suit—which he was likely to lose—Kent and his wife decided to donate 295 acres to the federal government, asking that they be made into a national monument. This acreage included the forty-seven endangered acres of redwoods that the water company wanted to acquire. A grateful President Roosevelt accepted this gift and proposed naming the park in honor of Kent and his wife. However, the couple insisted that it be named in honor of the Sierra Club's president and the state's leading conservationist, John Muir. Informing Muir of the gift, Kent wrote his friend, "I know the dreams we have will come true, and that men will learn to love nature." In response, Muir praised Kent for performing "in many ways the most notable service to God and man I've heard of since my forest wanderings began," adding, "That so fine a thing should have come out of money-mad Chicago! Whawad'a'thocht it!"[68] He predicted that Kent's magnificent gift would make him "immortal like your Sequoias, and all the best people of the world will call you blessed. . . . How such deeds shine amid the mean commercialism and apathy so destructively prevalent these days."[69]

Established in 1908, Muir Woods National Monument is located only 12 miles from San Francisco, making it one of the closest national parks to a major metropolitan area. It was also the first protected area to be donated to the federal government. In 1921, the Kents gave an additional gift of land to the monument. It now covers 554 acres, which lie adjacent to 6,000 acres of state-protected land, and is one of the most visited national parks in the

United States. Following his election to Congress in 1910, Kent became active in the Progressive Era–reform movement and played a critical role in the enactment of the 1916 National Parks Act. However, he disappointed Muir by supporting the Hetch Hetchy reservoir in Yosemite (see chapter 5).

SAVE-THE-REDWOODS LEAGUE

Efforts to protect the redwoods now moved up the coast to Humboldt County in northern California, where considerable timbering had been taking place since Highway 1 had opened up the area to lumber firms in 1915. The First World War had also substantially increased the commercial demand for redwoods, with the trees extensively used for railroad ties and piping at military bases in the United States and France. At the same time, the newly formed California Redwood Association began aggressively pursuing international markets opened up by the Panama Canal. As one scholar summed it up, "All in all, 1917 was a terrible year to be an old redwood."[70]

The effort to protect these trees was led by a new organization, the Save-the-Redwoods League. Like both its two predecessors, the league was founded in the San Francisco Bay Area. In 1918, a group of upper-class business leaders from the Bay Area and New York met at the Bohemian Grove in San Francisco and decided to establish an organization "to preserve the oldest trees in the world."[71] Within two years the league had a national membership of 2,000. During the interwar years, it replaced the Sierra Club as the state's and the country's most important conservationist organization.

In contrast to both the Sierra and the Sempervirens clubs, the league was dominated by socially prominent businessmen who had both the resources and the time to pursue civic interests such as nature conservation. But its membership also included natural historians, professional preservationists, foresters, landscape architects, botanists, biologists, paleontologists, and geologists who had a professional interest in redwoods protection. Also unlike the two previously established environmental organizations, the league was a national organization, with over one-third of its members living outside California. This broad base of support reflected the extent to which the state's redwoods had become a recognized natural resource.

The Save-the-Redwoods League's goal was to save as much as possible of the 2 million acres of redwoods that remained in private hands along California's coast. Its strategy in this task was to raise the funds to purchase the land from its private owners. The group then planned to give these holdings to the state of California to be made into state parks. The league engaged in an extensive national public relations campaign and solicited donations from wealthy individuals across the United States.[72] It also encouraged both contributors and potential contributors to visit the trees in order to increase national interest in and financial support for their protection.

Because of its upper-class leadership and the financial support it received from corporations involved in extractive industries, the league from the beginning had a private enterprise orientation. Accordingly, it opposed efforts to use the state's power of eminent domain to acquire redwood acreage. Rather, it sought to protect the trees though "friendly negotiation" and "just compensation" of the logging industry, a strategy that recognized what were believed to be the industry's legitimate claims to the land.[73] In contrast to the Sierra Club, which focused on public policies at the federal level, and the Sempervirens Club, which sought to affect state policies, the Save-the-Redwoods League relied upon private philanthropy, drawing on the nature protection strategy of William Kent.

Using their own wealth and that of their many affluent friends, the league established an influential and enduring green branch of American philanthropy. During the 1920s, it purchased several prime stands of trees along California's North Coast. By 1963, the league's purchases had been responsible for the state's ownership of 102,000 acres of redwood forests in four state parks on lands valued at over $11 million. By 2005, that figure had risen to nearly 180,000 acres at a total cost of $100 million.[74] The league's efforts, in cooperation with those of both the Sierra Club and the Sempervirens Club, led to the creation of four major redwood state parks: Humboldt Redwoods State Park, Prairie Creek Redwoods State Park, Jedediah Smith Redwoods State Park, and the Del Norte Coast Redwoods State Park—all located in the northwest corner of the state.

Expanding State Parks

Unlike national parks, which, with the notable exception of Muir Woods, were established on land already owned by the federal government, California's state parks were located on formerly private land. This meant that to acquire such lands, funds had to be either appropriated by the state or donated by private individuals. Notwithstanding these financial challenges, the number of state parks in California grew rapidly, reaching five, along with several historical monuments, by the mid-1920s.

However, several of these parks, such as Mount Diablo, were poorly developed, badly managed, and difficult for the public to access. The latter shortcoming defeated one of the primary purposes for which the parks were created. Moreover, the state's population growth during the first decades of the twentieth century, along with increasing urbanization and industrial development, meant that the open spaces and recreational opportunities that new parks might provide were rapidly diminishing, even as demand for them was growing.

Adding to these concerns was the importance of California's scenic and recreational attractions to the state's tourism industry. Duncan McDuffie, a prominent realtor and chair of the Save-the-Redwoods League's state parks committee, wrote after a review of the state's five parks in 1925:

> Next to our fertile soil, California's greatest single asset is the opportunity it offers for outdoor life. No industry except agriculture puts as much money into circulation in California as do the hundreds of visitors who come here seeking health, recreation, pleasure, sport and out-of-door life generally. Yet gradually many of the attractions that have made the state famous are being destroyed. . . . It would seem to be sound business for the state to see that its major opportunities for recreation and enjoyment of the out-of-doors are left open for the use and enjoyment of both its citizens and its visitors.[75]

In 1927, California's governor and state legislature established the State Parks Commission, marking another important expansion of the state's administrative capacity. That same year, California authorized the expenditure of $6 million in state funds, to be matched by an equal amount of privately generated funds, for the acquisition of additional parklands. A bond issue authorizing this expenditure was then submitted to the state's voters.

The campaign to ratify the state parks bond issue was both extensive and broad based. The bond issue was publicly endorsed and supported by every newspaper in the state, as well as 250 organizations, including local chambers of commerce; the American Legion; the California Real Estate Association; tourist and travel associations; automobile clubs; and conservation, education, and garden groups. During the last weeks of the campaign, local chambers of commerce, utility companies, and the Boy Scouts and Campfire Girls distributed approximately a million leaflets in support of the measure. Major oil firms as well as the California Farm Bureau Association sponsored radio announcements advocating a "Yes" vote. On November 6, 1928, the California State Park Bonds Act was approved by a nearly three-to-one plurality of California's voters.

Ironically, by depressing land and timber values, the stock market crash of 1929 that followed shortly after the bond issue vote facilitated the acquisition of new state parklands. The Great Depression both significantly reduced the costs of land acquisition and made many large property owners more willing to part with their landholdings. This was especially true of forestland, the commercial value of which declined during the 1930s as demand for new housing construction plummeted. In 1931, the Pacific Lumber Company agreed to sell thirteen acres of an old redwood forest in the Bull Creek and Dyerville Flats area of Humboldt County in northern California. Half of the $3.2 million purchase price was paid by the state, and the other half was raised by the Save-the-Redwoods League, which received a large contribution from John D. Rockefeller.

Other acquisitions made during this period, either through purchase or gifts, included half a mile of Southern California beachfront, eight miles of toll road adjoining 900 acres of land at Mount Diablo in the San Francisco Bay Area, and 1,600 acres of land at Palomar Mountain in northern San Diego County. All told, in 1931, fourteen miles of ocean beach were added to the park system, and total park acreage nearly doubled. By 1934, when state funds from the bond issue had been nearly exhausted, California had forty-nine state parks with a total land area of 300,000 acres. Between 1928 and 1934, the annual number of visitors to state parks, including those who made day trips to visit beaches, increased from 60,000 to nearly 6 million.

While the California park system was politically popular, its lack of a regular source of state funding restricted its further expansion. Financial constraints also limited its ability to maintain the parks and historical monuments that had already been acquired. During the mid-1930s, as the system struggled to find a solution to this problem, a potential funding source emerged from an unexpected direction: California's oil industry.

OIL DRILLING AND THE BEACHES

In 1936, Standard Oil decided to try an end run around local opposition to additional oil drilling in Southern California (discussed in chapter 4) by sponsoring a state ballot initiative to legalize slant oil drilling into offshore deposits. Southern Californians' opposition to this policy initiative, known as the State Lands Act, was intense. Every newspaper and elected official in the region opposed it, and chambers of commerce from West Los Angeles, Santa Monica, Venice, Manhattan Beach, Palo Verdes, Redondo Beach, Hermosa Beach, and Playa del Rey joined together to urge its defeat. These opponents characterized the ballot proposal as "vicious," "imprudent," "a medium for satisfying the private greed of certain large oil interests," and "a vehicle through which ruin and destruction will be carried through our beaches."[76]

But the oil firms then received support from a surprising source: the State Parks Commission. The commission agreed to support the initiative—provided that a share of state oil royalties was allocated to it in return. William Colby, a San Francisco mining lawyer who chaired the Parks Commission, promised that such revenue sharing would "make future park bond issues unnecessary and will provide for the entire park system at no future expense to taxpayers." Testifying before the state legislature, he dramatically argued that the redwood groves and beaches that needed protection would be destroyed if the park system didn't obtain a steady source of funding. With no new funds in sight, Colby reported, "the period of acquisition is nearing completion."[77] A business group, the Shoreland Planning Association (SPA), along with several civic park and beach groups, also agreed to support the initiative provided that 30 percent of oil royalties went to parks and beaches.

This rather unusual Baptist–bootlegger alliance between state park advocates and the oil industry proved politically effective. While the bond issue failed in Los Angeles, the majority of the state's voters approved it. The initiative's revenue-sharing provisions added roughly $700,000 a year to the budget of the State Parks Commission. This permitted the commission to increase its protection of both Southern California beaches and northern redwood groves. In 1941, the state legislature raised the share of state oil royalties dedicated to beaches and parks from 30 percent to 70 percent. In 1954, after California was given control of the revenues from offshore oil drilling, additional funds for park development and administration became available. Ultimately, while the beach–oil pact was contentious, with many developers and civic groups continuing to oppose oil drilling near the coasts, oil revenues played an important role in financing the expansion of California's public beaches and parks.

FURTHER EXPANSION

During the 1960s, public interest in and support for park and wilderness preservation grew throughout the United States. In 1964, President Lyndon Johnson signed the Wilderness Act. This legislation created the Land and Water Conservation Fund, which made federal money available for park and recreational purposes. California's elected officials in Washington played a major role in this law's enactment, and California was the first state to have its outdoor recreation plan approved for federal funding.

At this time, the need for better conservation programs and policies was particularly urgent in the state. Between 1950 and 1960, nearly 3 million people had moved to California. This population growth, along with increased highway construction, had heightened both public demands on the state's park system and political pressures to expand it. In 1963, the state legislature voted to submit a $150 million state park and recreation bond to California's voters. However, even if the bond initiative were approved, its proceeds would not become available for another eighteen months. Accordingly, California governor Edmund "Pat" Brown asked the legislature for an emergency appropriation of $19 million. These funds would be used to purchase 25,000 acres of prime beach and park property, including eight miles of ocean frontage now barred to the public—all of which, Brown warned, might be "lost to the people as a result of mushrooming subdivisions and rising prices."[78] The legislature approved the emergency funding.

As in 1928, the 1964 bond issue to finance park acquisition and management attracted widespread support from both conservation and business organizations as well as from media throughout the state and the governor, who actively campaigned on its behalf. On November 3, 1964, the initiative passed overwhelmingly, with a plurality of 1.5 million votes. By 1969, California had a total of 178 state parks, more than any other state.

Redwood National Park

During the 1960s, as national interest in nature conservation increased, redwood protection reemerged on the national political agenda. Due to the postwar housing boom, during the 1950s the number of trees harvested each year had tripled. In addition, some of the redwoods in the state parks were being threatened by erosion and highway construction. Conservationists became alarmed.[79]

THE SIERRA CLUB STEPS IN

In response to the new threats facing the redwoods, a revitalized Sierra Club spearheaded a national political effort to protect the remaining trees. By the mid-1960s, the Sierra Club had become a national organization with 21,000 members and a staff of thirty-three. Led by David Brower, it had become more politically active and assertive in its defense of wilderness protection. Breaking with the Save-the-Redwoods League's strategy of seeking accommodation with the private owners of forests and convinced that the expansion of the state park system was inadequate to protect the remaining trees, the Sierra Club began a campaign for federally funded land purchases. This approach would avoid what it described as the "apocalyptic destruction" of the redwoods by timber companies engaged in clear-cutting.

The Sierra Club leadership and staff accepted the recommendation of the National Park Service (NPS) that a new national park be established at Redwood Creek, a site that included the single largest block of old-growth coastal redwoods still in private hands. But the club wanted a considerably larger park than the one envisioned by the NPS—one that would include not only the iconic redwood groves but also the wilderness surrounding them. In keeping with its broader emphasis on wilderness protection, the club argued that a much larger park of at least 90,000 acres was needed to protect the "superior faunal variety, geological variety and geographical variety" that characterized the "unparalleled uniqueness of the area."[80]

A POLITICALLY CHARGED EFFORT

The creation of Redwood National Park fostered more debate than any other national park in the United States.[81] The politics surrounding its creation were markedly different and much more contentious than those that had influenced the establishment of the national parks in the Sierras during the late nineteenth century. On one hand, there were no economic or material benefits associated with establishing a large national park in Redwood Creek, which was located in the thinly populated and relatively remote northwest corner of the state. Such a park was neither likely to attract additional tourists to California nor located in an area close to a major population center. In fact, the Sierra Club argued that it was precisely the park's remoteness that would enable those visiting it to have an authentic wilderness experience. The club primarily wanted the redwoods and the surrounding wilderness to be protected for their own sake, and not for any human benefit—a vision that reflected a new environmental ethos about nature protection.

On the other hand, the economic costs of the park's creation were much more substantial than those associated with California's other national parks. Much of the land for the proposed park was not only privately owned but economically valuable. Five politically influential forestry companies were actively harvesting trees on it. These firms strongly rejected the claims of the Sierra Club that the redwoods were endangered, arguing that "America's Majestic Redwoods have [already] been saved" and that many of the remaining redwoods were not the "huge primeval trees" but "the sidehill stuff, which in many cases is half fir."[82] Even the Save-the-Redwoods League initially opposed the park's creation, arguing that the state had already preserved enough trees through representative groves.

Workers and local governments were also opposed to the park, while newly elected California governor Ronald Reagan voiced concern that the larger park envisioned by the Sierra Club would adversely affect the timber industry and the already-depressed economy of rural northern California. In this case, nature protection would be at the expense of the local community, in whose "backyard" the commercially valuable redwoods grew.

Finally, after prolonged and bitter debate, a compromise was reached, and in October 1968, Congress authorized a national park of 58,000 acres. Half of this acreage would come from three existing state parks, and the remainder would be purchased from or exchanged with private owners. At an eventual cost of $92 million—triple the amount that Congress had authorized—it was the most expensive park purchase ever made by the federal government.

While the Sierra Club heralded the park's creation as "a great victory" over "the monumental opposition of the most powerful combination of financial interests that ever stood against a park," the effort had only saved 10,876 acres of old-growth redwoods.[83] In addition, the final park had an ungainly, odd shape said to resemble a jerry-rigged congressional district or, equally uncharitably, a worm. While the creation of the park ensured the protection of the Tall Creek grove of trees—which included the world's tallest tree—virtually all of the watershed around the grove was left in private hands, making the trees vulnerable to erosion from upslope and upstream logging. Nonetheless, the establishment of Redwood National Park marked the first time the federal government had protected the coastal redwoods since the designation of Muir Woods as a national monument in 1906.

A SPLIT AMONG ADVOCATES

The establishment of Redwood National Park by Congress signaled a change in organizational advocacy for redwood protection. Previously, there had been a rough division of labor between the Save-the-Redwoods League and the Sierra Club, with the former focused on protecting the coastal redwoods through land purchases that created or expanded state parks and the latter focused on protecting the large sequoias on the western slope of the Sierras that were already under federal protection. By engaging in coastal redwoods protection though national political advocacy, the Sierra Club directly challenged this division.

The Save-the-Redwoods League, which was limited by its philanthropic traditions, business leadership, and tax-exempt status, was reluctant to endorse or support the Sierra Club's newly aggressive lobbying effort to create a national park to protect the coastal redwoods, especially as this approach involved the exercise of eminent domain rather than voluntary land purchases. In the debate over Redwood National Park, the league had initially backed an alternative smaller site for a park in an area that it judged less likely to produce controversy and only belatedly supported the Sierra Club's efforts. For the club, whose membership had steadily increased over the course of the campaign, the park's creation represented a reshaping of the organization's identity. Not only had the Sierra Club become the principal political protector of all the state's redwoods, but the fight also marked its emergence as an influential national lobby, serving as "a harbinger of more sophisticated campaigns ahead."[84]

PARK EXPANSION

After Redwood National Park's establishment, three timber companies, motivated by fears that the boundaries of the park might be expanded, accelerated their clear-cutting of the old-growth forests in the Redwood Creek area right up to the park's boundaries. As the Sierra Club had feared, the destruction of 90 percent of the approximately 150,000 acres of trees in the Redwood Creek watershed threatened the previously protected redwoods. Loads of gravel and sediment five to fourteen feet high began washing down Redwood Creek—reminiscent of the destructive debris generated by hydraulic gold mining a century earlier. In response, the Sierra Club launched a campaign to expand the park's boundaries. This time, even though the club's efforts were supported by the Save-the-Redwoods League and several other environmental organizations, the battle was even more heated. While the timber firms had earlier recognized that some form of national park was inevitable, they now went on the offensive, describing the park's expansion as a threat to private enterprise and an unnecessary burden on taxpayers and accusing the Sierra Club of scare tactics.[85] The firms not only rejected the government's requests for a voluntary moratorium on logging but actually increased their rate of clear-cutting. Loggers, backed by the AFL-CIO, organized caravans and demonstrations to oppose the plan. Gathering on the steps of the U.S. Capitol, they demanded that Congress "Save Our Jobs!"

Nevertheless, in March 1978, President Jimmy Carter signed legislation authorizing the taking of 48,000 additional acres—four-fifths of which had already been clear-cut, with the remaining 9,000 acres consisting of virgin redwoods. An upstream protection zone of 30,000 acres was also established. In an important concession to the state of California, the legislation established a federally funded unemployment program for displaced loggers. When the costs of worker protection and payments to the logging companies were totaled, the final costs of park expansion came to nearly $2 billion—over five times the original budget.

Redwood Protection

Today, approximately 350,000 acres of California's redwoods, which represent 45 percent of the remaining coastal redwoods, are now protected in four federal and state parks. Three of them, Humboldt Redwoods State Park, Redwood National Park, and Big Basin Redwoods State Park, contain a total of 98,500 acres of ancient coastal redwoods. But all told, only about 5 percent of the state's original coastal redwoods remain, demonstrating the enormous challenges California has faced in protecting them, as well as the lag in protecting them compared to the sequoias in the Sierras. These trees are major tourist attractions and have become more accessible to the public through the construction of a coastal highway. The "Avenue of the Giants," a thirty-one-mile stretch of Highway 1, runs through the world's largest stand of virgin redwoods in Humboldt Redwoods State Park.

In marked contrast to the Sierra sequoias, virtually all of which are in publicly owned and protected forests, the majority of coastal redwoods are still privately owned. They continue to be harvested to meet the strong consumer demand for their wood. This harvesting, however, is regulated by the California Forest Products Act of 1973. This statute, which is the strictest of any such state law in the United States, requires that all commercial harvesting be reviewed and approved by the California Department of Forestry and Fire Protection. California also has the most restrictive regulations on clear-cutting on private land in North America.[86]

Thanks to these state restrictions, along with continual replanting, the fact that young redwood forests grow extremely rapidly, and long-term improvements in commercial management practices, there has been sufficient "natural" production of redwood fiber to meet current and future construction needs without diminishing total redwood acreage. Some privately owned forests are open to the public and used for hunting, fishing, and camping. However, controversy over the management practices of the lumber industry remains, as do conflicts over the extent of private and public forest ownership.

Conclusion

This chapter has explored the long and multifaceted efforts that have been made over the years to protect several of the state's unique areas of scenic beauty. These efforts have engaged both the state of California and the federal government, with state political constituencies playing an important role in shaping federal policies. The federal initiative to protect Yosemite came from California, as did much of the political support for the creation of national parks in the Sierras. In addition to public intervention, private philanthropy has also played an important role in protecting many of California's scenic areas, with many of these funds coming from outside the state.

Through the first decades of the twentieth century, with the notable exception of forest conservation, California's management capacity lagged behind that of the federal government—hence the importance that Muir attached to returning Yosemite Valley to federal jurisdiction and Kent's decision to donate his land to the federal government rather than to the state of California. But around the turn of the century, the state began to develop the administrative capacities needed to protect its natural environment. Historically, the coastal redwoods were primarily protected in state parks. However, more recent efforts to protect the coastal redwoods have required federal support, largely because of the expense involved.

A critical factor shaping historical political support for conservation in California was its urban roots. A significant number of middle- and upper-class Californians, many of whom lived in the San Francisco Bay Area, placed a high value on protecting the state's areas of scenic beauty. The geographic foci of both the Sierra Club and the Sempervirens Club were closely linked to the material interests of their members: namely, their ability to enjoy the natural amenities located in the "backyard" of a major metropolitan area. While national in scope, the Save-the-Redwoods League drew strongly on the support of Bay Area residents to protect the natural environment around them, which they personally valued.

In this context, it is important to consider the significant roles played by both John Muir and William Kent. Neither man moved or returned to California because of his interest in wilderness protection. Muir became politically active and Kent a prominent "green" philanthropist *after* living in California and learning that the wilderness areas to which they had become emotionally attached were threatened. It was living proximate to the beauty of northern California that made them into what we would now call environmentalists. In short, the attractiveness of the geography of northern California played a critical role in creating public support for protecting it.

Equally important were the commercial benefits that could be derived from protection of the state's unusually attractive natural environment. Precisely because the state had many areas of extraordinary—and unusual—natural beauty, California had a significant potential to attract tourists. But this potential would not be realized without government protection. The railroads played a critical role in supporting public policies to protect the Sierras and the coastal redwoods, and a broad range of commercial interests backed the expansion of the state's parks. Interest in attracting tourists to California underlay the original efforts to protect Yosemite as well as the expansion of the state park system. Protecting the state's forests also had other economic benefits.

For this and other reasons, alliances between citizen groups and businesses were both frequent and important. The Southern Pacific Railway was John Muir's most influential supporter, providing him with critical backing at several key moments. The bizarre alliance between the oil industry and the State Parks Commission to finance park expansion was no less important. Within the citizenry, the Save-the-Redwoods League cultivated business support and received contributions of forestland from lumber companies as well as financial support from business leaders. Without the backing of segments of the business community and both local and national business leaders of influence, much less of the state's scenic landscape would have been protected.

Yet at the same time, it is also important to recognize that business interests also served as a constraint on forest protection. The economic value of the coastal redwoods considerably delayed and limited their protection. By contrast, more of the ancient trees survived in the Sierras in part because they were less accessible to loggers and of less commercial value.

California also benefited from the national value placed on its unusual scenic features. Thanks to the publicity from prominent individuals like Frederick Olmsted and Horace Greeley and the area's widespread representation in photographs and paintings, Yosemite became a national scenic icon. The sequoias in the Sierras were likewise seen as a unique national treasure. This visibility certainly contributed to the willingness of Congress to protect these trees. The same was true of the state's coastal redwoods, which were able to attract philanthropic support from donors throughout the United States. In short, while the primary public and business efforts to protect the state's scenic areas came from within its borders, the protection of California's forests was in part due to the fact that many of its "Big Trees" were valued by more than Californians.

4

Protecting California's Coast

California's 1,200-mile coastline along the Pacific Ocean has long been recognized as one of the state's most distinctive and beautiful geographic features. An early western visitor to the state wrote: "On no other coast that I know shall you enjoy, in calm, sunny weather such a spectacle of Ocean's greatness, such beauty of changing colour, or such a degree of thunder in the sound."[1] A more recent visitor observed: "One has only to stand at the continent's western edge, confronting the Pacific Ocean from the California coast, to understand the fascination so many people have for this memorable meeting place of land and water . . . the greatest of their state's natural treasures."[2] In addition to its aesthetic value and opportunities for recreation, the coast is a major economic resource. It enhances the value of property located on or near it, and the coastal area also contains substantial deposits of oil. Precisely because the coast is a scarce and valuable resource with so many competing uses, protecting it, like the coastal redwoods, has been highly contentious.

While the previous two chapters focused on environmental issues affecting northern California, this chapter has a broader geographic focus. It begins by exploring the conflicts over Southern California's beaches and coastal areas and then turns to efforts to protect the San Francisco Bay and the entire Pacific coast.

The public policies discussed in this chapter again demonstrate the broad dynamics that historically have shaped many of the state's environmental initiatives. First, an attractive environmental amenity—in this case, the coast—was threatened by economic development. Second, citizen groups

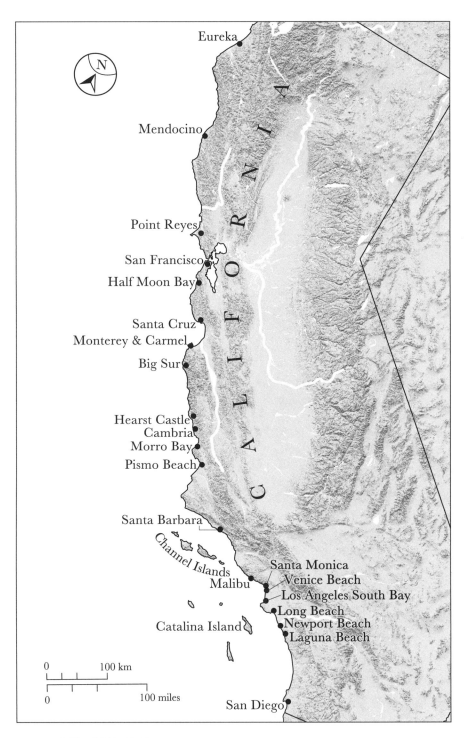

MAP 4. California's Pacific Coast

responded by engaging in political activity to protect or restore their ability to enjoy public goods that they valued. These grassroots campaigns mobilized large numbers of citizens to their cause. Third, divided business interests made possible alliances between citizen activists and segments of the business community. Fourth, the state was able to protect its environmental assets more effectively by expanding its administrative capacity—in this case, through agencies like the State Lands Commission and the Coastal Commission. But while the strengthening of government regulation had a measurable impact on improving the state's environmental quality, it did not occur until after considerable degradation, some irreversible, had already occurred—as in the cases of both hydraulic gold mining and forest protection explored in the two previous chapters.

However, on one important dimension, the dynamics of two of the important cases described in this chapter depart from the book's explanatory framework. The campaigns to establish the Bay Conservation and Development Commission, the world's first coastal protection agency, as well as the more sweeping California Coastal Commission, received no business support. In both cases, the interests of business were not divided. Rather, their creation was made possible by extensive citizen mobilization, an outcome that reveals the important role played by public support for environmental protection in California beginning in the middle of the twentieth century.

Oil and the Beaches

OIL IS DISCOVERED

Just as gold mining had adverse environmental impacts in northern California, so did the discovery of oil adversely affect the environment of Southern California. Oil was first discovered in California's San Joaquin Valley during the 1870s. Drilling began in 1892 at a well located about a mile from Los Angeles City Hall. Within a decade, more than a thousand oil wells had been drilled within the city's limits. North of Los Angeles, in Santa Barbara, oil firms at around the same time began to build derricks at the end of piers to recover offshore oil. By the turn of the twentieth century, there were more than 200 offshore oil wells in the state. By 1909, California led the United States in oil production. Several very rich oil fields were subsequently discovered in the Los Angeles Basin, and these soon accounted for 80 percent of the state's total oil output. The discovery of oil in the city touched off a stampede of economic activity similar to that produced by the Gold Rush more than a half-century earlier.[3] During the 1920s, oil was one of the major sources of economic growth in Los Angeles. Much of this drilling took place on or adjacent to the city's beaches and tidelands, as many of the most promising fields were located there.

DRILLING BECOMES UNPOPULAR

However, the drilling of oil in the city's residential areas proved extremely unpopular among private citizens. Operations were accompanied by numerous explosions of natural gas, along with loud noise, unpleasant odors, and sprayed or spilled oil. The wooden derricks, open oil tanks, and spilled crude often caught fire. One resident of Huntington Beach complained: "These oil men have taken everything except the food in the icebox. . . . My back yard is an oil well, a stump hole. My fence is gone and the inside of my house is a mess."[4] The city's beaches were soon filled with derricks, drilling piers, fences, pipes, and equipment and were often fouled by oil spills. Those seeking to enjoy them were often forced to walk through a maze of unsightly, noisy, and foul-smelling equipment, with their access often blocked by machinery or fences. It was not uncommon for people to sunbathe surrounded by oil rigs.

The extensive oil drilling along the region's attractive coastline threatened both tourism and the prosperity of shoreline communities in Southern California. In 1928, the state responded to public pressure by banning drilling off of piers. Governor C. C. Young described the measure as "a victory for the public in a long battle to protect the priceless California coast from private exploitation and ruin."[5] In fact, this measure was also supported by the major oil firms, since changes in technology meant that they no longer needed piers to access tideland oil. Rather, they now could drill diagonally from dry land into the tidelands—a method known as slant drilling. The oil firms also hoped that moving wells off the beaches would reduce public opposition to offshore drilling—an important priority for the industry, as many of the richest reserves were located offshore in the tidelands.

However, public and business opposition in Los Angeles to any oil drilling continued. The city's residents regarded the coast as a scenic and recreational resource rather than an industrial one. They disliked both the new rigs that were being built adjacent to the beaches and the unsightly old rigs that loomed offshore. The campaign to remove this equipment from both on- and offshore was led by the Los Angeles business community, including the city's chambers of commerce and real estate organizations—another important example of business backing for environmental protection. Several communities along the Santa Monica Bay went so far as to demand a ban on all drilling within a half mile of the water, arguing that this activity impaired beach recreation "to the detriment of the community as a whole."[6]

In essence, the fight boiled down to a competition between two major priorities—relaxation and recreation versus resource extraction—over the use of coastal resources.[7] This conflict echoed the earlier clash over the fate of the California redwoods. But just as Californians wanted to both consume the wood from the state's forests *and* protect and admire the trees, so too did they want to reap the benefits of the sprawling housing patterns of Southern California and automotive-based tourism made possible by oil drilling while also enjoying the beaches. It was thus no more possible to ban all redwood harvesting in northern California than it was to prohibit all oil drilling in the southern part of the state. In both cases, compromises were necessary.

As Southern California grew rapidly between the 1920s and the 1940s, coastal property owners as well as the local business community became increasingly worried about beach oil pollution. In 1929, political pressure from Southern California persuaded the legislature to block new oil development in tidelands along the entire coast. In 1932, the state's voters rejected a ballot initiative proposed by the oil industry to increase the exploitation of offshore reserves. While the measure's proponents had emphasized the importance of tax revenues, the state's electorate placed a higher priority on preserving the beaches for recreation. According to scholar Peter Asmus, they went to the polls "with their eyes and hearts instead of their pocketbooks," though presumably some Southern Californians living on or near the beaches also sought to protect their property values.[8]

However, as noted in chapter 3, two years later voters approved a ballot measure permitting additional oil development off the state's shores in return for the allocation of 30 percent of these operations' revenues to park development. This measure was strongly opposed by voters from the coastal areas of Southern California, whose opposition to oil drilling on and along the coast persisted. However, proceeds from the additional funds made available by the initiative did make possible state purchases of several additional beaches in Southern California and also expanded state parks throughout the state.

Subsequently, the State Lands Act of 1938 restricted drilling on state-owned lands to uplands or filled tidelands but exempted offshore drilling from the prohibition. At the same time, California established the State

Lands Commission to more closely regulate state land management. The decision to create this commission was prompted by the California Department of Finance's discovery of serious irregularities in the execution of a boundary line agreement in Malibu the previous year. State policymakers believed that the management and development of California's oil and gas resources would be better overseen by an autonomous board whose decisions were made in a public forum with opportunities for citizen participation. The commission's formation proved to be an important step in the development of the state's environmental administrative capacity.

The oil laws enacted by California in both 1929 and 1938 reveal a striking contrast between petroleum politics at the state and federal levels. California's restrictions on where oil could be drilled were more restrictive than those of the federal government. Paul Sabin has speculated that one source of this difference was political access: "Political lobbies like coastal real estate interests and small business groups had a voice at the state level that they lacked in Congress," he points out, while the oil industry was more powerful in Washington than in Sacramento.[9]

This discrepancy stands in marked contrast to the state and federal attitudes that had characterized the battle over Yosemite's recession that had taken place at the beginning of the twentieth century. At that time, environmental advocates had viewed the federal government as a better steward of California's natural environment than the state of California. But now, a few decades later, state policies had become *more* protective of the state's environment than those of the federal government. The oil drilling issue thus represented the beginning of a historical shift in the relative stringency of federal and state regulatory policies. This divergence would become highly contentious during the 1960s, when California insisted on the right to enact more stringent regulations for vehicle emissions than the federal government.

Protecting Beaches

If, as described in the previous chapter, public land use policies in northern California had focused on protecting the scenic areas of the Sierras and the coastal areas north and south of San Francisco, land use in Southern California placed a priority on public access to the region's beaches. Beach protection efforts lagged behind both sequoia and redwood protection efforts in northern California, which had begun in the 1860s for the former and around the turn of the century for the latter. By contrast, in 1930, sixty-four of Los Angeles County's seventy-one miles of beaches were in private hands and thus closed to the public.[10]

The drive to increase public beach access was spearheaded by the Shoreline Planning Association, an organization that brought together real estate, tourism, and commercial interests that sought to make the Southern California coast a more attractive place to visit and live. The SPA's objectives were similar to those of many of the region's residents, to whom the beaches were a major source of recreation—much as the Sierras and the coastal redwoods were for those who lived in the northern part of the state. Once again, local geography played a key role in shaping environmental policy in California, as did congruence between business and citizen interests.

On many issues, the (then) conservative, Republican-dominated counties of Southern California had very different political preferences than the largely Democratic, liberal communities of the northern half of the state. But both had a similar material interest in protecting their ability to "consume" the environmental amenities that were available in their respective "backyards" (or, in the case of Southern Californians, their "front yards").

BEACHES BECOME PUBLIC GOODS

As the century progressed, the ownership of Southern California's beaches began to change. The Depression, along with gasoline rationing during the Second World War, imposed financial hardships on several private beach clubs, which were eventually taken over by municipal authorities. In some cases, clubs were taken over by the military during the 1940s and then remained in public hands after the war. Several large private landowners, including the producer Louis B. Mayer and the actress Mary Pickford, donated their beachfront residences to local governments. In one case, a group of residents bought a heavily mortgaged private club and turned it over to Santa Barbara County for public use—an act that mirrored the philanthropic efforts of private citizens to protect the state's redwoods described in the previous chapter.

These changes, however, failed to satisfy the Shoreline Planning Association, which wanted a much more comprehensive and coordinated plan for beach property acquisition. Due to the accumulation of unspent royalties from oil drilling during the Second World War, public funds were available from the state; the challenge was how to use them. In December 1944, the Los Angeles County supervisors submitted a beachfront acquisition bill to the state legislature, which agreed to authorize $10 million in public funds to assist local governments with purchasing beachfront properties—with the proviso that those governments had to match the state grants with either cash or beachfront acreage.

The SPA then embarked on a public campaign to encourage local governments to match the state funds. Its reports and press releases described the beaches as the state's "greatest natural resource," one that deserved to be "owned, protected and developed by the State for the enjoyment of the people." The association's public relations materials also invoked the just-concluded Second World War, with one piece of literature stating: "Our armed forces used the 'beaches' to beat enemy forces. They should now be able to enjoy publicly owned beaches in peace."[11] Citizens were encouraged to donate funds in honor of fallen soldiers.

Consequently, public beach acquisition increased rapidly during the second half of the 1940s. By 1952, nearly all of the critical properties identified by the SPA had been acquired by either city, county, or state agencies. Moreover, oil drilling no longer took place on or close to the beaches. But subsequently, another environmental risk from oil drilling would threaten the beaches of Southern California.

Offshore Drilling in Santa Barbara

EARLY OIL COLLECTION

Patches of tar have long been found on the beaches of Santa Barbara. Native Americans used this tar to bind their woven baskets, and Spanish explorers relied on it to caulk their leaky ships. When the English explorer James Cook anchored his ship in the Santa Barbara Channel in 1778, his navigator wrote that the sea was "covered with a thick, slimy substance [and] had the appearance of dissolved tar floating on the surface, which covered the ocean in all directions."[12] During the later part of the nineteenth century, seeping natural asphalt was shipped from the area to San Francisco and used to pave that city's sidewalks and streets.

In 1896, operators in the Summerland Oil Field east of Santa Barbara began drilling into the ocean from piers they had constructed. Their operation made Santa Barbara the world's first site of offshore oil development. By 1901, 350 small wells had been drilled off Santa Barbara County's coast. At this time, Santa Barbara was a sparsely inhabited, predominately agricultural community whose citizens were eager for the revenue that could be gained from oil drilling. Indeed, there was considerable disappointment when operation of the wells was discontinued during the 1920s after seepages of seawater made them uneconomical.

OIL DRILLING FALLS OUT OF FAVOR

By the 1930s, Santa Barbara's economy had changed: the city had become a well-established resort community, with tourism serving as a major source of revenue, as well as a retirement community for many affluent easterners. In addition to weather warm enough for almost year-round swimming in the Pacific, the major geographic attraction of Santa Barbara was its coastline, which was considered one of the most beautiful in the nation, with, in the poetic words of Malcolm Baldwin, "a narrow plain hugging the shore, merging into rolling hills and rising to a mountain backdrop."[13]

This beauty, however, was now threatened by another feature of the city's geography. During the 1930s, geologists had discovered substantial oil reserves underneath the Santa Barbara Channel. Located in relatively shallow water, these reserves could be readily accessed by existing ocean-drilling technology. While the 1938 California State Lands Act had legalized oil leasing in state tidelands out to a three-mile limit, a protracted dispute between the federal government and the state over the ownership of this offshore oil had restricted offshore platform construction and drilling. In 1953, this dispute was resolved when Congress passed the Submerged Lands Act, which granted states ownership of all oil within three nautical miles of the shore; oil found beyond that point would belong to the federal government. This demarcation between state and federal jurisdiction, like that between the state park in Yosemite and the national park surrounding it, would prove both consequential and contentious.

OPPOSITION TO OIL

Because of the economic importance of tourism, wealthy landowners who sought to preserve their spectacular views of the shoreline, and the more general desire of the local community to preserve the attractive aesthetics of the coast, there was substantial local public opposition to the state's efforts to issue oil leases in the three-mile zone it now legally controlled. The residents of Santa Barbara instead wanted the state to create an oil-free sanctuary to preserve their views of the shoreline. After considerable debate in Sacramento, the state government agreed to establish a marine sanctuary extending sixteen miles along the coast of Santa Barbara. Oil drilling would be permitted in this channel only under very restrictive conditions. The county and city of Santa Barbara then enacted further zoning controls to regulate onshore production in the area that literally sat in their "front yard."

Subsequently, however, several major oil fields were discovered within the three-mile zone controlled by the state on both sides of the marine sanctuary, and in 1957, California began to grant leases to exploit them. Many of these wells yielded large amounts of oil, and by the mid-1960s there were more than 170 oil or gas wells along the coast of Southern California. None were located in the Santa Barbara Channel, though a few of them were visible from the city on a clear day.

The federal government now realized that it could also cash in on the rich oil fields within its jurisdiction. In 1965, a Supreme Court decision rejected California's claims to the continental shelf lands in the Santa Barbara Channel beyond the three-mile limit, holding that they were the property of the federal government. The following year, the federal Bureau of Land Management asked companies to submit proposals for the Santa Barbara Channel tracts they were interested in leasing.

This move alarmed the residents of Santa Barbara. In response to their protests, the Department of Interior agreed to prohibit any leasing in a two-mile buffer zone beyond the state sanctuary—which essentially restricted drilling up to five miles from the coast. Santa Barbara County had requested a larger protected zone, as well as the leasing of less acreage and fewer platforms, but the federal government denied these requests, although it did agree to require that large platforms be camouflaged in an effort to protect the aesthetic value of the coast. But notwithstanding these concessions, the federal government did permit oil drilling in the Santa Barbara Channel. Washington was understandably less interested in protecting the ocean views from Santa Barbara than was Sacramento. Once again, the state found itself with "greener" policy preferences than the federal government.

A TERRIBLE SPILL

In February 1968, the federal government sold $603 million worth of leases for offshore drilling off Santa Barbara's coast. Shortly afterward, Union Oil, the operator of these leases, discovered oil and received a permit for platform construction. The company's first oil rig—which was also the first oil platform located in federal waters off California—began drilling on September 14, 1968. Known as Platform A, or Alpha, it was sunk in 188 feet of water and located 5.8 miles from the shore, or just 0.8 of a mile beyond the buffer zone that the federal government had agreed to respect. The platform contained 57 slots for wells, which made it possible to drill diagonally into the oil reserves from several different angles.

Four and a half months later, on January 28, 1969, Platform A's fourth well was drilled to its final depth of 3,479 feet. As the drill was being withdrawn, a leak developed and an enormous amount of gas, oil, and drilling mud gushed up the hole and burst into the air. While the workers were able to plug the well, they failed to stop the blowout, leaving oil leaking into the ocean. A thick, bubbling oil slick began to grow and spread. In less than twenty-four hours, seventy-five square miles had been covered with oil. Within four days, the oil had begun to come ashore, coating beaches, boats, and oceanfront property with a black glaze.

The spill continued for several months. By the time the well was finally sealed, it had deposited between 2 and 3 million gallons of oil into the channel, impacted 800 square miles of ocean, and coated more than 35 miles of coastline with oil up to six inches thick. Rescuers counted 3,600 dead ocean-feeding seabirds as well as a large number of seals and dolphins. The spill also killed countless numbers of fish, devastated kelp forests, and displaced many endangered birds. All commercial fishing was suspended, and the beaches were closed until June. A year later, large areas of crude oil from the spill could still be seen in the ocean.

RESPONSE TO THE SPILL

The spill received extensive national media attention. A week after it began, on February 5, 1969, it was the major headline in many morning newspapers and was widely covered on radio and television. News coverage featured dramatic pictures of thousands of petroleum-covered birds and blackened Santa Barbara beaches. A U.S. Senate subcommittee hearing on the spill was covered by all three television networks and fifty reporters.

A highly dramatic and photogenic environmental disaster, the Santa Barbara oil spill had a major national political impact. Just as the "discovery" of Yosemite and the sequoia redwoods in California had increased national awareness of the importance of protecting areas of spectacular natural beauty, so too did the oil spill off the coast of Santa Barbara vividly demonstrate the environmental risks of offshore oil drilling. More broadly, by calling national attention to how the country's natural environment was being threatened, the spill helped inspire the growth of the national environmental movement—another important example of the national environmental impact of developments in California.

However, the most immediate political impact of the spill was in Santa Barbara. There, the crisis led to the political mobilization of the city's largely affluent, well-educated, and politically sophisticated residents, who sought to combat what they perceived as a colossal wrong, namely, "the pollution of their otherwise near perfect environment."[14] Unlike other coastal communities in California and elsewhere in the United States, Santa Barbara had chosen to give up substantial tax revenues in order to protect its offshore environment. But its residents were now facing the damages of the largest offshore oil spill in the United States to date.[15]

Led by a former state senator and a local corporate executive, the newly radicalized members of this politically conservative community (which would later become President Ronald Reagan's home) established an organization called "GOO," for Get Oil Out. Their petition to President Richard Nixon, which attracted more than 100,000 signatures, made three specific demands. They wanted all offshore oil operations in the Santa Barbara Channel to be immediately terminated, no further leases to be issued, and all oil platforms and rigs to be immediately removed from the channel. GOO's demands were echoed in hundreds of letters published in local newspapers and in additional petitions submitted to key members of Congress and officials in the Nixon administration. At one point, an angry mob of Santa Barbara residents gathered at a dock used by oil platform crews, blocked traffic, rocked cars, and marched to City Hall and back in a demonstration that lasted into the night.

The Department of Interior did agree to issue a temporary ban on drilling in the Santa Barbara Channel, but drilling was subsequently resumed under the five leases that had already been issued, albeit under stricter oversight. The wells operated under these leases, including those drilled from Platform A, continue to extract oil though the present day.[16] U.S. Secretary of Interior Walter Hickel did make one important concession: he removed fifty-three square miles of federal tracts near the Santa Barbara Channel from future leasing. But the federal government continued to hold offshore lease sales in the rest of California through 1982, when Congress directed that no federal funds be used to lease additional tracts off the coast of California.

Earlier opposition to oil drilling in Southern California had focused on the operations' aesthetic impact or interference with the recreational uses of the beaches. But the Santa Barbara spill dramatically revealed new environmental risks, which were taken extremely seriously in California. After the spill, the California State Lands Commission, which controls leasing on the state's three-mile seabed, halted all further leasing of state offshore tracts—a restriction made permanent by the 1994 California Coastal Act. However, nine active offshore drilling and production operations were allowed to continue. Today, California is the nation's third-largest oil-producing state, with most oil coming from drilling in the San Joaquin Valley, a predominately rural inland area located in the middle of the state. This region contains one of the four largest oil-producing fields in the United States, as well as several substantial untapped reserves.

Saving San Francisco Bay

A "VIRTUAL CESSPOOL"

The San Francisco Bay is one of the most attractive and best-known natural features of California. Along with the Golden Gate Bridge, which connects the bay and the Pacific Ocean, it is the first thing many people think of when they picture San Francisco. In 1869, Lake Merritt was created in the city of Oakland across the bay from San Francisco by damming off a section of the San Francisco Bay. Thanks to the efforts of Oakland's mayor, who loved ducks, the following year the state of California declared the lake a waterfowl refuge, the first such refuge to be established in the United States.[17]

But this early example of environmental protection in the San Francisco Bay was anomalous. As northern California industrialized during the latter part of the nineteenth century, the San Francisco Bay became increasingly polluted. Canneries, steel mills, smelters, and tanneries dumped their toxic wastes into both the bay and the rivers flowing into it. Making matters worse, ships also freely discharged their wastes into the bay's waters. By 1900, the bay was a "virtual cesspool," and nearly all of its formerly abundant schools of herring, sardines, and shrimp had disappeared.[18] As the East Bay began to develop in the early twentieth century, the increased discharge of municipal sewage further deteriorated water quality. In fact, the Oakland estuary became so foul that a channel had to be cut through the city to improve water flows—thus making Alameda into an island. Mocking the daily flow of the tides past San Francisco toward the southern end of the bay, in 1965 Tom Lehrer, a comedian playing in San Francisco, teased: "The breakfast garbage that you throw into the Bay/They drink at lunch in San Jose." His barbs hit home because they were so close to reality.[19]

Equally important, the bay was being rapidly filled in. During the Gold Rush, it was estimated to have contained 787 square miles of open water; by 1960, this had been reduced to 548 square miles. Less than a quarter of the original tidal marshlands that had historically surrounded the bay remained, with the rest being "reclaimed." The U.S. Army Corps of Engineers predicted that if all the remaining tidal and submerged lands were reclaimed, only 187 square miles of the bay would still be left.[20]

This infill was the result of many years of steady development. Anxious for additional land and benefiting from the bay's shallow shoreline that facilitated waterfront construction, the cities around the bay allowed a number of companies and operations to put down roots on the shore. Gradually the area was filled in by railways, docks, piers, airports, and, during the Second World War, military shipyards and airport expansion. Treasure Island was constructed in the middle of the bay for the 1939 World's Fair. The construction of military bases in Oakland and Alameda actually moved the shoreline of the East Bay a mile closer to San Francisco. During the 1950s, landfills by cities around the bay further defaced the shoreline, and several housing projects further reduced the bay's size. Eventually, only 4 miles of its 276-mile circumference below the delta remained open to the public.[21]

During the mid 1960s, several local governments were planning major landfills in shoreline areas of the bay to which they had legal title. The city of Oakland had applied for a permit to fill a two-square-mile area of the bay that would extend to Treasure Island, while San Francisco wanted to fill about a mile of the bay offshore of Candlestick Park, the baseball/football park located south of the city. The cities of Alameda, Emeryville, Richmond, San Rafael, and Corte Madera had similarly ambitious plans to take advantage of what was prime real estate. In Sausalito, an attractive town on a hillside in Marin County that looks over the surface of the bay to San Francisco, a developer was planning a $10 million commercial development to be built on fill extending 1,000 feet into the bay and stretching along seven blocks of the shoreline.

However, unlike earlier developments, these plans did not unfold smoothly. All of these planned fills were located in the bay's most critical ecological zones, namely, the shoreline areas that were the principal nurseries for fish and their food and the main feeding grounds for millions of waterfowl. These areas also moderated the weather along the shore, provided views of the water for Bay Area communities, and were used for shoreline and water recreation.[22] For the first time, groups began to push back against infill.

SAVE SAN FRANCISCO BAY ASSOCIATION

The initial effort to protect the bay came from the university town of Berkeley. In 1961, the city of Berkeley announced that it planned to double its physical size by filling in 4,000 acres of mudflats along the city's shoreline that it owned. Just as plans for offshore oil drilling threatened the ocean views of the residents of Santa Barbara, so did the Berkeley project threaten that city's aesthetics, outraging some residents. Three politically well-connected women, Kay Kerr (whose husband was president of the University of California), Sylvia McLaughlin (whose husband was a member of the University of California Board of Regents and president of the Homestake Mining Company), and Esther Gulick (who was married to a Berkeley economics professor), invited the leaders of thirteen environmental organizations to a meeting at the Gulick home in the Berkeley hills. There, they formed the Save San Francisco Bay Association. The group sent hundreds of letters to call public attention to the destruction of the bay. Their campaign received extensive media attention, and contributions poured in. In response, the city of Berkeley withdrew its development plans and began to work instead on developing the city's shoreline to promote recreation. Subsequently joined by a wide array of writers, naturalists, environmentalists, and civic leaders from communities throughout the Bay Area, by 1965 the association had 18,000 members.

Nearly every state legislator from the region now recognized the need to protect the bay. In 1965—only four years after the association had been formed in the Berkeley hills—California's legislature voted to create the San Francisco Bay Conservation and Development Commission as a temporary agency, marking another step in the development of the state's administrative capacity. The commission was charged with preparing a comprehensive and enforceable plan for protecting the bay and managing the development of its shoreline. To protect the bay while it was preparing its report, the commission was given the power to review and approve or reject all development projects.

The commission immediately exercised its regulatory authority by turning down several development projects, abruptly bringing to a halt more than a century of unrestricted filling in of San Francisco Bay. During the next three years, it prepared more than twenty reports, which served as the basis for the plan that it submitted to the governor and the legislature in January 1969. This plan recommended the creation of a permanent regional agency, the Bay Conservation and Development Commission (BCDC), which not only would have the ability to grant or deny permits for all bay-filling and dredging activities but would also be given authority over all developments around the bay extending 100 feet from the shoreline.

OPPOSITION TO PROTECTION

After the temporary commission submitted its report, several bills were introduced in the legislature that incorporated various aspects of its recommendations. But these measures faced strong opposition, spearheaded by two politically influential business firms. The first was the Leslie Salt Company, which was the largest landowner in the bay. It owned 52,000 acres of former marshland that had been turned into salt ponds, which the company now wanted to convert into housing developments. However, the commission wanted to keep the salt ponds in production as long as possible, as they both served as a wildlife habitat and supplemented the total surface area of the bay.

The second major business opponent was Westbay Community Associates. This joint-venture partnership had plans to develop a twenty-seven-mile-long recreational and housing complex along the bay's western shoreline. Massive amounts of landfill would create 10,000 acres of now-submerged land. Westbay realized that a permanent agency was likely to challenge these plans. Both it and Leslie Salt soon hired politically connected Sacramento lobbyists.

The creation of a permanent agency also faced opposition from local governments. The mayor of Oakland, one of the largest Bay Area cities, feared that restrictions on landfill would be harmful to the city's development. San Francisco, Albany, and Emeryville also expressed concerns about giving the proposed BCDC authority over shoreline development, as did local governments in Southern California. They argued that such an agency would violate the principle of "home rule," which gave local municipalities the right to control development, and would interfere with their plans for growth. The latter concern was particularly critical, as local property taxes were the primary source of income for local governments, giving them an important incentive to expand their boundaries and encourage real estate development.

All told, the establishment of a permanent commission faced formidable opposition. This resistance came not only from two major business firms but also from local governments throughout the state, including those from the more historically environmentally conscious Bay Area, whose support for environmental protection did not extend to giving up their right to fill in "their" bay.

SAVE OUR BAY ACTION COMMITTEE

To counter this opposition, as well as several powerful state legislators' lack of enthusiasm for the creation of a regional regulatory agency, activists established a new grassroots organization called the Save Our Bay Action Committee (SOBAC). The committee distributed 38,000 stickers with the slogan "Save Our Bay," which emphasized that the bay belonged to all the area's residents, and collected several hundred thousand signatures in support of legislation to establish a strong regional authority, which it then delivered to key leaders in the state legislature. By placing full-page ads along with contribution coupons in local newspapers, SOBAC was able to both compile a large mailing list and generate enough contributions to sustain its campaign. Toward that end, the committee depicted the business firms and politicians opposed to effective controls over the bay as "villainous despoilers" of this resource and widely circulated pictures of what the bay would like look if the current rate of landfill were to continue.[23]

Several factors contributed to the effectiveness of SOBAC's campaign. First, it was able to draw upon a large existing network of Bay Area conservation organizations such as the Sierra Club (which had 33,000 members in the Bay Area) and the Save the San Francisco Bay Association (which had more than 20,000 members). Second, the bay's value as a public resource was widely recognized: many residents could see it from their hillside windows or observe it on their daily commutes along its shorelines or across its several bridges. The public did not need to be told that the bay was worth saving: it was a highly visible and attractive, if not defining, feature of the area. To be spurred into action, the public only needed to be convinced that the bay was endangered. But even that was obvious: the public could readily observe several infill projects, ranging from housing developments to garbage dumps, that were already underway.

LEGISLATIVE SUPPORT FOR PROTECTION

Sustained grassroots pressure, including petition campaigns, persuaded key legislative leaders to change their position and support legislation to establish the BCDC—an important sign of the growing strength of grassroots environmental movements in California. To broaden its geographic support, SOBAC took its campaign to Southern California. There, it asked Southern Californians to support the creation of the BCDC on the grounds that the bay was a "special and unique natural resource" that belonged to all Californians—echoing the rhetoric used by the Save-the-Redwoods League that the redwoods belonged to all Americans.[24]

This effort was effective. After several amendments designed to weaken the temporary commission's authority were defeated, legislation to establish the BCDC was approved by a vote of twenty-four to ten in the Senate and fifty-five to four in the Assembly. When the bill reached the desk of Governor Ronald Reagan, its supporters presented him with a petition containing 200,000 signatures. In a dramatic gesture, the bill's supporters stretched the list of signatures more than three miles around the state capitol. On August 7, 1969, Reagan signed legislation that created the world's first coastal protection agency. The BCDC was granted permitting authority over all developments within 100 feet of the shoreline.

This legislation was a landmark achievement in the development of environmental law, one that transformed the coastal governance of the entire region. Its enactment reflected the extent of public support in northern California (and from some Southern Californian allies) for protection of a major natural resource in the face of private and local government opposition.[25] It also signaled important growth in the extent and influence of grassroots citizen mobilization in California. Notably, in the case of this environmental policy conflict, there were no prominent bootleggers—only Baptists.

In October 2015, the BCDC celebrated its fiftieth anniversary. While threats to the bay have continued to emerge, most notably from pressures to expand the Bay Area's ports and airports, on balance, the commission has been what Richard Walker has called "spectacularly successful, a model of environmental regulation for the public good, as well as efficiency, [and] effective government."[26] The size of the bay has actually expanded as hundreds of acres of formerly filled or diked lands have been opened up. It now includes the nation's largest urban wildlife refuge, and improvements in water quality have revived fishing. Public shoreline access to the bay has increased from 4 miles in 1969 to 200 in 2015,[27] with hundreds of miles of trails, parks, beaches, and promenades created on the site of former landfills, industrial areas, and working waterfronts. In attempting to balance conservation and development, the BCDC has also approved several commercial and public development projects on the shoreline, including restaurants, hotels, housing, fishing piers, marinas, museums, and a baseball park, which several BCDC commissioners have concluded "allow the public to enjoy the bay to an extent that was unthinkable 50 years ago."[28]

Somewhat ironically, given the lack of support for the establishment of the commission from both commercial interests and local governments, the BCDC's development plans and controls have increased commercial opportunities along the bay. Moreover, by expanding environmental amenities, the commission has made the Bay Area a more attractive place to live and work and thus promoted the region's economic growth. So successful has the BCDC been that it was cited by the first United Nations Conference on the Human Environment as a "model of citizens' initiative."[29] According to Peter Douglas, a consultant with the state legislature, the BCDC's achievements "inspired and fueled the greater movement on behalf of the coast."[30] This is the subject to which we now turn.

The Coastal Protection Initiative

THE ATTRACTION OF THE SEA

In 1931, California's legislature first began to recognize the importance of protecting the coast's natural beauty. According to a joint legislative report on seacoast conservation published that year, "one of the most valuable assets of the state of California lies in its coast line along the Pacific Ocean and in the land and water areas contiguous thereto."[31] Noting that a significant portion of the state's population lived relatively close to the coast, the report acknowledged "a need for general supervision of the beach area[,] both tidelands and uplands, so that development may be orderly" before concluding that "enforcement of existing and future laws with record to the seacoast should all be centered into one government agency."[32] But while the legislature did appropriate funds to study the problem of coastline conservation, it took no action.

Much of the state's subsequent population growth was concentrated near the coast. By 1970, 4.2 million people lived within five miles of the Pacific Ocean—more than the total populations of thirty-four American states at the time. California's fifteen coastal counties were home to 12.8 million people, or 63 percent of the state's total population. The coastal population density was particularly pronounced in the counties of Southern California, which contained an average of 16,896 people per mile of coastline.[33] More broadly, about 80 percent of the state's population resided within a half-hour drive of the Pacific Ocean.

THREATS TO THE COAST

As California's population grew, the coast became increasingly subject to demands for conflicting uses.[34] These conflicts raised important policy issues. Should wetlands be maintained in their natural state or turned into boat harbors and ports? Should the coast in northern California retain its wild character, or should some second-home subdivisions and resorts be permitted to be built there? What priority should be given to maintaining or increasing the coast's recreational opportunities? To what extent should open, undeveloped spaces be preserved? Should the coastal bluffs and beaches of Malibu be open to all 7 million people who lived in Los Angeles County or just to its residents? Should new power plants be placed along the coast where water was plentiful and the costs of construction were lower rather than further inland, where they would not disrupt coastal views or interfere with other uses?

While these dilemmas were similar in principle to those that had been raised by the redwoods, they were considerably more complex, as the number of alternative and competing uses of the coast was much greater. Nevertheless, the broader issue was the same. As had been true for Yosemite, the sequoias in the Sierras, the coastal redwoods, and the San Francisco Bay, an attractive environmental amenity was being threatened by rapid economic development.

During the 1960s, threats to the coast became more visible. High-rise buildings replaced smaller ones; farmlands were converted to housing and commercial facilities; signs, fences, and buildings increasingly blocked public access to formerly accessible land, including beaches; and new power plants were constructed to take advantage of the ocean's cooling water. While California's state constitution legally guaranteed public access to the coast, by the 1960s less than one-fifth of the area was available for public use. As Jared Orsi noted, "The coastline was vanishing before an encroaching frontier of development."[35] Surveys reported that the most widely perceived benefit of stopping or slowing coastal development was the "preservation of the natural beauty of the coast."[36] The public also expressed a strong preference for the establishment of more public recreation areas and campgrounds alongside the ocean.

For their part, marine scientists and a few early conservationists had for decades worried about the impact of the state's rapid economic and population growth on the ecology of the coast. By the 1960s, more than half of the coast's original wetlands had been developed, threatening wildlife habitats.

Sewage and industrial waste also degraded coastal water quality, which in turn endangered fishing. Most dramatically, the 1969 Santa Barbara oil spill had demonstrated the vulnerability of the coast to spills from offshore oil drilling, highlighting the need to put coastal protection on the public agenda.

INSTITUTIONAL CHALLENGES TO PROTECTION

The holding of tidelands—the area of oceanfront between high and low tides—in public trust is an old legal doctrine. With roots in Roman and English common law, the principle was recognized in California's constitution. But its implementation faced substantial political and institutional challenges. The local governments that were responsible for controlling coastal land use historically had a pronounced pro-development bias. This was due both to their dependence on property and sales taxes for revenues and to the important role played by the construction industry and building trades union in financing local political campaigns.

Over the years, coastal development decisions remained decentralized, subject to the competing jurisdictions of fifteen counties, forty-six cities, forty-two state agencies, and seventy federal agencies.[37] This meant that no one authority was responsible for or capable of dealing with the coast's scarce resources in an integrated or coordinated fashion. Nor was any public policy formulated that was capable of addressing spillover effects, or situations in which the decisions of one jurisdiction affected another. In consequence, the public trust provisions of California's constitution remained a dead letter when it came to the tidelands.

THE FIGHT FOR A COASTAL COMMISSION: PROPOSITION 20

In 1967, Ellen Stern Harris, a conservation activist in Southern California who was disturbed by what was happening to the coast in her immediate area, revived the idea of creating a state coastal conservation commission. At a legislative hearing held the following year, she argued that in order to stop the "squandering [of] our treasured coastline," the state needed to adopt a plan for regulating development along the coast, one modeled on the BCDC. Pointing out that no one entity was responsible for overall decisions about uses of the coastline, a representative from the Sierra Club called for the creation of a statewide or regional coastal commission that would have the authority to veto development projects.[38]

Between 1970 and 1972, the state legislature considered several bills to create a state coastal management agency. These proposals would have essentially extended to the rest of California's coastline the land use controls that the legislature had recently adopted for the San Francisco Bay. In 1971, Janet Adams, an activist previously involved with the Save the Bay campaign, organized the California Coastal Alliance to mobilize public support for these legislative proposals. During the next year, the number of organizations joining or endorsing the alliance increased threefold.

However, the alliance's efforts were unsuccessful. Legislation to create a coastal management agency was stalled by pro-development legislators in the state Senate's Natural Resources Committee. The proposals also faced determined opposition from the California Real Estate Association, the League of California Cities, the County Supervisors' Association, and the state's utility and oil firms.

By the spring of 1972, the leadership of the Coastal Alliance had become frustrated with the legislature's inaction. They decided to pursue an alternative political strategy. The group drafted the California Coastal Initiative, which it planned to submit directly to the state's voters on the upcoming election's ballot. With text identical to that of the bills that had died in the state Senate, the initiative sought to coordinate development along the coast and thus manage and balance conservation and development. Under its terms, a twelve-member state coastal commission as well as six regional commissions would be responsible for reviewing all new developments that could potentially affect the coast. All new development within 3,000 feet of the coastline would be prohibited, unless one of the commissions had issued a permit authorizing it. Such permits would only be issued if the project's developers could demonstrate that their plans would have no adverse environmental impact. Furthermore, public hearings would be held for any application whose impact was deemed "substantial." Finally, the state commission would be charged with designing a plan for a permanent coastal management system that would be submitted to the state legislature in 1976.

According to Jared Orsi, the alliance's strategy was to "institutionalize the ideal of coastal protection by harnessing citizen frustration over coastal environmental decline, the enthusiasm of the Save the Bay movement, and the horror of the Santa Barbara oil spill."[39] This aim was achieved: thanks to a massive volunteer effort backed by 100 organizations, the alliance was able to collect 400,000 signatures in only two months. Called Proposition

20—or the Coastal Zone Protection Act—the measure was placed on the November 1972 ballot.

What now followed was one of the most bitterly fought environmental battles in California's history. Both the degree of mobilization of the proposition's supporters and the intensity of the opposition it faced were unprecedented. Several factors made this conflict distinctive. One was the initiative process itself. While the use of the initiative and referendum in California dates from the turn of the twentieth century, the Coastal Zone Protection Act was the first time the initiative process had been used by environmentalists to attempt to do an end run around the state legislature and enact a major new policy. The second distinguishing factor concerned the scope of the proposition. Previous environmental policy decisions had primarily had a local or regional impact, typically affecting those who lived either in northern or Southern California. But thanks to the geography of California's long coast and the concentration of residents along it, the majority of Californians had a stake in Proposition 20's outcome. Statewide in its range, the proposal addressed residents' access to an important environmental amenity that most viewed as *local*.

Finally, the stakes for local governments, coastal property owners, and coastal development businesses throughout the state were equally significant. All were threatened with diminished access to or less control over extremely valuable real estate. Indeed, in the extent of its geographical scope, Proposition 20 may well have been among the most substantive and far-reaching challenges to private property and the authority of local governments in the United States to date.

THE "YES" AND "NO" CAMPAIGNS

After the proposition was placed on the ballot, its proponents mounted a broad grassroots campaign that sought to mobilize as many citizens and citizen associations as possible. The "Yes" campaign was led by the state's oldest and largest environmental organization, the Sierra Club, along with several other environmental groups; organizations of teachers, surfers, and senior citizens; the Planning and Conservation League; the League of Woman Voters; the California Parents and Teaching Association; the California Roadside Council; and the United Auto Workers. Ultimately, more than 15,000 organizations became involved.

Thousands of individuals volunteered their time and expertise in support of the proposition, sending personal notes to their friends and organizing phone banks to call voters. Cartoonist Hank Ketcham drew two *Dennis the Menace* panels lamenting the loss of beach access and asked that they be run on the comic pages of newspapers. *Sunset Magazine* editor Melvin Lane actively campaigned for the initiative, and artist Ansel Adams contributed photographs on its behalf. Several bands staged benefit concerts, and an artist donated a T-shirt logo for the campaign captioned, "Where's the beach?"

Several government officials also supported the "Yes" campaign. Among them were sixty state legislators, several House members and both U.S. Senate members from California, and several local officials. The president pro tem of the state Senate declared that "the public interest will only be served when the public itself rises up and demands protection of its own, irreplaceable coastline."[40]

Significantly, the measure's proponents did not describe or promote the proposition as an environmental measure. Rather, they focused on the issue that Californians cared most about: their access to *their* coast. Thus, the official "Yes" ballot statement, which was signed by legislators from both political parties, emphasized the loss of both physical and visual coastal access. This statement directly appealed to the material interests of the California public, arguing that their coastal land was special and thus merited a special kind of protection: "Our coast has been plundered by haphazard development and land speculators [who] bank their profits, post their 'no trespassing' signs and leave. . . . The public has been denied access to hundreds of miles of beaches and publicly owned tidelands. . . . Ocean vistas are walled off behind unsightly high-rise apartments and billboards. Increase public access to the coast. . . . VOTE YES."[41] The proposition's supporters emphasized that their goal was not to stop all economic development along the coast but rather to prevent haphazard development from restricting the public's access to "their" coast.

Opposition to Proposition 20 was led by a group called Citizens Against the Coastal Initiative. This organization warned the electorate that Proposition 20 would "lock up the beaches from the public" and described the initiative as "an essentially elitist piece of legislation for the benefit of a small minority of citizens."[42] Its broad coalition of business supporters included land developers such as the California Builders Association, the California Chamber of Commerce, and the state's oil and gas companies. While the latter financed most of the "No" campaign, the most active opposition to the proposition came from California's utilities. Pacific Gas & Electric predicted that its passage would lead to serious power shortages, while Southern California Edison included a letter in the billing statements mailed to its customers informing them that the proposition's passage would result in delays in new power construction, the costs of which would then be passed on to consumers.

Three of the state's major newspapers, the *San Francisco Chronicle*, the *San Diego Union*, and the *San Diego Evening Tribune*, opposed the proposition, as did several local governments, which argued that the creation of another bureaucracy would unnecessarily delay the approval of new projects and thus hurt economic growth and tax collection. The Los Angeles Building and Trade Council emphasized that the passage of the initiative would cost jobs.

While Proposition 20's opponents outspent its proponents by more than four to one, on November 7, 1972, the measure was supported by 55 percent of the electorate, winning approval by an 800,000-vote margin. The proposition carried twelve of the fifteen coastal counties, including all of the politically conservative counties of Southern California. In addition to the support it received from a wide range of organizations and a large number of volunteers, the "Yes" campaign succeeded because, in the words of William Duddleson, it "appealed to millions of Californians' imaginative pictures of what 'life in California' was about."[43]

MAKING THE COMMISSION PERMANENT

By taking planning authority away from local governments, Proposition 20's passage marked the most significant coastal planning and land use effort in U.S. history. However, its impact would be muted unless the legislature agreed to make the Coastal Commission established in 1972 permanent. In December 1975, this commission presented its 433-page Coastal Plan to the legislature. By this time, there was more support for coastal protection in Sacramento. Legislators did not want to be seen as ignoring the views of the majority of their constituents. At the same time, real estate and energy firms feared that if the legislature did not take action, another initiative might result in even stronger regulation. And environmentalists were not sure that they were capable of waging another successful public campaign. In short, no one wanted another ballot initiative.

The legislature spent seven months considering a bill based on the commission's findings that would establish a more permanent coastal management system. In an important breakthrough, the backers of the bill, called the Coastal Act of 1976, succeeded in securing the backing of the California Council for Environmental and Economic Balance (CCEEB). This alliance of labor, utility, oil, and development organizations had been formed in 1972 to challenge what they perceived as overly stringent environmental regulations—a category that had included a strong coastal bill.

CCEEB's endorsement of the Coastal Act reflected both compromises made by the bill's steering committee and the assessment of the bill's opponents that it was preferable to cooperate with the advocates of coastal protection rather than risk the outcome of another initiative. After CCEEB agreed to support the legislation, the League of Cities also changed its position and agreed to endorse it as well.

However, the bill still lacked sufficient votes for passage. To ensure its success, Governor Jerry Brown engaged in extensive negotiations with both environmental groups and organized labor, two of his most important political constituencies. Eventually, the AFL-CIO and the building trades unions announced their support, switching three votes in the state Senate and enabling the bill to pass. At the Coastal Act's signing ceremony, Assembly Speaker Kevin McCarthy credited the state's citizens with achieving "the single most important conservation act by the California legislature in a generation."[44] Two months later, in November 1976, the state's voters capped the "Year of the Coast" by approving a bond issue that included $130 million to purchase additional land for state and local beaches and coastal parks, as well as $10 million to fund the newly established—and permanent—California Coastal Commission.

A PERMIT SYSTEM

The legislation enacted in Sacramento gave the California Coastal Commission the authority to oversee the preparation of local coastal programs by local governments. Most important, it authorized the California Coastal Commissions—both state and regional—to establish and administer the establishment of a permit system that, according to Robert Healy, "for scope of coverage and strictness of environmental standards is without precedent in the nation's short history of direct involvement in land-use control."[45] The commission's wide-ranging power over coastal development meant that its decisions would have a broad impact, affecting issues as diverse as water quality, air pollution, coastal population density, the location of freeways, and the siting of power plants.

The commission's core mandate was to avoid further "irreversible and irretrievable commitments of coastal zone resources."[46] Permits were required for virtually all substantial development on or within 1,000 yards of the coast (as well as three miles out to sea), ranging from the building of single-family houses and the expansion of ranches to the paving of bike paths and the construction of nuclear power plants. In addition, a two-thirds vote of the California Coastal Commission was required to approve any development that adversely affected agricultural uses or interfered with the line of sight from the coastal highway to the sea.

All told, this commission is one of the most powerful bodies ever established in either California or the nation, controlling all development along the state's 1,100-mile coastline.[47] But this responsibility placed an enormous administrative burden on both the state and the temporary regional commissions. They have to make literally thousands of decisions on a case-by-case basis affecting development along a large coastline with highly diverse topographical, ecological, cultural, and political characteristics. Nor did they have any precedents to follow as no government had ever been asked to manage such a large and diverse shoreline.

Over the years, the substantial economic value of the coast has produced what reporter Adam Nagourney has called "an everlasting tug of war," with the interests of both wealthy coastal property owners and coastal developers often pitted against those of community groups opposed to further coastal development.[48] Not surprisingly, the commission has frustrated both environmentalists and property owners, who view it as favoring their opponents.[49] Both sides have their "horror stories," and cases that the commission appears to have mishandled have received considerable publicity. However, when the 1972 Coastal Zone Protection Act was due to expire in 1976 at the beginning of Jerry Brown's (first) governorship, the state legislature voted to extend the area it protected to five miles from the shoreline.

In marked contrast to the Bay Conservation and Development Commission, the California Coastal Commission continues to be controversial. Many of its decisions have proved unpopular, especially among developers and local governments. Between 1977 and 1981, the California legislature stripped the commission of several of its powers. When the regional bodies were phased out in 1981, pro-development local governments regained control over their own development plans. That same year the commission became less conservationist in its stance when coastal county officials were appointed to half of its seats. In 1983, Republican governor George Deukmejian significantly cut both the commission's budget and the size of its staff, though he was unable to deliver on his campaign promise to abolish it. Since then, conservationists on the commission have continued to find themselves on the defensive, and several commissioners have been removed for being too protectionist.

An important reason why the California Coastal Commission's efforts to protect public access have been so disputed is that for coastal property owners, the coast *is* literally in their front yard. The rights of such property owners have been repeatedly challenged by the commission, which has typically made the granting of construction permits conditional on the owners agreeing to allow public access to or adjacent to *their* private property. In marked contrast to the restrictions on oil drilling on beaches and off the coast of Southern California, which have benefited coastal property owners, the public access initiatives of the Coastal Commission have often disadvantaged such individuals. These residents have thus become a powerful source of opposition to the regulatory authority, the mandate of which represents a far-reaching and historic challenge to their private property rights.

In 1987, the U.S. Supreme Court heard a case brought by a conservative legal organization, the Pacific Legal Foundation, on behalf of the Nollans, appellants who owned private property along the coast.[50] At issue was whether the Nollans' renovation of their beachfront home in Malibu permitted the Coastal Commission to demand a public use easement across their property to facilitate public access to the beach. The Court had to consider whether this easement constituted a government "taking" of private property that required "just compensation" under the Fifth Amendment.[51] What made this issue so critical was that the commission lacked the financial resources to either purchase private properties or pay their owners compensation. Its only available tool *was* regulation.

The majority decision, written by Associate Justice Antonin Scalia, conceded that the commission could demand a concession from a property owner, in order, for example, to protect the public's view of the beach. However, the Nollans' construction project was not determined to reduce public access to the beach. Accordingly, the Court concluded that by holding a building permit hostage for a property rights concession that bore no relationship to the social harm the permit had caused, the commission was engaging in "out and out . . . extortion."[52] While this decision did provide the basis for future litigation, which affected regulatory policies in several states, its impact on the work of the commission was modest. This was due both to further court decisions that restricted the "regulatory takings" argument and to the Coastal Commission's ability to demonstrate the "social harms" caused by many of the developments it sought to restrict. Moreover, its mission remained popular with the state's electorate. In fact, in 1991, Republican governor Pete Wilson, who had previously supported coastal zone regulation as a state legislator, signed a bipartisan bill that expanded the commission's powers to halt controversial developments in ecologically sensitive areas by limiting judicial review of the commission's decisions.

Considerable controversy continues to surround the implementation of the California Coastal Act today. In 2016, a group of pro-development commissioners, echoing the concerns of developers that the commission's staff was "stifling legitimate growth," mounted a campaign to remove the agency's executive director.[53] Nevertheless, there continues to be strong support among the public for maintaining public access to the coast, with three out of four Californians visiting the coast at least once a year. Polls also report widespread barriers to coastal access such as a lack of affordable parking and limited opportunities for affordable overnight accommodations.[54] The continued growth of the state's population has made facilitating public access to the coast an ongoing challenge.

Conclusion

This chapter has documented the substantial environmental challenges that have confronted California's attractive coastal areas. Southern California's beaches and offshore areas, San Francisco Bay, and the state's coastline have all found themselves under threat over the state's history. Were it not for government regulation restricting oil drilling, the public acquisition of beachfront property in Southern California, and the authority given to both the San Francisco Bay Conservation and Development Commission and the California Coastal Commission, the state's magnificent coast would be much less attractive and publicly accessible.

Efforts to protect the coast can be divided into two broad categories: those that relied on Baptist–bootlegger coalitions and those that did not. Opposition to both on- and offshore oil drilling in Southern California, like the campaigns for forest protection in northern California described in the last chapter, involved a coalition of citizens and business interests and benefited from divisions within the business community. Those who lived on or near the coast in Southern California had a material interest in protecting the beaches and their ocean views. For pecuniary reasons, the shoreline development firms also favored restrictions on oil drilling in order to protect the attractiveness of California's southern coastline.

However, no such Baptist–bootlegger coalitions emerged in the public efforts to protect the San Francisco Bay or increase public access to the coast. These important environmental policy initiatives received no business backing, but much business opposition—notable exceptions in California's history of environmental protection. This was particularly striking in the case of Proposition 20, which succeeded in mobilizing virtually the entire state's business community against it. Presumably, no firm or industry could envision how stricter land use controls might benefit it but could readily understand how such controls might disadvantage it. However, the fact that both initiatives were successful without any business support is revealing, demonstrating the increased political strength of the state's pro-environmental constituencies. Previously, no important environmental regulations had been enacted in California without any business backing.

The extent of grassroots support for protecting the San Francisco Bay is both consistent with and reflective of the historic role of the Bay Area as a major center of both regional and national environmental activism.[55] The northern California region is home not only to the Sierra Club but also to the Sempervirens Club and the Save-the-Redwoods League, all of which played important roles in protecting the sequoias in the Sierras and the redwoods along the northern California coast. What this chapter demonstrates, however, is that citizen activism to protect the state's environmental amenities has not been confined to the Bay Area. The conservative Republican residents of Los Angeles and Santa Barbara were as strongly committed to protecting "their" beaches and coastal areas from oil drilling as the more politically liberal Bay Area residents were to protecting the redwoods being cut down by lumber companies. Legislators from Southern California provided important political backing for the statute that protected San Francisco Bay, while the highly controversial coastal initiative received as much support from voters in Southern California's coastal counties as it did from those in the northern part of the state. These cases reveal the broadening of geographic support for protecting highly visible features of the state's attractive natural environment—support that transcended both partisan affiliation and political ideology.

A noteworthy feature of the politics of coastal protection was the important role played by the initiative process, without which this policy initiative would have remained stalled in the legislature. But while many environmental policy initiatives have come before the state's voters over the years, almost all of those that proposed major policy changes have been defeated.[56]

Rather, to the extent that the initiative process has played an important role in affecting environmental policy in California, it has primarily been by defeating initiatives that aimed to weaken environmental regulations, as this chapter has illustrated and which will be seen again in chapters 5 and 7.

Finally, this chapter has documented the growth of the state's administrative capacity. The State Lands Commission, the San Francisco Bay Conservation and Development Commission, and the California Coastal Commission have all played important roles in protecting the quality of the state's environment. The work and accomplishments of the Bay Conservation and Development Commission served as a model for the later coastal initiative. With the notable exception of the issue of offshore oil drilling, the federal government played little role in any of these developments. In that case, its policy preferences were less supportive of environmental protection than were those of the state of California—a pattern of federal-state conflict that would be replicated in other policy areas.

At the same time, California's coastal protection efforts have had a national impact. Following the passage of what was the nation's first comprehensive coastal protection legislation, the federal government enacted the Coastal Zone Management Act, which encouraged all states to develop coastal zone management plans. By 1978, a dozen coastal and Great Lakes states had adopted coastal or shoreline management programs. While a few of those preceded California's, the state has nonetheless served as "the flagship of coastal management for the nation," with its coastal protection regulations being among the most stringent and best enforced in the United States.[57]

5

Managing Water Resources

California's geography has many attractive features: besides being very beautiful, the state has an abundance of natural resources such as gold, oil, fisheries, and forests and a good deal of fertile land, along with an unusually benign climate. But on one important dimension its natural environment is strikingly inhospitable—at least to many humans. That dimension is water. California is the only state with a truly seasonal rainfall pattern, with 75 percent of its annual precipitation taking place between November and March. Consequently, there is little or no rain in the summer and early fall when it is most needed for crops and watering lawns. This means that water must be saved and stored to make it available during the several months each year when there is no precipitation.

While the state does have substantial water resources, they are poorly located to meet the needs of its population and agricultural sector.[1] Two-thirds of California's total precipitation falls in the northern third of the state, primarily in the Sierra Nevada Mountains, and much of it in the form of rain or snow. By contrast, two-thirds of the state receives less than twenty inches of precipitation a year, while the driest one-third of the state collects only 0.1 percent of its annual runoff. While the San Francisco Bay Area typically receives twenty inches of rain each year—though concentrated during five months—Southern California, where most of the state's population lives and works, is drier than any part of the eastern half of the United States. In the five-county Los Angeles metropolitan region as well as the San Diego metropolitan area, annual rainfall approximates that of the Middle East,

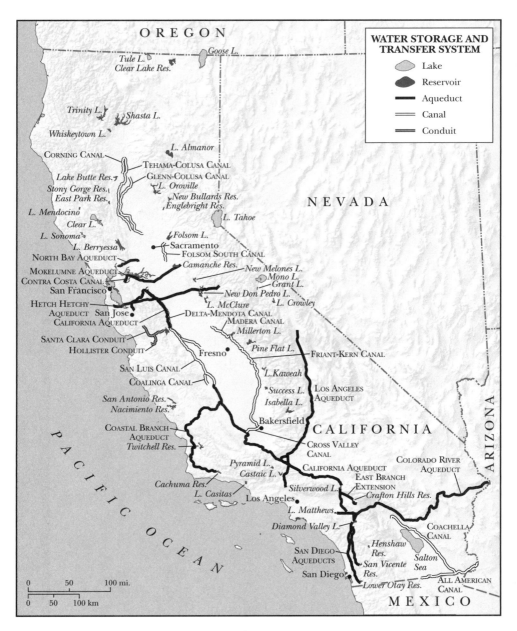

OREGON

Tule L.
Clear Lake Res.

Goose L.

WATER STORAGE AND
TRANSFER SYSTEM

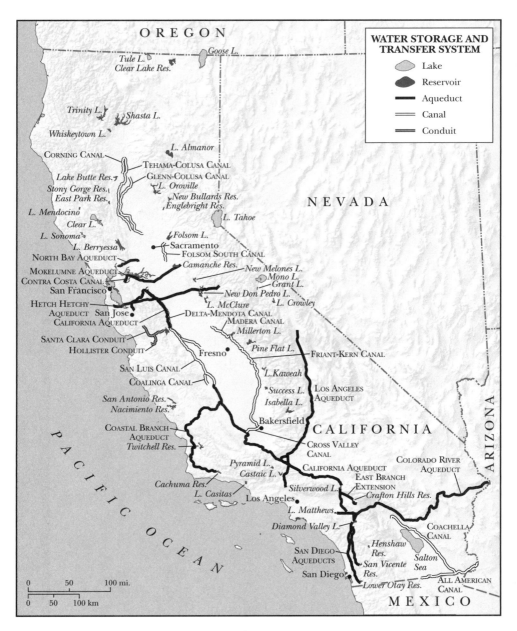 Lake

 Reservoir

━━━ Aqueduct

═══ Canal

─── Conduit

Trinity L.   _Shasta L._

Whiskeytown L.

CORNING CANAL

L. Almanor

TEHAMA-COLUSA CANAL
GLENN-COLUSA CANAL

Lake Butte Res.
Stony Gorge Res.
East Park Res.

L. Oroville
New Bullards Res.
Englebright Res.

L. Mendocino
Clear L.

L. Sonoma
L. Berryessa

NORTH BAY AQUEDUCT
MOKELUMNE AQUEDUCT
CONTRA COSTA CANAL
San Francisco

Folsom L.
Sacramento
FOLSOM SOUTH CANAL
Camanche Res.

New Melones L.
Mono L.
Grant L.

NEVADA

L. Tahoe

HETCH HETCHY
AQUEDUCT   San Jose
CALIFORNIA AQUEDUCT

SANTA CLARA CONDUIT
HOLLISTER CONDUIT

New Don Pedro L.
L. McClure
DELTA-MENDOTA CANAL
MADERA CANAL
Millerton L.

L. Crowley

Fresno

Pine Flat L.

FRIANT-KERN CANAL

SAN LUIS CANAL
COALINGA CANAL

L. Kaweah

Success L.
Isabella L.

LOS ANGELES
AQUEDUCT

San Antonio Res.
Nacimiento Res.

Bakersfield

CALIFORNIA

COASTAL BRANCH
AQUEDUCT
Twitchell Res.

CROSS VALLEY
CANAL

P A C I F I C

Pyramid L.
Castaic L.

CALIFORNIA AQUEDUCT
EAST BRANCH
EXTENSION

COLORADO RIVER
AQUEDUCT

Cachuma Res.
L. Casitas
Los Angeles

Silverwood L.
Crafton Hills Res.

L. Matthews

Diamond Valley L.

COACHELLA
CANAL

A R I Z O N A

O C E A N

SAN DIEGO
AQUEDUCTS

San Diego

Henshaw
Res.
San Vicente
Res.

Salton
Sea

ALL AMERICAN
CANAL

Lower Otay Res.

MEXICO

0   50   100 mi.
0   50   100 km

MAP 5. California's Water Storage and Transfer System

averaging five to ten inches along the coast and less inland. The Central Valley receives so little rainfall that it is considered a desert.

Fundamentally, California faces a structural imbalance between where the state's accessible runoff water is primarily found and where it is most needed for residential, commercial, and agricultural purposes. Compounding this challenge is the fact that California has one of the most variable rainfalls in the United States, with wide swings in precipitation from year to year. Its rainfall is never "normal"; rather, the state is periodically faced with years of too much or too little water.

As noted in chapter 2, an important reason why hydraulic gold mining proved so damaging was that the Sacramento Valley, which was the state's center of agriculture in the nineteenth century as well as the location of its capital and several other cities, lies in a floodplain. Many of the most fertile agricultural lands in Southern California are also located in floodplains. This means that during periods of unusually heavy rains, these water overflows must be actively managed to reduce flooding. At the same time, the state has also frequently faced prolonged periods of water scarcity. Most recently, California experienced severe droughts between 1986 and 1992 and between 2007 and 2009, with the years between 2011 and 2014 being the driest period in California's history since record keeping began. Following the end of the most recent drought in 2015–2016, the winter of 2016–2017 was the wettest on record in northern California.

Hydraulic mining demonstrated the technological feasibility and economic benefits of substantial investment in water storage and transportation. Without the development of an extensive water management infrastructure, gold mining would have become uneconomical after only a decade. The subsequent massive public sector investments in water infrastructure by both the federal government and the state would prove no less critical to the growth and prosperity of the state's urban and suburban population centers, especially in Southern California, as well as to the industry that succeeded gold mining as the state's most important business: agriculture. According to scholar Sarah Phillips, it was precisely California's intense "determination to wring every last drop of water from its highlands and transport it to its parched valley and coastal communities" that allowed it "to surpass New York as the most populous state and to generate the nation's most prolific agricultural and metropolitan growth."[2]

California's water management projects represent an important exception to its leadership in the area of environmental protection. *What is noteworthy is not the extent to which the state has protected its interior aquatic environment and the land surrounding it, but instead the degree to which it has so radically transformed and often degraded them.* Beginning early in the twentieth century and continuing through the 1970s, California, through the construction of 1,400 dams and 1,300 reservoirs, altered its natural watersheds more extensively than not only any other state, but any area of equivalent size in the world. The fact that much of California's agriculture and its large cities could not exist without massive water transfers means that much of the state resembles a garden rather than a wilderness.

California's approach to water management is distinctive from its other environmental policies described in this book in three important respects. First, the threats to the state's aquatic environment came from government, not business. It was public institutions, such as the water management authorities of the cities of San Francisco and Los Angeles and the state bureaucracies that funded and managed the water projects, that built California's "hydraulic empire." From this perspective, California's water management projects both were made possible by and reflected the expansion of administrative capacities at both the state and local levels, demonstrating the increasing strength of California's public institutions. But in marked contrast to the government bodies established to protect the state's forests and other scenic areas, the San Francisco Bay, and the coast, the public bodies that managed the state's water supplies transformed rather than protected its natural environment.

Second, with the notable exception of the battle over the damming and flooding of Hetch Hetchy around the turn of the century, until recently neither conservationists nor environmentalists challenged California's wide-ranging water management initiatives, despite the fact that many had deleterious environmental consequences. While California's forests, beaches, coast, and mountains were celebrated, valued, and often protected, its rivers were viewed, in the words of Joe Mathews, as "mere plumbing for our hydration convenience," pointing to an important limit of political support for nature protection within California.[3] The state's urban residents benefited as much—if not more—from California's water projects as they did from the wilderness and coastal protection policies described in the previous two chapters. They wanted to protect the trees and the coast, but they also wanted to consume as much water as possible.

Third, historically, business interests were *not* divided with regard to what to do (or not do) with California's water. Both agricultural and urban commercial interests were united in their strong support for the continued expansion of the state's hydraulic infrastructure. Thus, in this case, the public and business were on the same side. This situation only belatedly changed when some citizens became aware of the benefits of protecting the state's interior valleys, rivers, and lakes and when regional economic conflicts over water allocation divided business interests.

As was the case with the protection of forests and scenic areas, the federal government has also played an important role in shaping California's approach to water management. But in marked contrast to Washington's efforts to conserve Yosemite and the sequoias in the Sierras, in this policy area the federal government cooperated with the state of California by supporting the damming of its rivers and the flooding of its valleys. The federal government's initial legal backing of and subsequent financial support for the state's water management system has been critical in promoting the exploitation of not only the state's but the region's water resources.

Hetch Hetchy

SAN FRANCISCO AND THE NEED FOR WATER

Between 1860 and 1900, San Francisco's population increased sevenfold, making it into the nation's eighth-largest city.[4] Various engineering studies commissioned by the city concluded that it required more control over the sources and supply of its water. Since the 1870s, the city's water supply had been controlled by the Spring Valley Water Company, which had purchased nearly all the watersheds surrounding San Francisco. While the company could supply all the water the city required, it was also able to set its own prices, and its high rates had become politically controversial. Ending Spring Valley's monopoly on water became an important priority for San Francisco's turn-of-the-century Progressive movement. Moreover, finding additional sources of water had become critical to the city's long-term growth. Notwithstanding its winter rainfall, San Francisco sits on the edge of aridity, and the coastal fog that comes in from the Pacific is insufficient to relieve the dry summer months, when creeks vanish and grasses turn brown—or, as California boosters prefer to describe them, "golden."[5]

In 1900, the city was granted a new charter from the state that permitted it to own and administer its own utilities. But this authority meant little unless the city could locate an alternative source of water. Considerable quantities of water were available from the snow-filled streams of the Sierra Nevada Mountains, but the city still needed to find a way to access it. After reviewing several alternatives, the city's engineers decided that the best option was to draw water from the Tuolumne River and store it in a reservoir that would be built in the Hetch Hetchy Valley—a spectacular canyon in Yosemite National Park that was three and a half miles long and one- to three-quarters of a mile wide. The engineers were attracted by both the valley's "natural" water-storing capacity and the opportunity to create a water gravity system that would channel water originating high in the mountains through a lengthy aqueduct to San Francisco. The narrow gorge through the valley was also a perfect site for a dam, while the valley's elevation of 3,800 feet would minimize the need to pump the water to reach San Francisco. Moreover, the water stored behind the dam could also be used to generate power.

San Francisco's Board of Public Works was well aware that its proposed watershed and reservoir were located in the national park that Congress had recently established in 1890. But far from diminishing the suitability of Hetch Hetchy, that location was regarded as one of the site's attractions: it both reduced the likelihood of competing commercial claims and assured the water's quality. Because the valley was free of any encumbrances or private ownership, it also could be secured free of charge. The city officials who reviewed and supported this plan were confident that they could quickly obtain the necessary financing and federal approval for their project.

THE PLAN HITS SNAGS

However, it was precisely because Hetch Hetchy was located in a national park that the city's initiative led to a prolonged and bitter struggle. For John Muir, who was then battling to have all of Yosemite placed under federal protection, the proposed flooding of Hetch Hetchy was an outrage. He railed against the city's plans, lamenting that San Francisco might "as well dam for water-tanks the people's cathedrals and churches" and labeling the plan's supporters "temple destroyers" and "devotees of ravaging commercialism."[6] Muir argued that those who backed the reservoir idea were treating Yosemite in much the same way as the gold miners had treated the Sacramento Valley.[7]

The San Franciscans who supported the project were equally passionate. Muir was accused of acting in the interests of the Spring Valley Water Company. An unlikely ally of Muir, the company also opposed the reservoir's construction, though obviously for very different reasons. Muir and his followers were denounced as "mistaken zealots" who were "being used as catspaws by these grasping interests" and who wanted to deny the city's growing population access to an abundant supply of clean water. The *San*

Francisco Chronicle characterized those opposed to the Hetch Hetchy plan as "mushy esthetes."[8]

Supporters of the dam also argued that a narrow-minded obsession with preserving Hetch Hetchy blinded its critics to the recreational value of the lake that the dam would create. Was it not preferable for the public to be able to enjoy boating, fishing, and swimming rather than to preserve a canyon that was (then) largely inaccessible to all but the hardiest hikers? In fact, these supporters pointed out, only a few hundred people had ever visited the valley. A lengthy report prepared by San Francisco's engineering staff argued that far from damaging the beauty of the Yosemite Valley, the construction of the reservoir would actually enhance it and make it into a popular tourist destination. Muir indignantly responded, "As well may damming New York's Central Park . . . enhance its beauty!"[9]

The key issue in the Hetch Hetchy controversy was not whether the valley should be protected or developed. The dam's opponents also wanted to make the valley more accessible by developing an infrastructure of roads, hotels, and sporting facilities. The Sierra Club had long supported road construction into Yosemite, and, indeed, making the Sierras more accessible to the public was one of the organization's initial objectives. The real issue, then, was whether the valley should be developed for nature tourism or water storage. "The tragic irony of the Hetch Hetchy controversy," historian Robert Righter has written, "was that the city and its opponents were seeking to serve the public interest as each understood it."[10]

Given the way in which Hetch Hetchy pitted the "flourishing cult of wilderness" against Progressive Era views about the appropriate use of undeveloped natural resources, the conflict was inevitably a bitter one.[11] It also exposed a division among environmental advocates. Although environmentalists such as Muir were dead set against the Hetch Hetchy proposal, members of the Sierra Club who lived in San Francisco generally supported the city's plans: they wanted a secure, abundant, and clean supply of water to ensure the city's long-term growth. They also wanted to break up a local monopoly, an important Progressive Era goal.

Among those who supported the reservoir's construction was Sierra Club member William Kent, who had been elected to Congress in 1910. Kent was an active social reformer as well as a conservationist. In the Hetch Hetchy dispute, he chose to prioritize the former role, stating, "My idea of conservation would teach that if Niagara Falls could be totally used up in alleviating the burdens of the overworked sweatshops of New York City I should be glad to sacrifice that scenic wonder for the welfare of humankind."[12] Reflecting the importance that the Progressive movement attached to "responsible" use of the nation's natural resources, Gifford Pinchot, who then was head of the U.S. Forest Service, opined: "The thing seems to be clear beyond the possibility of arguments. To put it baldly—the intermittent esthetic enjoyment of less than one percent is being balanced against the daily comfort and welfare of 99 percent."[13]

On one level, the Hetch Hetchy controversy was similar to those that would surround the conflicts over the coastal redwoods or oil drilling in the coastal areas of Southern California: all three were about alternative uses of a scarce resource. But in the latter two cases, compromises were possible: oil drilling could take place farther offshore or inland, thus protecting the beaches and shorelines, while some of the vast acreage of redwoods could be harvested and other trees still protected. But, as in the case of hydraulic mining, no such compromise was possible when it came to Hetch Hetchy: the valley either would or would not be flooded.

THE HETCH HETCHY DAM PROJECT MOVES FORWARD

The large fire that destroyed so much of San Francisco following the 1906 earthquake increased public support for the project, with its supporters persuasively (although incorrectly) arguing that if water from the Sierra Nevada had been available, less of the city would have burned. Accordingly, in 1910, the voters of San Francisco approved a $45 million bond to finance construction of the dam, reservoir, and aqueduct. However, because this infrastructure was to be located in a national park, the federal government also had to give its approval. Accordingly, Muir turned to Washington, which he had always viewed as a better steward of the state's environment. His political campaign against Hetch Hetchy attracted the support of national park advocates from throughout the United States, including members of the Boston-based Appalachian Club and the American Civic Association. They argued that Yosemite National Park belonged to all Americans, not just to those who lived in San Francisco.

However, the project's opponents were unable to effectively challenge Pinchot's utilitarian position that a recreational reservoir would benefit more people than would a secluded valley. In 1913, legislation authorizing the project passed both houses of Congress—with the support of the entire congressional delegation from San Francisco—and was signed into law by President Woodrow Wilson in December of that year. Wilson stated: "I have signed this bill because it seemed to serve the pressing public needs of the region . . . and yet did not impair the usefulness or materially detract from the beauty of the public domain."[14] Muir was heartbroken and died the following year.

The construction of the dam, which buried Hetch Hetchy under 300 feet of water, and the 155-mile aqueduct to transport water from Yosemite to San Francisco were completed in 1934. The project was among the largest civil engineering endeavors of its time, exceeded in magnitude only by the Panama Canal and the project to bring water from the Catskill Mountains to New York City. The amount of water and electric power generated by the publicly owned Hetch Hetchy project far exceeded the needs of San Francisco, which then sold the surplus to neighboring communities. This proved so profitable that in 1961, the city's voters approved a $115 million bond to increase the aqueduct's capacity.

THE SIGNIFICANCE OF HETCH HETCHY

While it lost the battle to protect all of Yosemite, the prolonged conflict over Hetch Hetchy, which had played out both within California and in Washington over a nearly fifteen-year period, put the Sierra Club on the national political map and helped transform the organization from a primarily recreational club to one with a clear political agenda, namely, protecting national parks. As historian Michael Cohen has noted, "Remember Hetch Hetchy would become a battle cry for the Club for another century."[15] During the 1940s and 1950s, in what has been described as a "near repeat performance of the battle of Yosemite," the Sierra Club led a successful national campaign to prevent the construction of a dam at Echo Park inside Dinosaur National Monument on the Utah–Colorado border.[16]

Moreover, the extent and vigor of the opposition to the reservoir's construction both within California and among national parks advocates demonstrated the extent to which support for wilderness preservation had spread among the wider public.[17] According to Muir, "The conscience of the whole country had been aroused from sleep."[18] The failure to save Hetch Hetchy also contributed to the passage of the National Park Service Act in 1916, as well as to the creation of additional national parks.

Nonetheless, within the context of California's environmental history, the loss of the battle to save Hetch Hetchy raises several questions. By this time, San Francisco was already the state's as well as the country's center of environmental activism. Why, then, were so many of its residents willing to support the construction of a dam and reservoir in a national park? How was this aim consistent with the successful efforts concurrently taking place to protect the coastal redwoods and to place all of Yosemite under federal control—political campaigns that were strongly supported by all three of northern California's environmental organizations? Why was the membership of the Sierra Club divided over Hetch Hetchy, but not over any of the club's other conservation initiatives?

The explanation helps us understand not only the sources of public support for water management projects in California but also the limits of public support for environmental preservation. Protecting the Yosemite Valley and the iconic sequoias and redwoods in the Sierras and along the coast provided both environmental and pecuniary benefits: they protected scenic areas with which many Bay Area residents were familiar and which were valued for wilderness recreation and tourism. But no such benefits were associated with protecting Hetch Hetchy. Few local residents or tourists had ever visited this part of Yosemite or valued its aesthetics. Other than the Spring Valley Water Company, no business interests were disadvantaged by flooding the valley.

At the same time, building a dam and reservoir *would* provide important advantages to the residents of San Francisco: it would ensure the growing city a steady supply of fresh, clean water and shift control of their water supply from a private monopoly to a public authority. In short, for San Franciscans, the benefits of consuming the valley's water far outweighed the costs of protecting it. In this case, the politics of local geography worked *against* nature protection.

Los Angeles

A GROWING CITY WITH GROWING WATER PROBLEMS

Another major California city also faced significant challenges in ensuring an adequate water supply. Beginning in 1895, the city of Los Angeles won a series of important court decisions that affirmed its control of all water within a 500-square-mile area, including the very large reservoir that lay beneath the San Fernando Valley and fed the Los Angeles River. After these rulings, many nearby towns and communities wanted to be annexed by the city to gain access to the area's largest and most dependable water supply. Consequently, by 1900 the city had grown from its original twenty-seven to forty-three square miles. Thanks to both this geographic expansion and in-migration, its population doubled between 1895 and 1900.

Due to excessive pumping, however, by 1902 the river's flow had declined from 100 cubic feet per second in the 1880s to 45 cubic feet per second. This meant that, in effect, the city's population had become dependent on groundwater, the supply of which was uncertain.[19] While local water supplies may well have been adequate for the city's population during the later decades of the nineteenth century, they were clearly insufficient to sustain the city's expansion into a major metropolis in the twentieth century.

According to William Mulholland, the superintendent of the city's municipally owned water system, at the beginning of the century, "the time ha[d] come" for the city "to supplement its flow from some other source."[20] But as was the case for San Francisco, there was no sufficiently large water source nearby. The basin in which Los Angeles is situated is surrounded on three sides by deserts and on the fourth by an ocean. The nearest large rivers at the time were the Colorado and the Kern, but their low elevation made accessing their water technologically impracticable.

However, roughly 250 miles away, the Owens River flowed on the eastern side of the Sierra Nevada Mountains. While its distance from Los Angeles was considerable—roughly 100 miles greater than that between San Francisco and Hetch Hetchy—this water source had one important advantage: the river flowed into Owens Lake, which sat at an elevation of 4,000 feet. This meant that water from the lake could flow downward to Los Angeles, as the city is only a few feet above sea level.

The Owens Valley, through which the river of the same name flows, is an elongated trough that is about 120 miles long and between 4 and 6 miles wide. It lies between two high mountain ranges, the Sierra Nevada on one side and the Inyo and White Mountains on the other. Mount Whitney, the highest mountain in the continental United States, looms over the valley. Unusually for land located on the eastern slope of the Sierras, the valley receives a considerable amount of precipitation, much of which then flows into the Owens River and then into Owens Lake. In 1900, 7,000 people lived on farms and in small towns in the valley. Most of the area's 40,000 acres of farmland were used for cattle, as the soil was relatively acidic.

To succeed, the task of bringing water from the Owens River to Los Angeles had to overcome several challenges.[21] Los Angeles needed permission from the federal government to construct an aqueduct to transport the water to the city, because it would traverse federal lands. The city also had to gain control of land for this aqueduct and the associated water rights in the Owens Valley. Finally, it had to raise the necessary funds to both purchase those land and water rights and construct the aqueduct and other hydraulic infrastructure needed to transport the water over a considerable distance and through often-inhospitable terrain. The project was estimated to cost nearly $25 million, or about $675 million in today's costs.

LAND PURCHASE CONTROVERSIES

At the time, the water projects of Los Angeles had no politically salient environmental dimensions. Rather, the major controversy surrounding this project centered on the more than three decades of negotiations between the Los Angeles Department of Water and Power (LADWP) and the property owners in the Owens Valley who held the water rights the city needed to secure. Through 1935, the LAWPD paid a total of nearly $30 million to acquire ranches, farms, and town properties.[22] By 1938, Los Angeles owned almost 99 percent of the ranchland and 88 percent of the town and commercial lot acreage in Owens Valley, making it the largest landowner of any local government in the United States.[23] These property purchases gave Los Angeles the right to divert water from both the surface runoff and the valley's rich and easily accessible groundwater aquifers to the Los Angeles Aqueduct.

Even today, the Los Angeles Aqueduct raises strong emotions. According to the *Los Angeles Daily News*, "The story of the Owens Valley has taken on mythic proportions in the lore of the West, symbolizing the arrogance and disdain of the powerful cities toward rural areas." To many in the Owens Valley, the city's purchase of land and its accompanying water rights was little more than theft.[24] Reflecting on the project in 1986, the *Los Angeles Times* editorialized that the Owens Valley venture would "always enjoy a special aura of infamy. Mention the words *water* and *theft* in one breath, and someone will follow with *Los Angeles* and *Owens Valley* in the next."[25] That same year the *San Francisco Chronicle* recalled that "seventy years ago, the city of Los Angeles took most of the valley's water, bought nearly all of the land, killed off its agricultural industry, bulldozed the farms and turned it into an economic satellite."[26]

However, a detailed study of the hundreds of market transactions made as part of the project presents a more nuanced picture, finding that "most farmers appear to have been delighted to sell their properties . . . to a rich city like Los Angeles."[27] Far from being exploited, this study concludes, the "farmers in the Owens Valley were made better off by selling their water and land to Los Angeles than if they had remained in agriculture."[28] In addition, most sales took place during the 1920s and 1930s, when the national farm economy and thus agricultural property values were depressed. However, following extensive litigation as well as an investigation by the state, the city did subsequently agree to provide additional compensation to the owners of town parcels (which the city had not purchased) on the grounds that they had been disadvantaged by the decline in farming activity in the valley.

CHINATOWN: FOLKLORE AND FACT

Another part of the folklore associated with the transfer of water from the Owens Valley to Los Angeles was popularized in the 1974 movie *Chinatown* and questions the motives that underlay this enterprise. According to the film, the project's real proponents were the speculators who had purchased farmland in the San Fernando Valley, the city's northern suburb. The termination of the aqueduct in a large reservoir in this valley would enable them to irrigate their fields and thus profitably grow crops. In fact, however, the Los Angeles Aqueduct project was initiated not by private property owners or land speculators, but by three civil engineers. The most important of these was William Mulholland, who, according to Steven Erie, "viewed the aqueduct as his personal and professional gift" to the city of Los Angeles.[29]

While many investors did profit from the irrigation of the San Fernando Valley by Owens Valley water, a conspiracy was neither involved nor necessary. In this case, business and government interests were fully aligned. The objectives of the private individuals who had purchased land in the San Fernando Valley and the civil servants of Los Angeles were identical: both wanted additional water to facilitate the region's continued growth. Nor was there any conflict between the two, as there was more than enough water to meet the needs of both urban residents and farmers.

Moreover, the two interests of agriculture and urban growth were not as economically or geographically distinct as they subsequently became. Beginning around 1900 and continuing until mid-century, when urban sprawl exploded, Los Angeles County had a higher agricultural output than any other county in the United States. It contained more than a million orange trees and was among the nation's leading producers of fresh milk. In short, agriculture was an integral part of both the city's and the region's economic activity and benefited many urban businesses. This important alliance between the business interests of Southern California and the region's agricultural sector would endure even as its urban and suburban population centers and areas under cultivation became more geographically distant from one another.

SUPPORT FOR THE AQUEDUCT

The Los Angeles business community, represented by the city chamber of commerce, the Merchants and Manufacturers Association, and the Municipal League, had a clear financial stake in the city's long-term growth and strongly backed the Owens Valley water purchase and aqueduct project. The *Los Angeles Herald* proudly announced that after the construction of the aqueduct, lawns "could be kept perennially as green as emerald and greater Los Angeles could go on swimmingly in its metropolitan progress," while the *Examiner* predicted that the project's approval would produce enough water to supply a city of 2 million, thus allowing the city to grow by both annexation and in-migration.[30]

In September 1905, a $1.5 million bond issue to build the aqueduct was placed before the city's voters. Its supporters, aided by the *Los Angeles Times*, waged what amounted to a scare campaign, informing voters that their water supply was precarious. While in fact the city did have sufficient water to meet current demand—in recent years, rainfall had been above average—it was fortuitous for the aqueduct's backers that temperatures exceeded 100 degrees during the week before the election. Nevertheless, the city wasn't hedging its bets. To help ensure the positive outcome of the vote, the city's water utility created an artificial water famine, even dumping water reserves into sewers at night. Consequently, as Steve and Susie Swatt have noted, "the city's water supply became so scarce that, on the eve of the election, it passed an ordinance forbidding people to water their lawns and gardens."[31] Mulholland denied any subterfuge, claiming that any occasional water cutbacks were primarily due to faulty pipes and other infrastructure problems and that the dumping of water into the reservoirs was for the purpose of flushing them. While this controversy remains unresolved, it does point to the political influence that the city's water agency wielded.

In any event, much as their northern neighbors in San Francisco had supported the Hetch Hetchy project, the citizens of Los Angeles endorsed Mulholland's plan. Angelinos voted in favor of each of the two critical aqueduct bond issues by overwhelming margins: fourteen to one in 1905 and ten to one in 1907. With these and ten additional bonds approved through 1931, the voters of Los Angeles effectively, wrote Steven Erie, "mortgaged themselves and their posterity for the promise of unlimited water and thus perpetual growth."[32]

As was also the case for San Francisco, the federal government backed Los Angeles's water management project. A strong supporter of western irrigation, President Theodore Roosevelt was vocal in his support for the city's efforts to secure the necessary right of way from the federal government. Echoing Pinchot's support for the construction of the Hetch Hetchy reservoir, the president stated: "It is a hundred or thousand fold more important to the State and more valuable to the people as a whole, if [this water is] used by the city than if used by the people of the Owens Valley."[33] Like Hetch Hetchy, the Owens Valley project reflected a national Progressive Era value embraced by Roosevelt and many in the public.[34] Interestingly, both Los Angeles and San Francisco sought to access water from areas that were far away from "their backyards."[35]

Construction of the aqueduct, which, like the Hetch Hetchy project, was one of the largest public works projects to date, began in 1908. Second in size only to the Panama Canal, the building of the aqueduct required 240 miles of phone lines, 500 miles of new roads, 2,300 buildings, and 6,000 workers to dig tunnels, construct canals, and build other infrastructure. Five years after work began, in 1913, water from the Owens River began to pour into the San Fernando Valley, where it was stored in the local aquifer for distribution to the residents of Los Angeles. At the ceremony marking the first cascade of Owens water into Los Angeles, which was attended by 40,000 onlookers, Mulholland turned to the city's mayor and said, "There it is. Take it."[36]

Still, there was one important difference between Los Angeles's effort to secure its water supply and San Francisco's. While Hetch Hetchy had increased public awareness of the importance of protecting national parks, Mulholland's achievement had a very different political impact. It became a model for future water development projects in both the region and the state.

SUPPLYING LOS ANGELES WITH ADDITIONAL WATER

As Los Angeles continued to grow—its population tripled between 1900 and 1910 and by 1930 had reached 1.2 million—so did its need for more water. The city now turned its attention to the Mono Basin, located on the eastern slopes of the Sierra Nevada in the middle of the state near Hetch Hetchy. This basin had considerable quantities of high-quality water but less arable land and even fewer people than the Owens Valley. Most of it flowed into Mono Lake, a landlocked, highly alkaline body of water. An important attraction of the Mono Basin was that it was highly elevated. This meant that its water could be directed by gravity through the Owens River Gorge, which would in turn generate additional power. Los Angeles planned to build a tunnel to the Owens River drainage and then divert the water from the four streams that fed Mono Lake.

With the funds from a 1930 bond issue, land agents from the Metropolitan Water District began to acquire properties and water rights above and around Mono Lake. By the end of the 1930s, the city had purchased 30,000 acres. Dams on the tributaries that flowed into Mono Lake were then built to divert water from the lake to the city, and the Los Angeles Aqueduct was extended by an additional 105 miles. This $40 million construction project was completed in 1941. However, the city was unable to take advantage of the additional water available from Mono Lake because of the limited downstream capacity of its aqueduct. A second aqueduct, which was completed in 1970, increased the flow of water into the city by 33 percent. Both projects led to the severe depletion of Mono Lake.

State and Federal Water Projects

THE BOULDER DAM

Supplying water to support the growth of urban areas along the coasts of northern and Southern California was only one aim of California's water management system. A second, and at least equally important, objective was to promote agriculture. Farmers in the Imperial Valley, an area in the southern part of the Central Valley that is technically a desert, had long been faced with unpredictable water supplies from the Colorado River. With no significant dams upstream, river flows ranged from tepid to violent, with a large flood in 1905 proving particularly devastating. Farmers wanted a dam to be constructed across the Colorado River at the mouth of Boulder Canyon, Nevada. This would accomplish several goals: it would provide flood control; generate hydroelectric power; and supply water to Arizona, Nevada, and California. This plan would also enable the farmers of the Imperial Valley to receive water from the Colorado River, which flowed through neighboring states.

However, such a major project—the dam would be the world's largest—exceeded the financial capacity of California or its neighboring states. Complex negotiations involving the future distribution of water from the project followed, with California farmers and the Metropolitan Water District of Southern California eventually capturing a major share of the resulting water. In 1928, Congress authorized the construction of the dam, to be called Boulder Dam and since renamed the Hoover Dam. The project created a

28-million-acre-foot reservoir, later named Lake Mead. To address the water needs of Southern California, the federal government also authorized construction of two additional dams as well as a canal and aqueduct.

Completed in 1941, the Boulder Canyon Project both promoted agriculture in the Imperial Valley and facilitated the substantial urban growth of Los Angeles, Orange County, and San Diego both during and after the Second World War. Norris Hundley has noted that "the availability of Colorado River water beginning in the 1940s . . . had a profound psychological effect on city leaders and planners. It obliterated any sense of restraint about Los Angeles's capacity to absorb ever more people and industries. For surrounding communities, the abundant new supply . . . encouraged growth otherwise not possible."[37]

In 1940, the year before Colorado River water began arriving in the region, the population of the Los Angeles–Orange County–San Diego metropolitan area stood at 4 million. By 1970, it had increased to more than 10 million, further facilitating massive suburban sprawl, increasing automotive usage, reducing air quality, and creating more demand for water from northern California.

THE CENTRAL VALLEY PROJECT

California's next major water management project focused on the needs of the Central Valley. Since the days of the Gold Rush, Californians had recognized this region's significant agricultural potential. A rich, fertile, flat alluvial plain 450 miles long and 40 to 70 miles wide, the Central Valley is located between the Sierra Nevada Mountains on the east and the coastal ranges on the west. However, not only does the area receive little rainfall, but two-thirds of the water that flows into it naturally from the Sierras goes to the northern third of the valley (the part that had been most adversely affected by debris from gold mining in the Sierra foothills). Moreover, as noted in chapter 2, the Sacramento Valley in the northern part of the Central Valley is located in a natural floodplain and was thus prone to severe flooding from the Sacramento River and its tributaries. Scientists have since discovered that the intensity of flood conditions in the Sacramento Valley is greater than in any other American river system. Unlike the slow-rising Mississippi, for example, the water levels of the rivers flowing into the Central Valley rise in flash fashion, rather than gradually.[38]

Most farmers in California's Central Valley were thus dependent on groundwater. As the irrigated areas under cultivation grew, tripling between

1900 and 1930, the regional aquifers that supplied this groundwater became depleted. A 1930 government study concluded that "if an additional supply of water is not brought in, there will be an agricultural regression and the impairment of values that will affect . . . the entire San Joaquin Valley."[39] In response, the state, with the assistance of the federal government, developed an ambitious plan to transfer water from the wetter northern and mountainous regions of the state to the valley.

Dubbed the Central Valley Project, this effort involved the construction of a large dam on the Sacramento River, later called Shasta Dam, which would both control the flow of the river for flood management and distribute water to users in the Sacramento Valley, the Sacramento Delta, and the northern San Joaquin Valley. A smaller dam on the San Joaquin River would irrigate farmlands in nine central California counties.

This plan was authorized by the state legislature in 1933, and a bond issue was approved by the state's voters the same year. The onset of the Great Depression, however, prevented the state from selling the bonds its voters had authorized. In response, the Roosevelt administration proposed that the federal government fund it. Urging congressional approval of the administration's budgetary request, California congressman B. W. Gearhart stated: "We are asking not so much for the improvement of California for Californians alone, as for the development for the benefit of all the people of the United States, for the tens of thousands of people from all over the Union that are coming to California to establish their homes in its Great Central Valley."[40] Reflecting the New Deal's support for public infrastructure and agriculture, Congress agreed to authorize the necessary funds.

Over time, the project's scope steadily expanded. By the 1940s, it had come to encompass twenty dams, including structures on the Trinity, American, and Stanislaus rivers, and 500 miles of canals that managed 9 million acre-feet of water. This water was distributed to 2.5 million city dwellers and enabled the irrigation of 3 million acres of farmland in the Central Valley, including many thousands of acres of land that had not previously been cultivated. The largest purveyor of water in the state, the Central Valley Project helped promote a highly inefficient and wasteful water system that encouraged the growth of water-intensive agriculture and also resulted in the loss of habitat for fish such as salmon and steelhead trout.

At the same time, however, the project also had an ancillary benefit. The Shasta Dam created a reservoir that became the third-largest body of water in California, after Lake Tahoe and the Salton Sea. Because of its relatively accessible location, what has become known as Shasta Lake has become a major location for water recreation, widely used for boating, water skiing, camping, houseboating, and fishing—giving Californians another material benefit from transforming the state's hydraulic environment.

STATE WATER PROJECT

As the state's population and farm acreage continued to grow, so did its apparently inexhaustible demand for water. In 1951, California's Water Resources Board reported that notwithstanding the major water projects that had been undertaken, 40 percent of the runoff in California's rivers was still flowing unused into the Pacific along the state's northern coast. Accordingly, the board recommended the State Water Project (SWP). This effort would include the construction of a massive dam and a 3.5-million-acre-feet reservoir on the Feather River, one of the few remaining freely flowing rivers in the state. The water from the reservoir would then be distributed to both urban and agricultural areas in northern, central, and Southern California, with the latter receiving it via a long aqueduct. This water would be used to irrigate hundreds of thousands of dry acres in the San Joaquin Valley in the middle of the Central Valley and then would be sucked into the largest pumps ever built and lifted 2,000 feet up and over the mountains to Los Angeles.

This would be the largest state-built water management project in the United States and the most ambitious feat of engineering ever undertaken by a state.[41] The earthen dam at Oroville on the Feather River would be the tallest in the world, while the aqueduct that would move the water 444 miles south from the Sacramento–San Joaquin Delta to San Diego would instantly become California's longest river (if built in the East, it would have stretched from Boston to Virginia), as well as the world's longest aqueduct. As the Water Resources Board put it, the state's "greatest challenge was redistribution of the water supply from areas of surplus to areas of deficiency."[42] Each year, 2 million feet of water would be transferred from the north of the state to the south, providing water for 25 million Californians and irrigating 755,000 acres of farmland.

GOVERNMENT AND STATE SUPPORT

Democrat Pat Brown, who became California's governor in January 1959, decided to make the State Water Project a central legacy of his governorship. For the governor, the project's opponents lacked a vision of the state's future. He wrote to one newspaper publisher: "What are we to do? Build barriers around California and say nobody can come in because we don't have enough water to go around?" In his mind, the problem was simple: "We do not have enough water when and where we need it. We have too much water when and where we do not need it." One of Brown's senior aides declared that "by bringing water to the thirsty land," the government was "in effect doing the Lord's work."[43]

Thanks in large measure to the governor's skillful and energetic lobbying, the California legislature authorized the sale of $1.75 billion in general obligation bonds plus enough revenue from the state's offshore oil deposits to pay for the first phase of the project, which was estimated to cost $2.5 billion. The $1.75 billion bond measure was not only the largest in the state's history, amounting to three-quarters of the state's annual budget, but also the largest bond ever issued by any state.[44] Moreover, the state's commitment to the endeavor would be open-ended, with the legislature granting water officials the option of proposing any additional water projects that they deemed necessary. So broad was this mandate, Hundley declared, "that the second phase held the promise of never ending as long as a single drop of California water remained unused."[45]

While the legislature had thrown its support behind the SWP, the bond issue also required the approval of the state's voters—and for the first time in the state's history, a major water management bond faced serious opposition. This resistance came from voters in the northern part of the state, who believed that the proposed project would give away "their" water to Southern California. They also objected to its environmental impacts.

Nevertheless, the bond measure was approved in November 1960, with the more numerous voters of Southern California voting for it by sufficiently wide margins to overcome the opposition from the state's less populated northern counties. But its margin of approval was extremely narrow: it passed by only 174,000 votes of the 5.8 million cast. This margin, the narrowest of any election in the state's history, reflected a north–south divide that would increasingly dominate and complicate the politics of water in California.

The proposition's passage, according to Kevin Starr, "represented the fulfillment of nearly eighty-five years of vision" and "constituted a high point of postwar thought and action in the matter of what Californians, the majority of them at least, wanted their state to be: a modern commonwealth . . . embracing growth as its first premise."[46] However, it also turned out to mark the apogee of the state's water management programs. The Feather

River project was one of the last major water construction projects to be completed in California. As the environmental movement became more influential, the governor's view that a river that ran its natural course was "wasting water" found itself increasingly challenged. Consequently, Ethan Rarick has observed, "Brown's era was the last time Californians attempted so audaciously to remake their natural landscape."[47]

Backlash

STATE AND FEDERAL POLICY CHANGES

After the bond issue's passage in 1960, important policy changes took place simultaneously at the federal and state levels. Both the National Policy Act of 1969 and the California Environmental Policy Act of 1970 required that new water management and flood control projects include an assessment of their environmental impacts. The National Wild and Scenic Rivers Act of 1968 and a comparable state statute adopted in 1972 established protections for several rivers that had previously been identified as dam sites. The latter legislation specifically prohibited water diversions, except to meet local needs, on several rivers, including the Smith, the state's only major undammed river. Both federal and state endangered species legislation listed several native fish for protection, which also served to restrict additional water projects. These state and federal laws reflected the growth of public support for nature protection both in California and around the United States.

Among the public, too, water projects beginning in the late 1960s began to face increased opposition from community and citizen groups, environmentalists, and, most importantly, the residents and businesses of northern California. The result of this shift was to significantly slow down the further expansion of the state's hydraulic infrastructure.

SAVING ROUND VALLEY

The first successful effort in California to stop the construction of a dam and reservoir occurred in the late 1960s. The 196-mile-long Eel River in northwestern California had flooded in 1964, with more water flowing out of it in eight days than was required to irrigate the entire cotton crop of California for a year. Accordingly, the State Water Project planned to build a dam at Dos Rios, located in Mendocino County at the middle fork of the Eel River. The dam would be 700 feet high and would put the Round Valley behind it under 200 to 300 feet of water, which would then be stored and distributed, primarily to Southern California. This reservoir would become the largest manmade lake in the state.

Relatively few people lived in the Round Valley, which was located in a relatively remote location in the Sierra foothills 140 miles north of San Francisco. However, one of them, Richard Wilson, a farmer and rancher from an affluent California family who had decided to settle there because of the valley's isolation, became politically engaged. He subsequently formed the Round Valley Conservation League. At a public hearing, Wilson criticized those who wanted "to take out a beautiful valley and its surrounding mountains and turn it into a reservoir for flood control, water storage, and recreation." Echoing John Muir's defense of the sequoias, he added: "Perhaps it is because the state of California is so richly blessed with beauty and natural resources that we take this area for granted, but please let me say that it will not take too many more demands like this, and the children of future generations can look at the inland valley of our state in picture books only."[48]

However, the residents of the valley were divided on the issue. Some were pleased by the opportunity to sell their land and leave the valley or were attracted by the recreational opportunities and tourist income that the reservoir promised to bring. The Native Americans who lived in the valley had also been promised other land to which they could move.

Because the project required state approval, the debate over the valley's future reached the office of Governor Ronald Reagan. In 1969, Reagan, in a decision reflecting the growing political strength of the environmental movement in California, issued an executive order that effectively killed the Dos Rios Dam. This act saved the Round Valley from being flooded and protected the Eel River. In explaining his decision, the governor stated that he was concerned about destroying the valley's "great natural beauty" and negatively impacting the community of Covelo and the Round Valley Indians.[49] In November 1972, the legislature passed and the governor signed the so-called Wild Rivers bill protecting the Eel River and Round Valley for an additional twelve years, and presumably forever. Belatedly, California had woken up to the threats to its natural beauty posed by water projects—threats that had begun with Hetch Hetchy and continued with the construction of the state's additional dams, reservoirs, and aqueducts.

"REMEMBER THE STANISLAUS"

The first major public campaign to save a wild river was launched in opposition to the construction of the New Melones Dam, a project designed to fill up the New Melones Reservoir to increase the water supply, generate hydroelectricity, and improve flood control. While several dams had already been constructed on the Stanislaus River, a 13-mile stretch of it still flowed unimpeded through the Sierra foothills. Saving this stretch, which would be flooded once the dam was completed and the reservoir filled, became highly politically contentious.

There were several reasons why this particular water project attracted such public interest. The canyon in which the river flowed was extremely attractive: it had tall limestone cliffs, stunning spring wildflowers, and the distinctive flora and fauna of the Sierra foothills. Moreover, during the 1970s, public interest in whitewater boating had increased. The Stanislaus was one of the few remaining wild or partially wild rivers in California, and its challenging rapids had made it ideal for whitewater rafts and kayaks. The large number of people visiting the river—many of whom valued the experience of whitewater rafting, hiking, fishing, and camping in the mild climate of the lower Sierras—had created a constituency for saving it.

But even those Californians who had never seen the river became upset that such an attractive natural site—and one that had been visited, enjoyed, and valued by so many—was slated for destruction. Lasting more than a decade, the public campaign to "Save the Stanislaus" has been described as "the biggest citizen effort to save a river and stop a dam in American history."[50] The campaign included lobbying, letter writing, demonstrations, a legal challenge to the environmental impact statement filed by the dam's proponents that went all the way to the Supreme Court, and an unsuccessful 1974 grassroots effort to pass a proposition to stop the dam's construction. However, none of these efforts, including the opposition of the State Water Resources Board, were successful in blocking the project. The federal government filled the reservoir, and the remaining wild stretch of the river was flooded. Surprisingly, the federal government had managed to carry out a water project in California that was opposed by both the public and state government officials.

However, the intense public controversy surrounding the construction of this reservoir made it the last addition to the Central Valley Project. Indeed, New Melones was one of the last large dams to be built in the United States. Just as Santa Barbara had become a rallying cry in the opposition to offshore oil drilling and Hetch Hetchy in the fight to protect national parks, so did "Remember the Stanislaus" became a rallying cry for river protection. After the Stanislaus fight, the public added rivers to the list of natural areas that were deserving of public protection.[51] It now could no longer be assumed that developing the state's rivers to supply urban and agricultural needs was necessarily the best and most important use of water. The campaign to save the Stanislaus also led to the establishment of a new environmental organization, Friends of the River, which, along with other citizen groups, increased public support for river protection.

OTHER WATER PROJECTS

In 1981, U.S. Secretary of Interior Cecil Andrus added California's North Coast and lower American River to the National Wild and Scenic Rivers System. This act restricted water projects on these rivers—a significant development since, because of their significant water flows, they had been viewed as important potential sources of new water supplies. By the end of the 1990s, California had named eleven rivers to its own wild and scenic system and prohibited dam construction on a twelfth, though the scope of each of these protections were limited, applying only to portions of each river.

Nonetheless, pressures for new water projects have continued. The state's prolonged drought starting in 2011 prompted voters in 2014 to approve a $7.12 billion bond issue to improve the state's water infrastructure, which, due to pressures from agricultural interests, also included $2.7 billion for new water storage. While this funding put back on the agenda new water projects—including another dam on the San Joaquin River costing $2 billion and the $4 billion Sites Reservoir that would store water from the Sacramento River in wet periods—their construction remains problematic. This is in part, the *New York Times* reported, "because California already has so many dams and the best sites were used up long ago," meaning that "all that money would buy relatively little extra water."[52]

Protecting the Sacramento–San Joaquin Delta

THE GEOGRAPHY OF THE DELTA

Over the years, the most important and prolonged conflict over the social, economic, and environmental impact of water projects in California has centered on the Sacramento–San Joaquin Delta.[53] A unique geographic phenomenon, it is one of only two inland deltas in the world and is the largest estuary on the West Coast. Covering more than 75,000 square miles and including 700 miles of channels, it extends nearly 500 miles from the Cascade Range in the north to the Tehachapi Mountains in the south and is bound in the west by the Coast Range and in the east by the Sierras. Essentially, it is a valley that has been flooded by rising sea levels since the last Ice Age. Today, the delta consists of several major waterways, including the Sacramento and San Joaquin rivers. These rivers meet near Sacramento, forming a great inland delta created by the depression of the Sacramento–San Joaquin Valley. Prior to Western settlement, the combined waters of these rivers washed unrestrained over nearly a million acres before escaping into a channel that flowed into the San Francisco Bay.

The water flows from these rivers into the delta act as a hydraulic dam, holding back the seawater that also flows into the delta from the San Francisco Bay through the Carquinez Strait. While the delta has always contained both salt- and freshwater, the precise mix of the two varies from year to year. When river flows are high, the water in the delta is mostly fresh, but during drought years, its salinity levels rise as increased amounts of ocean water from the San Francisco Bay flow into it.

Nearly half of the precipitation that falls in California winds up in the delta's watershed. As the primary source of drinking water for two-thirds of the state's population, the delta lies at the heart of the state's hydraulic infrastructure. Both the State Water Project and the Central Valley Project expended substantial effort there, constructing a series of pumps, aqueducts, and bypasses to both prevent flooding in the area and funnel snowmelt from the Sierra Nevada to the 25 million people of the Bay Area, the Central Valley, and Southern California.

The delta irrigates 7,000 square miles of agricultural land, supporting $300 million in rice and other commodity crops. It also contains a wide range of aquatic habitats. Two-thirds of California's salmon pass through its waters en route to their spawning grounds in the rivers that flow on to the Pacific Ocean, and at least half of the state's migratory birds use its wetlands. Many of the delta's thousands of islands contain boat docks. It has been described as "a paradise for those who like to fish for striped bass, for duck hunters who build their blinds in the remaining marshes, and for people who like to float idly along canals between saloons and inns."[54]

During the 1960s, the intrusion of saltwater into the delta from the San Francisco Bay steadily increased as a result of both the increased consumption of freshwater by delta communities and farms and local population growth. In addition, much of the runoff from the Sierras that had previously flowed into the delta was now being diverted via aqueducts to meet local urban and business needs. Finally, and most importantly, the delta was being deprived of half its freshwater by diversions from the Sacramento and San Joaquin river systems. This water was then shipped to the Central Valley and to other parts of the State Water Project. At times, during periods of low water flows, ocean water from the San Francisco Bay advanced far enough inland to be sucked into the state and federal aqueducts transporting water to the south.

These changes in the ecological balance of the delta were disastrous to many native fish. Striped bass and king salmon found it difficult to adjust to the reverse movement of ocean water, and millions of eggs and fry, including the tiny delta smelt that were on the verge of extinction, wound up in the pumps that sucked water south. Salmon breeding grounds were disrupted and waterfowl habitats impaired by the discharge of pesticide-riddled drainage water from Central Valley farms. Ultimately, all but 8,000 acres of the 345,000 acres of tidal marsh disappeared, made into islands of farmland surrounded by levees.

Given its importance and the wide range of conflicting demands on it, it is not surprising that, like the California coast, the delta has been a perennial source of controversy. As Ted Simon has observed, "it has become, fittingly for such a convoluted ball of waterways, the Gordian knot of California water politics."[55]

PROTECTING THE DELTA: THE PERIPHERAL CANAL

State and federal planners had long recognized the need for new policies to protect the delta, as it occupied a central place in both the state's water management system and the ecology of northern California. In 1965, state officials designed a plan to protect the delta and also make additional water available for the San Joaquin Valley and Southern California by constructing a 43-mile-long, 400-foot-wide, 30-foot-deep unlined ditch in the shape of a broad eastward swing curve—hence its name, the Peripheral Canal. This waterway would begin at the Sacramento River fifteen miles south of the state capital and then go farther south, bypassing the eastern edge of the delta, and end up at the state and federal pumping plants near Tracy. To protect the delta's water quality, gates would be located along the canal that would release enough freshwater to prevent saltwater intrusion.

The canal, along with other related water projects, was expected to make 7.8 million acre-feet of water available annually for the State Water and Central Valley projects, as well as an additional 1.3 million acre-feet of freshwater to meet the needs of the delta. The project's cost was estimated at $170 million, with the majority coming from the federal government. The proposed canal attracted support from the southern part of the state, since it promised to ensure that the water shipped to the San Joaquin Valley would be of the same quality as that drawn from the upper reaches of the Sacramento River. The canal's promise of improving the ecosystems of the delta also attracted the support of the California Department of Fish and Game.

CIVIC OPPOSITION

But, as had been true in 1960 when the State Water Project was put to voters, the Peripheral Canal project generated strong opposition from the residents of northern California. Northern Californians resented having "their" water shipped to farmers in Southern California, who they argued were wasting it by inefficient irrigation practices. Particularly intense opposition came from the urban residents and farmers who lived along the delta, especially those in Contra Costa County, who had been most adversely threatened by saltwater intrusion. These residents did not want to give the Metropolitan Water District, the cooperative serving much of Southern California, the discretion to decide how much water would be released to maintain freshwater quality, fearing that the supply would be reduced during drought years. Moreover, they were wary of the fact that nowhere in the plans for the canal were the delta's water rights made explicit. For this reason, the water agencies of the central delta became the project's bitterest and most persistent opponents. As one of their representatives put it, "We don't want to give the Metropolitan Water District the plumbing to suck us dry in a drought year."[56]

Opposition to the Peripheral Canal proposal became a unifying force in the region, bringing together northern and central newspapers, local governments, businesses, and farm groups.[57] While the conflict over the canal had initially revolved around competing regional economic interests, the growth of environmentalism in the early 1970s added a new dimension to the dispute. Environmentalists were now questioning the logic behind the expansion of the state's water system, asking why the state should supply additional water to the already highly developed "megalopolis" of Southern California.[58] The Sierra Club argued that future water needs should be met by measures including conservation, wastewater reclamation, and development near existing water supplies and warned that the canal would threaten the wild and scenic status of North Coast rivers.[59] The alliance of environmental organizations, which included Friends of the Earth, the Planning and Conservation League, Friends of the River, and several other nature protection organizations, now came to lead the fight against the canal.

STATE LEADERS WEIGH IN

Both Governor Pat Brown and Governor Ronald Reagan had been strong supporters of the Peripheral Canal. The former had regarded it as a natural outgrowth of his State Water Project, while the latter's power base was located in the southern part of the state, which strongly backed the plan. Given his emphasis on an "era of limits," Governor Jerry Brown, who took office in 1975, had been expected to oppose the canal. But instead he chose to support it. His decision was influenced by the two-year drought that broke out in California shortly after he took office, highlighting the vulnerability of Southern California's water supplies and increasing political pressure from Southern California and agribusiness for the governor to support the project. But the same drought also intensified opposition to the canal, since it was precisely during such periods of water scarcity that the delta's freshwater was most likely to be at risk.

In order to address both the concerns of northern Californians about protecting water quality in the delta and the need of Southern Californians for additional water, the governor fashioned a compromise. To appease northern Californians, he proposed a constitutional amendment that would require any new storage projects on the North Coast rivers to receive a two-thirds rather than a majority vote of the legislature and would make the state rather than the federal government responsible for protecting water quality in the delta. To Southern California he promised that these constitutional guarantees would not become effective until *after* the canal was approved by the legislature. After considerable debate, a sharply divided legislature approved the compromise. The vote was along regional lines, and its substantial margin of support reflected the greater representation of legislators from the more populous southern part of the state rather than a broad stamp of approval.

At around the same time, in another compromise move, legislators from Southern California agreed to put the proposed constitutional amendment protecting the delta and the North Coast rivers on the ballot. These protections became Proposition 8, which appeared on the ballot in November 1980. The measure was approved by 54 percent of the electorate, with support now coming disproportionately from voters who lived in the San Francisco Bay Area and the Sacramento Delta.

REFERENDUM TO OVERTURN APPROVAL
OF THE PERIPHERAL CANAL

Emboldened by the approval of Proposition 8 but still lacking trust in both the state's and the federal government's commitments to protect the rivers in the northern part of the state, a coalition of delta residents and environmentalists now initiated a referendum that would overturn the legislature's approval of the Peripheral Canal bill. A broad coalition of anti-canal groups succeeded in collecting 850,000 signatures, and the matter was placed on the June 1982 ballot. Since Proposition 8 could not take effect unless the canal was approved, both proposals were in effect on the ballot.

The battle over Proposition 9, the Peripheral Canal referendum, was among the hardest fought and costly in the state's history. Somewhat surprisingly, the California Farm Bureau Federation, which represented fifty-four county agricultural associations, decided to back the effort. This was not because its members were opposed to the Peripheral Canal, which they strongly supported, but because the federation objected to Proposition 8's protection of the North Coast rivers and the delta. According to the federation's president, "We do not feel we should bankrupt our future by locking up the north coast rivers as the price for securing the Peripheral Canal."[60]

The J. G. Boswell and Salyer land companies, the largest farm owners in the state, contributed heavily to the campaign to overturn the canal approval. Their motives were similar to those of the California Farm Bureau Federation: what they wanted was a canal project that would be free from any environmental restrictions. A few years earlier, the state had reduced its water allocation to farmers in Tulare Lake in order to divert its waters to the delta to protect 230 species of birds and more than 50 species of fish. The Boswell and Salyer companies feared that the "fine print" of the Peripheral Canal bill would weaken their legal case against this diversion and facilitate future reductions of the water allocation on which they depended for their large cotton farms.

For their part, environmentalists also supported the referendum—though for very different reasons. While they feared the overturning of Proposition 8's protections by a two-thirds vote of the legislature, their main concern was with the Peripheral Canal itself. They claimed that southern farmers did not really need additional water, as it would be used to support the growing of crops of which there were already surpluses. They also argued that the delta's ecology was too fragile to permit such an extensive and complex project. In what has been described as "the oddest alliance since the Hitler–Stalin

Pact," both the state's largest farmers, who considered the canal's wildlife protections too strong, and its environmentalists, who considered them too weak, joined together to support the referendum—creating another bizarre California Baptist–bootlegger coalition.[61]

On June 2, 1982, the referendum repealing the Peripheral Canal legislation—and thus also Proposition 8—was decisively approved by a margin of more than three to two. It was backed by voters in the counties around San Francisco by margins of nine to one and by voters in Southern California by a narrower margin of two to one. Subsequent polling data revealed that the most important consideration for the state's voters was the canal's costs, which had grown to a projected $2.5 billion, though 40 percent also thought that the project would harm the environment.

The weather may also have played a role in the vote. 1976 was the third driest and 1977 the driest year in California's history. However, beginning in 1978, the state experienced several unusually wet years, including 1980, when a succession of subtropical storms hit Los Angeles. Marc Reisner observes: "It would be excessive to say that a string of five rain-laden years determined the outcome of the vote on the Peripheral Canal, but it would probably be true. Had the referendum been held in October of 1977, when most of the state had barely seen rain in a year and one half, Californians might have voted for anything, even dragging icebergs down from the North Pole."[62] Whatever the reason, the state's voters had turned down a significant expansion of the state's water management infrastructure, marking water developers' first major defeat.[63]

To help address the continued deterioration of the delta's ecology, which has placed many of the state's native fishes on the verge of extinction, in 1992 the federal government enacted legislation that required that a minimum amount of water be kept in the delta to protect wildlife. Since 2007, the state has restricted pumping in the area in order to protect the delta's fish. Under an agreement reached in 2010, the California Department of Water Resources has been obligated to restore 8,000 acres of intertidal and subtidal habitat for salmon and smelt. These environmental protections have, of course, reduced the outflow of delta waters for agriculture. This has in turn outraged the state's farmers, who have accused environmentalists of wasting water on fish at the expense of the state's economy—a concern exacerbated by the state's recent series of droughts. Both north–south regional disputes over access to water and conflicts over the extent to which the delta's fragile marine ecology should be protected at the expense of greater water availability will undoubtedly continue. Like the coast, the delta represents a valuable natural resource for which there are many conflicting uses and demands.

Restoring Two Lakes and a Sea

OWENS LAKE

The environmental impacts of the Los Angeles Aqueduct also belatedly became politically controversial. Due to the aqueduct's diversion of water that normally flowed into Owens Lake, by 1923 this body of water had dried up, leaving over sixty square miles of dry lakebed exposed to seasonal winds that pulverized its salty crest. By the early 1990s, Owens Lake was viewed as "the largest source of fugitive dust pollution in North America."[64] In October 1999, the LADWP agreed to implement dust control measures that would enable the area to meet federal air quality standards by 2006, with the costs borne by the city of Los Angeles. In 2001, shallow flooding of 11.9 square miles of the lakebed began. The amount of water necessary for adequate dust mitigation was projected to be more than 65,000 acre-feet annually, which would cover 29.8 square miles of lakebed.

Consequently, by 2013, half of the water carried by the Los Angeles Aqueduct was being used for environmental mitigation in the Owens Valley. By this time, the valley's role in bringing water to Los Angeles had diminished: it now provided just a third of the city's water needs. In 2013, on the 100th anniversary of the aqueduct's completion—an occasion celebrated in Los Angeles with a dramatic reenactment of its opening—the long-standing water feud between the city and the valley was finally resolved. "The city has accepted its responsibility," Los Angeles mayor Eric Garcetti said, adding, "We took the water."[65] Rather than continuing to flood the lakebed with 25 billion gallons of water a year in order to hold the dust in place, engineers began to till about 50 miles of the lakebed. This strategy created three-foot-high furrows capable of reducing the thick haze that often obscures visibility across the lake without requiring much additional water.

MONO LAKE

With the increased diversion of tributary flows into Mono Lake by the Los Angeles Aqueduct, the water level of that body had also steadily declined. By 1981, it had fallen about forty-six feet, its surface area had shrunk from ninety to sixty square miles, and its level of salinity had nearly doubled, becoming more than twice that of the ocean. These changes threatened both aquatic wildlife and the lake's migratory bird population. Too, as in the case of Owens Lake, the large amount of white salt crust that emerged in the wake of the receding waterline choked the air with alkaline dust during windstorms. Large dust storms increased levels of air pollution.

In 1978, the National Audubon Society, the Friends of the Earth, the Sierra Club, and the Mono Lake Commission sued in state court to restrict the export of water from the Mono Basin, citing the public trust doctrine, which they claimed applied not only to navigable waterways but also to streams used for recreation, wildlife habitat, and ecological study. In 1983, in *National Audubon Society v. Superior Court*, the state's Supreme Court agreed with the plaintiffs, holding that the state could limit the exercise of existing water rights to protect public trust values. According to the court, "water belonged to the people," and thus the State Water Resources Control Board was responsible for monitoring and allocating "its use in a manner consistent with the public trust."[66] This was a significant ruling: authorities would now be required to balance the city's need for water against the public's need for the lake and the preservation of its ecosystem.

Following an unsuccessful appeal to the U.S. Supreme Court, in 1983 the LADWP was ordered to reduce its diversions from the Mono Basin in order to permit the lake's level to be stabilized. During the next decade, there was considerable additional litigation. Finally, in 1993, an agreement was reached that permanently reduced the city's diversion of water from Mono Lake by about a third, with the state agreeing to supply additional water to enable the lake to rise to 6,392 feet, the level that had been determined would eliminate the dust problem.

One environmental activist exulted that "for the first time ever in California, water was removed from the grasp of an anointed appropriative user and assigned, not to some rival diverter, but to an environmental purpose."[67] The public trust doctrine that had made this achievement possible had been shown to be an effective means of restoring the environment.[68] This decision not only placed Los Angeles on the defensive but signaled an important change in the legal standards and public expectations for appropriate water use—one that would have implications both within California and throughout the West.

SALTON SEA

Controversy has also surrounded the fate of the Salton Sea, the largest lake in California, located in Southern California's Imperial Valley. The lake had been formed over millions of years as water from the Colorado River had flowed into the Imperial Valley. It has alternatively been a freshwater lake, an increasingly saline lake, and a dry desert basin, depending on the balance between water inflows and water losses from evaporation. Its current status as a "sea" dates from the beginning of the twentieth century, when what had been a dry lakebed was filled by water from the Colorado River. During the 1950s, the Salton Sea had some success as a resort area, but its increased salinity and pollution from agricultural runoff killed virtually all of its fish, and its tourist industry atrophied.

Over the next half-century, the condition of the sea steadily deteriorated, with much of the lakebed becoming dry and salt levels increasing as a result of reduced water inflows stemming from mandated water transfers to local metropolitan areas. The shrinking lake also interfered with bird migration and caused clouds of dust. During the 1990s, Congressman Sonny Bono initiated a campaign to "save" the Salton Sea that resulted in the establishment of the Salton Sea Authority. Various proposals by state authorities have called for the diversion of water by the local irrigation district to replenish the sea, but to date, the lack of sufficient additional water flows—which would need to be taken from local residents and farmers—has led to the sea's continued deterioration. However, in 2017 state regulators approved a plan to spend nearly $400 million over ten years to slow the shrinking of the Salton Sea in order to protect migratory birds and reduce dust levels.

The Impact of Water Management

It is impossible to exaggerate the importance of California's water management infrastructure. Ellen Hanak has declared, "The economic glories of California, its social and cultural achievements—indeed much of what state residents take for granted as quintessentially *Californian*—are attributable to its water projects, many enacted with federal support." These projects, she has pointed out, which include 1,400 dams on almost every river in the state and 1,300 reservoirs, have

> harnessed the rivers of the Coastal Range, the Sierra Nevada, and the Rocky Mountains, making it possible for farmers in Kern County to irrigate their crops with water from the Pit River in Madoc County, for businesses in the Silicon Valley to produce computer chips using runoff from Mount Lyell in the Yosemite back country, for Budweiser to brew beer in the San Fernando Valley with groundwater from the eastern

Sierra Nevada, and for the residents of San Diego to drink water that fell in snow outside Pinedale, Wyoming.[69]

Thanks to the construction of massive long-distance aqueducts, most Californians live within "virtual watersheds," with their water supply being significantly dependent on the runoff from distant snowpacks in the Sierra Nevada and Rocky Mountains. While virtually all of the state's population centers depend on water transported over long distances, diverted water has been particularly critical for the economic and population growth of Southern California. Steven Erie has noted that "very little of Southern California's staggering population growth and economic development to date could have occurred without an adequate supply of affordable imported water."[70] Without this "imported" water, it has been estimated that only 500,000 people could live in Los Angeles, and only 3 million could live in all of Southern California, where 18 million now reside.

California's weather has made it ideally suited to agriculture. It is one of only five major growing regions in the world that has a Mediterranean climate, and its extensive deep alluvial soils are also ideal for growing crops. But the state's preeminent agricultural sector would not have been possible without additional supplies of water, which have made California into one of the most intensively farmed landscapes in the world outside of the tropical rice zones. Today, the state accounts for 12 percent of the agricultural output of the United States and supplies one-third of the table food consumed by Americans.[71] For more than a half-century, California's agricultural output has been higher than that of any other state, making its farm sector "one of the wonders of the world."[72]

Most of the state's prime agricultural lands were irrigated between 1900 and 1930, largely from pumped groundwater. What the massive state and federal water projects from the 1930s to the 1970s achieved was to make agricultural production possible on the state's most marginal farmlands. These areas, located in the eastern and southern ends of the San Joaquin Valley and the interiors of San Bernardino, Imperial, and Riverside counties, receive fewer than five inches of rain per year.[73] The post-1930 water projects brought these lands into production, in addition to supplementing the groundwater from lands that had been previously farmed using irrigated water.

The Politics of Water Management

For more than half a century, California's public supported each of the state's increasingly ambitious water projects. Citizens voted for the Hetch Hetchy reservoir, the Owens River aqueduct and its extension to Mono Basin, the Colorado River Aqueduct, the original Central Valley Project, and the State Water Project. Most of these proposals were approved by wide margins. California's elected representatives also fought in Congress for the Boulder Canyon Project, as well as for the federal financing of other water management projects. While important business interests in the agricultural sector were behind and disproportionally benefited from many of the state's water projects, these enterprises were also backed by most urban residents as part of a Baptist–bootlegger alliance formed in support of economic development via water management. With the notable exception of Hetch Hetchy, it was not until the late 1960s that a water management project was challenged on environmental grounds. In this policy area, California's record of environmental protection has been far from exemplary: throughout U.S. history, no western state has more actively or aggressively transformed its rivers than California.

This raises an important question: Why did efforts to protect the state's interior aquatic environment lag behind the protection of Yosemite, the sequoias in the Sierras, the redwoods along the coast, and the coastal areas of Southern California? Why, during the same years that many Californians were working to protect the redwoods, were they largely indifferent to what was happening to the state's free-flowing rivers and interior valleys? An important part of the answer to this question is that California's citizens wanted additional water and protection from floods at the same time that they wanted to enjoy the state's natural beauty. The former goals required that nature be controlled and tamed; the latter that it be protected in more or less its "natural" state. Thus, somewhat paradoxically, the same state that has played a leadership role in environmental conservation is also the one that has most extensively and intensively transformed its interior aquatic environment.

California's water management policies thus reveal an important limit to its citizens' support for protecting its natural environment. Compared to restricting oil drilling or timber cutting or reducing pollution from cars, protecting the state's rivers and valleys bore a much higher cost. It was possible to limit both oil drilling and timber cutting without completely stopping them, while, as the next chapter will demonstrate, controlling air pollution in Los Angeles did not prevent citizens' continued use of cars. Similarly, when it came to protecting the coast and the San Francisco Bay, compromises between development and protection were possible. But throughout much of California's history, there appeared to be no viable alternative to building the water infrastructure that would support the state's continual economic and population growth. Only belatedly did both the costs of and alternatives to doing so become politically salient.

A related factor was the lack of any business opposition to the development of the state's and region's aquatic infrastructure. In this policy area, the state's business community was unified, not divided. No firm or sector stood to benefit from opposing the expansion of the state's water infrastructure, while many business interests—including, most notably, agriculture—stood to benefit from this development. What made the preferences of California agribusiness especially influential on this issue was that were no business interests on the other side.

Geography also played an important role in driving California's approach to water management. In contrast to the many scenic areas in the state that citizens had rallied to protect, dams and reservoirs were primarily located away from the state's major population centers and, equally importantly, in parts of the state that few Californians visited or valued. Most water projects were developed in the sparsely inhabited northern third of the state and in the Sierra foothills, which had much less dramatic scenery than the Sierras themselves, while Colorado River water came from outside the state. Thus, their environmental impact was largely invisible. As noted earlier, few Californians had ever visited Hetch Hetchy, and it is likely that virtually no one in Los Angeles had ever heard of, let alone visited, the Owens Valley or Mono Lake.

In short, in this important, exceptional case, each of the factors that had earlier promoted the protection of the state's natural environment now ironically served to undermine it.

Changing Public Attitudes

Over time, rivers came to be perceived not as sources of water that needed to be tamed and controlled but as natural resources that should be protected— like the coast, the redwoods, and the sequoias. No longer would a river that was allowed to run its natural course to the sea be viewed as "wasting" water. This shift began in the late 1960s and accelerated during the 1980s and 1990s. What happened? An important part of the explanation has to do with the increasing public interest in river recreation. The growth of recreational activities such as rafting, kayaking, fishing, and camping along riverbanks created a constituency for river protection in much the same way that the increased interest of middle-class Americans in "wilderness" tourism and hiking created substantial public support for protection of the scenic areas described in chapter 3. According to one estimate, while through 1930, only about 5,000 Americans had ever floated in a whitewater river, by the early 1990s, 35 million had done so.[74] In short, the perceived benefits of river protection grew as citizens became more affluent and mobile. At the same time, as parts of the state that had previously been inaccessible (like Hetch Hetchy) became available for recreation and relaxation, they became both visible and valuable.

Another factor in this shift was the growing importance of north–south regional differences. These differences historically had been muted: both San Francisco and Los Angeles had acted in parallel fashion to secure long-distance supplies of water. Notably, both the Colorado River Project and the Central Water Project were supported by voters throughout the state. But beginning with Governor Pat Brown's State Water Project, regional differences became more politically salient. Northern Californians voted against the bonds to finance this project not because they cared about its environmental impact, but because they had developed a proprietary stake in what they perceived as "their" water: it had become part of their "backyards." Consequently, they saw no reason to share it with the cities and farmers of the southern part of the state. In marked contrast to the coastal protection initiative, which unified northern and Southern Californians, the state's water policies increasingly divided them.

In this context, it is important to appreciate the political significance of the prolonged struggle to protect the delta, an effort that resulted in the first defeat of a major water management bond issue in the state's history. Much of the opposition to the Peripheral Canal was geographically based, stemming from the harms it threatened to those who lived and worked in and around the delta. Previous water management projects had primarily affected those who lived in rural areas far from the state's major population centers. But now, for the first time, the costs of such a project had "come home," and it was seen to threaten the financial and recreational interests of the significant number of people who lived around the delta.

Finally, to these factors must be added the more general expansion of public interest in and support for environmental conservation that took place both in California and nationally in the late 1960s and early 1970s. But by the time some Californians finally "woke up" to the environmental consequences of the state's hydraulic infrastructure, its interior rivers, lakes, and valleys had already been transformed beyond recognition.

Water and California's Future

As noted earlier, in 2014, in the midst of a severe multiyear drought, California's voters overwhelmingly approved a $7.5 billion water bond issue. But whatever changes in the state's water infrastructure take place because of these expenditures, they are unlikely to address its long-term water problem, which is likely to be exacerbated by climatic weather changes. Reallocating or storing more water will be of limited use if less of it is available in the first place.

California has historically exercised limited control over private water usage. This tendency is part of the legacy of the riparian law established during the Gold Rush that gave water access both above and below the ground to whoever claimed the land first. It was only in 2014, when the state had its lowest rainfall in recorded history, that California enacted the Sustainable Groundwater Management Act, a law that required those pumping groundwater to measure the amount of water they extract.

The historic lack of any regulation of groundwater pumping has become a serious problem, most notably in the Central Valley, where overpumping by farmers is actually causing the ground to sink and leading to the collapse of depleted aquifers—outcomes that effectively destroy the future ability of the ground to store water. According to one environmental lawyer from Orlando, "It's unusual for a state of the size and sophistication of California to have no code or legislation addressing the use of groundwater, which has been a mainstay in Florida for decades, if not hundreds of years."[75]

In response, California has finally begun to take water conservation more seriously. A state law enacted in 2009 required a 20 percent reduction in per capita water use. As a result of a 25 percent state cutback that Governor Brown ordered in 2015, water usage in California declined by 23.9 percent from its 2013 level. Notwithstanding record rainfalls in 2016–2017, the working assumption of state officials is that California will continue to grow drier, and thus the state will need to learn to adapt to life with less water. "California is facing a new climate realty, in which extreme drought is more likely," the New York Times reported. "The state's water rights, infrastructure and management were designed for an old climate that no longer exists."[76] According to Felicia Marcus, the chair of the state's Water Resources Control Board, "Our emphasis is on conservation as a way of life in California. We've had the luxury of taking our precious water for granted in the past, but we do not anymore."[77] Most ominously, Doug Parker and Faith Kearns of the University of California–Berkeley's Division of Agriculture and Natural

Resources conclude that "there is no solution to drought, only a change in our way of thinking about drought." They argue:

> Californians have always accepted, and at times even embraced, the uncertain nature in this beautiful diverse state. From the boom and bust of the Gold Rush to a new population living on fault lines, California's uncertainty is built into our lives. Drought is not different. We will always face times when water is scarce, so we must optimize water use while accepting uncertainty as an integral part of the California lifestyle.[78]

To the extent that Californians can begin to use water more efficiently—for households as well as agriculture—the trade-offs between protecting the state's aquatic environment and having sufficient water for human needs may become more manageable. As will be discussed in chapter 7, during the 1970s California policymakers devised a creative approach to ensuring adequate energy supplies while avoiding the construction of new power plants. Their solution was to promote energy conservation—a policy innovation that has proven remarkably successful. The state will now be challenged to formulate a similarly creative approach to managing its water.

6

Protecting Air Quality

California's struggles with air quality demonstrate the mixed and often-contradictory role played by the state's geography in its formation. On one hand, California's benign climate played an important role in the early growth of Los Angeles. Many people relocated there because they were attracted by its unusually pleasant and "healthy" weather. But on the other hand, thanks in part to its unique topography, by the 1940s the Los Angeles Basin had the worst air quality in the United States. Public and business demands for automobile control in the United States originated in Los Angeles, and pollution controls for motor vehicles were essentially initiated by the state of California. Following a successful national political campaign that pitted the interests of California against the nation's automotive manufactures, in 1967, Congress allowed California—and initially only California—to issue its own vehicle emissions standards. Thanks to the unique pollution problems of Los Angeles, the United States became and remains the only country to have two distinctive mobile-source pollution control standards.[1]

California's regulatory autonomy has enabled it to function as a kind of laboratory for the United States in which the state has adopted progressively more stringent regulations, many of which have then been diffused to the rest of the nation. This unique regulatory system of "iterative federalism" has played an important role in strengthening the regulations of both the federal government and several other states.[2] Supported by both the public and much of the state's business community, and implemented by the California Air Resources Board (CARB), a well-respected administrative agency with considerable technical skills, dramatic improvements in air quality have taken place throughout California, especially in its southern part.

Many of the themes described throughout this book are illustrated in this chapter. These include the importance of both citizen mobilization and business support for stronger environmental regulations and the progressive development of the state's regulatory capacity, from the creation of the Smoke and Fumes Commission in Los Angeles in 1945 to the organization of air pollution control districts in 1947 and finally the establishment in 1968 of the California Air Resources Board. This chapter also highlights the critical role played by alliances between citizens and the business community, both of which had a common interest in protecting California's air quality.

On two dimensions, the themes developed in this chapter are distinctive. First, they demonstrate the increasingly complex and often-conflicting relationship between the federal and state government. The control of air pollution was the first important policy area in which California's environmental policies were consistently more innovative and stringent than those of the federal government. Second, in no other area of environmental policy have California's regulations had as much impact outside the state as in air quality. The state's unique ability to establish its own automotive emissions standards continues to serve as the most important demonstration of the "California effect."

Controlling Urban Air Pollution

By 1912, virtually every city in the United States with a population over 200,000 had defined smoke as a public nuisance and established smoke abatement programs. One of these cities was Los Angeles, a city whose pollution control problems had emerged relatively early in its history. In 1903, when Los Angeles County had only about 100,000 residents, the city experienced such a severe smog attack that some residents mistook it for an eclipse of the sun. The *Los Angeles Herald* reported that "darkness spread over streets. . . . [S]moke fumes . . . obscured the sun and drove out daylight. . . . The smoke making nuisance is growing in volume and density." The City Council, the newspaper added, was "in favor of any kind of legislation that will lead to its abatement."[3]

Two years later, the city approved an ordinance that restricted emissions of dense smoke from flues, chimneys, and smokestacks. This law was then replaced by a more comprehensive measure drafted and supported by the Public Health Committee of the Los Angeles County Medical Association.

In 1907, the city employed the state's first environmental official, a smoke inspector. Between 1908 and 1937, Los Angeles enacted several additional pollution controls, including restrictions on smoke and fumes from industrial structures and emissions from oil-burning orchard heaters.

The Distinctive Problems of Los Angeles

While Los Angeles was certainly not unique among American cities in facing growing problems with air pollution, there were two reasons why the deterioration in its air quality during the first half of the twentieth century was particularly pronounced. The first had to do with the city's distinctive topography. Los Angeles lies at the bottom of a huge 1,600-square-mile natural inverted bowl, three sides of which are bound by mountains. The fourth side of the bowl faces the Pacific Ocean. Hot ocean air moves inland from the Pacific, while cold coastal currents cool the lower air levels. Because the lower layers of cooler air are heavier than the warmer ones, they remain close to the ground—often staying as low as 500 feet. These ground-level pollutants consequently remain trapped in the Los Angeles Basin by both the warm air above them and the mountains that surround the city. Exacerbating the impact of this unusual topography is the fact that Los Angeles, unlike many coastal cities, has relatively weak wind currents. The winds that do blow come from the west, but because of the mountain barriers to the east, they trap rather than disperse the region's pollution.

Ironically, Southern California's benign climate has worsened its air quality. The region's high-pressure atmosphere results in cloudless sunshine for much of the year: Los Angeles has more days of sunshine than any other major urban area in the country except Phoenix. Although this meteorological characteristic keeps its temperature relatively pleasant and stable, when combined with cooler air, it produces a temperature inversion that creates a "noxious photo-chemical brew."[4]

Taken together, these topographical features mean that air quality and visibility in Los Angeles would be adversely affected even if the region were relatively uninhabited. In fact, in 1542, Juan Rodriguez Cabrillo, the Spanish explorer who gave the state its name, observed that the smoke from Native American campfires rose only a few hundred feet and then spread out at the base of the mountains in the east, obscuring their visibility. He went on to label the San Pedro Bay near Los Angeles "La Bahia de Los Fumos," or the Bay of Smokes. Other explorers and early settlers also reported that the basin in which Los Angeles is now located frequently experienced a "natural tropical haze" and was often "so filled with smoke as to confine the vision to a small circumference."[5] As early as 1868, when the region was still sparsely inhabited, a five-day smoke episode severely restricted visibility.

This geographic vulnerability is analogous to that faced by the Sacramento Valley, the location of which in a floodplain means that it would have faced severe flooding even in the absence of debris from hydraulic gold mining. Both cases illustrate the environmental threats posed by distinctive features of the state's topography, threats that were then significantly exacerbated by human activity.

The second factor contributing to the region's particularly poor air quality was its rapid population and industrial growth. Between 1920 and 1940, the population of Los Angeles County increased from under 1 million to 2.7 million—a rate of growth that exceeded that of any other metropolitan area in the United States.[6] During the Second World War, the city became a major industrial center. Between 1940 and 1941, investments in large-scale industrial plants increased from $4.4 million to $38.5 million, while the number of workers employed in manufacturing grew from 152,000 in 1940 to 446,000 in 1943. In 1942, the city was awarded more than $3 billion in military contracts, an amount that tripled the following year.[7] Many of the industries involved in this war production—including the manufacture and processing of rubber, nonferrous metals, petroleum machinery, and chemicals—were substantial contributors to air pollution.

SMOG ATTACKS

As early as 1939, aviation authorities described the haze in downtown Los Angeles, Pasadena, and Altadena as a "serious menace to air flying."[8] By the 1940s, haze obscured Catalina Island off the coast of Los Angeles, as well as the mountains to the east. Frequently, low-lying smoke and fumes spread through the city, leaving its angry citizens coughing and crying.

Over time, "smog attacks" became a fixture of life in Los Angeles. The city experienced its first such attack in July 1940, followed by a string of others over the next two years as the ramping up of military-industrial production strained the capacity of the city's atmosphere to absorb additional effluents. During the first half of 1943, residents began to regularly complain about the "terrific smoke nuisance," while some workers in defense factories left their jobs rather than work in "gas-laden air." Trapped by the San Gabriel Mountains, polluted air from Los Angeles began to spread to residential communities outside the city limits, covering Pasadena, for example, from noon to nightfall. The Pasadena Chamber of Commerce worried that the fumes were "affecting health and the reputation of the community as a healthful city."[9]

On September 8, 1943, a day that became known as Black Wednesday, the city witnessed a "daylight dimout."[10] Citizens panicked. Blinded drivers struggled to the roadside to avoid collisions, while mothers took their frightened children into hotel and office lobbies to shelter them. The paint on cars became blistered and black, and greasy residues appeared on the curtains and furniture in hotels and restaurants. Rumors spread that the Japanese had attacked the city.

THE CITY INTERVENES

Additional smog attacks subsequently took place in September, October, and December 1944, sparking a wave of citizen complaints from Los Angeles, Burbank, Pasadena, and other parts of the county. The Los Angeles City Council responded by ordering an investigation of the "peculiar atmospheric condition" that had so visibly adversely affected the region. Public health officials recognized that the causes of the heavy acrid haze that had engulfed the city were both complex and long-standing. But city officials found themselves under intense public pressure to find a "villain." They decided to focus on one particular downtown industrial facility, a smoky, smelly synthetic butadiene plant owned by the Southern California Gas Company. Articles about the fumes produced by this plant appeared almost daily in the city's newspapers.[11] It was at this facility, whose fumes had spread to residential communities along the foothills of the San Gabriel Mountains, that the city chose to begin its battle to clean up its air.

Initially, the City Council tried to close the plant until it had installed proper abatement equipment. However, the federal government refused to allow the closure, as the plant produced a petroleum derivative that was critical to the war effort. This episode marked the first conflict between state and federal officials over the control of air pollution in California. Soon after the federal government's refusal, it became apparent that the industrial facility had been mistakenly targeted. Even after the plant was periodically shut down for trial periods and abatement equipment installed, the smog persisted.

In 1945, Los Angeles created a Smoke and Fumes Commission, the first of its kind in the United States and California's opening salvo in its fight to develop its regulatory capacity to address air pollution. The commission enacted limits on smoke emissions based on those adopted by other American cities. However, the commission's Office of Air Pollution Control mistakenly assumed that the causes of air pollution in Los Angeles were similar to those found in cities in the East and the Midwest, where emissions of sulfur and smoke were produced by the burning of coal. However, this was not the case for Los Angeles, whose industrial plants and utilities relied instead on hydroelectric power and oil. Not surprisingly, then, these regulations had little impact. The number of days when pollution in downtown Los Angeles reduced visibility to less than one mile actually increased from seven in 1941 to forty-seven in 1947. By 1949, the moviemakers who, initially attracted by the city's good weather and abundant sunshine, had made Los Angeles into the film capital of the world, were frequently cancelling plans for outdoor shoots. Small wonder that Los Angeles became "the poster city" for the postwar smog crisis.[12]

MOBILIZATION

Under the leadership of the politically influential publisher Norman Chandler, the Los Angeles Times played a central role in mobilizing public pressure to address the region's pollution control problems. Chandler, whose family had extensive investments in the region, stated in 1948 that the Los Angeles Times had "entered the [anti-smog] campaign in the public interest with the avowed purpose, if possible, of finding all the sources of air pollution, and [was] committed to the position of going forward without fear or favor of its effect upon any industry."[13] The Times followed up this commitment by publishing a series of lengthy articles about the city's growing pollution problems. To build political support for its clean air campaign, the newspaper established a Citizens Smog Advisory Committee.

In contrast to many other cities whose business and manufacturing organizations had opposed efforts to reduce soot and smoke, the city's most influential business organization, the Los Angeles Area Chamber of Commerce (LAACC), was a strong backer of government regulation. The threat to the city's growth posed by poor air quality was of particular concern to its economically important real estate industry, which feared that the city's worsening pollution problems would make it more difficult to attract new residents. In fact, much of the rapid growth of Southern California between the 1870s and the 1940s had been due to its well-publicized promise of a more attractive and healthy lifestyle. "Residents came to the region looking for respite from sooty, industrial cities," wrote Sarah Ekland, while "for decades boosters promoted the region as a natural sanitarium for those suffering from tuberculosis and other respiratory diseases."[14]

The region's air was a vital part of that attraction. A book promoting the region published in 1893 reported: "Southern California presents a most gloriously invigorating tonic, and stimulating climate, very much superior to anything. . . . [T]he air is so pure and much drier than at Mentone [on the Italian Rivera]. . . . [I]t has a most soothing influence on the mucous membrane, even more so than the climate of Florida."[15] A contemporary column in a British newspaper assured its readers that Southern California was a "land of promise for those threatened with, or suffering from, consumption, asthma, throat diseases, dyspepsia or physical prostration. . . . Infectious diseases are scarcely known here."[16] One of those who came to Los Angeles for his health was Norman Chandler's father, Harry Chandler, who arrived in 1888. He had been advised by his doctors to recuperate in a "warm and dry climate" following an illness he had contracted while at Dartmouth College.

During the 1920s, many wealthy retirees, especially from the upper Midwest, moved to Los Angeles for its abundant sunshine and relatively cool nights—the latter a particularly important attraction before the advent of air conditioning. Now the fact that the city's air was no longer "pure" or "invigorating" made a mockery of the extensive LAACC campaigns to promote the city's attractiveness—marketing efforts that had made Southern California one of the most widely publicized regions of the United States. A city that had formerly enjoyed a reputation as the nation's healthiest was now its most polluted.

Nor were urban residents and local business interests the only ones adversely affected by the city's deteriorating air quality. Notwithstanding the region's urban growth, by 1900, Los Angeles County was the state's and the nation's most economically important agricultural producer, measured by total value of agricultural output—a position the county would continue to hold for almost half a century. Southern California had more than a million orange trees, and its farms also grew beans, potatoes, sugar beets, olives, walnuts, spinach, and lettuce. The decline in air quality significantly damaged crops from Long Beach to the San Fernando Valley, with losses totaling several millions of dollars. Many farmers were forced to relocate or go out of business.

In sum, a broad coalition of business interests including the tourism, real estate, and agricultural sectors had a strong pecuniary stake in reducing air pollution in Los Angeles—a goal also shared by much of the city's citizenry. A Baptist–bootlegger coalition was in place; the challenge now was to figure out how to accomplish its goal.

Air Pollution Control Districts

The city's efforts to improve air quality initially focused on curbing stationary sources of pollution. Authorities believed that pollution could be adequately abated if controls on smokestacks, incinerators, steel plants, and foundries could be enacted and effectively enforced. The soundness of this approach was reinforced by a report commissioned by and widely publicized in the *Los Angeles Times* in 1946. Written by Robert Tucker, an air pollution expert from Washington University in St. Louis, it concluded that the primary sources of the city's poor air quality were discharges of fumes, smoke, odors, and dust from facilities such as chemical firms, refineries, food production plants, soap and paint plants, and railroads. The report noted that industrial operations in the city had nearly doubled during the previous five years. It was this rapid industrial growth, combined with the city's population explosion (it now had 3.7 million residents) and its warm, stagnant weather patterns, that Tucker declared had made its Mediterranean-like climate "traitorous."[17]

Tucker dismissed claims that the pollution was due to the automobile, stating that "although it is quite probable that the automobile does contribute to the nuisance, it is not in such proportion that it is the sole cause."[18] Accordingly, his report recommended essentially the same kinds of pollution control measures that had improved air quality in St. Louis—namely, reducing emissions from industrial, or stationary, sources. But however mistaken its diagnosis, his report did highlight one important shortcoming of current pollution control efforts in Southern California: the lack of a central administrative structure to enforce air pollution controls throughout Los Angeles County, including both incorporated and unincorporated areas outside the city's borders. Indeed, according to the city's mayor, Los Angeles's pollution problems were primarily a result of the "floating garbage" that originated in the towns that surrounded the city.[19]

Following Tucker's report, Los Angeles County asked the state to authorize the creation of the Los Angeles Air Pollution Control District (LAAPCD). This proposal was strongly supported by much of the region's local business establishment, including the Los Angeles Chamber of Commerce, the Pasadena Chamber of Commerce, and the Automobile Club of Southern California. The *Los Angeles Times* published several editorials on the subject. One such editorial rhetorically asked if the corporate wealth of heavy industry justified "the oppressive clouds of smoke and fumes in the region."[20]

However, not all business supported the creation of the LAAPCD. While improving the region's air quality was an economic imperative for many local businesses, this was not the case for the region's railroads, lumber companies, and oil refiners, which were less dependent on the local economy. The railroads claimed that the new regulatory body would unlawfully burden interstate commerce, while the oil companies objected to provisions in the proposed legislation that required any firm constructing or modifying an industrial facility to first receive a permit. For its part, the lumber industry feared that it would no longer be able to freely burn mountains of sawdust waste in Los Angeles County.

The oil firms proved the legislation's major opponent in Sacramento. However, the threat of adverse publicity from the *Los Angeles Times* persuaded them to change their position. At a meeting between a county official and representatives from Standard Oil, Union Oil, Texaco, General Petroleum, Shell, and Richfield Oil, William Strong, the vice president of Union Oil, acknowledged that smog was affecting not only the health of the community but also its future prosperity and announced that his firm would no longer oppose the legislation.[21] Each of the major oil companies then changed their position, as did the region's timber companies. This paved the way for the passage of the Air Pollution Control Act of 1947, which was signed into law by Governor Earl Warren.

This pioneering legislation—the first by a state to address air pollution—authorized the creation of air pollution control districts (APCDs) in every county of the state. The Los Angeles Air Pollution Control District was the first to form, becoming the nation's first pollution control authority to span existing political jurisdictions. With an initial budget of $178,000, it became the best-funded pollution control agency in the United States. By 1954, it had 117 employees and a budget that had grown to $700,000. Through 1957, it spent nearly $10 million on pollution control efforts.[22] In 1955, a second pollution control district was established in northern California. This Bay Area Pollution Control District included all or portions of nine counties.

The creation of these and other APCDs was an important milestone in the history of pollution control in California. It enabled the state to develop a substantial scientific and technical capacity to identify and address the problems of air pollution. Smog workers became respected professionals.[23] The development of administrative capacity and professional expertise increased the autonomy and influence of these regulatory agencies and officials, a development that would have a major long-term impact on the state's environmental policy trajectory.

INITIAL ACCOMPLISHMENTS

From the 1940s through the 1960s, Los Angeles led the nation and the globe in its efforts to fight air pollution.[24] Its innovative, stringent, and effectively enforced controls on pollution from iron foundries, open-hearth steel mills, oil storage tanks, and local refineries almost totally eliminated the visible, heavy particulate emissions of black smoke and soot that continued to affect many other American cities. During the second half of the 1950s, the number of smog alerts declined. According to a report issued by the LAAPCD in 1957,

> Los Angeles County has the world's biggest smog headaches, and certainly its most notorious. It also has the world's most complete air pollution control program, and its most effective. The deservedly acclaimed efforts made in cities such as Pittsburgh and St. Louis are a bare beginning compared to what has been done here. . . . Ours is the toughest air pollution program in the world, and we are blazing the trail in learning how to control it. . . . The fruits of a victory will not [only] be a more enjoyable future for us, but a valuable contribution to world science as well.[25]

This report also pointed to the broader national impact of Los Angeles's pollution control efforts. As the country's best-known battleground in the fight to improve air quality, Los Angeles served as a template for other cities' and states' air pollution controls. A top pollution control official from New York City acknowledged in 1962: "We copy them. . . . Their budget is five times ours. They investigate—we check."[26] Los Angeles had established itself as the premier jurisdiction for tackling air quality. Many scientists and pollution control officials from Los Angeles and California subsequently worked for other cities and states, while many federal environmental officials acquired their knowledge of air pollution controls through work in Southern California.

By the mid-1960s, the APCDs had issued more than 100 rules and regulations for stationary sources, which prevented emissions of an estimated 1,500 to 2,000 tons of harmful pollutants each day. But despite the APCDs' formidable accomplishments in reducing pollutants from stationary sources, the overall impact of their regulations on air quality remained limited. That is because the most important sources of air pollution in Southern California had yet to be controlled. These were emissions from mobile sources, namely, cars and trucks.

Automotive Emissions

Even though the Air Pollution Control Act of 1947 had exempted motor vehicles from the permitting requirement for pollution sources, the LAAPCD
did have the legal authority to regulate automobile emissions. However,
through 1949, motor vehicles were not part of the region's pollution control
efforts. The reason was a simple one: cars were still considered to have a
"relatively minor" impact on air quality when compared to the more visible emissions from industrial and municipal sources.[27] There was as yet no
scientific understanding of or appreciation for the role played by the largely
invisible pollutants from cars in creating smog. Nonetheless, the limited
reduction in smog levels achieved by the LAAPCD's controls over visible
pollutants from stationary sources led some authorities to suspect that pollution from automobiles might be making an important contribution.

These suspicions were strengthened by an event that occurred in 1949.
In November of that year, the University of California at Berkeley's football
team played a home game against Washington State University. During the
week prior to the game, the San Francisco Bay Area had experienced pollution conditions similar to those of Los Angeles. However, it was only on
the day of the game, and only in Berkeley, that many thousands of specta-
tors experienced the intense eye irritation that was the hallmark of Los Angeles smog.

A committee of the state assembly, which had been highly critical of the
pollution control efforts of the LAAPCD, decided to launch an investigation.
It found that weather conditions in the Bay Area during the week before the
game were identical to the type of inversion that periodically affected Los
Angeles. But why, then, did Los Angeles–style smog only occur on the day
of the game? The only unusual occurrence that day was a massive traffic jam
that had produced an unusually concentrated level of vehicular exhaust. The
football game had, in effect, produced a microcosm of conditions common
to Los Angeles, where the idling, stopping, and starting of traffic jams daily
produced clouds of exhaust.[28]

In short, the similarity between what had occurred that day in Berkeley
and what was occurring daily in Los Angeles was striking. As the eye irrita-
tions had occurred only on the day of and near the location of the football
game, it was impossible to escape the conclusion that automotive exhaust
was its cause. This discovery marked the first public recognition of the automobile's contribution to air pollution. But more research would be required
to establish a scientifically credible link.

SMOG SCIENCE

Part of the problem that scientists faced in establishing this link was that the chemical nature of smog was still not understood. It was not until the late 1940s that Dr. Arie Jan Haagen-Smit, a biochemist at Cal Tech, established the scientific basis for smog. Haagen-Smit had become interested in air pollution after his experiments demonstrated the negative effect of smog on plants. He and a colleague took a leave of absence from Cal Tech to head the research efforts at the LAAPCD. They subsequently found that smog aerosol contained unsaturated hydrocarbons, which are released from gasoline storage tanks, gasoline tanks in automobiles, and automobile exhaust.[29]

However, their conclusions were not widely accepted, and several scientific journals rejected their research. Research by the Stanford Research Institute funded by the Western Oil and Gas Association blamed Los Angeles smog on home heating and rubbish burning, among numerous other sources—none of which were related to the industry's products. Nor was Haagen-Smit's analysis welcomed by the auto industry. Indeed, when a Los Angeles County supervisor asked Ford Motor Company in 1953 if it was conducting any research on controlling exhaust pollution, the firm's news department replied: "The Ford engineering staff, although mindful that automobile engines produce exhaust gases, feels that these vapors are dissipated in the atmosphere quickly and do not represent an air pollution control problem."[30]

CITIZEN AND BUSINESS MOBILIZATION

During eighteen days in October and November 1954, Southern California experienced its worst smog attack to date. As a heavy blanket of smog lay across much of the metropolitan region, three infants died from respiratory causes, a child was temporarily blinded, and a man reported that his wife had attempted suicide because of headaches induced by the smog.[31] The next year, in September of 1955, Los Angeles experienced the highest recorded level of ozone in its history. The *Los Angeles Times* reported that "the densest smog on record grayed Los Angeles for hours . . . threatening closure of industry and curtailment of traffic."[32] Hospital admissions for respiratory complaints increased, airplanes had difficulty landing, and outdoor movie shoots were halted.

Citizens became outraged. In Pasadena, a citizen action committee demanded a grand jury investigation. Angry protestors waved signs that read

"SMOG HAS CHANGED SAN GABRIEL VALLEY TO DEATH VALLEY."
At a community meeting in Highland Park, attendees wore gas masks as a
form of protest. The Citizens' Anti-Smoke Advisory Committee organized a
grassroots antipollution campaign, and a group of concerned parents formed
an organization called Stamp Out Smog (or SOS). Petitions were circulated
against industrial polluters, and hundreds marched on local city halls. The
residents of Los Angeles County may have been indifferent—or, more likely,
oblivious—to the impact of the aqueduct they had supported on the ecology of Owens Valley and Mono Lake. But they were not indifferent to the
smog emissions that pervaded their city: they could be seen in the "yards"
all around them.

In addition to this upsurge in citizen mobilization, the increasingly severe
smog alerts of the mid-1950s also led to the establishment of a business-based
policy planning organization, the Air Pollution Foundation of Los Angeles.[33]
The organization's board of trustees was primarily drawn from locally ori-
ented firms, the prosperity of which depended on the continuing attraction
of residents and tourists to Los Angeles. Its members included the region's
utilities, its major department stores and banks, and local airlines.

The foundation assembled a professional staff to direct and coordinate a
broad research program investigating the causes of smog in Southern California. By the end of 1956, researchers had reached the important conclusion that since automobiles were the only remaining uncontrolled source
of unburned hydrocarbons in the city, "motor vehicles were the principal
contributors of (photochemical) smog to Los Angeles."[34] This conclusion by
a business-sponsored research team was a major political and policy breakthrough. It quickly led to a broad consensus, shared by technical experts,
politicians, and business leaders alike, that the key to improving air quality
in Southern California was to install pollution controls on automobiles.

After several years of denial, the automobile industry now acknowledged
that motor vehicle exhaust did produce smog and was a major contributor
to its existence in Los Angeles. Nonetheless, the car manufacturers insisted
that conditions in Los Angeles were distinctive. Since other cities were not
experiencing similar pollution problems, then, according to General Motors,
"some other factors" peculiar to Los Angeles "may be contributing to this
problem."[35] This claim, however, proved to be incorrect. In fact, both New
York City and San Francisco had also experienced episodes of eye irritation
and low visibility, and in 1957, "Los Angeles–type smog" had appeared for
the first time in Philadelphia.

CONTINUED DETERIORATION

Throughout the 1950s, reports of smog's effects on public health and damages to crops also began to surface in other parts of California, including Riverside, the San Fernando Valley, San Diego, Ventura, Fresno, and Bakersfield. In just a few years, air pollution was transformed from a local problem to a statewide one.[36]

While air pollution in many American cities steadily became worse during the 1950s, the deterioration of air quality was particularly pronounced in greater Los Angeles. In addition to the city's unusual topography, which trapped air pollutants at ground level, three other interrelated factors were at work. The first was Los Angeles's unusual population growth. During the 1940s, Los Angeles experienced a greater rate of population growth than seen in any American state. In just six years, between 1950 and 1956, the county grew by 1.2 million people. By the mid-1950s, it contained 5 million inhabitants—more residents than lived in all but eight of the forty-eight American states and as many people as the total population of the entire Rocky Mountain West. Second, during this period the city's businesses expanded at a significantly higher rate than in the rest of the United States. In 1953, new commercial and residential construction in Los Angeles exceeded the combined totals of such construction in seven major American cities. Third, cars played a uniquely important role in the daily lives of Los Angelinos.

The Automobile and Los Angeles

The unusual reliance of Los Angelinos on motor vehicle transportation reflected the region's historical pattern of urban development as a dispersed series of communities. The city developed horizontally rather than vertically because land was abundant, a geographical opportunity that was actively promoted by the city's politically powerful real estate firms. While most American cities became more suburban in the postwar period, Los Angeles, according to Scott Bottles, "decentralized earlier and to a greater extent than other cities," both because it had urbanized later and because its capacity for spatial expansion was less physically restricted than that of other cities.[37] Between March 1923 and March 1924, local developers subdivided 84,000 new lots and constructed 125,000 single-family homes.[38]

Los Angeles's unusually low population density was also possible because it initially developed and grew during a period when streetcars and inter-urban railroads enabled residents to live in single-family homes located in suburbs spread across the countryside, far away from the urban core. The Pacific Electric Railway served the entire Los Angeles Basin, laying more than 1,000 miles of track by the 1920s. The railway was the largest electric inter-urban transportation system in the world, designed to move both commuters and shoppers from the outlying areas where they resided to downtown businesses and stores.

But by 1950, the railway's passenger service had been almost entirely discontinued. In a widely publicized and frequently quoted report presented to the Senate Judiciary Committee in 1974, Bradford Snell, a U.S. Senate legislative analyst, stated that the city's transportation system had been destroyed by the automobile industry. He claimed that the industry had purchased a controlling interest in the urban railway and then replaced the trolleys with more inefficient diesel coaches, thus forcing urban residents to turn to the automobile as their only means of transport. This sales strategy turned people who previously had relied on the rail system away from public transport and toward automobile travel, making Los Angeles into an "ecological wasteland" that served corporate wants instead of social needs.[39] Snell's account was bolstered by the fact that in 1949, a federal grand jury had convicted General Motors and other firms of "conspiring to replace electric transportation systems with buses and to monopolize the sale of buses" in Los Angeles.[40]

But Snell's saga of virtuous inter-city rail firms destroyed by the "greedy" automobile industry does not stand up to scrutiny. The city's rail transportation system did play a critical role in the initial dispersion of its population. But the public was far from happy with the service it provided. As Bottles has reported, "In seeking to operate their business profitably, railway officials, in the minds of many citizens, deliberately ran too few cars, refused to build necessary crosstown lines or tracks into lightly populated areas, ignored the safety of the public, and bribed elected officials for favors."[41] Indeed, the increasing dispersion of the city's workplaces and residential developments may have made a fixed rail system no longer practical.

In 1920, the *Los Angeles Record* published a major exposé on the state of local rail transport. Headlined "Los Angeles Street Car Service Is Intolerable," the article reported that "condemnation of the traction companies of Los Angeles was never so general and bitter as it is today," specifically citing crowded car conditions, inexperienced drivers, and poor scheduling. The newspaper subsequently received complaints from hundreds of citizens about inadequate rail service. In fact, a central policy objective of the

Progressive Era reform movement in Los Angeles during the first decades of the twentieth century was to establish a utility commission that would require the owners of the rail systems to better serve the public—efforts that were unsuccessful because of the strong political sway of the railway.

LOS ANGELINOS AND THEIR CARS

In fact, Los Angeles's unusual dependence on automotive transportation long predated the demise of the rail system during the 1930s and 1940s. In 1924, Frederick Law Olmsted, Jr., the son of the great Central Park planner, wrote that "the place of the automobile in the transportation problem of Los Angeles is far more important than in the cities of the East." He attributed this situation to Southern California's favorable climate, "the widely scattered pollution and the almost universal housing in detached single family dwellings."[42] As early as 1915, Los Angeles had one car for every eight residents, compared with a national average of one vehicle per forty-three citizens. Automotive registration in Los Angeles County increased nearly fourfold between 1918 and 1923, growing to 430,000. By 1925, every other person in Los Angeles owned a vehicle, three times the national average of one car for every six people. Moreover, the residents of Los Angeles drove their cars more frequently: in 1924, nearly half of those who entered the central business district drove there.

Automobile registration more than doubled again in the decade following the Second World War. By 1956, there were nearly 3 million cars registered in Los Angeles County. This represented roughly 5 percent of all motor vehicles registered in the United States and constituted the greatest concentration of motor vehicles in the world.[43] In fact, the residents of the Los Angeles Basin owned more automobiles than the citizens of any other country except the United Kingdom, Canada, and France. Between 1936 and 1954, daily gasoline consumption grew from 1.8 million to nearly 4.8 million gallons. Because automobile engines expelled between 7 and 10 percent of their intake as whole unburned hydrocarbons, by 1954, automobiles and other vehicles in Los Angeles were emitting more than a quarter-million gallons of gasoline directly into the air every day.[44]

The increasingly important role of the automobile in Los Angeles was linked to its perception as a "democratic piece of urban technology."[45] By offering their owners flexibility and efficiency, they served as "a symbol of urban and industrial progress."[46] Automobiles enabled the residents of Los Angeles to live *where* they wanted—rather than close to where the streetcar lines happened to be located—and *how* they wanted, which was largely in single-family dwellings located far from downtown. This pattern of residential growth further contributed to the region's decentralization, as businesses and shopping districts relocated to sites throughout the region. In short, Los Angeles became dominated by what Wyn Grant has described as "sprawling low-density single family homes, monoculture communities, . . . long commutes and the addiction to gas."[47] As one observer wrote: "Driving, after all, was one of the main points of living in Los Angeles."[48] Southern Californians and cars "went together like celebrities and sunglasses."[49]

THE DILEMMA OF THE AUTOMOBILE

The residents of Los Angeles wanted to be able to continue to rely on automobile transportation. But this dependence on the automobile had created a dilemma, for it was precisely the central role of the automobile in the otherwise highly appealing Southern California lifestyle that had led to the deterioration of the region's air quality. According to the LAAPCD, in 1960, mobile sources of emissions accounted for 80 to 90 percent of the smog in the South Coast Air Basin.[50] How could this important consumer and lifestyle preference—which was also shared by the region's political and business elites—be reconciled with the equally strong preference for cleaner air?

The most politically viable solution was to force the automobile industry to build cars that emitted fewer pollutants. This abatement strategy, in addition to placing no restraints on the lifestyle of Southern Californians—such as by, for example, restricting urban sprawl or reviving mass transportation—also had the advantage of placing the burden of installing pollution control technologies on an industry that was both headquartered outside the state and had relatively few production sites in it. (In 1963, the economic importance of "motor vehicles and parts," measured by value added, ranked first in the United States but only fifth in California; forty years later, in 2003, the state had fewer than 37,000 vehicle-sector jobs.[51]) The relative lack of automotive production in California was politically significant: it weakened business and union opposition within the state to imposing mobile-source pollution controls and essentially exported much of the immediate cost of pollution abatement to firms, workers, and consumers in other states. Moreover, the fact that California accounted for approximately 10 percent of all cars sold in the United States (with Los Angeles accounting for half of this total) meant that the car companies would have little choice but to design and produce vehicles that met the state's pollution control standards. It was this purchasing power that gave the state considerable leverage.

But while the automobile may have occupied a particularly prominent position in Southern California, other policies related to its use were state-wide. As early as 1910, shortly after the automobile was invented, California's voters had approved an $18 million bond issue for road construction. By 1925, California was crisscrossed by a network of 6,400 mostly paved high-way miles. During the Second World War, planners at both the state and local levels envisioned a significantly expanded program of highway construction. In 1947, the state approved legislation that raised both the gasoline tax and registration fees for automobiles to establish the Highway Trust Fund. As a result, California became a pioneer in modern highway construction.

By 1950, more than 10 million motorists were driving 4.58 million vehicles on California's 14,000 miles of state highway annually.[52] Gaso-line and diesel taxes were increased again in 1953. In 1959, Governor Pat Brown signed the Freeway and Expressway Act of 1959, which envisioned a $10.5 billion freeway/expressway construction program over the next twenty years. Today, the state has nearly 400,000 miles of roads, nearly all of which are "free." In short, the embrace of the automobile in Southern California may have been especially pronounced, but it was far from atypical for the state as a whole. The automobile remains an important symbol of California, and its citizens continue to rely heavily on individualized transportation. Significantly, exhaust from motor vehicles accounts for 60 percent of the state's air pollutants, more than in any other state.

Federal Action

THE FEDERAL AIR POLLUTION CONTROL ACT OF 1955

The "alarm bell" that first brought the nation's air pollution problems to the attention of the federal government took place not in Los Angeles, but in Donora, Pennsylvania. In 1948, six days of smog led to twenty deaths and 6,000 illnesses. This incident attracted considerable national publicity, espe-cially because shortly afterward, 800 people died during an outbreak of air pollution in London. The U.S. Public Health Service conducted an extensive study of the Donora episode, which provided the first clear evidence that air pollution could adversely affect public health. During the early 1950s, the LAAPCD urged the federal government to support additional research, calling smog "a problem of . . . national import." "There is no good reason why Los Angeles County should bear the entire costs of research efforts which are of concern, and will be of benefit to the entire . . . nation," the district declared.[53]

Congress responded by enacting the Federal Air Pollution Control Act of 1955. This federal initiative was strongly influenced by California's experience, marking the beginning of the state's impact on federal air pollution policies.[54] Moreover, one of the key proponents of this legislation was California senator Thomas Kuchel. However, the legislation left the responsibility for regulating air pollution with state and local governments. The role of the federal government would be limited to funding research and supplying local governments with technical assistance.

THE STATE RESPONDS

The Air Pollution Control Act allocated a significant proportion of federal funds to the LAAPCD as well to the University of California, the University of Southern California, and several California state agencies. Federal personnel were loaned to the state of California, and several were subsequently transferred to the LAAPCD, which established the state's first motor vehicle control laboratory in 1955.

The federal government's emphasis on research rather than regulation was initially paralleled at the state level. In 1954, a severe two-week smog episode in Los Angeles had prompted renewed demands for state action. Although California governor Goodwin Knight had been assured by a group of doctors and scientists that public health was not endangered, he acknowledged the need for additional research. Accordingly, he announced a program "to throw all the state's technical resources" into the effort. The University of California received emergency funds to test and develop a "practical and inexpensive" automotive pollution control device, while the California Department of Public Health was awarded $100,000 to undertake "a broad attack on health problems arising from smog conditions."[55]

Political and public pressure for the state to take a more active role increased. The Los Angeles City Council asked the state for financial support for pollution abatement on the grounds that smog did not respect political jurisdiction boundaries. The city of Riverside urged the state to establish uniform air contamination standards on similar grounds. But at the same time, the League of California Cities argued that the state needed to respect the autonomy of local governments. Governor Knight wavered between the two positions, but in the end, he opposed state regulation on the grounds that the smog problem was essentially a local one. State legislation enacted in 1955 required the Department of Public Health to play a more active role in the issue by supporting additional research, monitoring pollution levels, and providing assistance to local agencies. But it too left the responsibility to regulate and control air pollution in the hands of local governments.

The Growth of State Regulation

Severe pollution episodes in 1955, 1956, and 1957 continued to increase pressure for state regulation. In 1958, the LAAPCD announced its support for statewide automobile emissions standards, to be accompanied by the testing, inspection, and mandatory installation of pollution control devices in all cars. This proposal represented a major policy shift, since it would make the state of California, and not local governments, responsible for regulating mobile-source emissions. In 1960, the state legislature, strongly supported by Los Angeles County, passed the Motor Vehicle Pollution Control Act, the first statute authorizing the regulation of automotive emissions in the United States. The law established a new state regulatory body, the Motor Vehicle Pollution Control Board (MVPCB), which was given the responsibility for certifying new pollution control devices. Once two such devices had been certified, drivers would be required to install them on all new and used vehicles within one year.

However, the legislature did not include the provisions for statewide inspection and enforcement that Los Angeles had requested. This failure was due to strong pressures from northern and rural legislators, many of whom regarded air pollution from vehicles as a problem unique to Los Angeles and did not want their constituents to be unnecessarily burdened, especially by requiring their (used) cars to be inspected. Accordingly, the legislation allowed any county to "opt out" of the state's emissions controls for used vehicles, though the approved devices would still be required to be installed on all new vehicles sold in the state.

The MVPCB certified four kinds of catalytic converters, or "afterburners," that were able to work with leaded gasoline. The converters, versions of which would become a key component of federal emissions standards, were developed by independent manufacturing firms from Southern California— not the automotive companies.[56] They were required to be installed on all new cars sold in California beginning in June 1965 and represented the first emissions control requirements for automobiles in the United States. In 1964, the state of California continued its automotive pollution control program by enacting the nation's first tailpipe emissions standards. These regulations restricted emissions of carbon monoxide and hydrocarbons for new cars beginning with the 1966 model year.

Upset by the prospect of losing their control over emissions technologies, the automobile manufacturers announced that they had developed their own engine modification devices, which they claimed were superior to the add-on devices developed by the independent manufacturers. Furthermore, the manufacturers' devices would also meet the state's 1966 model emissions standards.

Finally, more than fifteen years after the fateful Cal–Washington State football game and a decade after the importance of pollution from automobiles had become widely recognized, the state had mandated the adoption of the nation's first automotive emissions technologies and established its first emissions standards. These important initiatives marked a historic step in the regulation of air pollution from mobile sources in the United States. Governor Edmund Brown declared that he intended to make California "the ecological gold standard" for other states affected by pollution, adding that "our problems apply to every state in the country. . . . California is a good place for these problems to be studied and their solution found."[57]

The Growth of Federal Regulation

In 1960, Congress had approved legislation that required the U.S. Surgeon General to study the effect of motor vehicle exhaust on public health. While abatement and enforcement efforts remained in the hands of state and local governments at this time, only fifteen states had adopted any pollution control program, while more than half of all state pollution control expenditures had been made by California—and of those, nearly four-fifths had been made by the city of Los Angeles.[58] Three years later, Congress passed the Clean Air Act, which among other provisions directed the Department of Health, Education and Welfare (HEW) to encourage the automobile industry and oil companies to develop devices and fuels that would reduce the discharge of harmful pollutants.

The federal government's interest in curbing automotive emissions subsequently increased. In 1964, a Senate subcommittee chaired by Senator Edmund Muskie (D-Maine) held a series of public hearings on the issue at various locations throughout the United States. Significantly, the first such hearing was held in Los Angeles. During it, Governor Brown testified that while California had begun to address automotive emissions, its accomplishments remained modest: the state needed help from the federal government. He argued that "the automobile industry is in interstate commerce and the Federal Government clearly has jurisdiction."[59] Recognizing that auto exhaust represented up to half of the nation's air pollution, the subcommittee decided that uniform national standards were needed and recommended that they be based on those of California.

The U.S. Conference of Mayors and the National Association of Counties supported the subcommittee's proposal, as did the head of the U.S. Public Health Service's Division of Air Pollution, which, echoing Brown's argument, noted that since the nation's 85 million vehicles freely crossed state and local boundaries, the case for national controls was "self-evident."[60] The automotive manufacturers disagreed, claiming that the problem was regional and therefore that standards should vary by location. But once both Pennsylvania and New York also began to consider establishing emissions controls on mobile sources—with the latter's proposed standards being even stricter than California's—the industry recognized that it had lost the battle.[61] Accordingly, it now reversed its position and backed the establishment of uniform federal standards.

With the support of the auto industry, the 1965 Motor Vehicle Air Pollution Control Act required HEW to establish emissions standards for new cars. The following year, the department issued the federal government's first vehicular emissions standards. These rules, which became effective for new cars beginning with the 1968 model year, were identical to those that California had adopted two years earlier.

Pressure for More Regulation in California

Within California, strong public pressures for tough pollution controls persisted. The state continued to grow rapidly, adding 600,000 people and 830,000 new vehicles annually. Unless automotive emissions dropped dramatically, Los Angeles's 1940 smog level was predicted to double by 1975. Already, a curtain of smog periodically overlaid a 250-mile area stretching from Santa Barbara to the Mexican border. Pollution control advocates in Los Angeles had also become increasingly frustrated by the shortcomings of the state's Motor Vehicle Pollution Control Board, which they criticized for being too cautious and lacking either the political will or technical skills to approve and require the automotive pollution control technologies necessary to improve air quality. In addition, while the 1965 federal legislation did not address the issue of federal preemption, pollution control advocates in California feared that new federal air pollution standards would make the MVPCB's role irrelevant.

In an effort to strengthen the state's lagging air pollution control efforts, in 1967, the legislature merged the MVPCB and the Bureau of Sanitation into a new regulatory body, the California Air Resources Board. Dr. Haagen-Smit, the scientist who had earlier been instrumental in identifying the scientific link between automobiles and smog, became the CARB's first chairman.[62] The new agency was given much broader regulatory responsibilities than its predecessors, including the ability to regulate stationary pollution sources throughout the state. California was divided into air basins, and air quality standards were established for each. In addition to expanded authority, the CARB and the regional control districts were given substantial scientific and technical resources. The board's budget came directly from user fees rather than from the state's general fund.

Federal–State Tensions

Los Angeles was not the only city preoccupied with air pollution. The federal government also faced growing public concern about air pollution in several urban areas and widespread dissatisfaction with the regulatory efforts of state and local governments. Indeed, in 1967, less than half of the nation's urban residents lived in cities or states that had adopted any controls on air pollution. In response, Congress once again revisited the role of the federal government in air pollution control policy. One of the most contentious issues it now faced was the relationship between federal and state automotive emissions standards. California officials had already determined that the existing federal standards were not sufficiently stringent to protect air quality in Los Angeles. At the congressional hearings convened by Senator Muskie, city officials from Los Angeles had testified in support of allowing California to continue to establish its own emissions standards. As Chip Jacobs and William Kelly explain, state officials "decided to take matters in their own hands." Accordingly, they sought a waiver from the federal government that would allow the state to set emissions standards stricter than those imposed at the federal level.[63]

THE FIGHT FOR A WAIVER

The waiver was first proposed by California senator George Murphy as an amendment to the Air Quality Act of 1967. His proposal, however, quickly met with strong opposition from both HEW and the Automobile Manufacturers Association. The former testified that such a waiver would result in a wasteful duplication of federal standards, while the latter predicted that it would create chaos and harm consumers. The industry had earlier favored state standards because it had assumed that this would mean no standards except in California. Now the industry wanted to prevent any state, including California, from establishing its own regulations.

In the House of Representatives, John Dingell, whose Michigan congressional district was home to the Ford Motor Company, proposed an amendment that would allow federal laws to preempt more stringent state regulations. As a pleased auto industry representative put it: "The tail is not going to wag the dog, and Los Angeles is the tail."[64] The Dingell amendment was approved in committee and then brought to the floor of the House of Representatives. California felt betrayed: not only had the federal government given it little or no help in addressing its air pollution problems, but it was now going to prevent the state from doing more on its own.

Senator Murphy immediately launched a national campaign to oppose federal preemption. With unusual solidarity, the issue was strongly supported by every member of the state's normally fractious congressional delegation. One member commented: "Air pollution is a bigger issue than Vietnam in California, and every Democrat and Republican in the delegation will fight to the last ditch on this."[65] The delegation circulated pictures of Los Angeles enveloped in a brown haze along with cans of smog marked "poison" to their colleagues. State and local pollution control officials from California visited Washington to inform the nation's legislators that federal preemption not only would violate states' rights but would mean that "the interests of Detroit auto makers [had] prevailed over the interests of California's 20 million people."[66] At the suggestion of Senator Robert Kennedy (D-New York), California's congressional delegation solicited the support of senators and representatives from the South by defining the issue as one of states' rights. Opposition to federal authority had allied the interests of California environmentalists with those of southern segregationists: both wanted to maintain the ability of states to set their own rules.

In California, a Los Angeles radio station aired a multipart program titled "A Breath of Death: The Fatality Factor of Smog." Declaring that "Southern California is on a collision course with disaster," the program reported that during the preceding decade, air quality in the Los Angeles area had been unhealthy nine out of ten days.[67] It emphasized the health effects of smog—which it labeled "Dingell's dust"—and exposed the automobile industry's role in drafting and supporting the Dingell amendment. These broadcasts mobilized the California electorate, which deluged Congress with 500,000 letters and postcards from around the state, setting what appeared to be a record for citizen mobilization on a single piece of national legislation. Providentially, a long, intense smog episode took place between August and October of 1967—precisely the time that the House of Representatives was debating the Dingell amendment and that Dingell himself paid a visit to the state.

After one of the most heated conflicts between the state and federal government over environmental policies to date, the state's campaign was successful. The California exemption was restored in the House version of the legislation and then accepted by the conference committee. The final Air Quality Act of 1967 established uniform national standards for emissions from new cars but exempted from those standards any state that had controlled automotive emissions prior to March 30, 1966. Only one state met this requirement: California. The state was permitted to request a waiver from HEW (and, after 1969, the Environmental Protection Agency) to permit it to adopt more stringent standards than the federal government whenever it was able to demonstrate a "compelling" need for them.

THE SIGNIFICANCE OF CALIFORNIA'S WAIVER

Thanks to the bipartisan efforts of the state's congressional delegation, the work of its pollution control officials, and the grassroots lobbying of its citizens—as well as those southern congressmen and senators persuaded by the value of the federalism argument—California had successfully challenged one of the nation's most important and politically powerful industries. This accomplishment was and remains unprecedented: to date, no other state has been granted a permanent waiver in a federal regulatory statute. As a spokesman for the LAAPCD recalled, "We were jubilant and tried not to dance in the streets. The waiver was going to change the face of air pollution in the United States, it was that historic."[68]

What is particularly striking about the waiver debate is how markedly the policy preferences of the California electorate and the state's policymakers had changed between 1959 and 1967. In 1959, there was still substantial opposition to the adoption of statewide emissions standards for vehicles, especially from rural areas. But by 1967, every local and state pollution control official, along with the entire state congressional delegation and a massive segment of the public, supported the state's efforts to adopt more stringent emissions standards than the federal government.

The successful Washington lobbying campaign not only reflected the extent to which a wide advocacy coalition in favor of more restrictive controls on air pollution had become influential within the state but signaled the state's commitment to maintaining its regulatory independence from the rest of the United States. The 1967 amendments to the Clean Air Act are today a footnote in the history of national environmental policy, but they mark a critical milestone in California's history of environmental politics and policies. After 1967, being "greener" than the rest of the country became a source of state pride. This identification in turn would set a pattern of Californian regulatory autonomy and national leadership that would subsequently extend beyond automobile emissions. In a wide range of policy areas, including energy efficiency, chemical safety, and climate change, California would develop its own health, safety, and environmental standards, and these regulations would typically be more innovative, comprehensive, and stringent than those of the federal government as well as other states.

The timing of the 1967 waiver was also important. The amendment was approved just two years before a major environmental movement swept the nation. The year 1969 would become known as the "Year of the Environment," when high levels of public support for environmental protection emerged across the country. Congress responded to these national pressures by transferring the primary responsibility for environmental regulation from the states to the federal government. But thanks to its own earlier pollution control initiatives and the 1967 exemption it received from the federal government, California had *already* staked out its own distinctive role in environmental policy formation—a role that has persisted to the present.

However, conflict between federal and state authorities has continued.[69] In 2003, for example, the CARB adopted rules to reduce air pollution from small engines used in lawnmowers, leaf blowers, and other non-road equipment. While these regulations only applied to engines sold in California, a major manufacturer of the engines based in Missouri threatened to close its manufacturing facilities and move outside the United States, leading to the loss of 2,000 jobs, if they were adopted. Senator Christopher Bond (R-Missouri) introduced an amendment to an appropriations bill blocking California's regulations. While this amendment was approved in committee, it was dropped in conference committee thanks to aggressive lobbying by California's two Democratic senators, Barbara Boxer and Dianne Feinstein, along with California's new Republican governor, Arnold Schwarzenegger, and the state's large House delegation.

Subsequent Policy Developments through 1989

Congress passed the 1967 federal waiver just in time. While Southern California had made considerable progress in reducing air pollution from stationary sources, the steady increases in both the total number of registered motor vehicles and the total number of vehicle miles driven in the state threatened to set back the progress that the APCDs' stationary-source controls and the state's automobile emissions standards had made. The Los Angeles area now had more than 4 million motor vehicles, which were collectively responsible for 90 percent of all of the state's air pollution by weight, 64 percent of all its air pollutants other than carbon monoxide, and nearly 100 percent of its emissions of carbon monoxide.[70]

In 1968, the state used the regulatory waiver it had just received from the federal government to enact the Pure Air Act. This legislation established increasingly stringent standards for vehicular emissions of both hydrocarbons and carbon monoxide, to go into effect between 1970 and 1974. It also issued the nation's first emissions standards for nitrogen oxides. Like the statute creating the CARB, this legislation was enacted with bipartisan support. In signing it into law, Governor Ronald Reagan cited the measure as another example of the state's leadership in pollution control, stating that he was "gratified to see that the concern for improving our air quality is recognized as being of equal importance with the conservation of our other natural resources."[71]

The automobile industry inadvertently played a key role in assisting the Pure Air Act's passage. The industry's support for federal preemption had already made it very politically unpopular in the state, and the first lobbyist it sent to Sacramento antagonized legislators by claiming that further emissions controls were impossible to achieve. By this time, however, the staff of the California Assembly's Office of Research had developed considerable expertise in air pollution as well as automotive emissions technology. Staff testimony before the legislature effectively challenged the industry's arguments and helped to mobilize public support for stricter controls.

Both federal and California standards for cars produced in 1970 were roughly similar.[72] However, California also required that auto firms install evaporative control systems—a requirement that the federal government adopted the following year. This initiated a pattern of the federal government frequently following California's lead, typically adopting the state's more stringent standards within two to five years.[73] Overall, between 1963 and 2005, California issued a total of seventeen standards for light and medium on-road vehicles. Of these, all but five, including standards for nitrogen oxides, hydrocarbons, and carbon dioxide, were subsequently adopted by the federal government.[74] Unleaded gasoline, the two-way catalytic converter, standards for particulate matter, and evaporative control systems were also first introduced in California and then required by the federal government. Federal standards for health-related pollutants from motor vehicles have typically tracked those of California, though often with a time lag and with some minor differences.

However, the federal government has also played a role in strengthening California's regulations. The 1970 Clean Air Act amendments authorized the EPA to establish ambient air standards and to require each state to submit implementation plans stating how it planned to meet them. Not surprisingly, air quality in Los Angeles fell significantly below these standards. This in turn forced California to tighten its automotive emissions standards, which the 1967 federal waiver had permitted it to do.

The 1970 amendments also tightened standards for automotive emissions of carbon monoxide, hydrocarbons, and nitrogen oxides. Had they actually been adopted by 1975, as the legislation required, federal standards for the first time would have been more stringent than California's.[75] However, the automobile industry claimed that unless the standards' implementation was delayed, it would not be able to meet the fuel economy standards that the federal government had imposed following the energy crisis of the early 1970s. That crisis and the major economic downturn that accompanied it had shifted the emphasis in the national conversation about automotive emissions from pollution control to fuel economy. Both the EPA and Congress now chose to prioritize the latter and repeatedly delayed the implementation of the 1970 pollution control standards.

California, however, decided to buck this trend and instead strengthen its mobile-source emissions requirements. One reason why the federal government in 1981 was finally able to require that the 1975 standards be implemented was that California had successfully demonstrated that the two policy objectives were not incompatible. By this time, the emissions levels for California cars were even lower than 1977 levels, with no loss—and, in some cases, even a gain—in fuel economy.[76]

In 1984, California began to require smog checks for used vehicles, which rural legislators had previously opposed. Vehicles were required to be inspected every other year, as well as every time they were sold or registered for the first time in the state. These inspections were now widely accepted by the public, even though the unusual stringency of the state's testing requirements meant that more vehicles failed them than in any other state. They were also effective: between 1984 and 1991, the state's vehicle inspection programs reduced harmful emissions by 17 percent.[77] Reflecting the fact that 5 percent of the state's (primarily older) vehicles were responsible for nearly half of its automotive emissions, a few pollution control districts established voluntary accelerated vehicle retirement programs, which enabled heavily polluting vehicles to be purchased and then taken off the road.

State and Federal Regulations during the 1990s

In 1990, the California Air Resources Board developed new emissions regulations based on vehicle types.[78] These new laws required the phased introduction of low-emissions vehicles and the cleaner fuels needed to operate them. Rather than creating a single performance standard, vehicles were divided into four categories: transitional low-emissions vehicles (TLEVS), low-emissions vehicles (LEVs), ultra-low-emissions vehicles (ULEVs), and zero-emissions vehicles (ZEVs). Emissions standards, which become known as LEV I, were then established for each category. The state also added an ambitious requirement intended to force the development of new, more efficient technology: each large automotive company was required to make 2 percent of the cars it sold in California ZEVs by 1998, with the percentage rising to 5 percent by 2001 and 10 percent by 2003.

The CARB had assumed that in order to meet these standards, the automotive firms would need to develop substantially new technologies, including alternative fuel engines. But the firms were able to improve their existing technologies so quickly that their emissions were far lower than had been thought possible in 1990. As CARB chairman Alan Lloyd observed: "We've seen the near impossible accomplished with gasoline vehicles: zero evaporation emissions, exceedingly clean exhaust—cleaner, in some cases, than the outside air entering the cabin for ventilation purposes, and emission control systems that are twice as durable [as] their conventional forbears, forecasted to last an astonishing 150,000 miles."[79]

The LEV I mandate was so successful that in 1998, California adopted new emissions standards, known as LEV II. These standards extended the same requirements imposed on passenger cars to light-duty trucks—including sport utility vehicles—and strengthened the standard for emissions of nitrogen oxide by an additional 75 percent. However, it proved extremely difficult to develop a battery electric vehicle that met both cost and performance goals, and the state was forced to postpone its ZEV mandate requirement. Up to 2002, there were never more than 3,900 ZEVs in California at any given time, half of which were owned by government or utility fleets.

At the federal level, the 1990 Clean Air Act amendments also established new emissions standards for mobile sources. The "Tier I" requirements, which were phased in between 1994 and 1996, were identical to California's 1993 standards for light vehicles. But while the federal government had permitted these standards to be implemented over time, California required that all vehicles adopt the 1993 standards that same model year. In 1999, the EPA adopted "Tier II" automotive emissions standards that were based on California's earlier LEV II requirements. The agency also followed California's lead by dividing the automotive fleets into different categories and creating separate emissions standards for each. The federal government's vehicle categories and emissions standards became roughly similar to those established by the state, though some of the federal standards do permit emissions levels greater than those allowed in California. As Ann Carlson has written, "It is hard to imagine the federal government would have achieved such regulatory success absent California's successful experimentation."[80]

The 1990 federal legislation also regulated fuel content for the first time. Again, California played a critical role in this development. The fact that the state's aggressive technology-forcing standards had already established that the refining industry could meet the standards the federal government was now considering played an important role in the regulations' adoption. While similar in many respects, California's standards for reformulated gasoline, or "clean fuels," are more stringent than those of the federal government in an attempt to limit the concentration of ozone-forming hydrocarbons during the summer months. This effort has largely been successful: the state's clean-burning gasoline that came to market in 1992 reduced emissions of reactive organic gases by 220 tons a day.

The 1990 Clean Air Act amendments also regulated emissions from diesel vehicles, requiring that trucks and buses using this fuel reduce their emissions from late 1980s levels by more than 90 percent by 2010. This mandate, however, only applied to new vehicles and engines, leaving the states free to regulate existing automobiles. With an estimated 900,000 diesel-powered heavy-duty trucks and diesel-powered buses accounting for 30 percent of the state's nitrogen oxide emissions and 40 percent of its particulate emissions—pollutants linked to the inflammation and aggravation of lung diseases—California chose to do so, issuing regulations that required the phased retrofitting or replacement of older diesel vehicles, along with several other restrictions on various categories of existing diesel vehicles. By contrast, Texas chose to apply its regulations only to new diesel engines.[81] Since 1993, California's regulations to restrict emissions from diesel engines have been progressively strengthened and made more comprehensive.

Air Quality Improvements

The impact of regulatory standards for mobile-source emissions and other pollution sources on the air quality in both Southern California and the state more broadly has been substantial.[82] Overall, California vehicles today are more than 99 percent cleaner than they were in 1970.[83]

In 1990, the South Coast Air Quality Management District recorded the maximum one-hour ozone concentration at 0.33 parts per million (ppm)—a reduction of 0.6 ppm since 1985—even though the state now had 23 million registered vehicles that had traveled a total of 242 billion miles. That same year, nitrogen oxide and hydrocarbon vehicle emissions totaled 1.4 million tons—200,000 tons less than in 1980, notwithstanding an increase of 87 billion vehicle miles driven since that year. In 1990, Southern California exceeded the Stage 1 smog alert level (0.29 ppm ozone) on only forty-two days—an improvement of forty-one days since 1985 and of seventy-six days since 1975.[84]

By 1996, the South Coast Air Quality Management District's maximum one-hour ozone concentration had been reduced to 0.24 ppm—a 59 percent improvement from 1965. The region experienced Stage 1 smog alerts on only 7 days that year, compared to 111 days in 1975.[85] Overall, the statewide averages for nitrogen oxide and hydrocarbon emissions per vehicle declined by 58 percent and 80 percent, respectively, from 1970 levels. By 2000, California's population had reached 34 million, with 23.4 million registered vehicles being driven 280 billion miles a year, 40 billion more miles than had been recorded for the previous decade. Nonetheless, that year vehicle emissions for nitrogen oxides and hydrocarbons totaled 1.2 million tons—a decrease of 200,000 tons from 1990.

Between 1955 and 2013, the amount of particulate pollution—small dust particles that are harmful to public health—declined by 80 percent. Since 1960, pollution emissions of all smog-causing chemicals have declined by 98 percent. In 2014, ozone levels in Los Angeles were 40 percent of what they had been in the mid-1970s despite a doubling of the number of cars being driven. Throughout the 1970s, Los Angeles had averaged 125 Stage 1 smog alerts per year. But beginning in 1999 and continuing through 2015, the city had no Stage 1 alerts and averaged only seven bad air quality days each year. The recorded smog level in 2015 was the lowest since reporting began.[86]

These are remarkable accomplishments for a city whose residents breathed some of the dirtiest air in the world in the 1940s, 1950s, and 1960s and that had become a national symbol of urban air pollution. Moreover, these improvements have taken place even as both population and vehicular traffic have grown substantially. While people may no longer flock to Southern California to improve or restore their health, the region's air quality no longer threatens its attractiveness as a place to live and work. It would be hard to imagine the region continuing to grow so rapidly had its air quality not improved so substantially.

Nonetheless, compared to the rest of the United States, air quality in Southern California, as well as in other regions of the state—most notably the San Joaquin Valley, the topography of which exhibits some of the same pollution-trapping features as Los Angeles—remains *relatively* poor. Of the seven cities in the United States judged to have the worst air quality, six, including Los Angeles, are in California—even though the state has the most stringent regulations in the country.[87]

The reasons for the city's ongoing problems are twofold. One is the continued increase in automotive usage, which has strained the carrying capacity of the region's air. The second is the intense truck traffic on Los Angeles's freeways. This traffic is largely due to the increasingly important role of the city's ports, which today employ more than 130,000 workers and receive more than 80 percent of all American imports from Asia. Roughly 40 percent of the goods that flow into the port are subsequently moved away from the coast on diesel trucks. While, as noted earlier, the state and Los Angeles have imposed increasingly strict restrictions on emissions from diesel engines, this traffic still negatively affects the city's air quality.[88]

Statewide, California faces another challenge. Due to both the state's job growth and its housing shortages, commute times are increasing. Between 2014 and 2015, they grew by 4.6 percent, while during that same period, trips by public transportation declined by 4.8 percent.[89] The increased amount of time many Californians are spending driving to and from work has in turn increased motor vehicle pollution. In short, notwithstanding its regulatory accomplishments, California's effort to improve air quality by controlling automotive emissions remains a continuous challenge.

The Importance of Curbing Automotive Emissions

Clearly, Californians' continued dependence on cars has been a central driver of the state's leadership in vehicle emissions requirements since the 1960s. The steady increase in vehicle usage has required a continual reduction in pollution from motor vehicles, lest air quality decline in the parts of the state where much of its population resides and most of its cars are driven. California remains the nation's largest automobile market, accounting for 12 percent of national sales. Motor vehicle exhaust remains the most important source of health-related air pollutants throughout the state. When asked why California has historically led the nation in automotive air pollution controls, a senior state pollution control official replied: "L.A."[90] He then added: "Californians have a high reliance on motor vehicles."[91]

According to Mary Nichols, who chaired the California Air Resources Board between 1978 and 1983 and chairs it again today, "The political will to require cleaner cars in California goes back to the discovery of smog, no question about that. But that will is backed up by the fact people are well aware that we really are breathing a lot of pollution that's created by our desire and need for mobility." Furthermore, she added, Californians are willing to pay for "the satisfaction of knowing that [they] are helping to move the automobile industry in the direction of producing clean cars."[92] Whether or not Californians are as satisfied as she suggests—after all, CARB rules are the primary reason why they pay an average of fifty additional cents per gallon of gasoline—the state has continued its ongoing efforts to reduce pollution from mobile sources.

As described in this chapter, both local business interests and citizen groups have played important roles in the drive to improve air quality in Los Angeles. But it is also critical to recognize the role played by the CARB. Over nearly five decades, the board has developed considerable technical expertise in automotive emissions, including knowledge of what technology is capable of accomplishing.[93] It has also helped promote and develop a close working relationship with the business clusters in the state that specialize in the development of new emissions control technologies. Thanks in part to the state's regulatory leadership, seventy-five advanced automotive technical centers are located in Southern California.

It is clear that without its development of technical expertise, aided by a well-trained and well-funded staff of engineers, lawyers, and policy experts, California would not have been able to take advantage of the regulatory authority granted to it by the federal government. Moreover, without its highly visible accomplishments in improving a dimension of environmental quality on which Californians have historically placed a high value, it would have lacked the political backing to continue to innovate in this area. Indeed, without the substantial scientific and administrative expertise in pollution control that both Southern California and the state had previously developed, California would have been less likely to have had its waiver granted in the first place. In short, the state's development of administrative and technical expertise has played a critical role in its pollution control efforts.

At the same time, it is important to recognize that the political route California chose to curb emissions from motor vehicles accepted rather than challenged or even questioned the primacy of motor vehicle transportation. The real burdens of developing and installing the technologies required to reduce these emissions were placed on the automobile manufacturers, which were headquartered far from California, manufactured few cars in the state, and thus had little political presence or economic influence in it. Likewise, this pollution abatement strategy financially benefited those local business interests that relied on residents and tourists who wanted cleaner air. Thus, California's long-standing focus on regulating mobile-source emissions reflected the balance of business power within the state as much as it did the unusual and distinctive pollution abatement problems of Southern California.

Finally, this chapter has revealed the limits of what Los Angelinos have been willing to do to improve their air quality: in short, they were willing to support pollution controls provided they did not interfere with their reliance on automobiles. Unlike the hydraulic gold miners, these residents were fortunate that the government was willing and able to develop technology-forcing regulations that made it possible for them to continue their automotive-based suburban lifestyle, while at the same time breathe cleaner air. In the absence of such regulations, Los Angeles would be virtually uninhabitable.

The "California Effect"

The regulation of automotive emissions in the United States demonstrates the critical importance of federalism in shaping American environmental policies. The control of automotive emissions in the United States originated in the state of California. Thanks to the 1967 Air Quality Act and the more than 115 waivers granted to the state by the federal government, California continues to lead the nation in the stringency of its mobile-source regulatory standards. But California's impact has extended far beyond the state.

First, as noted earlier, the federal government has frequently adopted the state's regulations after a time interval. By allowing the state to establish its own automotive emissions standards, California has essentially functioned as a "superregulator," adopting innovative regulations that can then be "exported" to the rest of the United States. Pollution control officials in California are both aware and proud of the state's critical role as a testing ground.[94] In addition, the fact that California is the only state that can enact more stringent vehicle emissions standards than the federal government may well have given the state an important incentive to do so. After all, if California does not act, no other state can.

Second, in 1977, the federal government, recognizing the value of allowing auto emissions standards to vary to reflect local conditions, permitted other states the option of adopting either California or federal emissions standards—a policy option that Congress subsequently clarified. Under the terms of the 1990 Clean Air Act amendments, states that are in violation of federal standards can choose between the adoption of California's automotive emissions standards or the federal government's. No state, however, can select any other standard. This two-standard strategy represented a compromise between protecting economies of scale in automotive production and enabling states to accelerate their improvements in air quality by drawing on California's regulatory expertise.

Several states have taken advantage of this policy option. Currently, thirteen states plus the District of Columbia, which account for approximately one-third of the national automotive market and have a combined population of 113 million people, have adopted California's low-emission vehicle standards. These standards have been continually strengthened since they were first introduced in 1991. California and twelve other states that collectively accounted for 40 percent of the market for new trucks have adopted emissions limits for trucks and industry that are more stringent than federal standards. In short, as Wendy Leavitt has written, "what happens in California never stays in California for very long, and that is especially true when it comes to vehicle emissions regulations."[95] In no other area of environmental policy has California had such a direct and substantial impact on environmental policy outside the state's borders.[96]

7

Energy Efficiency
and Climate Change

For four decades, California has been at the forefront of national efforts to improve energy efficiency and reduce greenhouse gas emissions. These initiatives began with policies to reduce energy use in order to avoid the construction of additional power plants and went on to include progressively more stringent energy efficiency standards and renewable energy mandates, additional curbs on automotive emissions, and a cap-and-trade program designed to reduce statewide GHG emissions. The emergence and expansion of these efforts demonstrates the importance of the factors that have shaped environmental policy innovations in other areas—namely, perceived threats to the state's attractive and vulnerable environment, strong civic support for environmental protection, a divided business community that has made possible alliances between environmental activists and business firms, and the growth of the state's administrative capacity.

At the same time, these policies are also distinct from those described in the previous five chapters. First, they developed more incrementally, with some backsliding, much conflict, and frequent compromises. Second, some of their policy triggers—most notably, the 1973 energy crisis and California's 2000–2001 energy deregulation fiasco—were unrelated to environmental risks or threats. Third, their scope, diversity, and economic impact have been more substantial than those of the state's regulations protecting land use, coastal areas, and automotive emissions. The significance of these policies in turn has shaped business responses to them, creating more complex and shifting alliances and conflicts among firms and industries than have characterized developments in other environmental policy areas.

Finally, and perhaps most importantly, in marked contrast to the state's other environmental policy threats, California cannot protect itself from the risks of global climate change. This means that the state has a critical stake in promoting a "California effect" that will encourage other political jurisdictions both in and outside the United States to also restrict their emissions of greenhouse gases.

Energy Efficiency

PROJECTED ENERGY NEEDS

The origins of California's efforts to promote energy efficiency date from the early 1970s. In 1972, the RAND Corporation issued the results of a three-year study of the state's energy needs that predicted that the state's energy consumption would increase fourfold by 1991.[1] The report went on to project that unless the state was able to reduce its energy consumption growth rate, which was currently between 7.5 and 8 percent annually and thus was set to double every ten years, it would need to construct the equivalent of 130 new power plants by 2002. Policymakers in Sacramento were also warned that unless the approval of new power plants was expedited, the state would likely face power outages. While California's utility firms were eager to build new facilities, they were also concerned that constructing so many additional plants would produce friction with community groups and environmental activists. Such projects faced significant siting challenges after the passage of the 1970 California Environmental Quality Act, which required extensive reviews of the environmental impacts of both public and private development projects and often led to considerable delays in project approvals.

At hearings held by the California Assembly's Committee on Planning and Land Use, the legislators also learned several disturbing facts. First, the state had no long-term energy policy. Second, the state's utilities were actively working to promote electricity use through such strategies as subsidizing builders and contractors who agreed to install energy-intensive appliances. Third, the utility industry's plans for meeting increased consumer demand included the construction of additional nuclear power plants—a measure opposed by the state's increasingly powerful environmental organizations, which viewed nuclear power as both too expensive and too dangerous.

These groups also challenged the accuracy of the utility industry's demand forecasts and criticized the state for making no effort to promote conservation, which they argued would reduce the need for new power plant construction in the first place. Environmentalists also claimed that the California Public Utility Commission (CPUC) had focused too narrowly on rate regulation and ignored the larger policy issues surrounding energy supply and demand. They urged the legislature to establish a new regulatory body that would have both the analytical expertise to critically evaluate the utilities' requests for new power plant construction and the authority to mandate energy conservation initiatives.

THE CALIFORNIA ENERGY COMMISSION

In 1973, both houses of the Democrat-controlled state legislature narrowly approved a law establishing the California Energy Resources Conservation and Development Commission. This legislation not only consolidated the approval process for new power plants but also granted the new commission broad powers over the state's energy supply and demand, including the responsibility for both forecasting supply and demand and reducing the latter through conservation and energy efficiency standards. The bill was opposed by the state's utility firms, which wanted an agency that would be responsible only for expediting siting decisions, and the building industry. The nation's appliance firms had also lobbied against the legislation, as they did not want to give the state authority over the design of their products. This broad business opposition led Republican governor Ronald Reagan to veto the legislation.

Four days after the governor's veto, however, war broke out in the Middle East, precipitating the Organization of the Petroleum Exporting Countries oil embargo, gasoline shortages throughout the country, and a major national energy crisis. These events drew nationwide attention to energy use, but in rapidly growing California, already sensitized to environmental threats issues, the problem caused particular concern.[2] In May 1974, during the atmosphere of crisis, Governor Reagan reluctantly signed a similar version of the legislation he had previously vetoed—notwithstanding the continued opposition of appliance and construction firms and the state's utilities.

This landmark legislation, called the Warren-Alquist Act of 1974, established a new state regulatory body, the California Energy Commission (CEC). Its scope was extremely broad. In addition to being granted the authority to approve or deny site applications for large power plants, it was made responsible for addressing the state's long-term energy needs. The CEC was also specifically charged with establishing energy-efficient building and appliance standards, with appliances that did not meet the state's standards after July 1, 1977, no longer permitted to be sold in California. Finally, the CEC would fund research, development, and demonstration projects for technologies that used renewable, alternative, and cleaner energy, all of which would be financed by a $16 annual surcharge on electricity users. The commission's establishment signaled an important broadening and strengthening of the state's administrative capacity as well as its national leadership in the area of energy efficiency.

Assemblyman Charles Warren (D-Los Angeles), one of the law's biggest supporters, described the legislation as "the most comprehensive energy conservation program in the United States."[3] He expressed the hope that it would serve as a model for other states. The *Sacramento Union* characterized the ten-page bill as "the weightiest document in the state's history in the energy field, a product of years of technical and legislative efforts to bring order to the energy jungle."[4] The *Sacramento Bee* editorialized, "California is one of the greatest consumers of energy to fuel its high-geared economy and therefore it is incumbent upon this state to provide more leadership in . . . providing proper future supplies without ruining the environment or the citizen's way of life."[5]

A NEW BUSINESS MODEL FOR UTILITIES

After Democrat Jerry Brown replaced Reagan as governor in January 1975, California initiated a new approach to electric utility resource planning that fundamentally changed how its utilities forecasted energy demand. Rather than assuming that economic growth required increased energy consumption and thus the construction of new power plants, the CEC developed an end-use forecasting model. This approach would allow policymakers to explore how increasing the efficiency of utility consumers could act as an alternative to expanding supplies of energy. Conservation and energy efficiency would become, in effect, new sources of supply, thus reducing the need to construct new power plants.

Under this new regulatory approach, the CEC would periodically project the demand for energy by end users and then either identify existing new sources of supply or require a reduction in energy use. After forecasting the net need for new energy resources (calculated by subtracting existing supply from the forecasted demand), the agency would adopt its own efficiency requirements and/or request support for conservation programs from the CPUC, which had control over utility rates.

Significantly, a utility would only be given permission to build a new facility if it could demonstrate that there was a need for additional energy supplies that could not be met by reducing demand. The CPUC, in turn, would cooperate with the CEC by applying a least-cost planning strategy that required that the costs of energy reduction be compared to the costs of adding new supply. Ratepayer funds were allocated to promote energy efficiency activities, and the state's investor-owned utilities were authorized to administer a wide range of energy efficiency programs.

It was fortuitous timing for the state to make a commitment to meet its current and future energy needs through improvements in energy efficiency. As energy prices soared, consumers could recognize the benefits of energy-efficient practices.[6] Energy efficiency was also growing as a topic of academic study in the United States as scholars and policymakers increasingly recognized that energy use could be reduced without reducing economic growth; after all, Europeans were using half as much energy per capita as Americans. *What consumers wanted, policymakers increasingly understood, was not to consume energy, but to have access to the goods and services that energy consumption made possible.*

In 1982, the CPUC formally adopted a new regulatory strategy for the state's utilities. Labeled "decoupling," it removed their financial disincentive to promote energy efficiency and conservation. Under the new system, a utility that saved energy by subsidizing energy-efficient appliances or light bulbs for its customers would receive revenue for its lost electricity sales. This new regulatory approach, which in effect made "negawatts" as valuable as "megawatts," had long been advocated by the Environmental Defense Fund, whose research had also informed it.[7] But the plan had been strongly opposed by the state's utilities, whose business model had been based on increasing energy consumption. The utilities were pressured into adopting this strategy only after being fined by the CPUC.

However, over time, the state's utilities began to accept and recognize decoupling's advantages, persuaded by California's initial improvements in promoting energy efficiency and continued high oil prices.[8] In an important policy shift, decoupling thus made utilities into advocates of energy efficiency. In 2007, under a regulatory approach labeled "decoupling plus," the CPUC increased the utilities' incentives to help their customers use less energy in order to further reduce the need to build new power generation facilities. Utilities were also given performance incentives if they met or exceeded their energy efficiency targets.

California was the first state to adjust its utility rate regulations to financially incentivize energy efficiency and conservation. Federal legislation adopted in 2009 conditioned a state's receipt of federal funds to promote energy efficiency on the creation of regulatory policies that aligned utility incentives with efficiency goals. Currently, nearly half the states in the country have adopted some form of utility revenue decoupling. This trend again demonstrates California's national leadership and its important role as a "laboratory" for policy innovation.

ENERGY EFFICIENCY RESEARCH

Just as scientific studies on the impact of motor vehicles on air pollution helped change state emissions regulations, academic research in California played a critical role in shaping public policy on energy efficiency. The state became a major site for research on energy efficiency. In 1973, the Lawrence Berkeley National Laboratory (LBNL) established its Energy and Environment Division, and John Holdren inaugurated a doctoral program in energy resources at the University of California, Berkeley. The establishment of the CEC created a market for the academic research being produced at Berkeley, and this research in turn helped make the CEC more effective. Art Rosenfeld, a physics professor at Berkeley working at the LBNL, recalled: "The fortunate convergence of our policy requirements and scientific knowledge was a key factor behind California's leadership in energy efficiency. In the years before the Commission's in-house research capability was developed, it relied upon local scientists for data forecasting, testing protocols, and analytical tools."[9]

One of the CEC's first initiatives was to draft energy efficiency performance standards for buildings. Rosenfeld and his colleagues substantially revised this draft using data from a software program they had designed that better measured heat flows in buildings. The 1977 issuance of the nation's first energy efficiency building standards marked the beginning of "a symbiotic relationship between CEC and the research community" that proved enduring. By funding academic research, the CEC helped build what W. Michael Hanemann has described as "a rigorous foundation for energy efficiency regulations that CEC subsequently promulgates."[10] A critical component of the state's ongoing and long-term efforts to reduce its energy use, California's energy efficiency standards for buildings have been continually updated and have had a national impact: today, five other states have equally strict building codes.[11] Legislation adopted in 2015 set a new goal of doubling the energy efficiency savings from existing and new buildings by 2030.

APPLIANCE STANDARDS

While building codes had long been recognized as a responsibility of state governments, appliance standards had been traditionally viewed as a federal responsibility because of their links with interstate commerce. Within California, the appliance industry was more concentrated and better politically organized than the more fragmented construction sector, which had been unable to resist new building code standards. But in the late 1970s, political pressures in California were also building to regulate the energy efficiency of appliances.

Ultimately, the battle over appliance standards came to be linked with the battle over nuclear power plants. After a 1976 ballot proposition that would have banned the construction of new nuclear power plants was defeated by voters, the legislature placed a moratorium on further nuclear development until a permanent solution to the disposal of nuclear waste was put in place. But the moratorium on new nuclear power plant construction meant that the state would be forced to construct more fossil fuel power plants, which would in turn increase harmful air pollutants.

Despite the legislative moratorium, the San Diego Gas and Electric Company had moved forward with plans for the Sundesert nuclear power plant, and legislation was proposed that would exempt the facility from the 1976 ban. After being informed that California refrigerators were using the equivalent of five Sundeserts and that even minimal efficiency standards would eliminate the need for the equivalent of 1.5 Sundeserts at no additional cost to consumers, Governor Brown threw his political support behind energy efficiency.[12] His stance helped persuade the legislature to overcome the opposition of the appliance industry and to authorize the state to adopt efficiency standards for appliances. Later that year, California issued the nation's first appliance efficiency regulations, which applied to refrigerators and freezers.[13]

Refrigerators, whose energy efficiency steadily improved even as their size tripled, became the poster product for the positive effects energy efficiency standards could have. As Rosenfeld explained, "The coincidence of California's first performance standards with the market entry of better-performing models began a positive reinforcing cycle. . . . Targeted, government-assisted R&D helps make possible the introduction of increasingly efficient new models, which themselves become the basis for tightening the efficiency standards, because they demonstrate that meeting a tighter standard is technologically feasible."[14]

The state's standards were subsequently tightened in 1980 and 1987, followed by comparable federal standards issued in 1990, 1993, and 2001—another important example of California's policy leadership. In each instance, the appliance industry was able and willing to comply with these regulations, demonstrating a "government-industry partnership that has served society very well."[15] The CEC also established efficiency standards for room and central air conditioners. The list of California-regulated products subsequently expanded to include space and water heaters, plumbing fittings, fluorescent ballasts, and large air conditioners, showerheads, and faucets.[16]

During the 1960s, the prospect of multiple states adopting their own automotive emissions standards had prompted the car industry to support uniform federal standards. A similar pattern now occurred. After six other states adopted California's appliance standards, the appliance manufacturers asked Congress to establish national standards. The resulting National Appliance Energy Conservation Act of 1987 represented a compromise between the states on one hand and the federal government and the appliance trade associations on the other. This legislation stipulated that any standard issued by the federal government would preempt any state standard, but that the states would remain free to adopt efficiency standards for products *not* covered by federal standards.

In 1988, 1992, and 2005, federal legislation established efficiency standards for several products previously regulated at the state level, including light bulbs, electric motors, and commercial heating and cooling equipment. Most of these standards replicated those set earlier by California—though the time lag between their passages was often considerable. For example, the 1988 federal standard for fluorescent lamp ballasts was based on one set by California in 1978. Today, California's standards remain the most stringent and comprehensive in the nation. The CEC set new energy efficiency standards for seventeen products in 2004 and added an additional twenty-two in 2009. The latter included the world's most rigorous efficiency standards for televisions, which reduced the electricity usage of new flat-panel products by half.

In 2016, following four years of negotiations with business firms and environmental groups, California issued the nation's first energy efficiency requirements for desktop computers and monitors.[17] These regulations were projected to reduce the state's carbon dioxide emissions by 730,000 tons and save consumers $170 million in electricity bills annually. California's desktop standards today are 30 percent more stringent than the voluntary standards manufacturers must meet in order to qualify for the EPA's Energy Star label. Because the state is home to one in eight Americans, it is likely that California's new computer efficiency standards will not only become de facto national standards but also be adopted internationally by global brands—another example of the "California effect." It has been estimated that if these standards were adopted throughout the United States, American carbon emissions would decline by 14 million tons and consumers would save about $3 billion in electricity bills annually. For its part, the technology industry described the state regulation as "ambitious, but achievable."

California's energy efficiency standards now cover more than fifty products, more than any other state, and the number of products regulated by the state continues to steadily increase. Through 2014, twelve states in addition to Washington, DC, adopted appliance efficiency standards for sixteen types of appliances not covered by federal standards. While each state is free to enact its own standards for appliances not (yet) regulated by the federal government, most states have simply adopted those crafted by California, leading to the coexistence of two de jure appliance efficiency standards, one set in Washington and the other in Sacramento.[18] In fact, however, rather than design and produce two different sets of products, most appliance manufacturers have adopted California's standards nationwide—another important example of the "California effect."

POLICY IMPACT

Between 1974 and 2014, residential energy consumption per capita remained nearly constant in California while increasing nearly 75 percent in the rest of the United States.[19] California today is the second most energy efficient state in the United States after Massachusetts. The steady strengthening of its performance standards for buildings and appliances, as well as the initiation of utility company programs that have promoted the adoption of more energy-efficient technologies, including commercial lighting retrofit incentives and residential appliance rebates, have all played a role in this achievement.

However, other nonregulatory factors have also made an important contribution to stabilizing the state's energy demands.[20] These include the state's relatively high residential electricity prices (which since 1970 have increasingly risen above those in the United States as a whole), a shift in its housing mix toward more multifamily and attached housing, a shift in the state's manufacturing economy away from highly energy-intensive sectors, and its relatively benign climate. According to a study by Mark Levinson, "nearly 90 percent of the gap between residential electricity consumption in California and other states in 2009 can be explained by differences unrelated to California's regulations."[21]

Nonetheless, between 1975 and 2015, the state's energy-saving program, building codes, and appliance standards reduced the energy bills of Californians by nearly $90 billion, significantly ameliorating the impact of the state's high utility rates. The state's energy efficiency regulations and programs also resulted in the construction of thirty fewer large power plants, which in turn improved air quality and protected several scenic areas.[22]

According to Levinson, were the rest of the United States as energy efficient as California, "total national energy consumption by 2009 would have been reduced by an amount sufficient to achieve the Obama's Administration's goal of reducing U.S. greenhouse emissions to 17 percent below 2005 levels by 2020."[23] Within California, the state's wide-ranging and long-standing leadership in promoting energy efficiency, as well as its policy accomplishments, helped lay the foundations for its subsequent policy initiatives to reduce greenhouse gas emissions, since energy use is an important contributor to carbon emissions.

Preliminary Efforts to Promote Alternative Energy

Beginning in the 1970s, California, often with the assistance of the federal government, began to promote alternative energy. In 1976, it provided a tax credit for solar energy equipment, and in 1978, it added a more generous tax credit for investment in small wind and solar systems. The state also allowed projects utilizing alternative energy sources to issue bonds that would be exempt from state taxes. The primary purpose of these policies was to reduce the state's dependence on oil, which in the mid-1970s had supplied nearly half of the electricity used in California and had made the state highly vulnerable to the 1973 global spike in oil prices.

During the 1980s, California had the largest geothermal industry in the world. By the end of the decade, taking advantage of its large agricultural and forestry sectors, the state also hosted the world's largest biomass industry. By 1985, California had built more than 12,000 wind turbines, giving it

87 percent of the world's wind power capacity. In 1991, the state government built renewable energy mandates into its public utilities code that required that a (unspecified) portion of the state's total energy portfolio be derived from renewable sources. Five years later, as part of its restructuring of the state's energy industry, the state created the Renewable Energy Fund, which provided $540 million in subsidies and incentives for renewable producers, purchasers, and providers.

However, several factors subsequently converged to halt and reverse these developments. They included the expiration of federal tax incentives, a sharp decline in global oil prices, and the 1982 election of Republican governor George Deukmejian, who was opposed to tax credits for renewable energy. During the 1980s, no renewable energy plants were built. By 1998, 73 percent of the state's utility contracts for wind energy had expired, as had 78 percent of solar contracts. Many biomass plants closed, and hundreds of wind turbines were dismantled. California-based Kenetech, once the largest wind energy company in the world, went bankrupt, while another large wind energy firm, the Zond Corporation, found itself in financial difficulty and was sold to Enron. Thus, in marked contrast to the other state environmental initiatives described in this book, these initial efforts were not durable.

However, in 1995, California did enact one sustainable renewable energy policy. This was net metering, which allowed consumers to receive credit for electricity produced onsite. The purpose of this innovative policy, which required utilities to buy back the surplus power generated by their consumers, was to encourage small-scale solar and wind energy projects. The first net metering law had been enacted by Minnesota in 1983, followed by six other states. In California, the practice was backed by the California Solar Energy Industry Association, which was attracted by the proposal's business opportunities, since all existing residential solar installations had so far only been used to heat water.

The legislation introduced in Sacramento was extremely modest. The electricity produced under the net metering program was limited to 0.1 percent of the utilities' peak demand, and no installation could be larger than ten kilowatts. Nevertheless, this proposal was vigorously opposed by the state's private utility companies: Pacific Gas & Electric, for example, characterized net metering as a "bold scam by the solar power industry to force our electric customers to subsidize the sale of expensive residential photovoltaic systems."[24]

Nonetheless, the legislature was persuaded to approve the measure because of its modest size and the fact that it would not cost the state any money. An important feature of this legislation required the utilities to connect to any system that met specific technical standards, thus removing a major barrier to residential installations. However, because residential solar installations remained expensive and state tax incentives for installing them modest, through 2002 there were only 2,200 net metering customers in the state. But the California legislation did help spark a major wave of net metering policies: by 1999, fifteen more states had adopted them, and by the end of 2016, forty-one states were providing renewable credits and reduced rates via net metering and other compensation programs—another example of the state's national impact on the spread of "green" technologies.

Tackling Climate Change

THE ISSUE EMERGES

As in the case of energy efficiency, the research conducted and disseminated by citizen organizations played an important role in shaping public attention to and public policy regarding climate change. In 1999, the Union of Concerned Scientists and the Ecological Society of America initiated and coordinated a study by several prominent California scientists on the potential impacts of climate change on the state's ecosystems. Their report highlighted several threats to the state's economy and residents, including a rise in summer temperatures, an increased risk of forest fires, and a reduction in the size and density of the Sierra snowpack runoff that supplied a third of the state's water. Known as the "Green Book," this report was distributed widely to state agencies and played an important role in educating California policymakers about the local consequences of climate change.[25]

In 2000, the state legislature created an independent organization, the California Climate Action Registry. Its purpose was to allow organizations to voluntarily register their greenhouse gas emissions and then track their reductions. By establishing GHG emissions baselines, companies and other organizations would be able to receive credit for meeting future GHG emissions reduction requirements. The registry program also standardized GHG reporting tools as well as the protocols for certifying them and sought to encourage voluntary efforts to increase energy efficiency and reduce GHG emissions. Again, California played an important leadership role in this effort: by 2007, thirty-nine states and two Canadian provinces had established uniform protocols to measure, report, and verify GHG emissions from their industrial sectors.[26]

RENEWABLE PORTFOLIO STANDARD

What spurred the revival of interest in renewable energy in California in the early 2000s was an unusual and extraordinary event that had nothing to do with climate change. During 2000–2001, the state experienced a major electricity crisis, accompanied by rolling blackouts, electricity emergencies, and, most importantly, a nearly fourfold increase in the wholesale cost of electricity. This crisis had a number of important political impacts.[27] Besides highlighting the need to diversify energy supplies, it underlined the important role that energy conservation could play in addressing supply shortages and lowering prices and, by shaking public confidence in market solutions to energy problems, led to stronger public support for a more active role by the government in regulating energy supplies.

In 2002, California adopted its first renewable portfolio standard (RPS). While several states had preceded California in adopting an RPS, California's was the most stringent. It required that investor-owned utilities and other retail sellers increase their use of renewable energy sources from the current rate of 12 percent to 20 percent by 2017. This put the state, Kevin Golden has noted, "back on track to lead the country in creating a stable, competitive sustainable energy market."[28] By 2003, sixteen states had adopted renewable portfolio standards for electricity generation.[29]

In supporting this legislation, environmental organizations had persuasively argued that not only would the standard improve air quality but it would also help buffer the state from natural gas price spikes, which had been a major cause of the 2000–2001 state energy crisis. Significantly, climate change was *not* a driving force behind the law's enactment. Indeed, the law's text did not even mention the issue. Rather, the establishment of the RPS was primarily driven by the state's urgent need to diversify its energy sources and decrease its reliance on fossil fuels, thus reducing its vulnerability to future price hikes. Supported by 85 percent of the state's population, it was approved by large margins in both the state Assembly and Senate.[30]

Regulating Automobile Emissions

President George W. Bush's 2001 rejection of the Kyoto Protocol, an international commitment to reduce greenhouse gas emissions, helped set the stage for California's first substantive restrictions on GHG emissions. Assembly Bill 1493, popularly known as the Pavley bill after its author, the Southern

Californian Democratic legislator Fran Pavley, directed the California Air Resources Board to limit GHG emissions from automobiles. Pavley argued that California should lead the nation in this effort because it was "going to be more impacted by global warming than other states," echoing the conclusions of the 1999 Union of Concerned Scientists report.[31] Moreover, she pointed out, a higher share of California's energy was consumed by transportation than the national average: 38 percent versus 28 percent.

In support of the initiative, the Natural Resources Defense Council argued that "California is uniquely positioned to provide leadership and a standard for the rest of the country."[32] Under the terms of the federal Clean Air Act, California was the only state that could establish its own tailpipe emissions standards. Other states could then adopt California's requirements, but only after California had done so. In light of federal inaction, this effectively meant that if California did not regulate GHG emissions from cars and light trucks, they would not be regulated. More broadly, the marked slowdown in the expansion of federal environmental regulation that had begun in the 1990s and continued under the administration of George W. Bush (2000–2008) meant that any new environmental policy initiatives would have to come from states such as California.

SUPPORT AND OPPOSITION FOR THE PAVLEY BILL

The Pavley bill was backed by a broad coalition of environmental and public health organizations, as well as the governments of Los Angeles and San Jose. As has often been the case in California, the interests of business were divided on the issue. Several business associations, including the California Chamber of Commerce, the California New Car Dealers Association, and the Western States Petroleum Association, opposed the bill. However, it was supported by the business–environmental alliance known as the Clean Power Campaign, as well as Environmental Entrepreneurs, a group of Silicon Valley firms that had partnered with the National Resource Defense Council. The backing of the latter groups was critical in alleviating the fears of some legislators about the law's potential negative economic impacts. Nonetheless, the legislation was extremely controversial: auto dealers ran print ads and radio spots that claimed that it would lead to higher gas taxes, lower speed limits, and fees on gas guzzlers. Two radio disc jockeys from Los Angeles led a caravan of SUV drivers to Sacramento to loudly express their opposition for the measure.[33]

Two of the bill's key nonbusiness supporters were the Sierra Club and the League of Conservation Voters. These groups were quite successful in framing the issue as a conflict between the national automobile industry—whose credibility had been undermined by its long-standing opposition to any state regulation that aimed to reduce mobile-source emissions—and the desire of Californians to purchase less-polluting vehicles. This argument echoed that heard in the debate over federal preemption of air quality standards in 1967, which had pitted the interests of Californians against those of the nation's automobile manufacturers.

Besides this rhetorical focus, these groups' extensive lobbying campaign for the Pavley bill also emphasized the impact of automotive GHG emissions on air pollution and public health—issues of long-standing concern to Californians—as well as on climate change. Roger Karapin has pointed out that the droughts and wildfires that occurred in California in the early 2000s further affected the debate on the Pavley bill.[34] Once again, highly visible threats to California's vulnerable geography had played a critical role in increasing public support for environmental regulation.

But while previous statutes regulating automobile emissions had received strong bipartisan support, with many passing unanimously, voting on the Pavley bill divided along partisan lines. Every Republican member of both the Assembly and the Senate opposed the measure, reflecting both the extent of business opposition to the legislation and national partisan divisions over climate change. The vote signaled both the increasing political divisiveness that would characterize California's climate change initiatives and the critical policy impact of Democratic Party control of the legislature.

The Pavley bill was signed into law by Governor Gray Davis on July 22, 2002. Significantly, its text was only eight pages long. Rather than specifying any GHG emissions standards or providing detailed procedures for developing them, the law gave the CARB broad discretion to determine what constituted the "maximum feasible and cost-effective" strategy for issuing such standards. It was the CARB's scientific and technical expertise and its demonstrated achievements in improving the state's air quality—discussed in more detail in the previous chapter—that had made it politically possible for the agency to be given such broad discretion. Pavley herself considered legislators' confidence in the CARB to have been key to its passage.[35]

According to Barry Rabe, while other nations "have struggled with an array of voluntary and incentive programs," California was the first government to mandate reductions of greenhouse gases from automobiles.[36] The first important public policy in the United States to explicitly address the risks of climate change, the California statute was popular with the state's public, received a considerable amount of positive national publicity, and encouraged national environmental groups to pressure the government for federal climate change legislation, although their effort proved unsuccessful.

THE CARB SETS STANDARDS

The CARB issued its first GHG emissions standards in 2004. They required a reduction of 30 percent of fleet average emissions per new vehicle—measured in terms of carbon dioxide equivalent per miles driven—to be phased in between 2009 and 2016. These standards were similar in design to the LEV program established in 1993 (see chapter 6), with the important difference being that California was now also regulating emissions of carbon dioxide, methane, and other greenhouse gases. These standards were expected to add between $1,100 and $1,900 to the cost of a new car, which the CARB estimated would be recouped through reduced fuel consumption.

For the automotive manufacturers, the rules were the equivalent of being hit with a "$33 billion sledgehammer." According to an industry trade association official, they were "probably the most far reaching and expensive regulation the auto industry has ever faced."[37] What concerned the industry was not so much having to meet California's standards as it was the tendency of other states and the federal government to adopt automotive emissions standards set by the CARB.[38] In short, the industry feared another "California effect."

In December 2004, the industry sued to block the CARB standards on the grounds that only the federal government had the authority to regulate automobile fuel economy. It argued that California's regulations to reduce GHG emissions were essentially "an end-run" around Washington's failed effort to increase fuel efficiency standards. An industry spokesman predicted that "California's motorists are going to be extremely angry when they find that they are going to lose access to SUVS, trucks and minivans."[39]

Russell Long, executive director of a San Francisco advocacy group that had helped draft the 2002 legislation, however, responded that "California led the nation with the introduction of the catalytic converter, unleaded gasoline, hybrid vehicles, and now we will lead on global warming." He pointed out that California had "proven time after time that protecting the environment is consistent with protecting the economy" and that other states were likely to adopt the California standards.[40]

Confirming both Long's expectations and the industry's fears, by 2007, seventeen states, representing more than 40 percent of the U.S. population and accounting for nearly 50 percent of new vehicle sales, had adopted

California's greenhouse gas vehicle emissions standards. In his 2003 State of the State address, New York Republican governor George Pataki urged the state to "reduce greenhouse gases by adopting the carbon dioxide emission standards . . . recently proposed by the State of California."[41] However, before California, and thus any state, could implement them, the state needed to receive a waiver from the EPA. California had every reason to expect to receive such a waiver, as they had been granted repeatedly since 1968.[42]

But after delaying its decision for three years, in 2008, for the first time, the EPA rejected California's waiver request. According to Stephen Johnson, the agency's chief administrator, California did not have "compelling and extraordinary reasons" why its fuel economy standards should exceed federal ones, since climate change was an international rather than a regional problem. Johnson had overruled the advice of his staff, who had written a memo stating that "California continues to have compelling and extraordinary conditions . . . [that] are vulnerable to climate change" and that "California exhibits a greater number of key impact concerns than other regions," such as potential water shortages, wildfires, rising sea levels, and more threatened and endangered species than any other state in the continental United States. The EPA's denial was criticized by several governors, while sixteen states and five environmental groups sued the Bush administration to reverse it.

The EPA's inaction and then denial delayed the implementation of the CARB's GHG emissions standards by both California and other states that had wanted to adopt them until the end of the George W. Bush administration. Upon assuming office in January 2009, President Barack Obama asked EPA Administrator Lisa Jackson to reconsider California's waiver request, which the agency then granted on June 30, 2009. But at this point the automotive industry, worried about a potential patchwork of state rules and responding to pressure from the White House, agreed to back stronger national fuel efficiency standards that were similar to those of California, while California in turn modified its standards to match those of the federal government. Once again, California's "bottom-up" tactics had had a national impact.[43] According to William Reilly, "We would not be where we are today if California had not kept up the pressure for cleaner cars."[44]

The State's Role Expands

By 2002, California had adopted a range of policies that reduced GHG emissions, though many were not identified or intended as such. These included energy efficiency standards for new appliances and buildings, GHG emissions standards for automobiles (the implementation of which had been delayed), a renewable energy mandate, and changes in utility regulations to promote energy efficiency. But what was still lacking was the political leadership necessary for the enactment of more ambitious policy goals to reduce statewide GHG emissions. Such leadership became possible in 2003, when an unprecedented gubernatorial recall election removed Democratic governor Gray Davis. While Davis had signed both the expanded renewable energy and fuel economy statutes, he had done so reluctantly and was disinclined to play a leadership role in this policy area.

The front-runner among those seeking to replace Davis was Arnold Schwarzenegger, a liberal Republican. In campaigning for the governorship, Schwarzenegger not only expressed strong support for the Pavley bill but, on the advice of his brother-in-law, Robert Kennedy, Jr., emphasized his commitment to environmental protection. Schwarzenegger won the replacement election by a substantial plurality and became governor in 2003.

In 2004, an influential report initiated by the Union of Concerned Scientists provided a specific quantitative estimate of how California might be adversely affected by climate change. This report, entitled *Choosing Our Future*, predicted that California would experience a significant rise in summer temperatures, which would both increase the risk of forest fires and reduce the size of the snowpack in the Sierras. This in turn would significantly deplete the state's water supply. *Choosing Our Future* received considerable media and scientific attention, and its findings were presented to both state agencies and the governor's office.[45] The report's impact was heightened by the timing of its release, in the wake of several years of drought and wildfires.

With public attention focused on the impact of global warming on the Sierra snowpack and thus the state's freshwater supply, Governor Schwarzenegger decided to take an aggressive position on climate change. In a June 2005 speech at the United Nations World Environment Day conference in San Francisco, the governor stated: "I say the debate is over. We know the science. We see the threat. And we know the time for action is now."[46] Furthermore, he added, "California will not wait for our federal government to take strong action on global warming."[47] The governor subsequently signed an executive order requiring the state to reduce its current GHG emissions to their 2000 levels by 2010 and to reduce them 80 percent below their 1990 levels by 2050.[48] This was a popular position: Californians were now more likely than other Americans to believe that "climate change had already begun," and for the first time a majority considered global warming a "very serious threat to the state's future economy and quality of life."[49]

Two-thirds of residents wanted the state to address this issue independent of the federal government.[50]

What made the achievement of these goals more feasible was that between 1990 and 2005, California's overall GHG emissions had increased by only 7 percent, which was about 40 percent below the national average—a rate matched only by states with much lower populations and rates of economic growth.[51] In 1999, the state's per capita GHG emissions were already only half the national average, "making California look more like Germany than the United States," according to Ann Carlson.[52] At the same time, the state faced important future challenges as it grew rapidly. California had added 400,000 people each year since 1980, and its population was expected to increase by more than 40 percent, or 4 million people, by 2020. In addition, California continued to lead the country in miles driven, and its GHG emissions from the transportation sector were steadily growing.[53]

The Debate over AB 32

Following the issuance of the governor's executive order in June 2005, the locus of policymaking now shifted to the state legislature. Senator Fran Pavley introduced an amendment to Assembly Bill 32 that would grant the CARB the authority to implement the emissions reductions specified in the governor's executive order. Schwarzenegger preferred that regulatory responsibility be given to California's Environmental Protection Agency, a body that he directly controlled. In a compromise, the legislature agreed to give the governor authority to delay the law's implementation by the CARB if there was "threat of significant economic harm." AB 32 also required that one-third of all energy consumed by the state come from renewable sources by 2020. In addition, because emissions trading was opposed by environmental justice advocates, who were concerned that it would increase air pollution in low-income communities, the law permitted this policy approach but did not require it.

All of California's environmental organizations campaigned for the legislation. So did the building and construction trade unions, which were attracted by the employment opportunities of renewable energy. Forty-nine of California's cities as well as several religious organizations and the state's three major newspapers also endorsed it. Many of the bill's proponents touted the economic benefits the state would realize by taking a leadership role in climate change.[54] In the same vein, the text of the legislation described the threats posed by global warming as impacting "the economic well-being, public health, natural resources and the environment of California" and having "detrimental effects on some of California's largest industries," including agriculture and tourism—echoing the economic rationale for the air pollution controls initiated by the city and county of Los Angeles a half-century earlier.[55] According to a state environmental official, because the state's balmy climate helps maintain its economy, both its tourism and agriculture industries were threatened by global climate change.[56] In short, the legislation and its supporters identified economic and environmental risks from not regulating emissions and promised economic benefits from doing so.

BUSINESS DIVISION

Business preferences, however, were sharply divided on the bill. Because the legislation would create a larger and more stable market for clean technologies, high-technology firms and venture capitalists in Silicon Valley strongly supported it. By 2006, nearly $2 billion in venture capital had been invested in clean technology in California—five times the 2003 level of investment.[57] As one state policymaker predicted, "If you pass the legislation, it sends a signal to people that there is a market where people can invest. The amount of venture capital support pouring into the Bay Area now is incredible. . . . So what started as an environmental issue in 2001 or 2002 has garnered a lot of business support."[58]

Overall, the legislation was backed by more than 200 individual firms and business associations, including sixteen firms from the agriculture and food-processing sector, fifty-eight from clean tech industries, fifteen from the entertainment business, forty-nine from venture capital and other financial services, and twenty from the technology sector. The San Francisco Chamber of Commerce, the California Ski Industry Association, and state-level wind and solar energy associations also supported the measure.[59] In addition, the Environmental Defense Fund, a long-standing advocate of emissions trading, joined with several multinationals in a "Partnership for Climate Action" to back the proposed statute, while the governor personally persuaded Pacific Gas & Electric to support it.

Despite this support, however, most business associations strongly opposed the climate change bill. The opposition was spearheaded by the California Chamber of Commerce, the California Business Roundtable, and state trade associations representing manufacturers, mining, retailers, and automobile wholesalers. They were joined by several business associations from outside the state, including the Alliance of Automobile Manufacturers, the Association of International Automobile Manufacturers, and the Western States Petroleum Association.

AB 32 was approved on a nearly party-line vote; due to the extent of business opposition, as well as partisan divisions on climate change regulations, only one Republican assemblyman voted for it. However, three-quarters of the state's electorate supported the legislation.[60] On September 27, 2006, the governor signed what became known as the Global Warming Solutions Act of 2006.

THE SIGNIFICANCE OF THE GLOBAL WARMING SOLUTIONS ACT

AB 32 most obviously built upon the substantial and continuing progress made by California since the 1970s in stabilizing its per capita energy consumption. But the legislation also drew upon the more than four decades of state efforts to improve air quality. It was California's demonstrated accomplishments in controlling harmful air pollutants that gave both legislators and the public confidence in the state's capacity to also reduce GHG emissions. Once again, the text of this sweeping legislation was remarkably brief. Only twelve pages long, it left the details of implementation to the CARB, giving the board considerable regulatory authority.

With AB 32, California became the first state to adopt a strategy of comprehensive and enforceable GHG emissions reduction.[61] Specifically, the statute mandated a cut in GHG emissions to 1990 levels by 2020. Eleven other states had previously set GHG emissions reductions targets, and nine of them had established more stringent targets for 2020 than California's. But these goals were either not legally binding or narrower in scope than the California law. AB 32 thus was and remains, according to Barry Rabe, "the most ambitious climate change legislation enacted anywhere in North America and among the most aggressive policies in the world."[62] Indeed, it enabled the state to lay claim to world leadership, as many of its emissions reductions goals exceeded those of many member states of the European Union.

The law's passage received both national and international press attention. *Newsweek* placed Schwarzenegger on its cover, declaring, "California's Hummer-loving governor is turning the Golden State into the greenest in the land, a place where environmentalists and hedonism can coexist."[63] Schwarzenegger also become active in what has been termed "GHG diplomacy," signing an agreement with British prime minister Tony Blair to cooperate on clean energy technology and a memo of understanding with the governors of several western states to develop a regional target for reducing greenhouse gases.

Residential Solar Energy

The state also moved to increase residential solar adoption.[64] In 2006, the legislature approved the California Solar Initiative, the goal of which was to help Californians install 1 million solar electric rooftops on homes and businesses by 2018. This legislation was supported by several environmental organizations, a grassroots advocacy organization called Environment California, and a number of solar companies but opposed by the California Manufacturers and Technology Association and the California Chamber of Commerce on the grounds that it would further increase the state's already high electric rates. Thanks in part to a public campaign by the group Vote Solar, which generated 50,000 emails to legislators, the "Million Solar Roofs" bill was passed with broad legislative support and was signed into law, making California's residential solar program the second most ambitious in the world after Germany's. Raising the cap of net metering installations to 5 percent of a utility's electric sales, the law also provided substantial rebates to lower the costs of new solar installations and extended the tax credit for doing so. Large homebuilders were now required to offer solar energy systems as a standard option. This legislation, along with the state's relatively high electricity rates and a generous federal tax subsidy, made solar installations much more commercially feasible in California.

Political Backlash

Compared to every other environmental policy described in this book, California's climate change initiatives were unusual in their scope and goals. Not surprisingly, they also produced the strongest political backlash of any state environmental regulation.[65] This response was exacerbated by the fact that the state was particularly hard hit by the national recession that began in 2008. Through 2010, its unemployment remained stubbornly high at 12.4 percent—just as the regulatory burdens of AB 32 on the state's business firms and consumers were about to take effect.

AB 32's opponents decided to take advantage of this political opportunity. Using a time-honored tool in California politics, they chose to bypass the state legislature and go directly to the voters. They proposed an initiative that would suspend the implementation of AB 32 until the statewide unemployment rate fell to 5.5 percent for at least one year. Since that level of unemployment had only been reached three times since 1976, this requirement would effectively repeal AB 32. After receiving 800,000 signatures from registered voters, almost twice the number required, the initiative qualified for the November 2010 ballot as Proposition 23, the California Jobs Initiative.

Proposition 23 was a historic development. Never before had business mounted such a sweeping challenge to a major state environmental initiative. But likewise, never had an environmental policy had such a broad impact. While the other environmental regulations described in this book had primarily burdened a particular economic sector, AB 32 regulated virtually the entire state economy. Moreover, its anticipated costs were far more substantial.

The "Yes on 23" campaign raised approximately $10 million, nearly all of which came from oil firms—the industry that has been the primary opponent of virtually all of the state's environmental and climate change regulations. Its principal financial contributors were Valero and Tesoro, Texas-based oil companies whose business operations in California depended on low-margin gasoline refining and thus were highly vulnerable to any decline in gasoline consumption. Moreover, both firms had invested in capital-intensive refineries with significant energy inputs. Occidental Petroleum of Los Angeles also contributed $300,000 to the campaign, while the California Manufacturers Association threw its support behind the proposition, emphasizing the burdens of AB 32 on California's already depressed economy.

The "Yes" campaign had every reason to be optimistic. Survey data revealed that the deep recession had reduced public support for environmental regulation, both nationally and in California. Moreover, just two years earlier, the state's voters had turned down two propositions favored by environmental groups that would have promoted renewable energy and alternative vehicles.

THE POLITICS OF PROPOSITION 23

Not surprisingly, the state's major environmental organizations campaigned heavily against Proposition 23. These groups contributed $10 million to the effort, or roughly one-third of the funds spent on the "Yes" campaign. Communities United Against the Dirty Energy Proposition, a coalition of 130 ethnic, environmental, health, religious, and clean energy groups, mobilized 3,000 volunteers. As its name suggests, the group's campaign emphasized the air pollution and health risks of "dirty" energy (namely, oil), as contrasted with the health and environmental benefits of "clean" energy.[66] This was a clever strategy, as it linked the defense of the state's climate change legislation not to the threats posed by global warming, but to the "immediate social costs" of air and water pollution.[67]

Because Proposition 23 had been both initiated and primarily funded by Texas oil companies, its opponents were able to frame the issue in geographically populist terms: in this framing, "outside" business interests representing "dirty" oil firms were trying to dictate California's environmental policies. This rhetoric was strikingly reminiscent of the successful framing of the conflict over the preemption provisions of the Clean Air Act amendments in 1967. In both cases, claims about "states' rights" were effectively enlisted to challenge opposition to California's environmental regulations by firms from outside the state.

BUSINESS REACTIONS TO PROPOSITION 23

Two aspects of business involvement with Proposition 23 are particularly noteworthy. The first was the increasing economic importance and political influence of the state's clean technology sector, which attracted nearly $6.6 billion in investment between 2006 and 2008.[68] Between 2006 and 2010, California also attracted between 40 and 50 percent of the total venture capital investment in renewable energy/clean tech in the United States.[69] Moreover, employment in renewable energy firms grew by 150 percent between 2002 and 2010.[70] Not surprisingly, all the major trade associations from Silicon Valley opposed Proposition 23. The Silicon Valley Leadership Group, the worldwide revenues of which totaled more than $2 trillion, stated: "Our members believe that reducing greenhouse gas emissions and our dependence on fossil fuels presents an opportunity to transform the economy from one based on coal, oil and gas to one that runs on clean renewable energy."[71]

Clean tech venture capitalists also donated substantial amounts to the "No" campaign. John Doerr and Vinod Khosla and their spouses contributed $3 million, while Thomas Steyer gave $5 million. The opposition also received substantial contributions from a number of wealthy individuals, including executives at Google, Intel, and the Gap, continuing the tradition of northern Californian upper-class support for environmental protection that dated back to William Kent's donation of Muir Woods more than century earlier.

The second significant feature of business involvement with Proposition 23 was the change in the positions of many firms on emissions regulation between 2006 and 2010. In 2006, the vast majority of the state's business community had opposed SB 32. But only four years later, many of those same firms and business associations either remained neutral or even supported the "No" campaign in the fight over Proposition 23. Chevron, one of the world's largest oil companies, with both its headquarters and many of its refining facilities in the state, had opposed AB 32 but stayed neutral in the Proposition 23 campaign, presumably because of the investments it had already made to improve the energy efficiency of its California operations.

Similarly, the Western States Petroleum Association, which had opposed AB 32, declined to contribute to the Proposition 23 "Yes" campaign, and the state Chamber of Commerce, which had strongly opposed AB 32, took no position on the issue—in contrast to the National Chamber of Commerce, which endorsed the "Yes" campaign. Pacific Gas & Electric, one of the state's largest utilities, actually contributed to the "No" campaign. The firm had already made considerable investments in renewable energy and other low-carbon energy projects, and since 1982 it had operated under state utility regulations that had rewarded energy conservation. Eric Biber concludes that California's "long history of . . . aggressive efforts to develop energy policy that increases efficiency and reduces dependence on fossil fuels" has over time "created an interest group landscape that is supportive of stricter efforts to reduce carbon emissions and hostile to efforts to repeal energy efficiency and renewable energy mandates."[72]

Strikingly, the "No" campaign outspent the "Yes" campaign by a margin of three to one—and Proposition 23 failed by the substantial margin of 61.6 percent to 38.4 percent. An unusually complex Baptist–bootlegger coalition had triumphed.

Advanced Clean Cars

In 2012, the CARB announced its Advanced Clean Cars Program, an initiative that integrated the control of smog-causing pollutants and GHG emissions into a coordinated package of new requirements for cars from model years 2017 through 2025. With 26 million cars now on the road, California needed to substantially strengthen its mobile-source pollution standards to prevent its air quality from deteriorating. The new standard mandated a 75 percent reduction in smog-forming emissions and a 50 percent reduction in vehicle GHG emissions by 2025, linking air quality and climate change.

To achieve these goals, the state hoped to place more than 1.4 million zero- or low-emission vehicles—electric, plug-in hybrid, or hydrogen fuel cell cars—on the road by 2025. If successful, this would represent a substantial increase from the 10,000 such vehicles in the state in 2012. According to CARB director Mary Nichols, this program represented "a new chapter for clean cars in California and in the nation as a whole. Californians have always loved their cars. We buy a lot of them and drive them. Now we will have cleaner and more efficient vehicles."[73]

California's previous efforts to promote alternative fuel vehicles, most notably the zero-emissions mandate discussed in the previous chapter and an initiative of the Schwarzenegger administration to power cars using hydrogen fuel cells, were noticeably unsuccessful. But now, a commercially viable electric car industry had emerged. In 2010, Tesla Motors had relocated its headquarters to northern California and began vehicle production at a previously closed automobile plant in Fremont, assisted by financial support from the state. By 2016, company employment had increased sixfold, to 6,000. By July 2015, the Fremont plant had produced 21,500 vehicles, and by the middle of 2016, it was producing 2,000 vehicles per week. Tesla is anticipating a steady increase in sales and has plans to expand the capacity of its Fremont plant to produce as many as 500,000 cars per year, which will be sold throughout the world.[74]

Many of the firm's suppliers are also located in northern California, including ten in the San Francisco Bay Area, and several firms have opened facilities in the region in order to be close to Tesla. Other electric vehicle startups have opened design plants in the state, as have the major automotive manufacturers, attracted by the growing size of what has become the nation's largest market for plug-in electric vehicles and the availability of clean technology engineers from Silicon Valley.[75] According to the CEO of electric vehicle producer Proterra, "the Bay Area is absolutely the epicenter of electric vehicle technology."[76] Just as Southern California became a national center for firms involved in developing technologies to reduce automotive emissions, so has northern California become a global hub for electric vehicle design and manufacturing.

To promote a national market for electric cars, in 2012, the CARB issued updated zero-emission vehicle (ZEV) mandates. Nine other states, including New York, New Jersey, Connecticut, and Massachusetts, have since adopted them, which means they will affect the future design of vehicles throughout the United States. ZEV standards require that by 2018, 4.5 percent of each company's total sales in the ten covered states must be zero-emission vehicles, a goal that increases to 22 percent by 2025. "Zero-emission" vehicles can be either fully electric, plug-in hybrids or cars powered by hydrogen fuel cells. The firms can also choose in which states to sell them. Moreover, an automotive manufacture company can comply with the standards by buying "credits" from other manufacturers whose production exceeds the program's standards. This emissions trading scheme has been a boon to Tesla, which has sold hundreds of millions of dollars in credits to other car companies. It has also incentivized mainstream car firms to increase their own production of electric cars. Even if these companies do not make money on each electric vehicle, they can use those sales to keep selling more profitable gas-powered cars in the ten states that have adopted California's ZEV rules.

To date, Californians have bought or leased 200,000 pure electric vehicles, along with 107,000 plug-in hybrids.[77] These figures represent roughly half of all such vehicles sold in the United States and are attributable to both the state's tax subsidies and other incentives and its relatively large charging station infrastructure. While only 1.7 percent of all new cars in California run solely on electricity, virtually all the major global automotive companies have begun to develop and manufacture them—driven by the need to comply with both the requirements of the ten ZEV regulation states and a 2012 federal regulation requiring that average fuel economy increase to 54.5 miles per gallon by 2025. While their long-term future remains uncertain, electric cars are becoming less expensive, their range is increasing, and the infrastructure to sell, charge, and maintain them is improving, particularly in California. Demand for these vehicles has also been driven up by federal and state tax credits. The original buyer of an all-electric vehicle can reap up to $7,500 from the federal tax credit, while CARB offers rebates of $2,500 to buyers of battery-powered electric cars and $5,000 to buyers of fuel-cell vehicles.[78] However, in contrast to California, some states have reduced the financial incentives for the purchase of such vehicles.[79]

Cap-and-Trade

In 2012, acting under the authority granted to it by AB 32, the CARB began to implement a cap-and-trade program. It objective was to progressively reduce GHG emissions by establishing a price for them that would drive long-term improvements in energy efficiency. The GHG emissions covered by the system were initially capped and then required to be reduced by 2 percent in 2013 and 2014 and then by 3 percent a year through 2020.

Firms were issued permits for their carbon allowances. Those that reduced their emissions more rapidly than the cap required could sell or trade their permits, while those that polluted beyond their quota were forced to buy credits from either other firms or the state, with their prices set by auction.

The program initially included in-state electricity generators, electricity importers, and industrial facilities that emitted 25,000 tons of carbon dioxide equivalent per year. These included the state's utilities as well as its oil refineries, cement makers, food processors, manufacturers, and municipal governments and universities. Michael Dicapua, the head of North American analysis at Bloomberg Finance, called the launch of the market "an incredible development." "At the federal level the idea of regulating carbon through a market was given up for dead two years ago," he noted. "But California is prepared to go it alone."[80]

Within the United States, the Regional Greenhouse Gas Initiative preceded California's cap-and-trade initiative but was nevertheless less comprehensive. A mandatory trading program that began with ten northeastern states, the RGGI had been formed in 2005 and went into effect in 2009. However, unlike the California program, the initiative only covers carbon dioxide emissions from the electric power sector, which are responsible for approximately a fifth of GHG emissions in the participating states.[81]

California's rollout of cap-and-trade sparked a backlash from business. An official from the California Manufacturers and Technology Association labeled cap-and-trade "Recession: The Sequel" and predicted that it would "have a horribly negative effect on jobs and manufacturing investment" in California, since no other state had adopted similar requirements.[82] Several businesses, led by the state's petroleum firms, launched an advertising campaign in an unsuccessful effort to persuade Governor Jerry Brown to postpone the initial auction.

However, the state did attempt to reduce the program's initial burdens on business, distributing allowances totaling 90 percent of previous emissions to businesses for free in its first year. To further increase flexibility, the program provided for both offsets and multiyear compliance periods. The first rounds of auctions proceeded smoothly, with the price per ton of carbon emitted increasing from $10.09 at the first auction in November 2012 to $12.73 in November 2015.

The CARB subsequently added to the program distributors of transportation fuel, natural gas, and other fuels, whose emissions accounted for 37.6 percent of the state's GHG emissions. This expansion was strongly opposed by the oil industry, which claimed that it would lead to a substantial increase in energy prices and place the state at a major economic disadvantage. Sixteen Democratic members of the state assembly representing less affluent communities expressed their opposition as well. Nonetheless, transportation fuels were added to the program in 2015, making California one of the few jurisdictions to include such businesses in cap-and-trade programs and raising gasoline prices by an estimated ten to twelve cents a gallon.[83] Cap-and-trade now included facilities that produced 85 percent of the state's greenhouse gas emissions; only those emissions generated by agriculture, forestry, and waste management were excluded.

Through 2015, the auctions from the sales of emissions rights generated $4 billion. A quarter of this sum was allocated to the governor's high-speed rail project, with another 25 percent used to support solar installations, affordable housing, and drought relief in disadvantaged communities. The program's revenues were also rebated to California households in the form of climate credits, and funds have been used to promote clean energy and offer rebates for the purchase of more fuel-efficient vehicles.

CAP-AND-TRADE CHALLENGES

For all the national and international attention that California's cap-and-trade system has received, within the state its implementation has been challenging.[84] In 2012, the California Chamber of Commerce filed a lawsuit arguing that the program's permit fees were actually a tax and therefore, under state law, had required a two-thirds vote of the legislature—a supermajority that AB 32 had failed to receive. Reflecting both the possibility of an adverse judicial ruling and the uncertainty surrounding the program's continuation by the legislature after 2020, in May 2016, sales of auctions dropped dramatically, with only 10.5 percent of available credits sold. Even before that, the program's revenues had been less than anticipated—in 2014, they were $600 million lower than the governor's forecast of $2.4 billion—and it has also been criticized for not delivering sufficient reductions in air pollutants to disadvantaged communities.[85]

In enacting cap-and-trade, California had anticipated that the system would also be adopted by neighboring states, many of which share its power grid, thus strengthening the effectiveness of emissions trading. California did organize six American states and two Canadian provinces into the Western Climate Initiative, which established a regional GHG emissions reduction goal identical to that of AB 32 and unveiled plans to develop a regional market to help implement it. But by 2011, all the participating states and provinces had left the initiative except California. Today, California's only formal partnership for cap-and-trade is with the province of Quebec, which has held joint auctions with the state since fall 2014. Ontario has also announced that it plans to join.

The contraction of the Western Climate Initiative was not the only setback for cap-and-trade in North America.[86] The Midwestern Greenhouse Gas Reduction Accord, signed by six midwestern states and one Canadian province, also completely collapsed. By 2012, more than half the states and three-quarters of the Canadian provinces that had made formal commitments to participate in a regional emissions trading agreement had withdrawn them. In the United States, only California and the nine northeastern states that remain in the Regional Greenhouse Gas Initiative (New Jersey left in 2011) now employ cap-and-trade.

Revisiting Home Solar Power

In 2013, the legislature revisited the state's renewable energy goals and policies. This reexamination led to a prolonged and bitter conflict between electricity utilities and solar companies.[87] The dramatic decline in the price of solar cell panels, combined with creative financing options, net metering, and various federal and state tax incentives, had spawned the growth of a large solar installation industry in the state. Of the 6,100 solar companies in the United States today, 1,700 are doing business in California.[88] California accounts for half of all rooftop solar panel installations in the United States, with more than 300,000 residential and small businesses adopting the technology, which produce 5 percent of the state's energy—more than in any other state. California also represents a quarter of the nation's solar energy jobs, with 500,000 people employed in the state's renewable energy sector.[89]

For the solar companies, net metering has been critical to growth, as installing rooftop solar installations reduces homeowners' utility bills. But the practice also presents a problem for utility firms, since such homeowners are not paying their fair share for maintaining the state's electricity grid. The more customers take advantage of net metering, the greater the financial burdens on the firm's remaining customers to maintain the fixed costs of power generation. According to the president of Southern California Edison, nonsolar customers are subsidizing solar users by as much as $17 billion a year.[90] With net metering set to expire in 2014, the future of the program became a matter of political urgency for both the utility firms and the solar installation industry.

Ultimately, the legislature passed a compromise bill granting the CPUC the authority to impose a fixed monthly charge of up to $10 on all its customers while expanding the number of homeowners and small businesses that could take advantage of net metering. This legislation left much of the future of net metering and the compensation system that underlies it in the hands of the CPUC. Nor is California the only state in which net metering has become controversial. Under pressures from the utility industry, nearly every one of the more than forty states that have adopted net metering have been reviewing their support for rooftop solar programs, with Hawaii, Nevada, Arizona, Maine, and Indiana deciding to phase out the practice.[91]

Reducing Oil Consumption

In 2015, Governor Brown proposed legislation requiring the state's petroleum consumption to be cut 50 percent by 2030. While California appeared to be on target to meet the interim goal of reducing its emissions to 1990 levels by 2020, the governor had concluded that meeting the state's more ambitious 2050 target required that the rate of reduction be significantly accelerated. "In North America, California is now setting the pace, and we're very serious about it," Brown declared. "We're going to take whatever steps are needed to get the job done, because our future depends on it."[92] Noting that "the rest of the world is watching very closely what is happening in California," state Senate Democratic leader Kevin de León called it "absolutely critical that this measure passes, because it will be a big blow to the rest of the states and the whole country if it doesn't."[93]

But the Western States Petroleum Association labeled the bill "the California Gas Restrictions Act of 2015." The group's president claimed: "I can't figure out any way to reach a 50 percent reduction in that time frame without doing some pretty dramatic measures. If it isn't gas rationing, what is it?"[94] Industry-sponsored advertisements warned that the mandate would lead to fuel rationing and bans on sport utility vehicles. Kristin Olsen, the Assembly Republican leader, argued, "We want to be leaders, but not when there are no followers. At some point we have to look at the fact that no one is following California's lead."[95]

After passing the state Senate, the petroleum reduction legislation faced strong opposition in the Assembly. Resistance came from both sides of the aisle and included several Democratic legislators representing communities in central California that were suffering from high unemployment and slow economic growth. In response to what was widely viewed as an example of regulatory overreach by both the governor and the CARB, de León agreed to drop the petroleum mandate.

But while the resultant bill has been described as a "huge win for the oil companies," in fact its major beneficiaries were the state's three large private utilities.[96] Senate Bill 350 also required the state's Public Utility Commission to make it easier for California's 23 million drivers to purchase vehicles that ran on electricity rather than gasoline. This aim was to be met by permitting utility companies to install electric charging stations throughout the state, making them a part of their grid infrastructure. Pacific Gas & Electric subsequently teamed up with Ford and General Motors to offer discounts on electric cars to their employees, while Southern California Edison announced plans to install 30,000 electric vehicle chargers in office buildings, apartment complexes, and parking lots. For the utility companies, increasing the number of electric cars on the road will help offset the decline in electricity demand resulting from the increasing number of rooftop solar installations. As an executive from Pacific Gas & Electric put it, "We want to see people using electricity as a transportation fuel. We think that it's great for our business."[97]

Strengthening Renewable Energy Targets

In 2016, California strengthened its renewable energy targets by requiring 50 percent of the state's energy to come from renewable sources by 2030. Under these regulations, neither household rooftop solar nor large hydropower or nuclear power count toward these targets, with the latter two exclusions reflecting strong environmental opposition to these energy sources. By 2016, the state's three major utilities were generating one-third of their power from more than 200 large-scale renewable energy sources, making them compliant with the state's interim mandate of generating 33 percent of its energy from renewable sources by 2020.

However, the state's aggressive renewable portfolio standard has come at a price.[98] These regulations are a major reason why California's retail energy prices are 50 percent above the national average. Ironically, the installation of large-scale renewable electricity generation facilities has been too successful: they have generated more power than the state requires. Since 2010, about 80 percent of the state's new electricity generation capacity has come from renewable sources, many of which would not have been built were it not for the RPS. But the costs of these new facilities, along with the considerable expense of building new transmission facilities to move the power they generate from deserts to urban areas, is charged to energy users. At the same time, because the power generated by renewable energy sources remains unreliable and concentrated in certain parts of the day, the utilities must still have sufficient conventional power generation capacity available as a backup, the costs of which must then be borne by their customers.

Whether the state can meet its more ambitious 2030 renewable energy goals will depend in part on the development of battery energy storage facilities that can make renewable energy available during the evening hours of peak energy demand. While California has invested considerable resources in energy storage facilities, their capacity remains limited, and constructing such facilities remains extremely costly.[99] Additionally, the development of such facilities will require the state to restructure its energy transmission lines. Maintaining the reliability of the state's energy supplies in the face of its increasing reliance on intermittent supplies of renewable energy may prove challenging.

Extending and Increasing Climate Change Goals

In 2014, state Senator Fran Pavley introduced legislation to extend the state's climate change reduction goals beyond their 2020 expiration. Her bill codified an executive order requiring the state to reduce its GHG emissions to 40 percent below their 1990 levels by 2030—an interim target for Governor Schwarzenegger's more ambitious goal of reducing the state's GHG emissions to 80 percent below 1990 levels by 2050. Pavley's proposal faced opposition from several Democratic legislators, who argued that the less affluent communities they represented had not seen the benefits of the state's climate change policies. Nevertheless, the bill was approved in 2016, giving California a deeper GHG reduction target than President Obama had proposed for the United States and one more ambitious than that contemplated by virtually any country. At the same time, the legislature also enacted a companion statute that granted it more oversight of the state's air pollution officials and required them to give priority to reducing emissions from industrial facilities located in poor, heavily polluted areas, located primarily in the state's Central Valley.

The Renewal of Cap-and-Trade

Because California's cap-and-trade program was due to expire in 2020, supporters realized that it would not be available to help the state meet its recently enacted ambitious 2030 GHG reduction goals. The political campaign to persuade the legislature to extend cap-and-trade through 2030 was led by Governor Jerry Brown, who dramatically told a state Senate committee: "What am I? 79? Do I have five years more? This isn't for me, I'm gonna be dead. It's for you, and it's damn real."[100] For the governor, President Donald Trump's June 2017 decision to withdraw the United States from the Paris Climate Accord had made it especially critical for California to demonstrate that the United States was not abandoning the fight against climate change. Brown publicly stated, "I want to do everything we can to keep America on track, keep the world on track."[101] Climate concerns were not the only reason to push for cap-and-trade's continuation, however: the revenues from auctioning off pollution permits were a key funding source for a planned high-speed train connecting San Francisco and Los Angeles—another important priority for the governor.

In order to insulate the program from future legal challenges, cap-and-trade's proponents needed the extension to be approved by a two-thirds vote of both houses of the state legislature (even though the Chamber of Commerce lawsuit questioning the original law's constitutionality had been unsuccessful). Because some Democrats were opposed to the extension this meant that the legislation also required Republican votes. To craft sufficient political support, the bill's backers made a number of compromises, the most important of which was to require the CARB to set a ceiling on permit prices. This provision was designed to address concerns that a strict cap might limit the state's economic growth: should the price of permits spike, the state would act to increase their supply, thus lowering their cost. Companies were also permitted to continue to use offset credits to meet their compliance obligations, though the availability of this tool would be limited over time. Additional tax breaks were provided for manufacturers and power companies, special provisions were made for industries at risk of relocating, and the regulatory burdens on petroleum refineries and oil and gas facilities were reduced. The statute also included an unrelated provision that suspended the state's fire prevention tax. Primarily levied on rural property owners, this tax had long been a target for repeal by Republican legislators.

The compromise legislation received broad political support, even from organizations that had usually been at cross-purposes, such as the Environmental Defense Fund and the Natural Resources Defense Council on one hand and the California Chamber of Commerce, the California Business Roundtable, and business associations representing agricultural interests on the other. Oil firms, while refraining from publicly supporting the bill, privately backed it. Although much of the state's business community had fought cap-and-trade in the past, it now regarded the system's market-based approach to pollution control as less burdensome and more cost effective than the imposition of direct regulations to meet the state's 2030 reduction goals. For their part, the state's mainstream environmental groups also backed the legislation, notwithstanding the compromises that had been made to get business and Republican support. However, activists from the California Environmental Justice Alliance and the Sierra Club opposed the bill—as did a few Democratic legislators—because they believed it had made too many concessions to industry in general and to oil and gas firms in particular.

In July 2017, Assembly Bill 398 was approved by a two-thirds majority of fifty-five to twenty-four in the Assembly and twenty-seven to thirteen in the state Senate. While previous major California climate change policies had never gained more than one or two votes from members of the state's minority party, eight Republican legislators voted for the measure. Assembly Republican leader Chad Mayes, who had urged members of his caucus to work with Democrats on shaping the terms of the legislation, observed that "California Republicans are different than national Republicans. Many of us believe that climate change is real and that it's a responsibility we have to work to address." Assemblyman Devon Mathis (R-Visalia) made an emotional speech, telling his fellow legislators: "We have to make decisions as legislators—do we do what is right or do we do what is politically right?"[102]

The extent of Republican support for cap-and-trade's extension in part reflected poll data that indicated that while the views of Democratic and Republican voters on this policy issue still differed, a substantial number of California Republicans did regard the risks of climate change as credible and supported state efforts to address the problem. Some political cover was also provided by establishment Republicans. Former Secretary of State George Shultz wrote that late President Reagan "would be proud to see" cap-and-trade-receive bipartisan support, while former Republican governor Pete Wilson endorsed the legislation.[103]

The ceremony at which Governor Brown signed the program's extension was attended by his predecessor, Republican governor Arnold Schwarzenegger, who had signed the 2006 legislation that provided the foundation for cap-and-trade in the same location eleven years earlier. Brown told attendees that to pass the legislation, "Republicans and Democrats set aside their differences, came together and took courageous action. That's what good government looks like."[104] Schwarzenegger called the bill's passage "a message that we have a functional government in California where Democrats and Republicans work together."[105] An editorial in the *New York Times*, while noting that the legislation was "not perfect," stated that the bipartisan support behind its passage sent "a strong signal to the world that millions of Americans regard with utmost seriousness a threat the Trump administration refuses to acknowledge."[106]

However, the extent of bipartisan consensus on climate change legislation in California should not be exaggerated: the extension was only supported by one Republican in the state Senate, while all but seven Republicans in the state Assembly voted against it. Republican state senator Ted Gaines stated, "Gov. Brown and his cadre of climate change extremists won't be happy until California leads the nation on wind, solar and poverty."[107] And the conservative-leaning California Policy Center declared:

> The governor's insistence on using cap-and-trade revenues to fund his $68 billion-plus high speed-rail boondoggle highlights what's fundamentally wrong with the current cap-and-trade system. Rather than combat climate change, it's basically a tax on business use to fund myriad unrelated items. . . . It's hard to see how dramatically raising Californians' gas prices . . . thus increasing not only our driving costs, but the costs of transporting and manufacturing every manner of food and consumer good—is going to save the planet.[108]

Past and Future Policy Impacts

In 2014, California's GHG emissions were 9.5 percent lower than their historic 2004 peak of 487.63 million tons.[109] Since 2006, the state's annual climate-warming emissions have declined by 35 million metric tons. Between 2014 and 2015, they fell by an amount equivalent to removing 300,000 vehicles from the state's roads. By 2017, the state's GHG emissions had nearly returned to their 1990 levels, putting California on track to meet its 2020 GHG emissions reductions goal. These results are in large measure due to the transformation of the state's power generation sources in the decade since 2006. The share of the state's energy generated by small hydro, solar, wind, geothermal, and biomass sources increased from 11 percent in 2006 to 24.4 percent in 2016. California ranks sixth in the United States in the generation of its electricity from renewable sources if hydropower is excluded and ninth if it is included. The state leads the United States in electricity generated from solar. Its proportion of electricity generated from coal-burning electric generation plants—all of which are located outside California—declined from 7.6 percent to 3 percent over the past decade, while the percentage produced from natural gas increased from 46.5 percent to 59.9 percent.

While California's absolute emissions are the second highest in the United States (after Texas)—a function of the unusually large size of its economy as well as its extensive reliance on automotive transportation—the state's per capita carbon dioxide emissions decreased by 12 percent between 2000 and 2012. On a per capita basis, the state's emissions are the third lowest in the United States, after Washington, DC, and New York, both of which use considerably less motor fuel. But by another measure, the carbon intensity of California's economy—measured by carbon dioxide emissions per unit of economic output—declined by only 26.6 percent between 2000 and 2014, putting it in twenty-eighth place among the fifty states.[110] The latter shortcoming was primarily due to two factors, a drought that reduced the supply of hydroelectric power and a reduction in energy generated by nuclear power, both of which have increased the state's reliance on power generated by fossil fuels.

Because California has already reduced its GHG emissions substantially, achieving each additional increment of emissions reduction will become progressively more difficult.[111] To meet its 2030 target, the state's annual GHG emissions must decrease by 183 million metric tons —equivalent to what the state's transportation sector now produces each year. In addition to developing the technologies and infrastructure necessary to accommodate the state's increasing reliance on renewable energy, the number of low- or zero-emission vehicles on the road will need to substantially increase. California will also have to further increase the efficiency of its already highly energy-efficient buildings and begin to capture methane emissions from agriculture, among other policy initiatives. In addition, a larger portion of emissions reduction will be required to come from cap-and-trade.

The fact that California is pursuing such a diversity of strategies to reduce its GHG emissions means that not all of them must be equally effective, especially as some complement one other.[112] But clearly, many must play a more important role. What makes California's achievement of its emissions reduction goal even more challenging is that the state plans to shut down its last nuclear power plant by 2030. Finally, regulations aside, the state's future levels of GHG emissions will also be significantly affected by its rates of economic and population growth. Should either or both significantly increase, California will find it proportionately more difficult to achieve its long-term emissions reduction goals.

Broader Policy Impacts

Since California only produces 1.3 percent of global GHG emissions, by themselves the state's regulations will not reduce the threat posed by climate change to California—or the globe.[113] However, it is worth noting that if all fifty states had adopted California's standards in 2005, by 2020, American GHG emissions would have been 2.6 percent lower than they are currently projected to be, which would have had a global impact.[114] In any event, California clearly has strong incentives to encourage other governments to follow its example. Consequently, the state has become an important national and international advocate for climate change policies. State officials have worked to cooperate with and coordinate their climate action policies with those of other subnational governments. California has actually established a de facto State Department, and it has installed a deputy secretary for border and intergovernmental relations in the California Environmental Protection Agency who is responsible for administering the growing number of international environmental agreements that the state has signed.

Around the world, 165 local jurisdictions have signed onto the Global Climate Leadership Memorandum of Understanding established jointly by California and the German state of Baden-Wurttemberg. This agreement commits these subnational governments to keeping global temperatures from rising more than 2 degrees Celsius—hence its common nickname "2 MOU." Signatories include the states of Oregon, Washington, and Vermont, as well as the provinces of British Columbia and Ontario in Canada, the states of Baja California and Jalisco in Mexico, and Wales. While this agreement is not legally binding, it does reflect the frustration of many local governments—including that of California—with the slow progress of national climate change reduction efforts, as well as the fact that local governments do regulate housing, construction, energy, and transportation, all of which constitute important sources of GHG emissions. CARB officials have also served as international climate advisors, working with other governments to help them adopt programs similar to those of California.

California's policy impact has been particularly noticeable in China, where the state has served as a technical advisor to 100 Chinese cities. California's regulatory officials have held numerous meetings with their Chinese counterparts. According to Sophie Lu, the director of a Beijing-based energy research firm, "China has always looked to California. It is definitely a role model."[115] Hal Harvey, who runs a research firm based in San Francisco and has frequently travelled to China, has observed, "The reference point for China is not Washington, it's California. They would rather learn from California than any other jurisdiction."

Shortly after President Trump announced the withdrawal of the United States from the Paris Climate Accord, California governor Jerry Brown made a highly publicized visit to China, where he signed an agreement for the two governments—one the world's sixth-largest economy and the other its second largest—to cooperate in reducing GHG emissions. The governor subsequently solidified his reputation as America's de facto leader on climate change by announcing that California would host an international summit to bring together both business executives and government officials who had pledged to reduce their GHG emissions.[116]

More informally, the state hopes to lead by example. California officials, led by Governor Jerry Brown, believe that the state's core accomplishment to date—namely, demonstrating the ability of the world's sixth-largest economy to reduce its GHG emissions while continuing to grow—will spur other local and national governments to adopt more ambitious policies and goals.[117] According to Robert Stavins, director of the Harvard Environmental Economics Program, policymakers in Europe and China are "very aware of what's going on in California. It does affect their thinking."[118] Andrew Jones, the director of a nonprofit think tank, has said: "California's efforts set a pace and tone for other states.[119] In short, California is anticipating—if not depending upon—both a national and a global "California effect."

Nevertheless, the impact of that "effect" will be affected by the state's ability to meet its increasingly ambitious GHG reduction targets without impairing the growth of its economy. As Severin Borenstein of the Energy Institute at the Haas School of Business has observed, California has made itself into "a giant laboratory" for climate change. If the state succeeds in its experiment, it will provide a model that other political jurisdictions can emulate, especially if California is able to develop new cost-effective emissions reduction technologies. Alternatively, if the state cannot achieve its climate change reduction goals or its efforts to do so prove too costly, then, according to Borenstein, "other states and countries will be watching that too."[120]

Conclusion

As they have with many of the state's environmental policy initiatives described in this book, policymakers and citizens have acted in response to a wide range of perceived threats to the state's environmental quality in their fight against climate change. Californians are well aware that they live in a highly vulnerable natural environment, with frequent floods and mud-slides, periodic droughts, high risks of wildfires, and the ever-present danger of earthquakes. Climate change either adds to or exacerbates some of these already credible environmental risks. Such change is likely to mean more frequent droughts, while warmer winters will reduce the size of the Sierra snowpack, on which much of the state's water supply depends. Drier winters and hotter summers will increase the number and intensity of forest fires, which can affect communities throughout the state.[121] A warmer planet will raise sea levels along the state's large coastline, while a reduction in precipitation threatens the redwoods, the sequoias, and the agricultural industry, all of which require large amounts of water. In short, global climate change—both current and potential—clearly does threaten California's already highly vulnerable and fragile natural environment.[122]

But it is also politically significant that California has structured many of its climate change–related regulations in ways that provide both immediate pecuniary and environmental benefits to its citizens. The two most important examples of this strategy are the state's promotion of energy efficiency and its push for renewable energy. Both of these initiatives predate the emergence of climate change on the state's policy agenda, though they have expanded as climate change has become more politically salient. California may well have continued to pursue both policies even if the risks of global climate change had never emerged, because they save consumers money and reduce their dependence on high and volatile fossil fuel prices.

These initiatives have also served to limit the construction of new power plants in general and "dirty" fossil fuel plants in particular, which in turn helps protect the state's air quality—historically a major state environmental priority. An important reason for the extent of political support for renewables—and a critical factor behind the defeat of Proposition 23 in 2010—is that in California, renewable energy has come to be identified with "clean" energy.[123]

Much of the same dynamic holds for the state's ambitious initiatives to regulate automotive emissions. The fact that a majority of the state's air pollution comes from motor vehicles and that their number keeps growing means that California is forced to intensify its regulations just to maintain its air quality. Absent a concern about climate change, the regulations adopted by the state may well have been different, but not substantially so, since reducing GHG emissions from transportation also improves air quality. In sum, an important reason for the degree of public and political backing for several of the state's GHG emissions reduction goals and policies has been their ability to deliver ancillary benefits.

Patterns of business support and opposition have also been critical. As Karapin notes, "California is an important exception to the generally negative relationship between fossil fuel production and climate policy."[124] While California does not have any coal—an industry that has served as an important obstacle to climate change initiatives in several states and countries—it does have a large petroleum sector. The state holds 16 percent of U.S. crude oil reserves and is the third-largest oil producer in the country. California produces about 12 percent of the nation's oil—a level consistent with its share of the national population. Roughly 11 percent of the nation's refining industry is located in the state, and Chevron, one of the world's largest energy companies, is headquartered there. The state is also a major oil importer: net imports of fossil fuels recently amounted to half of its total energy consumption. Not surprisingly, it is the oil sector whose interests have been most adversely affected by the state's climate change initiatives and which has led much of the opposition to them.

But it is the wide divergence of business preferences that has made possible California's adoption of such a wide range of increasingly stringent energy efficiency standards and GHG reduction goals. United business opposition to such measures has been elusive because particular state regulations have advantaged various business sectors. These include, most notably, its clean tech sector: California is the birthplace of a wide range of clean technology firms, including Sunpower, Tesla, Silver Spring Networks, SolarEdge, Sun Run, and Bloom Energy. The state has become an important center of clean energy and has received more venture capital investment in this sector than all other states combined. State regulations have also created an important solar installation industry, promoted the production and sale of electric cars, and led to major investments in renewable energy facilities. In addition, earlier state policy initiatives changed the economic and thus the political preferences of the state's utilities, making them into supporters of both energy conservation and renewable energy and allies of electric car manufacturers seeking to wean drivers off gasoline.

In this context, feedback effects have been critical: state regulations have helped create and expand business sectors that have benefited from its energy efficiency and climate change regulations, and these in turn have become influential constituencies for defending such regulations, often lobbying for their further expansion. As Rabe insightfully notes, while "the actual economic ramifications of aggressive climate regulation are highly debatable, it has become common practice across partisan and institutional lines in California to argue that what is good for the climate is also good for California's economic development."[125] Whether that is in fact the case, putting the state on a less carbon-intensive growth trajectory has certainly benefited important segments of the state's business community, making possible the several Baptist–bootlegger alliances described in this chapter. In fact, virtually every policy initiative described in this chapter has received at least *some* business backing.

Finally, it is important to recognize the importance of California's history of environmental policy leadership. The state has played a critical role in improving air quality, most notably by controlling pollution from mobile sources—an effort that dates to the 1960s (discussed in chapter 6). Had California's regulations to reduce air pollution from motor vehicles been unsuccessful, policymakers—and the public—might have been less willing or able to support the state's even more ambitious effort to reduce GHG emissions. The two policy areas are thus linked: it was California's highly visible and effective efforts to control pollution from motor vehicles that positioned it to assume a leadership role in reducing greenhouse gas emissions; revealingly, the agency responsible for the former was placed in charge of the latter.[126] From this perspective, the genesis of the state's GHG regulations during the twenty-first century lay in mid-twentieth-century Los Angeles. All told, the links between automotive emissions and climate change in California demonstrate that "regulatory expertise and environmental leadership . . . are mutually reinforcing."[127] They also underscore the importance of public administrative capacity and policy accomplishments as necessary conditions for the exercise of environmental leadership.

8

California's Regulatory Leadership: Broader Implications

As this book has demonstrated, California's long-standing regulatory leadership in the area of environmental policy has been shaped by both its geography and the combined impact of a high level of citizen engagement, frequent business support, and the growth of the state's regulatory institutions.

Studies of environmental politics have tended to overlook the critical importance of geography. But geography is critical to understanding California's environmental challenges and opportunities. *The state has prioritized environmental protection because its geography has both made it continually threatened by environmental degradation and meant that it had more to gain by protecting its fragile but beautiful natural environment.*

Gold mining literally created the state of California. But because of how this resource was mined and where it was located, gold mining also had extensive negative economic and environmental consequences. The state's magnificent old-growth trees in the Sierras and along the coast were a major scenic feature and tourist attraction. But their economic value led many of them to be harvested. The discovery of oil made California the nation's leading energy producer. But its extraction threatened the attractiveness of the Southern California coast and public enjoyment of the region's beautiful beaches. The cities surrounding the San Francisco Bay, along with the bay's shallow coastline, made the region ideally suited for public and private development. But those projects shrunk the size of the bay. The state has abundant supplies of freshwater. But because this water is located far from its population centers, the state was forced to dam its rivers and flood many of its valleys. The benign weather of Los Angeles made the city an attractive place to live. But its distinctive topography undermined its air quality.

Public pressure to protect the state's unusually attractive but also highly vulnerable and continually threatened natural environment underlies virtually every environmental policy enacted in California. This pressure began with the efforts of a handful of prominent individuals to protect the unique natural beauty of the Yosemite Valley and the sequoias in the Sierras and then expanded into more organized efforts and campaigns to place Yosemite under federal control, protect the coastal redwoods, and expand state parks. The opposition of Southern Californians to oil drilling on and off their beaches pressured the state legislature to restrict drilling, while strong grassroots campaigns led to the passage of state policies to protect San Francisco Bay and the California coast.

Citizen activism played an important role in the enactment of first local and then state regulations to protect air quality in Los Angeles, most importantly by restricting emissions from automobiles. Extensive citizen mobilization subsequently proved instrumental in protecting California's ability to maintain and strengthen its own automotive pollution controls. More recently, a wide coalition of environmental and other citizen organizations, along with substantial public support, has limited the construction of new power plants; promoted conservation, energy efficiency, and the expansion of renewable energy; strengthened automotive emissions regulations; and, more broadly, backed regulations to address the risks that global climate change poses for California.

But while citizen pressures have been essential to the strengthening of environmental regulations in California, business backing has also been critical. The campaign to end hydraulic mining was led by Sacramento Valley farmers. Political support for protecting the Yosemite Valley came from steamship companies, backed by road builders and railways, all of which hoped to profit by attracting more tourists to California. For similar reasons, the Southern Pacific Railroad lent its considerable political influence to the fight to protect the sequoias in the Sierras. The Shoreline Planning Association was instrumental in increasing public access to the beaches of Southern California after the Second World War in order to make the region a more attractive place to visit and live. The Los Angeles business community, including the city's influential real estate developers, was a strong advocate for local, regional, and state regulations to protect the region's air quality. In addition, a wide range of business interests have benefited from and supported California's innovative and wide-ranging energy efficiency and climate change initiatives.

A third factor contributing to California's regulatory leadership has been the progressive growth of its regulatory institutions. This process began with the creation of the Office of State Engineer (1878) and the State Forestry Commission (1885) and subsequently expanded to include the establishment of the State Park Commission (1927) and the State Lands Commission (1938). More recently, the Bay Conservation and Development Commission was established in 1969, the California Coastal Commission in 1976, the California Air Resources Board in 1968, and the California Energy Commission in 1974. Equally importantly, these public institutions have been able to draw on the considerable expertise of the state's major universities and research centers. Dr. Haagen-Smit, the first director of the CARB, did his pioneering research on smog while at the California Institute of Technology, while the California Energy Commission initially relied on research conducted at the University of California Berkeley and the Lawrence Berkeley National Laboratory.

Broader Implications

What are the broader implications of this analysis of California's regulatory leadership? Three points are particularly critical: the importance of the local dimension of environmental policies, the role of business in environmental politics, and the limits of environmental regulation.

GEOGRAPHY AND LOCAL POLITICS

It would be an exaggeration to claim—to paraphrase Tip O'Neill—that "all environmental politics are local." Nevertheless, looking at environmental politics through the lens of a state, city, or region reveals the extent to which many environmental issues *are* rooted in geographic threats to people's "backyards." As Sarah Phillips notes, "Nothing strikes the local resident more concretely than sudden shifts in land use or the despoliation of the air, a river, or a favorite natural haunt. . . . [E]nvironmental concerns often percolate from the bottom up."[1] Similarly, Daniel Esty insightfully writes: "People regard themselves as part of an ecologically defined community. . . .

Many people have important aspects of their political identity established by their *proximity* to the Chesapeake Bay, the Gulf of Mexico, the Mississippi River, the Great Plains, the Rocky Mountains, Puget Sound, or the Central Valley."[2] One can readily add to this list the Everglades and the White Mountains, along with the Yosemite Valley, the sequoias in the Sierras, the redwoods along the northern coast, the San Francisco Bay, the beaches of Southern California, and the Pacific coast.[3]

For the residents of New York City, the Hudson River that flowed throughout the state and into their city was in their "backyard" and became an important focus of political activity to protect it. In 1902, downstate residents with a recreational interest in the state's mountains created the Association for the Protection of the Adirondacks. Its goal was to preserve "the Adirondacks forest, water, game and fish, and the maintenance of healthful conditions in the Adirondack region."[4] Thanks in part to the association's efforts, by 1904, New York owned more than 1.4 million acres in the Adirondacks and 104,000 acres in the Catskills. The latter had, in the words of David Stradling, "become invested with a wealth of legendary and historical association which gives them a peculiar and exclusive charm."[5] Their proximity to New York City made them an ideal location for those seeking a rural retreat from urban life.

Clearly, citizens can and do also care about protecting natural environments far away from where they live. Iconic natural places such as Niagara Falls, Yellowstone, and the Grand Canyon belong, in a sense, to all Americans. Americans who have never seen or are unlikely to ever see a caribou have opposed oil drilling in Alaska or wanted to protect endangered species in international waters and other countries. Nor have Californians been alone in valuing the state's natural environment. There was substantial support from throughout the United States to protect the redwoods—which were viewed as a unique natural resource—as well as widespread opposition to the flooding of Hetch Hetchy. Nonetheless, an insight that can be drawn from California is that an important basis of public support for many environmental policies comes from the threats that directly affect citizens and communities. How people define their "neighborhoods" shapes what they care about and want to protect.

BUSINESS AND ENVIRONMENTAL REGULATION

A second broader implication of California's historical regulatory leadership has to do with the role of business in environmental policymaking. A primary claim of the extensive literature on business and the environment is that it is *the political power of business that constrains a government's ability to adopt stronger environmental regulations*.[6] But the pattern of environmental policymaking in California reveals a more complex pattern. The most important source of opposition to more stringent environmental regulations in the state *has* been business, most notably the automotive and oil industries. But segments of the business community have also been important and influential *advocates* of more stringent environmental standards.

The significance of business support for stronger environmental regulations extends beyond lobbying and other forms of political influence. Much public opposition to stronger environmental protections is rooted in their anticipated negative economic impacts, especially on employment. While many such fears have proven exaggerated, certainly not all have. However, such concerns are more likely to be successfully addressed if environmental regulations also create economic opportunities. Thus, it is the business benefits of renewable energy initiatives that have prompted many states to promote them. Likewise, for those states wanting to attract service sector and high-technology firms or to appeal to tourists, retirees, or those purchasing vacation homes, an attractive natural environment—including natural scenic amenities and good air quality—can be an important competitive advantage. As Pennsylvania's Office of the Governor noted in 2004, "In the new economy environmental quality has become important not simply as an end in itself, but as a prerequisite for attracting new talent."[7] According to Rabe and Mundo, states are increasingly valuing environmental quality "both as a public health concern and as an essential ingredient for economic development."[8]

During the second half of the nineteenth century, California led the world in gold production. It has also long been the nation's third-largest oil producer and a major presence in the forestry sector. What has enabled these three economically important but often environmentally destructive industries to be challenged—though often with considerable difficulty and with varying success—has been the availability of alternative sources of wealth creation and employment. Thus, the restrictions on hydraulic gold mining made possible the growth of agriculture. The economic restrictions on harvesting redwoods were in part counterbalanced by opportunities for nature tourism. Restrictions on oil drilling in Southern California promoted the growth of coastal communities and encouraged tourism. Conversely, an important reason for the political strength of the state's agricultural sector, notwithstanding its several adverse environmental impacts, has been the lack of alternative economic opportunities in rural counties. Historically, it was the absence of any perceived economic benefits of protecting the state's inland rivers, lakes, and valleys that made possible the expansion of the state's water management system.

The absence of countervailing business opportunities also helps explain the lack of support for stronger environmental regulations in other states. States with substantial coal deposits such as West Virginia, Kentucky, and Wyoming have opposed stricter environmental controls. The state of Alaska has resisted restrictions on oil drilling. Louisiana's polluting chemical industry is weakly regulated.[9] James Willard Hurst has documented the complex legal arrangements that made it possible for Wisconsin's forests, which originally occupied 30 million of the state's 35 million acres, to be exhausted by timbering in a relatively short period of time.[10] A similar fate befell the cypresses and pines of Florida, barely 3 percent of which have survived.[11]

In each of these cases, an important reason for the lack of adequate environmental regulation was *not* that business was too politically powerful. *It is rather that the political preferences of each state's business community were not sufficiently divided.* More specifically, there was a notable lack of firms or industries that stood to benefit from and thus were willing to *support* stronger environmental controls. If environmental regulations impose major economic burdens on an important economic sector, those impacts must be at least partially counterbalanced by the benefits they provide to another sector. If such a sector does not exist or has not become politically mobilized, the imposition of environmental controls becomes much more difficult.

The claim that business can be a supporter of environmental protection is not novel. Samuel Hays's influential study of the Progressive conservation movement demonstrates that much of Progressive Era conservation policy was in fact in the interest of and backed by business.[12] State forest protection policies in New York and New England during the latter part of the nineteenth century and the early part of the twentieth also received broad business backing, including support from local property owners who wanted to promote tourism, hunting, and fishing. The politics of urban air pollution control from the Progressive Era though the 1940s reveals selected business backing for ordinances to improve air quality by restricting coal burning.[13] However, as noted earlier, the importance of business support for environmental protection has often been overlooked by many recent studies of business and environmental policy, including my own work.[14] But this book has repeatedly demonstrated that *without substantial business backing at critical moments, California's environmental quality would be much poorer.*

It is certainly possible for environmental regulations to be enacted without business support. The creation of Redwoods National Park, the protection of the San Francisco Bay and the California coast, and the creation of the California Energy Commission are all examples. But without any business backing, enacting strong environmental regulations is more difficult. The experience of California suggests that strong and effective environmental regulations are *more* likely to be enacted if they advantage and are supported by influential segments of the business community.

THE LIMITS OF REGULATION

In addition to demonstrating the potential of environmental regulation, California's history also illustrates some of its limitations. One such limitation has to do with the costs of environmental protection, which can be considerable. It took three long decades of struggle before hydraulic mining was finally banned, notwithstanding its widespread and widely known agricultural, economic, and environmental devastation. The reason for the delay was simple. Gold mining was both highly profitable and an important source of regional employment. While banning hydraulic mining may have been in the long-term economic interests of northern California, its immediate impacts were highly negative. Not only were local communities devastated, but it is unlikely that the 20,000 miners who lost their jobs were able to find equally remunerative employment in wheat farming. Economic factors also explain why the coastal redwoods were protected much later and less extensively than the sequoias in the Sierras. The wood from the former was much more commercially valuable than that of the latter. Today, the continued importance of oil production to the state's economy is an important reason why California has regulated but not banned fracking.

The most important example of the limits of California's "greening" has to do with its water management. Californians supported the construction of an extensive hydraulic infrastructure because they considered it essential to the growth and prosperity of both the urban and rural parts of the state. This infrastructure subsequently became as critical to the state's growth in the twentieth century as gold mining had been to its economic development in the nineteenth century, despite the fact that both natural resource developments had adverse environmental consequences. Finally, California's continued reliance on automobiles, and its placement of most of the burdens and costs of protecting its air quality on the manufacturers of these vehicles rather than on their drivers, points to the limits of what Californians have been willing to do to protect their air quality. These examples reveal some of the important economic and political constraints on environmental policies.

Federalism and Environmental Protection: Race to the Bottom or Race to the Top

An important theme highlighted in this book is the importance of federalism. The significance of states in shaping environmental policies has often been overlooked as a result of the disproportionate attention scholars have paid to environmental politics at the federal level.[15] But while California may have been historically distinctive in the extent to which it has adopted more stringent environmental regulations than the federal government, it has not been alone. New York created the Adirondack and Catskill forest preserves in 1885, six years before Congress passed legislation allowing the president of the United States to set aside federal forest preserves.[16] This pioneering policy initiative, according to David Stradling, represented "a new doctrine of state functions" and "a significant leap forward in establishing government authority over the environment."[17] Air pollution controls in the United States during the late nineteenth and early twentieth centuries were initiated by American cities. By 1916, seventy-five American cities had passed smoke control statutes, preceding federal regulations by half a century.[18] Furthermore, during the same period, states in northern New England pioneered efforts to halt and then reverse deforestation.[19]

In 1989, *Newsweek* reported that "a new era of environmental federalism has dawned. In a stunning switch the states are no longer merely implementing federal standards but . . . are passing more and more stringent controls on pollution than Congress had ever considered . . . protecting ground water, recycling garbage, mandating 'clean fuels' and reducing acid rain."[20] Some states enacted regulations for wetlands protection and land conservation that were more stringent and innovative than federal standards. In 1992, eight northeastern states announced an agreement to reduce the amount of nitrogen oxides emitted by electric utilities, imposing more stringent controls than those subsequently issued by the EPA. Several states have adopted one or more ambient air standards that exceed federal requirements, while eight states have adopted new stationary-source performance standards that are more stringent than those of the federal government.[21] Following federal legislation that permitted states to adopt either California or federal vehicle emissions standards, several states have adopted the former, as described in the two preceding chapters.

More recently, climate change policies have been characterized by "upside-down cooperative federalism," in which states have become the major source of policy innovation.[22] In this way, states have filled the voids left by the federal government's failure to move environmental policy forward, becoming "dominant players in an area conventionally thought to be the province of the federal government and international authorities."[23] These developments, which are described in detail in the previous chapter, have led to a revival of studies of state environmental policies and politics.[24]

The fact that some states are as capable—if not more capable—of strengthening their regulatory standards as the federal government does not mean that the fears of a "race to the bottom" that helped motivate the prior expansion of federal regulation are misplaced. Many states have been and remain regulatory laggards. Some have relaxed their environmental standards in order to attract or retain business investments.[25] David Konitsky argues that these states have responded "to the regulatory enforcement efforts of competitor states where their own enforcement effort may plausibly put them at a competitive disadvantage."[26] Local business pressures in several states have undermined enforcement efforts related to the cleanup of hazardous wastes, water pollution, and the protection of natural resources.[27] Moreover, nearly half of the state legislatures have enacted laws that prohibit state regulatory agencies from issuing standards that go beyond federal minimum requirements. More recently, many states have welcomed the Trump administration's efforts to repeal the Obama administration's climate change policy initiatives or have cut back on their previous carbon reduction programs. Clearly, state policy preferences remain highly diverse, and, for many states, federal rules and regulations have played a critical role in improving environmental quality.

RATCHETING UP AND POLICY LEARNING

At the same time, state policies have also strengthened federal standards. During the mid-1960s, an important reason why the automotive industry reversed its opposition to federal emissions controls was because two economically important states, New York and California, had adopted or were about to adopt their own regulations. The industry preferred uniform federal standards to a multiplicity of state ones. During the 1970s, a similar dynamic occurred with respect to energy efficiency standards for appliances. After several states, led by California, adopted their own standards, the industry decided to support federal regulation, which Congress then enacted. Most recently, the passage of chemical safety reform legislation by Congress in 2016 owed much to the policies of several states, most notably California and Massachusetts, which had adopted chemical safety regulations more stringent than those of the federal government. In each of these cases, state regulatory initiatives prompted an expansion of federal regulation. Clearly, environmental policy initiatives can come from "below" as well as unfolding from the "top down."

Multilevel governance in the United States has promoted policy innovation, experimentation, and learning.[28] States can and have functioned as regulatory laboratories, developing new policy approaches that can then be adopted by other political jurisdictions. The policy fragmentation that federalism makes possible has been an important source of policy innovation in the United States, and within that context, California has played an important role as a policy laboratory. For example, the Environmental Protection Agency has learned much from the California Air Resources Board about the feasibility of progressively more stringent air pollution controls. Absent California's ability to go beyond federal air pollution control requirements, federal vehicle emissions control standards would have strengthened at a much slower rate. Since 1967, California has received more than 115 waivers from the EPA to adopt its own motor vehicle air pollution controls; many of these waivers have since become important sources of new state and federal regulations. Similarly, other states as well as the federal government have learned from California's coastal land use controls. The adoption of many similar greenhouse gas reduction and energy efficiency initiatives by other states also reflects this pattern of policy learning. Looking back historically, the federal government's initiatives to promote forest conservation during the Progressive Era were able to draw upon the experiences and expertise of the northern New England states that had already acted to reverse widespread deforestation.[29]

The economic feasibility and environmental impact of several of California's wide-ranging and ambitious climate change initiatives, including cap-and-trade, its automotive regulations, its energy efficiency standards, and its renewable energy mandates, remain unclear. But these policies do provide other states with the important opportunity to learn from California's accomplishments and shortcomings and then to develop or adjust their own regulations accordingly. An important advantage of state regulation is that the costs of policy failure are likely to be more modest than they would be at the federal level. When California "overregulates," its citizens and business firms bear most of the costs. But when its regulations prove effective, other governments can then benefit by adopting them.

A NEW ERA

The respective merits and shortcomings of regulatory centralization and decentralization have been and continue to be widely debated.[30] But regardless of the strengths and weaknesses of environmental policymaking at the federal and state levels, what is clear is that the latter is becoming increasingly important. When we place the current period in historical perspective, we may view it as being in the midst of a structural shift in the relationship between federal and state regulatory authorities. During the late nineteenth century and the first half of the twentieth, there was a rough division of labor between these levels of governance. Both the federal government and several states were active in the conservation and protection of natural resources, while states and cities were primarily responsible for controlling air and water pollution. But beginning in the late 1960s, federal legislation became dominant in shaping environmental programs. Across multiple policy areas, the regulatory role of the states became primarily one of implementing and enforcing federal regulations—a relationship known as "cooperative federalism."[31]

Today, we may be well into a third era, one in which an increasing share of regulatory policy innovation and leadership is taking place at the state level. California may well herald the future of American environmental regulation—not in the sense that other states or the federal government will necessarily follow its lead, but rather because the slowdown or retreat in the federal government's strengthening of environmental standards means that a growing share of environmental policymaking in the United States will be done by states.

Some states will likely respond to the absence of federal pressures or the rollback of federal requirements by weakening their environmental regulations, while others, like California and New York, will choose to maintain or even strengthen them. This will make environmental policy in the United States more diverse, decentralized, and fragmented; will focus more public attention on state regulation; and is likely to change the dynamics of federal–state relations. Historically, much of the conflict between the federal government and the states over environmental regulation has revolved around state opposition to more stringent federal standards: the "sage-brush" rebellion and the "wise use movement," both of which have challenged federal land use policies as overly restrictive, are notable examples.[32] But now, such challenges may increasingly focus on state efforts to maintain their more stringent standards from challenges by the federal government.

In 1967, New York Democratic senator Robert Kennedy advised California's congressional delegation to invoke the doctrine of "states' rights" in order to enlist the support of southern legislators to vote against federal preemption of automotive emissions standards. That advice may prove prophetic. While states' rights has historically been associated with conservative principles and support for smaller government, following the 2016 election, the doctrine has been increasingly embraced by advocates of environmental regulation. Because of its long history of protecting its regulatory prerogatives against Washington's assaults, California will likely remain at the forefront of political and legal efforts to oppose federal policy initiatives that require states to weaken their own environmental standards.[33]

The Economic Benefits of Environmental Regulation

One important reason why California has been able to consistently adopt more stringent regulations than those of the federal government and other states is that many of its improvements in local and state environmental quality have been a source of competitive *advantage*. The improvements it has made in air quality—most notably in Los Angeles—its protection of the trees in the Sierras and along the Pacific, and its land use controls along the coast and around the San Francisco Bay have all made California a more attractive place to move to, invest in, and visit. While the location of Silicon Valley cannot be attributed to the state's environmental policies (or even to California's weather), northern California's attractive environment may well have played a role in the region's continual ability to attract highly educated, geographically mobile knowledge workers and the firms that employ them.

To be sure, many of California's environmental regulations have imposed economic, administrative, and bureaucratic burdens. Had some been less stringent or not adopted in the first place, California may well have been or would now be more prosperous. The expansion of its national and state parks have restricted its forestry, state regulations have reduced its oil drilling, and its coastal regulations have interfered with many commercial developments. Environmental impact requirements and other land use controls have also impeded many building projects, while strict building codes have increased

construction costs. Local zoning restrictions, some of which have been justified on environmental grounds, have raised housing costs. Californians pay
more for gasoline than drivers in any other state in the continental United
States, and their energy prices are among the nation's highest. Such state and
local environmental rules and restrictions are certainly a part of why California is considered a relatively unfriendly state in which to do business.[34]

Reasonable people can and do disagree about the *net economic impact* of
California's wide-ranging environmental policy initiatives. But absent the
adoption of many of them, it is also hard to imagine the state would be as
economically successful as it is today. Certainly, the continued deterioration
of its air quality would have impeded the economic and population growth
of Los Angeles, undermining the advantages of its weather. Such a development might well have prevented it from becoming the global entertainment
capital, as well as the location of many affluent residential communities.
Southern California would be a much less desirable place to live and visit
if its beaches and coastal areas had been filled with oil wells. Tourism has
long been one of the state's most important industries, and an important
reason why many people visit California is because of the beauty of its natural environment. But much of that beauty would not exist without extensive government regulation. Absent public policies, there would be fewer
state and federal parks, smaller groves of the magnificent sequoias and redwoods, more oil wells along the Southern California coast, a smaller San
Francisco Bay, a less accessible Pacific coast, and many more power plants
emitting harmful air pollutants.

Its environmental regulations are certainly not the main reason why California has had the largest state GDP since the early 1960s, is now the world's
sixth-largest economy, grew more rapidly than every other state between
2013 and 2016, and since 2000 has grown more rapidly than the United States
during all but three years.[35] The state has also benefited from its abundant
natural resources, its mild weather, its major research universities, its location on the Pacific coast, a high rate of immigration, and an ethos that values
innovation. *But environmental regulation may well be a necessary condition
for this economic success.* California convincingly demonstrates that government regulation matters, that economic growth and stringent environmental regulation can be compatible, and that environmental protection can be
consistent with and even contribute to economic growth.

While no state is likely to rival California's long-standing record of green
policy leadership across multiple policy areas anytime soon, its history does

demonstrate the considerable potential of local government to protect and improve its environmental quality as well as that of the nation. At this moment in our nation's history, as we enter an era in which environmental protection will lie more in the hands of states than those of the federal government, California's successes and challenges in forging ahead with innovative environmental policies over more than 150 years offer important insights that other states—as well as other governments—can emulate.

NOTES

Chapter 1: Introduction

1. Josef Chytry, *Mountain of Paradise: Reflections on the Emergence of Greater California as a World Civilization* (New York: Peter Lang, 2013), 13. The title of Chytry's volume is based on the suggestion that the word *California* may have been borrowed from the Persian term *Kari-iform*, which means "mountain of paradise," but this claim remains contested. Peter Schrag's highly critical portrait of the state is entitled *Paradise Lost: California's Experience, America's Future* (Berkeley: University of California Press, 1998).

2. Cass Sunstein, *Conspiracy Theories and Other Dangerous Ideas* (New York: Simon and Schuster, 2004), 71–72.

3. William Reilly, "Preface," in *Protecting the Golden Shore: Lessons from the California Coastal Commissions*, ed. Robert Healy, Jon Banta, John Clark, and William Duddleson (Washington, DC: Conservation Foundation, 1978), xi.

4. Kevin Starr, *Americans and the California Dream, 1850–1915* (New York: Oxford University Press, 1973), 174.

5. William Lowry, *The Dimensions of Federalism* (Durham, NC: Duke University Press, 1992), 96.

6. Gerald Nash, *State Government and Economic Development: A History of Administrative Policies in California, 1849–1933* (Berkeley: Institute of Governmental Studies, 1964), 1.

7. Richard Walker, "California's Gold Road to Riches: Natural Resources and Regional Capitalism, 1848–1940," *Annals of the Association of American Geographers* 191, no. 1 (2001): 166–199.

8. Scott Hamilton Dewey, *Don't Breathe the Air: Air Pollution and U.S. Environmental Politics, 1945–1970* (College Station: Texas A&M University Press, 2000), 55.

9. *New York State Ice Co. v. Liebmann*, 285 U.S. 262, 311 (1932) (Louis Brandeis, dissenting).

10. In *Trading Up: Consumer and Environmental Regulation in a Global Economy* (Cambridge, MA: Harvard University Press, 1995), I coined the term "California Effect" to illustrate how trade could enable governments with relatively stringent regulatory standards to raise those of their trading partners. In this book, I use the term more broadly to refer to how California has affected the environmental policies of other states and the federal government.

11. Wendy Leavitt, "The California Effect," *Fleet Owner*, March 1, 2010.

12. Barry Rabe, *Statehouse and Greenhouse: The Emerging Politics of American Climate Change* (Washington, DC: Brookings Institution Press, 2004), 142.

13. William Reilly, "California Driving Clean-Air Future," *San Francisco Chronicle*, January 23, 2012.

14. Carolyn Lochhead, "California Set to Fight Washington over Environmental Protections," *San Francisco Chronicle*, January 24, 2017.

15. David Vogel, "Trading Up and Governing Across: Transnational Governance and Environmental Protection," *Journal of European Public Policy* 4, no. 4 (December 1997): 562. See

also Richard Perkins and Eric Neumayer, "Does the 'California Effect' Operate Across Borders? Trading- and Investing-Up Automobile Emission Standards," *Journal of European Public Policy* 19, no. 2 (March 2012): 217–37.

16. Coral Davenport and Adam Nagourney, "Fighting Trump on Climate, California Becomes a Global Force," *New York Times*, May 23, 2017.

17. James Parsons, "The Uniqueness of California," *American Quarterly* 7, no. 1 (Spring 1955): 45.

18. Kevin Starr, *California: A History* (New York: Modern Library, 2007), 89–90.

19. James Farmer, *Trees in Paradise: A California History* (New York: W. W. Norton & Company, 2013), 66.

20. James Krier and Edmund Ursin, *Pollution and Policy* (Berkeley: University of California Press, 1977), 54–55.

21. Chip Jacobs and William Kelly, *Smogtown: The Lung-Burning History of Pollution in Los Angeles* (New York: Overlook Press, 2008), 162.

22. Jared Orsi, "Restoring the Common to the Goose: Citizen Activism and the Protection of the California Coastline, 1969–1982," *Southern California Quarterly* 78, no. 3 (Fall 1996): 258–59.

23. Schrag, *Paradise Lost*.

24. Michael Cohen, *The History of the Sierra Club, 1892–1970* (San Francisco: Sierra Club Books, 1988), 11.

25. Norris Hundley, Jr., *The Great Thirst: Californians and Water: A History* (Berkeley: University of California Press, 2000), 563.

26. Richard Walker, *The Country in the City: The Greening of the San Francisco Bay Area* (Seattle: University of Washington Press, 2007), 6–7.

27. The term "Baptist–bootlegger coalition" was coined by Bruce Yandle, who used it to refer to the "unholy" alliance between Baptists and bootleggers in the American South. Both groups wanted to prohibit the sale of alcohol on Sunday, the former in order to respect the Sabbath and the latter to create a market for illegal liquor sales. The term is now commonly used to refer to a political coalition between public and private interests. Bruce Yandle, "Bootleggers and Baptists—The Education of a Regulatory Economist," *Regulation* 7 (1983): 12–16.

28. Ann Carlson, "Regulatory Capacity and State Environmental Leadership: California's Climate Policy," *Fordham Environmental Law Review* 24 (2012): 65.

29. Jack Ewing, *Faster, Higher, Farther: The Volkswagen Scandal* (New York: W.W. Norton, 2017)

30. David Pettit, "Why Is California 'Worst'?," CNN, May 2, 2014, http://www.cnn.com/2014 /05/02/opinion/pettit-california-pollution/.

31. Richard Walker and Suresh Lodha, *The Atlas of California* (Berkeley: University of California Press, 2013), 64.

Chapter 2: Gold Mining

1. Norris Hundley, Jr., *The Great Thirst: Californians and Water: A History* (Berkeley: University of California Press, 2011), 1.

2. Benjamin Madley, *American Genocide: The United States and the California Indian Catastrophe* (New Haven, CT: Yale University Press, 2016), 23.

3. Hundley, *Great Thirst*, 5.

4. Ibid., 8.

5. Ibid., 8.

6. Ibid., 32–33.

7. Gerald Nash, *State Government and Economic Development* (New York: Arno Press, 1979), 3.

8. Ibid., 2.

9. Quoted in Carey McWilliams, *California: The Great Exception* (Berkeley: University of California Press, 1949), 25.

10. Kevin Starr, *California: A History* (New York: Random House, 2005), 80.

11. McWilliams, *California*, 35; Starr, *California*, 80.

12. Henry W. Brands, *The Man Who Saved the Union: Ulysses Grant in War and Peace* (New York: Doubleday, 2012), 57.

13. Ibid., 57.

14. Henry W. Brands, *The Age of Gold: The California Gold Rush and the New American Dream* (New York: Anchor Books, 2003), 269.

15. McWilliams, *California*, 49.

16. Quoted in ibid., 41.

17. Michael Hanemann, Caitlin Dyckman, and Damien Park, "California's Flawed Surface Water Rights," in *Sustainable Water: Challenges and Solutions from California*, ed. Allison Lassiter (Berkeley: University of California Press, 2015), 53.

18. Andrew Isenberg, *Mining California: An Ecological History* (New York: Hill and Wang, 2005), 32.

19. Morton Horwitz, *The Transformation of American Law, 1780–1860* (Cambridge, MA: Harvard University Press, 1977), 31. The classic work on this subject is J. Willard Hurst, *Law and the Conditions of Freedom* (Madison: University of Wisconsin Press, 1956). See also Donald Worster, *Rivers of Empire: Water, Aridity, and the Growth of the American West* (New York: Oxford University Press, 1985).

20. Donald Pisani, "The Gold Rush and American Resource Law," in *A Golden State: Mining and Economic Development in Gold Rush California*, ed. James Rawls and Richard Orsi (Berkeley: University of California Press, 1999), 139.

21. Isenberg, *Mining California*, 33.

22. Hundley, *Great Thirst*, 71.

23. Isenberg, *Mining California*, 23.

24. Robert Kelley, "Forgotten Giant: The Hydraulic Gold Mining Industry in California," *Pacific Historical Review* 23, no. 4 (November 1954), 343.

25. Hundley, *Great Thirst*, 77.

26. Marilyn Ziebarth, "California's First Environmental Battle," *California History* 63, no. 4 (Fall 1984): 276.

27. Kelley, "Forgotten Giant," 354.

28. Quoted in Douglas Littlefield, "Water Rights During the California Gold Rush: Conflicts over Economic Points of View," *Western Historical Quarterly* 14 (October 1983): 418.

29. Hundley, *Great Thirst*, 77–78.

30. Quoted in Isenberg, *Mining California*, 39.

31. Ziebarth, *California's First Environmental Battle*, 276.

32. Starr, *California*, 89–90.

33. Quoted in Isenberg, *Mining California*, 41.

34. Richard Rice, William Bullough, and Richard Orsi, *The Elusive Eden: A New History of California* (Boston: McGraw Hill, 1988), 289.

35. This quotation is taken from both Isenberg, *Mining California*, 41; and Randall Rohe, "Mining's Impact on the Land," in Carolyn Merchant, ed., *Green Versus Gold: Sources in California Environmental History* (Washington, DC: Island Press, 1989), 130.

36. Robert Kelley, *Battling the Inland Land: Floods, Public Policy, and the Sacramento Valley* (Berkeley: University of California Press, 1989), 202.

37. Matthew Booker, *Down by the Bay: San Francisco Between the Tides* (Berkeley: University of California Press, 2013), 120.

38. Rohe, *Mining's Impact*, 130.

39. Robert Kelley, "The Mining Controversy in the Sacramento Valley," *Pacific Historical Review* 25, no. 4 (November 1956): 332; Kelley, *Battling the Inland Land*, 107.

40. Quoted in Isenberg, *Mining California*, 42.

41. Quoted in ibid., 46.

42. E. A. Stevenson, "A Federal Agency Assesses Mining's Impact on the Indians, 1853," in *Green Versus Gold: Sources in California Environmental History*, ed. Carolyn Merchant (Washington, DC: Island Press, 1989), 109–110.

43. Madley, *American Genocide*, 347.

44. Isenberg, *Mining California*, 37.

45. Ibid., 177.

46. Quoted in Narda Zacchino, *California Comeback: How a "Failed State" Became a Model for the Nation* (New York: St Martin's Press, 2016), 172.

47. Quoted in Kelley, *Mining Controversy*, 333.

48. Kelley, *Battling the Inland Land*, 202.

49. Isenberg, *Mining California*, 169.

50. Ziebarth, *California's First Environmental Battle*, 278.

51. Ibid., 279.

52. Ibid., 279.

53. In 1891, the California legislature did again permit hydraulic mining in response to a national economic recession on the condition that no debris reach the floor of the Sacramento Valley. The expense of building effective debris dams proved prohibitive, however, and while gold mining did continue in California, it employed other extractive technologies that did not discharge debris into rivers. Two years later, the U.S. Congress approved the Caminetti Act, named for its sponsor, California Rep. Anthony Caminetti, and strongly supported by the California state legislature. This act created the California Debris Commission, which was given the authority to license hydraulic mining operations, provided that the tailings were appropriately contained, and established the nation's third river commission.

54. Raymond Dasmann, "Environmental Changes Before and After the Gold Rush," in Rawls and Orsi, *Golden State*, 118.

55. Ziebarth, *California's First Environmental Battle*, 276.

56. Richard Orsi, *Sunset Limited: The Southern Pacific Railroad and the Development of the American West, 1850–1930* (Berkeley: University of California Press, 2005), xvii. In fact, one of the railroad's four leading partners, Leland Stanford, had earlier appointed Sawyer as a district judge in San Francisco when he served as the state's governor. In 1887, three years after the Sawyer decision, Stanford invited the judge to present the main address at the laying of the cornerstone for Stanford University, named in honor of his deceased son. Sawyer also served as the first president of the university's Board of Trustees. See Kelley, *Gold vs. Grain*, 124–125.

Chapter 3: Protecting the Land

1. Robert Binnewies, *Your Yosemite: A Threatened Public Treasure* (Ashland, OR: White Cloud Press, 2015), xi.

2. Ibid., 46.

3. Ibid., 47.

4. Francis Farquhar, *History of the Sierra Nevada* (Berkeley: University of California Press, 1965), 74.

5. Binnewies, *Your Yosemite*, 76.

6. Justin Martin, *Genius of Place: The Life of Frederick Law Olmsted* (Boston: Da Capo Press, 2011), 251.

7. Starr, *Americans and the California Dream*, 182.

8. John Sears, *Sacred Places: American Tourist Attractions in the Nineteenth Century* (New York: Oxford University Press, 1989), 122.

9. Starr, *Americans and the California Dream*, 183.

10. Sears, *Sacred Places*, 130.

11. Mark Stoll, *Inherit the Holy Mountain: Religion and the Rise of American Environmentalism* (New York: Oxford University Press, 2015), 100.

12. Sears, *Sacred Places*, 128.

13. All U.S. senators were appointed by state legislatures until ratification of the 17th Amendment in 1913, which established the present system of direct election.

14. Binnewies, *Your Yosemite*, 82.

15. Robert Righter, *The Battle over Hetch Hetchy: America's Most Controversial Dam and the Birth of Modern Environmentalism* (New York: Oxford University Press, 2005), 22.

16. Horace Greeley, *An Overland Journey from New York to San Francisco in the Summer of 1959* (1860), ch. 29, in Yosemite Online Library, http://www.yosemite.ca.us/library/greeley/big_trees.html.

17. *Economist*, "Climbing the World's Biggest Tree," December 24, 2016, 101.

18. Sears, *Sacred Places*, 130.

19. Sears, *Sacred Places*, 130.

20. Donald Worster, *A Passion for Nature; The Life of John Muir* (New York: Oxford University Press, 2008), 170.

21. Michael Cohen, *The History of the Sierra Club, 1972–1970* (San Francisco: Sierra Club Books, 1988), 3.

22. Starr, *Americans and the California Dream*, 182.

23. Quoted in Douglas Brinkley, *The Wilderness Warrior* (New York: Harper Perennial, 2010), 76.

24. Olmsted's influence on landscape development in California went beyond Yosemite. He also laid out the designs for both the University of California at Berkeley and Stanford University.

25. The Supreme Court subsequently invalidated Hutchings's claim to his property in Yosemite, and Congress then appropriated funds to buy his hotel as a way of keeping all of Yosemite in the public domain.

26. Cohen, *History of the Sierra Club*, 3.

27. Worster, *A Passion for Nature*, 165.

28. Stephen Fox, *John Muir and His Legacy: The American Conservation Movement* (Boston: Little Brown and Company, 1981), 56.

29. Ibid., 56.

30. Worster, *A Passion for Nature*, 162.

31. Cohen, *History of the Sierra Club*, 17.

32. John Muir, *The Yosemite* (1912), 256, in Sierra Club, http://vault.sierraclub.org/john_muir_exhibit/writings/the_yosemite/.

33. Fox, *John Muir*, 105.

34. Fox, *John Muir*, 106.

35. Worster, *A Passion for Nature*, 329.

36. Cohen, *History of the Sierra Club*, 11.

37. Susan Schrepfer, *The Fight to Save the Redwoods: A History of Environmental Reform, 1917–1978* (Madison: University of Wisconsin Press, 1983), 10.

38. Binnewies, *Your Yosemite*, 116.

39. Starr, *Americans and the California Dream*, 190.

40. Cohen, *History of the Sierra Club*, 12.

41. Fox, *John Muir*, 120.

42. Frank Graham, *The Adirondack Park; A Political History* (New York: Alfred Knopf, 1978), 114.

43. Worster, *A Passion for Nature*, 368; Joseph Engbeck, Jr., *State Parks of California from 1964 to the Present* (Oregon: Graphics Acts Center Publishing, 1980), 27.

44. Stoll, *Inherit the Holy Mountain*, 158.

45. Binnewies, *Your Yosemite*, 132.

46. Fox, *John Muir*, 128.

47. Worster, *A Passion for Nature*, 399.

48. The California grizzly bear is now extinct but appears on the state's flag. The last one was killed in 1922.

49. Jared Farmer, *Trees in Paradise: A California History* (New York: W. W. Norton & Company, 2013), 20, 18.

50. Ibid., 20.

51. Starr, *Americans and the California Dream*, 174.

52. Worster, *A Passion for Nature*, 234.

53. Farmer, *Trees in Paradise*, 32.

54. Farmer, *Trees in Paradise*, 41.

55. Worster, *A Passion for Nature*, 320.

56. William Tweed, *King Sequoia* (Berkeley, CA: Sierra College Press, 2016), 195.

57. Donald Pisani, "Forests and Conservation, 1865–1890," *Journal of American History* 72, no. 2 (September 1965), 345.

58. Andrew Eisenberg, *Mining California: An Ecological History* (New York: Hill and Wang, 2005), 177.

59. Samuel Hayes, *Conservation and the Gospel of Efficiency: The Progressive Conservation Movement, 1890–1920* (New York: Atheneum, 1974), 24.

60. In prehistoric times, the trees grew throughout the United States. Now they are only found in California.

61. Farmer, *Trees in Paradise*, 45.

62. Harry Merlo, "Redwoods—Romance and Reality," 2, http://foresthistory.org/Research/documents/Redwoods_HarryMerlo.pdf.

63. Farmer, *Trees in Paradise*, 46.

64. Ibid., 46 (italics added).

65. Gerald Nash, *State Government and Economic Development* (New York: Arno Press, 1979), 195.

66. Farmer, *Trees in Paradise*, 63.

67. Righter, *Battle Over Hetch Hetchy*, 123.

68. Fox, *John Muir*, 135–136.

69. Righter, *Battle Over Hetch Hetchy*, 123.

70. Farmer, *Trees in Paradise*, 66.

71. Farmer, *Trees in Paradise*, 66.

72. Richard Walker, *The Conquest of Bread: 150 Years of Agribusiness in California* (New York: New Press, 2004), 32.

73. Farmer, *Trees in Paradise*, 67.

74. Walker, *Conquest of Bread*, 32.

75. Engbeck, *State Parks*, 47.

76. Sarah Ekland, *How Local Politics Shape Federal Policy: Business, Power, and the Environment in Twentieth Century Los Angeles* (Chapel Hill: University of North Carolina Press, 2001), 78.

77. Paul Sabin, *Crude Politics: The California Oil Market, 1900–1940* (Berkeley: University of California Press, 2005), 95.

78. Engbeck, *State Parks*, 101.

79. Schrepfer, *Fight to Save the Redwoods*, 111.

80. Ibid., 128.

81. Farmer, *Trees in Paradise*, 80.

82. Schrepfer, *Fight to Save the Redwoods*, 151; Simon, Ted, "River Stops Here," *Hastings West-Northwest Journal of Environmental Law and Policy* 2 (1994): 5, 213.

83. Schrepfer, *Fight to Save the Redwoods*, 159.

84. Ibid., 161.

85. Farmer, *Trees in Paradise*, 81.

86. Constance McDermott, Benjamin Cashore, and Peter Kanowski, *Global Environmental Forest Policies: An International Comparison* (London: Earthscan, 2010), 107.

Chapter 4: Protecting California's Coast

1. Janet Adams, "Proposition 20—A Citizens' Campaign," *Syracuse Law Review* 24 (1973): 1019.

2. William Reilly, "Preface," in *Protecting the Golden Shore: Lessons from the California Coastal Commissions*, ed. Robert Healy, John Banta, John Clark and William Duddleson (Washington, DC: Conservation Foundation, 1978), xi.

3. Quoted in Sarah Ekland, *How Local Politics Shape Federal Policy: Business, Power and the Environment in Twentieth Century Los Angeles* (Chapel Hill: University of North Carolina Press, 2011), 22.

4. Quoted in ibid., 23–24.

5. Quoted in ibid., 25.

6. Quoted in ibid., 26.

7. Paul Sabin, *Crude Politics: The California Oil Market, 1900–1940* (Berkeley: University of California Press, 2005), 56.

8. Peter Asmus, *Introduction to Energy in California* (Berkeley: University of California Press, 2009), 32.

9. Sabin, *Crude Politics*, 80.

10. Ekland, *Local Politics*, 32.

11. Ekland, *Local Politics*, 44.

12. R. F. Yerkes, H. C. Wagner, and K. A. Young, *Petroleum Development in the Region of the Santa Barbara Channel* (U.S. Geological Survey, 1971), 67-B, 14.

13. Malcolm Baldwin, "The Santa Barbara Oil Spill," *University of Colorado Law Review* 42 (1970): 38.

14. Harvey Molotch, "Oil in Santa Barbara and Power in America," *Sociological Inquiry* 40 (Winter 1970): 131.

15. As of 2016, the Santa Barbara spill ranks third after Deepwater Horizon and Exxon Valdez, but remains the largest in California's history.

16. Through 2010, they had produced 260 million barrels of oil.

17. Richard Walker, *The Country in the City: The Greening of the San Francisco Bay Area* (Seattle: University of Washington Press, 2007), 63.

18. Ibid., 112.

19. Matthew Morse Booker, *Down by the Bay: San Francisco's History Between the Tides* (Berkeley: University of California Press, 2013), 175.

20. Janine Dolezel and Bruce Warren, "Saving San Francisco Bay: A Case Study in Environmental Legislation," *Stanford Law Review* 23, no. 2 (January 1971): 350.

21. Walker, *Country in the City*, 111.

22. Harold Gillam, *Between the Devil and the Deep Blue Sea: The Struggle to Save San Francisco Bay* (San Francisco: Chronicle Books, 1969), 83.

23. Dolezel and Warren, "Saving San Francisco Bay," 356.

24. Ibid., 364.

25. Ibid., 365.

26. Walker, *Country in the City*, 115.

27. Michael Storper, Thomas Kemeny, Naji Makarem, and Taner Osman, *The Rise and Fall of Urban Economies: Lessons from San Francisco and Los Angeles* (Stanford, CA: Stanford University Press, 2015), 154.

28. Zack Wasserman and Barry Nelson, "Challenges to the Future of the San Francisco Bay," *San Francisco Chronicle*, October 11, 2015.

29. Walker, *Country in the City*, 115.

30. Stanley Scott, *Governing California's Coast* (Berkeley, CA: Institute of Governmental Studies, 1975), 18.

31. Adams, "Proposition 20," 1020.

32. Scott, *Governing California's Coast*, 17.

33. Paul Sabatier and Daniel Mazmanian, *Can Regulation Work?: The Implementation of the 1972 California Coastal Initiative* (New York: Plenum Press, 1983), 32.

34. Ibid., 29.

35. Jared Orsi, "Restoring the Common to the Goose: Citizen Activism and the Protection of the California Coastline, 1969–1982," *Southern California Quarterly* 78, no. 3 (Fall 1966): 258–259.

36. Sabatier and Mazmanian, *Can Regulation Work?*, 33.

37. Peter Douglas, "Coastal Zone Management—A New Approach in California," *Coastal Zone Management Journal* 1, no. 1 (1973): 1–2.

38. William Duddleson, "How the Citizens of California Secured Their Coastal Management Program," in Healy, *Protecting the Golden Shore*, 9.

39. Orsi, "Restoring the Common," 161.

40. Orsi, "Restoring the Common," 262–263.

41. Duddleson, "How the Citizens of California," 13.

42. Orsi, "Restoring the Common," 263.

43. William Duddleson, "How the Citizens of California," 11.

44. Duddleson, "How the Citizens of California," 59.

45. Robert Healy, "The Role of the Permit System in the California Coastal Strategy," in Healy, *Protecting the Golden Shore*, 67.

46. Robert Healy, "An Economic Interpretation of the California Coastal Commission," in *Protecting the Golden Shore*, 140.

47. Adam Nagourney, "A Commission's Power Struggle Clouds California's Coast," *New York Times*, February 9, 2006.

48. Nagourney, "Commission's Power Struggle."

49. Orsi, "Restoring the Common," 273.

50. *Nollan v. California Coastal Commission*, 483 U.S. 825 (1987).

51. Jefferson Decker, "Pacific Views: Private Rights, the Regulatory State, and American Conservatism," *Journal of Policy History* 28, no. 4 (2016): 667.

52. Ibid., 669.

53. Nagourney, "Commission's Power Struggle."

54. Jon Christensen and Phillip King, "Beach Access Hard to Preserve," *San Francisco Chronicle*, December 16, 2016.

55. See, e.g., Walker, *Country in the City*; and Christopher Ansell, "Community Embeddedness and Collaborate Governance in the San Francisco Bay Area Environmental Movement," in *Social Movement and Networks*, ed. M. Diani and D. McAdam (New York: Oxford University Press, 2003), 125–143.

56. The two notable exceptions are Proposition 9, the 1982 Peripheral Canal initiative (discussed in the next chapter), and Proposition 65, the Safe Water and Toxic Enforcement Act of 1986.

57. Orsi, "Restoring the Common," 278.

Chapter 5: Managing Water Resources

1. David Carle, *Introduction of Water in California* (Berkeley: University of California Press, 2009), 3–6.

2. Sarah Phillips, "Resourceful Leaders: Governors and the Politics of the American Environment," in *A Legacy of Innovation: Governors and Public Policy*, ed. Ethan Sribnick (Philadelphia: University of Pennsylvania Press, 2008), 34.

3. Joe Mathews, "Fighting over Water Seems Easier Than Making Peace," *San Francisco Chronicle*, December 4, 2016.

4. For the Hetch Hetchy controversy, see Robert Righter, *The Battle over Hetch Hetchy: America's Most Controversial Dam and the Birth of Modern Environmentalism* (New York: Oxford University Press, 2005); Kendrick Clements, "Engineers and Conservationists in the Progressive Era," *California History* 58, no. 4 (1979): 282–303; and Roderick Frazier Nash, *Wilderness and the American Mind* (New Haven, CT: Yale University Press, 2001), 161–181.

5. Righter, *Battle over Hetch Hetchy*, 38.

6. Norris Hundley, Jr., *The Great Thirst: Californians and Water: A History* (Berkeley: University of California Press, 2001), 180.

7. Donald Worster, *Rivers of Empire: Water, Aridity, and the Growth of the American West* (New York: Oxford University Press, 1985), 425.

8. Hundley, *Great Thirst*, 181.

9. Righter, *Battle over Hetch Hetchy*, 73.

10. Quoted in ibid., 91.

11. Nash, *Wilderness and the American Mind*, 162.

12. Righter, *Battle over Hetch Hetchy*, 124.

13. Ibid., 195.

14. Hundley, *Great Thirst*, 186.

15. Michael Cohen, *The History of the Sierra Club, 1972–1970* (San Francisco: Sierra Club Books, 1988), 29–30.

16. Neil Maher, *Nature's New Deal: The Civilian Conservation Corps* (New York: Oxford University Press, 2008), 8.

17. Nash, *Wilderness and the American Mind*, 181.

18. Ibid., 180.

19. Marc Reisner, *Cadillac Desert: The American West and Its Disappearing Water* (New York: Penguin Books, 1993), 60–61.

20. Hundley, *Great Thirst*, 141.

21. For detailed accounts of Los Angeles and its water policies, see Gary Libecap, *Owens Valley Revisited: A Reassessment of the West's First Great Water Transfer* (Stanford, CA: Stanford University Press, 2007); Les Standiford, *Water to the Angels: William Mulholland, His Monumental Aqueduct, and the Rise of Los Angeles* (New York: HarperCollins, 2015); and Steven Erie, *Beyond Chinatown: The Metropolitan Water District, Growth, and the Environment in Southern California* (Stanford, CA: Stanford University Press, 2006). See also Steve Swatt and Susie Swatt, *Game Changers: Twelve Elections That Transformed California* (Berkeley: Heydey and California Historical Society, 2015), 39–58.

22. Libecap, *Owens Valley Revisited*, 64.

23. Ibid., 117.

24. Robert Reinhold, "Accords Reached Over Water, L.A. Yields Some Mono Lake Rights," *Los Angeles Daily News*, September 25, 1969, quoted in Libecap, *Owens Valley Revisited*, 19.

25. *Los Angeles Times*, "For Shame, San Francisco," September 2, 1986, quoted in Libecap, *Owens Valley Revisited*, 19.

26. Carl Nolte, "A Woeful Tale of Stolen Water, Quaking Earth," *San Francisco Chronicle*, September 4, 1986, quoted in Libecap, *Owens Valley Revisited*, 20–21.

27. Libecap, *Owens Valley Revisited*, 27.

28. Ibid. This assessment is echoed by Erie, *Beyond Chinatown*, 39.

29. Erie, *Beyond Chinatown*, 36. This controversy is also described in detail by Hundley, *Great Thirst*, 159–162.

30. Hundley, *Great Thirst*, 152.

31. Swatt and Swatt, *Game Changers*, 41.

32. Erie, *Beyond Chinatown*, 40.

33. Hundley, *The Great Thirst*, 155.

34. Ibid., 195.

35. Stephanie Pincetl, *Transforming California* (Baltimore: Johns Hopkins University Press, 1999), 51.

36. *Economist*, "A Hundred Years of Soggy Tubes," November 9, 2013, 35.

37. Hundley, *The Great Thirst*, 231.

38. Robert Kelley, *Battling the Inland Sea: Floods, Public Policy, and the Sacramento Valley* (Berkeley: University of California Press, 1989), 12.

39. Worster, *Rivers of Empire*, 239.

40. Worster, *Rivers of Empire*, 242.

41. Ethan Rarick, *California Rising: The Life and Times of Pat Brown* (Berkeley: University of California Press, 2005), 209.

42. Quoted in Hundley, *Great Thirst*, 279.

43. Rarick, *California Rising*, 210–211.

44. Hundley, *Great Thirst*, 284.

45. Ibid., 280.

46. Kevin Starr, *Golden Dreams: California in an Age of Abundance, 1950–1963* (New York: Oxford University Press, 2009), 269.

47. Rarick, *California Rising*, 227.

48. Ted Simon, *The River Stops Here: Saving Round Valley, a Pivotal Chapter in California's Water Wars* (Berkeley: University of California Press, 2001), 166.

49. Ibid., 325.

50. Alexander Gaguine, "The Campaign to Save the Stanislaus River—1969 to 1982 and Its Historic Importance," *Headwaters*, April 18, 2009.

51. Quoted in Hundley, *Great Thirst*, 373.

52. Justin Gillis, "A Rush of Dilemmas," *New York Times*, December 22, 2015; see also Carolyn Lochhead, "A Future of Dams," *San Francisco Chronicle*, August 28, 2015.

53. Carle, *Introduction of Water in California*, 42–43.

54. Simon, *River Stops Here*, 263.

55. Ibid., 264.

56. Hundley, *Great Thirst*, 323.

57. Richard Rice, William Bullough, and Richard Orsi, *The Elusive Eden: A New History of California* (Boston: McGraw Hill, 2002), 592.

58. Hundley, *Great Thirst*, 323.

59. Rice, *Elusive Eden*, 593.

60. Hundley, *Great Thirst*, 327.

61. Quoted in Mark Arax and Rick Wartzman, *The King of California: J. G. Boswell and the Making of a Secret American Empire* (New York: Perseus Book Group, 2003), 352.

62. Reisner, *Cadillac Desert*, 366.

63. Arax and Wartzman, *King of California*, 359.

64. Libecap, *Owens Valley Revisited*, 129.

65. Adam Nagourney, "A Century On, the 'Chinatown' Water Feud Ebbs," *New York Times*, January 21, 2013.

66. Libecap, *Owens Valley Revisited*, 140.

67. Hundley, *Great Thirst*, 346.

68. Ibid., 346.

69. Ellen Hanak, Jay Lund, Ariel Dinar, Brian Gray, Richard Howitt, Jeffrey Mount, Peter Moyle, and Barton Thompson, *Managing California's Water: From Conflict to Reconciliation* (San Francisco: Public Policy Institute of California, 2011), 53–54.

70. Erie, *Beyond Chinatown*, 58.

71. Gillis, "A Rush of Dilemmas."

72. Richard Walker, *The Conquest of Bread: 150 Years of Agribusiness in California* (New York: New Press, 2004), 1.

73. Ibid., 178.

74. Referenced in Reisner, *Cadillac Desert*, 510.

75. Susan Kostal, "Drought Sheds Light on California's Water Law Deficiencies," *ABA Journal—National Pulse*, March 1, 2016.

76. Noah Diffenaugh and Christopher Field, "A Wet Winter Won't Save California," *New York Times*, September 19, 2015.

77. Ian Lovett, "As Drought Becomes the New Normal, California Acts to Preserve Its Water Supplies," *New York Times*, May 10, 2016.

78. Doug Parker, "California's Water Paradox: Why Enough Will Never Be Enough," *Conversation*, May 19, 2015.

Chapter 6: Protecting Air Quality

1. Even the European Union has the same vehicle emission standards for each of its twenty-seven member states.

2. Ann Carlson, "Energy Efficiency and Federalism," *Michigan Law Review* 107 (2008): 68.

3. Quoted in James Krier and Edmund Ursin, *Pollution and Policy: A Case Essay on California and Federal Experience with Motor Vehicle Air Pollution, 1940–1975* (Berkeley: University of California Press, 1977), 45.

4. Starr, *Golden Dream*, 260.

5. Quoted in Krier and Ursin, *Pollution and Policy*, 45.

6. Ibid., 44.

7. Marvin Brienes, "Smog Comes to Los Angeles," *Southern California Quarterly* 58, no. 4 (Winter 1976): 517–518.

8. Ekland, *How Politics Shape Federal Policy*, 56.

9. Brienes, "Smog Comes to Los Angeles," 520.

10. Krier and Ursin, *Pollution and Policy*, 53.

11. Brienes, "Smog Comes to Los Angeles," 520.

12. Starr, *Golden Dream*, 259.

13. Quoted in George Gonzalez, "Urban Growth and the Politics of Air Pollution: The Establishment of California's Automobile Emission Standards," *Polity* 33, no. 2 (Winter 2002): 223.

14. Ekland, *How Politics Shape Federal Policy*, 8.

15. Quoted in David Carle, *Introduction to Air in California* (Berkeley: University of California Press, 2006), 79.

16. Quoted in John Baur, *The Health Seekers of Southern California, 1870–1900* (San Marino, CA: Huntington Library, 1959), 31.

17. Chip Jacobs and William Kelly, *Smogtown: The Lung-Burning History of Pollution in Los Angeles* (New York: Overlook Press, 2008), 30.

18. Krier and Ursin, *Pollution and Policy*, 61.

19. Jacobs and Kelly, *Smogtown*, 36.

20. Quoted in ibid., 36.

21. Quoted in Gonzalez, "Urban Growth," 225.

22. Ibid., 225.

23. Wyn Grant, *Autos, Smog and Pollution Control: The Politics of Air Quality Management in California* (Aldershot, UK: Edward Elgar, 1995), 31.

24. Scott Hamilton Dewey, *Don't Breathe the Air: Air Pollution and U.S. Environmental Politics, 1945–1970* (College Station: Texas A&M University Press, 2000), 55.

25. Ibid., 58.

26. Ibid., 56.

27. Krier and Ursin, *Pollution and Policy*, 74.

28. Ibid., 76.

29. National Academy of Sciences, "Biography of Haagen-Smit," in *Biographical Memoirs*, Vol. 58 (Washington, DC: National Academies Press, 1989), 197.

30. Quoted in Carle, *Introduction to Air in California*, 135.

31. Starr, *Golden Dream*, 260.

32. Scott Harrison, "California Retrospective: 'Smog Sieges' Often Accompanied September Heat from the 1950s to '80s," *Los Angeles Times*, September 9, 2015, http://www.latimes.com/local/california/la-me-heat-smog-20150910-story.html.

33. Gonzalez, "Urban Growth," 226.

34. Ibid., 227.

35. Quoted in Krier and Ursin, *Pollution and Policy*, 89.

36. Ibid., 91.

37. Scott Bottles, *Los Angeles and the Automobile: The Making of a Modern City* (Berkeley: University of California Press, 1987), 5.

38. Ibid., 107.

39. Quoted in ibid., 2.

40. Quoted in Grant, *Autos, Smog and Pollution Control*, 38.

41. Bottles, *Los Angeles and the Automobile*, 4.

42. Quoted in ibid., 92.

43. Jacobs and Kelly, *Smogtown*, 162.

44. Dewey, *Don't Breathe the Air*, 59.

45. Bottles, *Los Angeles and the Automobile*, 15.

46. Ibid., 69.

47. Quoted in Grant, *Autos, Smog and Pollution Control*, 40.

48. Quoted in ibid., 38.

49. Jacobs and Kelly, *Smogtown*, 162.

50. Jeffry Fawcett, *The Political Economy of Smog in Southern California* (New York: Garland Publishing, 1990), 84.

51. Paul Rhode, *The Evolution of California Manufacturing* (San Francisco: Public Policy Institute of California, 2001), 31. Barry Rabe and Philip Mundo, "Business Influence in State-Level Environmental Policy," in *Business and Environmental Policy*, ed. Michael Kraft and Sheldon Kamieniecki (Cambridge, MA: MIT Press, 2007), 282.

52. Starr, *Golden Dream*, 249.

53. Quoted in Krier and Ursin, *Pollution and Policy*, 106.

54. Ibid., 109.

55. Ibid., 113.

56. "Oxy-Catalyst Gears for Auto Exhaust Market: Timing Depends on California's Approval of Exhaust Control Devices, but Company Is Set to Make Converters and Catalyst," *Chemical Engineering News* 40, no. 19 (1962): 36–37, http://pubs.acs.org/doi/pdf/10.1021/cen-v040n019.p036.

57. Jacobs and Kelly, *Smogtown*, 169.

58. Krier and Ursin, *Pollution and Policy*, 171.

59. Ibid., 173.

60. Dewey, *Don't Breathe the Air*, 75.

61. Ibid., 76.

62. National Academy of Sciences, "Biography of Haagen-Smit," 200.

63. Jacobs and Kelly, *Smogtown*, 175.

64. Dewey, *Don't Breathe the Air*, 77.

65. Jacobs and Kelly, *Smogtown*, 176.

66. Krier and Ursin, *Pollution and Policy*, 182.

67. Jacobs and Kelly, *Smogtown*, 177.

68. Ibid., 178.

69. This paragraph is based on Christopher McCrory and David Sousa, *American Environmental Policy, 1990–2006: Beyond Gridlock* (Cambridge, MA: MIT Press, 2008), 280–281.

70. Krier and Ursin, *Pollution and Policy*, 209.

71. Ibid., 189.

72. Data in this paragraph are from Ann Carlson, "Iterative Federalism and Climate Change," *Northwestern University Law Review* 103 (2009): 1116, 1118.

73. Quoted in ibid., 1115.

74. National Academy of Sciences, *State and Federal Standards for Mobile-Source Emissions* (Washington, DC: National Academy Press, 2006), 94–95; see 92–93 for a detailed statistical comparison of California and federal standards between 1966 and 2003. See also Carlson, "Iterative Federalism," 1116–1117.

75. Carlson, "Iterative Federalism," 1113–1115.

76. Ibid., 1097.

77. William Lowry, *The Dimensions of Federalism: State Governments and Pollution Control Programs* (Durham, NC: Duke University Press, 1992), 92. The state inspection program is also discussed by Krier and Ursin, *Pollution and Policy*, 214–215.

78. This discussion is based on David Calef and Robert Goble, "The Allure of Technology: How France and California Promoted Electric and Hybrid Vehicles to Reduce Urban Air Pollution," *Policy Sciences* 40 (2007): 6–13.

79. Carlson, "Iterative Federalism," 1120.

80. Ibid., 1124.

81. Dorothy Thornton, Robert A. Kagan, and Neil Gunningham, "When Social Norms and Pressures Are Not Enough: Environmental Performance in the Trucking Industry," *Law and Society Review* 43, no. 2 (2009): 410–413.

82. See the California Air Resources Board website at https://ww2.arb.ca.gov/.

83. Carlson, "Energy Efficiency and Federalism," 68.

84. California Air Resources Board.

85. Ibid.

86. Gregg Esterbrook, "Let's Modernize Our Pollution Laws," *New York Times*, October 8, 2015.

87. David Pettit, "Why Is California 'worst'?," CNN, May 2, 2014, http://www.cnn.com/2014/05/02/opinion/pettit-california-pollution/.

88. Michael Storper, Thomas Kemeny, Naji Makarem, and Taner Osman, *The Rise and Fall of Urban Economies: Lessons from San Francisco and Los Angeles* (Stanford, CA: Stanford University Press, 2015), 108.

89. *San Francisco Chronicle*, "How Housing Shortage Takes Toll on Environment," April 27, 2017.

90. Lowry, *Dimensions of Federalism*, 80.

91. Ibid., 96.

92. Paul Rogers, "California's 'Clean Car' Rules Help Remake U.S. Auto Industry," *Environment 360*, February 8, 2012.

93. Ibid.

94. Lowry, *Dimensions of Federalism*, 94.

95. Wendy Leavitt, "The California Effect," *Fleet Owner*, March 1, 2010.

96. For its international impact, see George Hoberg and Gordon McCullough, "The 'California Effect' on Canadian Energy and Climate Policies," *Green Policy Prof* (blog), July 6, 2009, http://greenpolicyprof.org/wordpress?p=263.

Chapter 7: Energy Efficiency and Climate Change

1. Timothy Duanne, "Regulation's Rationale: Learning from the California Energy Crisis," *Yale Journal of Regulation* 19 (2002): 482.

2. Arthur Rosenfeld and Deborah Poskanzer, "A Graph Is Worth a Thousand Gigawatt-Hours: How California Came to Lead the United States in Energy Efficiency," *Innovations* 4, no. 4 (2009): 57–79.

3. Jerry Gillam, "Reagan Signs Bill to Create State Energy Control Board," *Los Angeles Times*, May 22, 1974.

4. *Sacramento Union*, "Energy Planning Bill Offered," December 2, 1973.

5. *Sacramento Bee*, "Governor Should Sign Energy Bill," September 20, 1973.

6. Rosenfeld and Poskanzer, "Graph Is Worth," 62.

7. For a personal narrative of how this policy shift came about and the challenges faced by the Environmental Defense Fund in persuading the CPUC and the utility firms to adopt it, see

David Roe, *Dynamos and Virgins: An Advocate's Personal Account of the Struggle to Force a New Idea, and a New Future, on the Nation's Power Companies* (New York: Random House, 1984).

8. Rosenfeld and Poskanzer, "A Graph Is Worth," 70.

9. Ibid., 64.

10. W. Michael Hanemann, "How California Came to Pass AB 32, the Global Warming Solutions Act of 2006" (University of California at Berkeley: Department of Agricultural and Resource Economics, 2007), 6.

11. Arik Levinson, "California Energy Efficiency: Lessons for the Rest of the World," *Journal of Economic Behavior and Organization* 107 (2014): 289.

12. Roger Karapin, *Political Opportunities for Climate Policy: California, New York, and the Federal Government* (New York: Cambridge University Press, 2016), 129.

13. Rosenfeld and Poskanzer, "Graph Is Worth," 67–69.

14. Ibid., 70.

15. Ibid., 70.

16. This and the next paragraph are based on Hanemann, "How California Came to Pass," 7–8; and Steve Nadel, Andrew deLaski, Jim Kleisch, and Toru Uubol, "Leading the Way: Continued Opportunities for New State Appliance and Equipment Efficiency Standards," Report No. ASAP-5/SCEEE-A051, January 2004, 1–3.

17. Tatiana Schlossberg, "California Will Regulate the Energy Efficiency of Desktop Computers and Monitors," *New York Times*, December 16, 2016.

18. Ann Carlson, "Energy Efficiency and Federalism," *Michigan Law Review First Impressions* 107 (2008), http://repository.law.umich.edu/cgi/viewcontent.cgi?article=1083&context=mlr_fi.

19. Arik Levinson, "California Energy Efficiency: Lessons for the Rest of the World or Not?," National Bureau of Economic Research Working Paper 19223, June 2013.

20. Cynthia Mitchell, "Stabilizing California's Demand," *Fortnightly Magazine* (March 2009). See also Dan Walters, "Economist Questions California's Energy Conservation Claims," *Fresno Bee.com*, July 29, 2013.

21. Levinson, "California's Energy Efficiency," 271.

22. Lara Ettenson, "Report: California an Energy Efficiency Powerhouse, but Meeting Long-term Energy and Climate Goals Requires More," *National Resources Defense Council Expert Blog*, August 20, 2015, https://www.nrdc.org/experts/lara-ettenson/report-california-energy-efficiency-powerhouse-meeting-long-term-energy.

23. Levinson, "California's Energy Efficiency," 272–273.

24. Umair Irfan, "Solar, Utility Companies Clash over Changes to New Metering," *ClimateWire*, September 2, 2013.

25. Guide Franco, Dan Nayan, Amy Luers, Michael Hanemann, and Bart Croes, "Linking Climate Change Science with Policy in California," *Climate Change* 87, suppl. 1 (2008): S7–S20.

26. Kristen Engel and Barak Orbach, "Micro-Motives and State and Local Climate Change Initiatives," *Harvard Law and Policy Review* 2 (2008): 125.

27. Karapin, *Political Opportunities*, 139.

28. Kevin Golden, "Senate Bill 1078: The Renewable Portfolio Standard—California Asserts Its Renewable Energy Leadership," *Ecology Law Quarterly* 30 (2003): 712.

29. Barry Rabe, *Statehouse and Greenhouse: The Emerging Politics of American Climate Change Policy* (Washington, DC: Brookings Institution Press, 2004), 53.

30. Golden, "Senate Bill 1078," 703.

31. Garry Polakovic and Miguel Bustillo, "Davis Signs Bill to Cut Greenhouse Gases," *Los Angeles Times*, July 23, 2002.

32. Greg Lucas, "Push to Pass Greenhouse Gas Measure," *San Francisco Chronicle*, January 22, 2002.

33. Danny Hakim, "Steering California's Fight on Emissions," *New York Times*, December 9, 2004.

34. Karapin, *Political Opportunities*, 150.

35. Ibid., 143.

36. Barry Rabe, "Governing the Climate from Sacramento," in *Unlocking the Power of Networks*, ed. Stephen Goldsmith and Donald Kettl (Washington, DC: Brookings Institution Press, 2009), 40.

37. Stuart Brown, "California Rocks the Auto Industry," *Fortune*, September 1, 2004, 154.

38. Ibid.

39. William Booth, "California Takes the Lead on Curbing Auto Emissions," *Washington Post National Weekly Edition*, July 29–August 4, 2002.

40. Ibid.

41. Rabe, *Statehouse and Greenhouse*, 141.

42. Through 2001, more than seventy waiver requests had been granted and only seven denied; the latter, however, were on narrow technical grounds and of marginal importance. Barry Rabe, "Leveraged Federalism and the Clean Air Act: The Case of Vehicle Emissions Control," paper presented to the American Academy of Arts and Sciences, June 30, 2017, 32–35. The quotations in this paragraph are from Zachery Collie, "Behind EPA's Rejection of State Emission Rules, *SFGate*, January 24, 2008.

43. *Economist*, "Gold and Green," March 16, 2013, 29.

44. William Reilly, "California Driving Clean-Air Future," *San Francisco Chronicle*, January 21, 2013.

45. Franco et al., "Linking Climate Change Science."

46. Alexander Farrell and W. Michael Hanemann, "Field Notes on the Political Economy of California Climate Policy," in *Changing Climates in North American Politics*, ed. Henrik Selin and Stacy D. VanDeever (Cambridge, MA: MIT Press, 2009), 87.

47. Nine Hall and Ros Taplin, "Environmental Nonprofit Campaigns and State Competition: Influences on Climate Policy in California," *Voluntas* 21 (2010): 64.

48. The previous year, the governor of Oregon had set of target of reducing GHG emissions 10 percent below 1990 levels by 2020 and 75 percent below 1990 levels by 2050. The numbers Schwarzenegger selected were designed to make California's targets the most ambitious. Farrell and Hanemann, "Field Notes," 107.

49. Daniel Mazmanian, John Jurewitz, and Hal Nelson, "California's Climate Change Policy: The Case of a Subnational State Actor Tackling a Global Challenge," *Journal of Environment and Development* 17, no. 4 (December 2008): 409.

50. Hall and Taplin, "Environmental Nonprofit Campaigns," 75.

51. Rabe, "Governing the Climate from Sacramento," 38.

52. Ann Carlson, "Federalism, Preemption, and Greenhouse Gas Emissions," *University of California, Davis, Law Review* 37 (2002): 291.

53. Ibid., 281.

54. Farrell and Hanemann, "Field Notes," 102.

55. Mary Nichols, "California's Climate Change Program: Lessons for the Nation," *UCLA Journal of Environmental Law* 27 (2009): 188.

56. Matthew Garrahan, "California Sunshine Is Source of Power," *Financial Times*, September 12, 2012.

57. Next 10, *California Green Innovation Index*, 6th ed. (Next 10, 2014), http://www.next10 .org/sites/next10.org/files/2014%20Green%20Innovation%20Index.pdf, 18, 31; Patrick Burtis,

Creating the California Clean Tech Cluster (Natural Resources Defense Council, Environmental Entrepreneurs, September 2004); Nina Kelsey and Alice Madden with Juliana Mandell and Sean Randolph, "The United States: Local Green Spirals, National Ambiguity," in *Can Green Sustain Growth?*, ed. John Zysman and Mark Huberty (Stanford, CA: Stanford University Press, 2014), 135.

58. Janelle Knox-Hayes, "Negotiating Climate Change Legislation: Policy Path Dependence and Coalition Stabilization," *Regulation and Governance* 6, no. 4 (2012): 555.

59. Karapin, *Political Opportunities*, 160.

60. Mazmanian, Jurewitz, and Nelson, "California's Climate Change Policy," 409.

61. Timothy Duane, "Greening the Grid: Implementing Climate Change Policy Through Energy Efficiency, Renewable Portfolio Standards, and Strategic Transmission Investments," *Vermont Law Review* 34 (2010): 736.

62. Barry Rabe, "A New Era in States' Climate Policies?" in *Changing Climate Politics: U.S. Policies and Civic Action*, ed. Yael Wolinsky-Nahmias (Los Angeles: Sage Publications and University of California Press, 2013), 67.

63. Karen Breslau, "The Green Giant," *Newsweek*, April 16, 2007.

64. John Farrell, "California Seeks a Million Solar Roofs by 2018," *Energy: Democratizing the Electricity System* (blog), Institute for Local Self-Reliance, March 9, 2005, https://ilsr.org/california-seeks-million-solar-roofs-2018/.

65. For a more general discussion of the growth of political opposition to state climate change initiatives, see Leah Stokes, "Power Politics: Renewable Energy Policy Change in US States" (unpublished Ph.D. diss., Massachusetts Institute of Technology, June 2015).

66. Stephen Ansolabehere and David Konisky, *Cheap and Clean: How American Think About Energy in the Age of Global Warming* (Cambridge, MA: MIT Press, 2014), 173.

67. Ibid., 173–174.

68. Eric Biber, "Cultivating a Green Political Landscape: Lessons for Climate Change Policy from the Defeat of California's Proposition 23," *Vanderbilt Law Review* 66, no. 2 (2013): 421–422.

69. Kelsey and Madden, "Local Green Spirals," 135, 130.

70. Next 10, *California Green Innovation Index*, 31, 41.

71. Marc Lifshwer, "Ballot Initiatives Divide a Usually United Business Front," *Los Angeles Times*, October 31, 2010.

72. Biber, "Cultivating a Green Political Landscape," 401.

73. Associated Press, "California Passes Sweeping Auto Emission Standards," *Fox News*, January 28, 2012, http://www.foxnews.com/politics/2012/01/28/california-passes-sweeping-auto-emission-standards.html.

74. Tesla, "Tesla First Quarter 2016 Update," May 4, 2016, http://files.shareholder.com/downloads/ABEA-4CW8X0/1034511691x0x889927/27EE2FDA-9C77-4D6A-8CEE-E8DFE45227BA/Q1_2016_Tesla_Shareholder_Letter.pdf.

75. California Air Resources Board, "Advanced Clean Cars Summary," http://www.arb.ca.gov/msprog/clean_cars/acc%20summary-final.pdf, 2.

76. David Baker, "State's Climate Fight Showing Progress," *San Francisco Chronicle*, September 25, 2016.

77. Ibid.

78. Kathleen Pender, "Electric Vehicle Tax Credit at Risk," *San Francisco Chronicle*, February 26, 2017.

79. Hiroko Tabuchi, "Behind the Quiet State-by-State Fight over Electric Vehicles," *New York Times*, March 11, 2017.

80. Matthew Garrahan, "California Sunshine Is Source of Power," *Financial Times*, September 12, 2012.

81. For a comprehensive study of emissions trading in the United States Europe, see Leigh Raymond, *Reclaiming the Atmospheric Commons: The Regional Greenhouse Gas Initiative and a New Model of Emission Trading* (Cambridge, MA: MIT Press, 2016).

82. David Baker, "Foes See Disaster; Backers See Boon to Factories, Jobs," *San Francisco Chronicle*, November 12, 2012.

83. *Wall Street Journal*, "California's Cap-and-Trade Bubble," May 31, 2016.

84. David Baker, "Uncertainty Dogs Future of Cap-Trade in California," *San Francisco Chronicle*, August 7, 2016; see also David Roberts, "California's Signature Climate Policy Is Struggling Through Its Awkward Teen Years," *Vox*, June 21, 2016.

85. Mark Chediak and Joe Ryan, "California Fights to Save Market Plan to Cut Carbon Emissions," *Business Week*, September 7, 2016.

86. Barry Rabe, "The Durability of Carbon Cap-and Trade Policy," *Governance* 29, no. 1 (2016): 103–119.

87. David Baker, "Compromise Gives New Life to Far-Reaching Bill on Energy," *San Francisco Chronicle*, September 13, 2013.

88. David Baker, "Surviving Solar Firms See Explosive Growth," *San Francisco Chronicle*, January 20, 2014.

89. John Diaz, "Keeping the California Climate Green," *San Francisco Chronicle*, December 11, 2016.

90. Mark Hertsgaard, "Big Electric Shocks Big Oil," *Business Week*, October 22, 2015.

91. Hiroko Tabuchi, "After Rapid Growth, Rooftop Solar Programs Dim Under Pressure from Utility Lobbyists," *New York Times*, July 9, 2017.

92. Chris Megerian and Michael Finnegan, "California's Greenhouse Gas Emission Targets Are Getting Tougher," *Los Angeles Times*, April 29, 2015.

93. Adam Nagourney, "Bill to Slash Emission of Carbon Opens Up a California Divide," *New York Times*, September 6, 2015.

94. Ibid.

95. Ibid.

96. Hertsgaard, "Big Electric Shocks Big Oil."

97. Benjamin Elgin, "Skip the Esso, Let's Stop at the PG&E," *Business Week*, May 5, 2016.

98. James Bushnell, "Breaking News! California Electricity Prices Are High," *Energy Institute Blog*, University of California, Berkeley Energy Institute, February 21, 2017, https://energy athaas.wordpress.com/2017/02/21/breaking-news-california-electricity-prices-are-high/.

99. Anne Mulkern, "Can the Golden State Go 100% Green?," *E&E News*, March 13, 2017, https://www.eenews.net/stories/1060051344.

100. *Economist*, "Paris-on-Sea," July 22, 2017, 23.

101. Brad Plumer, "Just How Far Can California Possibly Go on Climate?," *New York Times*, July 27, 2017, https://www.nytimes.com/2017/07/26/climate/california-climate-policy-cap-trade.html.

102. Melanie Mason and Chris Megerian, "California Legislature Extends State's Cap-and-Trade Program in Rare Bipartisan Effort to Address Climate Change," *Los Angeles Times*, July 17, 2017, http://www.latimes.com/politics/la-pol-ca-california-climate-change-vote-republicans-201 70717-story.html.

103. Ibid.

104. Ibid.

105. Associated Press, "California Knocks Trump as It Extends Climate Change Effort," *Newsmax*, July 26, 2017, http://www.newsmax.com/US/US-California-Climate-Change/2017/07/26 /id/803830/.

106. *New York Times*, "California Leads, Again, on Climate," July 24, 2007.

107. Associated Press, "California Knocks Trump."

108. Steven Greenhut, "Cap-and-Trade Passage Is About Raising Taxes, Divvying Up the Spoils," California Policy Center, July 19, 2017, http://californiapolicycenter.org/cap-trade-passage-raising-taxes-divvying-spoils/.

109. The data in this paragraph are based on Baker, "State's Climate Fight."

110. Eduardo Porter, "Progress Stunted by a Nuclear Hurdle," *New York Times*, January 18, 2017.

111. Plumer, "Just How Far."

112. For a good analysis of the state's regulatory strategies and the interaction among them, see Michael Wara, "California's Energy and Climate Policy: A Full Plate, but Perhaps Not a Role Model," *Bulletin of the Atomic Scientists* 70, no. 5 (2014): 26–34.

113. This section is based on Carolyn Lochhead, "Brown Takes Lead in Climate Battle," *San Francisco Chronicle*, November 27, 2016; Jon Lappen, "California Champions Cross-Border Climate Innovations," *American Prospect*, October 26, 2016; Megerian and Finnegan, "California's Greenhouse Gas Emission Targets."

114. This estimate is based on 2005 projections. See Kristen Engel and Scott Saleska, "Subglobal Regulation of the Global Commons," *Ecology Law Quarterly* 32, no. 2 (2005): 183–233.

115. Chris Megerian, John Myers, and Jessica Meyers, "Gov. Brown, America's Unofficial Climate Change Ambassador in the Trump Era, Heads to China," *Los Angeles Times*, June 1, 2017.

116. Lisa Friedman, "Governor of California Plans Summit on Climate," *New York Times*, July 7, 2017.

117. Megerian and Finnegan, "California's Greenhouse Gas Emission Targets."

118. Ibid.

119. Jennifer Madina and Matt Richtel, "Carbon Goal in California Is 'Milestone' on Climate," *New York Times*, August 26, 2016.

120. Plumer, "Just How Far."

121. According to one study, between 8 and 27 percent of the state's 2013–2015 drought can be attributed to global warming. See Park Williams, "How Much Has Global Warming Worsened California's Drought? Now We Have a Number," *Conversation*, August 20, 2015, https://the conversation.com/how-much-has-global-warming-worsened-californias-drought-now-we-have-a-number-46445; see also Noah Diffenbaugh and Christopher Field, "A Wet Winter Won't Save California," *New York Times*, September 19, 2015.

122. John Diaz, "Grim Glimpse into Climate's Future," *San Francisco Chronicle*, September 3, 2017.

123. The political importance of this linkage is a central argument in Ansolabehere and Konisky, *Cheap and Clean*.

124. Karapin, *Political Opportunities*, 81.

125. Rabe, "Governing the Climate from Sacramento," 43.

126. The links between earlier state efforts to control air pollution and California's more recent enactment of climate policies is emphasized by Karapin in his study of both New York and California. Roger Karapin, *Political Opportunities for Climate Policy: California, New York, and the Federal Government* (New York: Cambridge University Press, 2016).

127. Carlson, "Regulatory Capacity," 65.

Chapter 8: California's Regulatory Leadership: Broader Implications

1. Sarah Phillips, "Resourceful Leaders; Governors and the Politics of the American Environment," in *A Legacy of Innovation: Governors and Public Policy*, ed. Ethan Sribnick (Philadelphia: University of Pennsylvania Press, 2008), 26.

2. Daniel Esty, "Revitalizing Environmental Federalism," *Michigan Law Review* 95 (1996): 641–642 (italics added).

3. See, e.g., David Stradling, *The Nature of New York: An Environmental History of the Empire State* (Ithaca, NY: Cornell University Press, 2010); Frank Graham, Jr., *The Adirondack Park* (New York: Alfred Knopf, 1978); David Stradling, *Mountains: New York City and the Catskills* (Seattle: University of Washington Press, 2007); Ellen Stroud, *Nature Next Door: Cities and Trees in the American Northeast* (Seattle: University of Washington Press, 2012); Jack Davis and Raymond Arsenault, eds., *Paradise Lost?: The Environmental History of Florida* (Gainesville: University Press of Florida, 2005); Howard Ernst, *Fight for the Bay: Why a Dark Green Awakening Is Needed to Save the Chesapeake Bay* (Lanham, MD: Rowman & Littlefield, 2010).

4. Stradling, *Nature of New York*, 102.

5. Ibid., 104.

6. See, e.g., Sheldon Kamieniecki, *Corporate America and Environmental Policy: How Often Does Business Get Its Way?* (Stanford, CA: Stanford University Press, 2006); Judith Layzer, *Open for Business: Conservative Opposition to Environmental Regulation* (Cambridge, MA: MIT Press, 2012); and several of the essays in Michael E. Kraft and Sheldon Kamieniecki, eds., *Business and Environmental Policy: Corporate Interests in the American Political System* (Cambridge, MA: MIT Press, 2007).

7. Rabe and Mundo, "Business Influence," 274.

8. Ibid.

9. See Arlie Russell Hochschild, *Strangers in Their Own Land* (New York: New Press, 2016).

10. James Willard Hurst, *Law and Economic Growth: The Legal History of the Lumber Industry in Wisconsin, 1836–1915* (Cambridge, MA: Harvard University Press, 1964).

11. Jack Davis, "Florida by Nature," in *The History of Florida*, ed. Michael Gannon (Gainesville: University Press of Florida, 1996), 279–384.

12. Samuel Hayes, *Conservation and the Gospel of Efficiency: The Progressive Conservation Movement, 1890–1920* (New York: Atheneum, 1974).

13. See, e.g., Christine Meisner Rosen, "Businessmen Against Pollution in Late Nineteenth Century Chicago," *Business History Review* 69, no. 3 (Autumn 1995): 351–397. For a historical study of water pollution control at the state level that pitted the Pennsylvania Railroad against several coal companies, see Nicholas Casner, "Polluter Versus Polluter: The Pennsylvania Railroad and the Manufacturing of Pollution Policies in the 1920s," *Journal of Policy History* 11, no. 2 (1999): 179–200.

14. David Vogel, *Fluctuating Fortunes: The Political Power of Business in America* (New York: Basic Books, 1989). Two recent exceptions on whose work I have drawn are Sarah Ekland, *How Local Politics Shape Federal Policy: Business, Power, and the Environment in Twentieth-Century Los Angeles* (Chapel Hill: University of North Carolina Press, 2011); George Gonzalez, *The Politics of Air Pollution: Urban Growth, Ecological Modernization, and Symbolic Inclusion* (Albany: State University of New York Press, 2005).

15. A typical book on American environmental policy devotes one chapter or essay to state environmental policies. See, e.g., Christopher Klyza and David Sousa, "The States and Environmental Policy," in their volume *American Environmental Policy: Beyond Gridlock* (Cambridge, MA: MIT Press, 2013), 247–286; Denise Scheberle, "Environmental Federalism and the Role of States and Local Governments," in *The Oxford Handbook of U.S. Environmental Policy*, ed. Sheldon Kamieniecki and Michael Kraft (New York: Oxford University Press, 2013), 394–412; and Barry Rabe, "Racing to the Top, the Bottom, or the Middle of the Pack?: The Evolving State Government Role in Environmental Protection," in his volume *Environmental Policy: New Directions for the Twenty-First Century* (Washington, DC: Sage and CQ Press, 2016), 33–57.

16. Klyza and Sousa, *American Environmental Policy*, 237.

17. Stradling, *Nature of New York*, 103.

18. See David Stradling, *Smokestacks and Progressives* (Baltimore: Johns Hopkins Press, 1999).

19. Richard Judd, *Common Lands, Common People: The Origins of Conservation in Northern New England* (Cambridge, MA: Harvard University Press, 1997).

20. *Newsweek*, "E Pluribus Plures: Without Leadership from Washington, the States Set the Environmental Agenda for the Nation," November 13, 1989, 70.

21. Matthew Potoski, "Clean Air Federalism: Do States Race to the Bottom?," *Public Administration Review* 61, no. 3 (2001): 337.

22. Vivian Thomson and Vicki Arroyo, "Upside-Down Cooperative Federalism: Climate Change Policymaking and the States," *Virginia Environmental Law Journal* 29 (2011): 1–62.

23. Rabe and Mundo, "Business Influence," 292.

24. See, e.g., Barry Rabe, Michael Roman, and Arthur Debelis, "State Competition as a Source Driving Climate Change Mitigation," *New York University Law Journal* 14 (2005): 1–53; Barry Rabe, *Statehouse and Greenhouse: The Emerging Politics of American Climate Change Policy* (Washington, DC: Brookings, 2004); and Kristen Engel, "State and Local Climate Change Initiatives," *Arizona Legal Studies*, Discussion Paper No. 06–36 (September 2006), 1–17. See also Roger Karapin, who compares climate change policy in California, New York, and Washington in *Political Opportunities*; and several essays in Barry Rabe, ed., *Greenhouse Governance: Addressing Climate Change in America* (Washington, DC: Brookings Institution Press, 2010).

25. For an extensive review of this literature, see Kristen Engel, "State Environmental Standard-Setting: Is There a 'Race' and Is It 'To the Bottom?" *Hastings Law Journal* 48 (1977): 271.

26. David Konisky, "Regulatory Competition and Environmental Enforcement: Is There a Race to the Bottom?," *American Journal of Political Science* 51, no. 3 (2007): 869. However, another study concludes that "the degree to which states relax environmental standards for economic gain remains unclear." Potoski, "Clean Air Federalism," 336.

27. Scheberle, "Environmental Federalism," 406.

28. For a comparative analysis of the impact of multilevel environment governance, see Sonja Walti, "How Multilevel Structures Affect Environmental Policy in Industrialized Countries," *European Journal of Political Research* 43 (2004): 599–634.

29. Judd, *Common Lands, Common People*.

30. See, e.g., Richard Revesz, "Rethinking the 'Race to the Bottom,'" *New York University Law Review* 67 (1992): 1210–1254; Richard Revesz, "The Race to the Bottom and Federal Environmental Regulation: A Response to Critics," *Minnesota Law Review* 82 (1997): 535–564; Henry Butler and Jonathan Macey, *Using Federalism to Improve Environmental Policy* (Washington, DC: American Enterprise Institute, 1996); and Esty, "Revitalizing Environmental Federalism," 570–651.

31. For a detailed study of intergovernmental policy implementation, see Denise Scheberle, *Federalism and Environmental Policy: Trust and the Politics of Implementation* (Washington, DC: Georgetown University Press, 2004).

32. Jacqueline Switzer, *Green Backlash: The History and Politics of Environmental Opposition in the U.S.* (Boulder, CO: Lynne Reiner, 1997).

33. See, e.g., Adam Nagourney and Henry Fountain, "At Forefront of Climate Fight, California Plans an Offensive," *New York Times*, December 18, 2016.

34. See, e.g., *Economist*, "The Not So Golden State," January 25, 2014, http://www.economist.com/news/business/21594967-all-silicon-valleys-vibrancy-california-can-be-lousy-place-do-business-not-so?zid=309&ah=80dcf288b8561b012f603b9fd9577f0e.

35. Refer to World Bank, *United States GDP Growth Rate 1996–2016* (2017), http://data .worldbank.org/indicator/NY.GDP.MKTP.KD.ZG?end=2016&locations=US&start=1996; Statistica, *Annual Percent Change of the Real GDP in California from 2000 to 2016* (2017), https:// www.statista.com/statistics/306775/california-gdp-growth/; U.S Congress Joint Economic Community, *Table of Real GDP Growth by State* (2016), https://www.jec.senate.gov/public/index .cfm/democrats/2016/12/table-of-real-gdp-growth-by-state.

INDEX

Adams, Ansel, 107

Adams, Janet, 105

administrative capacity, 12; and approach to managing natural environment, 46; commissions and (*see* commissions, California state); and enforcement of standards and regulations, 102, 114, 161–63, 173, 174, 209, 239; and expertise, technical and regulatory, 16, 17, 22–23, 42, 46, 133, 162, 180, 186–88, 191, 203, 230; growth of, 114; and implementation of policy, 41–42, 104, 181, 197–98, 207, 209, 215–16, 241; institutional or bureaucratic infrastructure and, 15–16 (*see also* commissions, California state); and leadership on environmental issues, 231; Office of State Engineer and early, 22–23, 233; permit systems and, 99–100, 105, 109–12, 215–16, 222; policy learning and, 239–41

Advanced Clean Cars Program, 213–15

aesthetic value: administrative capacity and protection of, 90; and California's geography, 12, 48; of California's natural environment, 1–9, 12, 90, 231; citizen mobilization and, 59, 81–82, 103, 150, 232; of coastlines, 1, 13, 84, 87, 92–93, 97, 102, 112, 231; conservation and, 81; as an economic asset, 53; Muir's nature ethic and, 56–57, 121; and nationwide mobilization for protection, 82–83; of rivers, 135–37, 149–50; scenic attractions and tourism, 3, 53–54, 69–70, 73, 82, 231, 243; of wilderness, 58, 151–52; Yosemite and, 3, 50–54

agriculture: as agribusiness, 44, 142, 143; air pollution and damage to, 160, 167; as ally of urban business, 127–28; Central Valley Project and, 131–33; climate change as threat to, 228; economic and political power of, 39–45, 235–36; and forest management, 69; hydraulic gold mining opposed by, 14–15, 22, 36, 38–40, 42; irri-

gation and demand for water, 10, 20, 33–34, 44, 118, 127, 130–36, 142, 148; in Los Angeles County, 127–28, 160; in Owens Valley, 126–27; productivity of California, 148; and Sacramento-San Joaquin Delta, 139

air pollution, 4–5, 10; administrative capacity and regulation of, 154–55; and agricultural damage, 160, 167; automobile exhaust as (*see* automotive emissions); business and response to, 159, 165, 166 (*see also* automobile industry); California as leader in fight against, 7–8; citizen mobilization against, 158–60, 165–66; control districts established, 161–63; costs of abatement of, 170; dust pollution, 145–46, 147; and energy production, 10; federal regulation and control of, 145, 171–72, 174–75, 176–77; hydrocarbons, 38, 165–66, 169, 174, 180–81, 183, 184; and improvements in air quality, 163; industrial sources of, 38, 157, 161–62; inversions and, 156–57, 164, 232; jurisdiction and regulation of, 158, 172–73, 176–79; limited visibility caused by, 158; as national problem, 166, 171–72, 177; and ozone levels, 165, 183, 184–85; particulates, 184–85 (*see also* dust pollution *under this heading*); as public health issue, 160, 165–67, 172–73, 183–84, 203; regulatory legislation addressing, 162, 176–77, 178; contribution of small engines to, 179–80; smog attacks, 155–58, 164–65; smog science, 164–65, 171–72; Smoke and Fumes Commission (LA), 153, 158–59; standards established for, 174; stationary sources of, 21, 38, 155–7, 161–62, 163, 176, 180, 221; as threat to economic development, 15; waiver for California's stringent standards on, 176–79. *See also* greenhouse gases

Air Pollution Control Act (1947), 162

Air Pollution Foundation of Los Angeles, 166
Air Quality Act, 176–77, 178
Alameda, 96, 97
Albright, Horace, 8
Alliance of Automobile Manufacturers, 208–9
alternative energy: biomass industry, 198–99, 224; geothermal industry, 198–99, 224; promotion of, 198–200; solar power, 198–200, 208, 210, 217, 218–19, 224; wind power, 198–99, 208, 224. *See also* renewable energy
amenities, local environmental, 13, 81, 90, 102, 103, 113, 235
American River, 138; effects of mining debris on, 35, 37
Andrus, Cecil, 138
Anti-Debris Association of Sacramento Valley, 39, 42
appliances: Energy Star certification for, 197; industrial opposition to conservation and efficiency standards for, 190–92, 195; industry preference for uniform federal standards for, 239; standards established for, 5, 8, 195–97, 198, 205–6, 239–40
aqueducts, 33–34, 133; Boulder Canyon Project and, 130–31; California Water Project, 133, 139; and desert irrigation, 34; environmental impacts of, 139–40, 145, 149; Hetch Hetchy water project, 120, 122–23, 149; Los Angeles Aqueduct, 125–30, 145; map of, *116*; and Sacramento–San Joaquin Delta, 139–40; use of in hydraulic mining, 32–34. *See also* canals
aquifers, 125, 126, 129, 131–32, 148, 152
Armes, William, 58
Army Corps of Engineers, 97
Asmus, Peter, 88
Assembly Bill 32, California Global Warming Solutions Act, 207–11; and employment triggers, 210–11; Proposition 23 and opposition to, 210–13, 228
Assembly Bill 398, 223
Association of International Automobile Manufacturers, 208–9
automobile industry: and air pollution (*see* automotive emissions); California policies and regulations opposed by, 15, 176–78; and California's consumer leverage, 170–71, 179, 186, 204–5, 214–15; and catalytic converter technology, 7, 173, 181, 204; climate change legislation opposed by, 202–3, 208–9; and costs of environmental regulation, 237; and incentives

for purchasing electric vehicles, 220; and new technologies (hybrid, electric, etc.), 8, 182, 183, 204, 213–15, 225 (*see also* zero-emissions vehicles [ZEVs]); public transportation and, 168
automotive emissions, 161, 164–71; as air pollution, 154, 164–65, 170, 228; automobile industry and opposition to California's regulation of, 165, 176–78, 239; awareness of, 164; Baptist-bootlegger coalitions and support of controls on, 151; California standards for, 5, 7–8, 15, 154, 180–84, 240; catalytic converters and reduction of, 7, 173, 181, 204; and "clean fuels," 183, 238; commercial trucking and, 185; diesel engines and, 183–84, 185; and evaporative control systems, 180–81; as exempt from Air Pollution Control Act of 1947, 164; federal regulation and control of, 174–75; industry preference for uniform federal standards for, 239; industry responsibility for abatement of, 170; and nitrogen oxide standards, 180–84; Pavley bill and limits to, 201–2; private car ownership and responsibility for, 19, 167–70, 225; and unleaded gasoline, 7, 173, 181; and used vehicles, 173, 181–82; vehicle categories and standards for, 182–83; and Volkswagen "dieselgate" scandal, 16; zero-emissions vehicles (ZEVs) mandates, 7, 182, 214–15, 225. *See also* greenhouse gases
Ayers, Thomas, 51

balanced use, 101, 103, 105, 146
Baldwin, Malcolm, 92
Baptist-bootlegger coalitions, 15, 143–44, 246n27; and air pollution, 151, 155, 160, 202; and beach protections, 90; and climate change, 205; and coastal redwood protections, 69, 82; and coastline protections, 86, 112; and defeat of Proposition 23, 212–13; and greenhouse gas limits, 202; oil industry and state parks as, 74–75, 82; and Peripheral Canal project, 143–44
battery electric vehicles, 183
Bay Conservation and Development Commission (BCDC), 18, 86, 98–101, 233
beaches, 74, 84; map of, *85*; as public goods, 89–91, 113. *See also* coastlines
Bear River, 35
Berkeley, 98, 164
Biber, Eric, 213
Big Basin Redwoods State Park, 68–69, 80
Bond, Christopher, 179

Bono, Sonny, 147

Borenstein, Severin, 227

Bottles, Scott, 167

Boulder Canyon Project, 130–31, 149

Boxer, Barbara, 179–80

Brower, David, 76–77

Brown, Edmund "Pat," 76, 133–35, 142, 171, 174–75

Brown, Jerry, 8, 109, 142, 152, 195, 216, 219, 222, 223

building codes, energy efficiency and, 5, 194–95, 198, 242–43

Bunnell, Lafayette, 50–51

Bush, George W., 205

business: as advocate of regulation, 12, 14–15, 108–9, 159–60, 232–33, 235; agri-culture as ally of, 127–28; in Baptist-bootlegger coalitions, 149, 234–35; divi-sions within, 22, 43–44, 48, 82, 92, 119, 162, 229; as opponent of environmental regulation, 237; and preference for uni-form standards, 239–40; and Progressive Era agenda, 236; and recession of Yosem-ite to federal control, 61–62; and water resources, 118–19. *See also specific sectors*

Butler, Nicholas, 60

Cabrillo, Juan Rodriguez, 3, 156

Calaveras Big Tree National Forest, 64

California: auto ownership in, 167–71; envi-ronmental beauty of, 1, 3; "green state" political identity of, 14, 179; naming of, 3; Yosemite as cultural symbol of, 51–52

California Air Resources Board (CARB), 7, 16, 154–55, 240; and Advanced Clean Cars Program, 213–15; establishment of, 176; and Global Warming Solutions Act implementation and enforcement, 209–10; and greenhouse gas emissions standards, 204–5; and local air quality standards, 176; Reagan and, 18; regulatory responsibilities of, 176; and research and development, 186; technological advances reflected in standards set by, 182–83

California Business Round Table, 208, 222

California Chamber of Commerce: and cap-and-trade, 217, 222; and Pavley Bill greenhouse gases regulation, 202, 208; and Proposition 20 coastal protections, 107–8; and solar energy development, 210

California Climate Action Registry, 200

California Coastal Act, 112

California Coastal Alliance, 105

California Coastal Commission, 16, 86, 104–14, 233

California Council for Environmental and Economic Balance (CCEEB), 108–9

California Department of Fish and Game, 141

California Department of Water Resources, 144

"California Effect," 7–9, 155, 187–88, 190, 197, 204, 227

California Energy Commission (CEC), 16, 18, 191–96, 233

California Energy Resources Conservation and Development Commission, 191

California Environmental Justice Alliance, 223

California Environmental Policy Act (1970), 135

California Environmental Quality Act, 18, 190

California Game and Fish Protective Associ-ation, 68–69

California Manufacturers Association, 211

California Public Utility Commission (CPUC), 191–94, 219

California Real Estate Association, 105

California Redwood Association, 67

California Solar Energy Industry Associa-tion, 199

California Solar Initiative, 210

California State Lands Commission, and oil leases, 96

California Water Resources Board, 133, 137

camping, 59–60

canals: map of, *116*; Peripheral Canal and Sacramento–San Joaquin Delta, 140–41; water management and construction of, 32–34. *See also* aqueducts

Candlestick Park, 97

Cannon, Joe, 61

cap-and-trade, 19, 189, 215–18, 221–24, 225, 240

Carlson, Ann, 16, 183, 207

Carquines Strait, 139

cars: and air pollution (*see* automotive emis-sions); and California culture, 167–71, 185–86, 237. *See also* automobile industry

Carter, Jimmy, 79–80

catalytic converters, 7, 173, 181, 204

Central Park, New York, 53–54

Central Valley: and flooding caused by hy-draulic mining, 35–36; natural resources of, 24

Central Valley Project, 131–33

Chabot, Anthony, 31

Chandler, Harry, 160
chemical regulation, 21, 240
Chinatown (film), 127
Choosing Our Future (Union of Concerned Scientists), 206
Chytry, Josef, 1
Citizens' Anti-Smoke Advisory Committee, 166
Citizens Smog Advisory Committee, 159
Clean Air Act, 179
Clean Power Campaign, 202
clean technology sector, 15, 205, 208, 212–14, 229
Cleveland, Grover, 66
climate, of California, 1; agriculture and, 148; as attraction, 25, 154, 160; droughts and, 117, 138, 144, 152; and immigration of settlers, 25–26; and precipitation, 20, 32, 69, 115–17; as vulnerable, 227–28, 232
climate change, global: AB 32 (California Global Warming Solutions Act) and, 207–11; Baptist-bootlegger coalitions and, 205; and bipartisan support of regulation, 223–24; California's policy to address, 4, 8; as economic threat, 207–8; and energy production, 10; environmental threats linked to, 10; and frequency and severity of droughts, 152; and Paris Climate Accord, 9, 222, 227; regulations and incentives relating to, 228; and rising sea levels, 10; as threat to California, 20, 190, 206–7; and water resources, 10, 20; and wildfires, 10. *See also* greenhouse gases
Coastal Management Commission, 108
coastal redwoods: "Avenue of Giants," 80; and citizen mobilization, 13–14, 68–69, 82; climate change as threat to, 228; commercial lumber value of, 9, 66–68, 74, 80, 237; competing resource values of, 67–68; contrasted with sequoia giants, 66–67; as endangered species, 77–78; Muir Woods, 69–71; national support for protection of, 82–83; private ownership of, 80; protection of, 48, 237; reforestation and planting of, 80–81; Sempervirens Club and protection of, 68–69; state parks created to protect, 69–74
coastal resources, Native Americans and, 24
Coastal Zone Management Act, 114
Coastal Zone Protection Act (1972), 105–6, 110
coastlines: aesthetic value of, 84, 102, 112; beaches, 74, 84, 89–91; Coastal Commission established for protection of,

16, 104–12; Coastal Protection Initiative, 102–12; degradation of, 10; economic development and threats to, 84; legislative protections of, 104–12; as a local issue, 106; map of, *85*; oil spills and (*see* oil spills); permitting system and planned development of, 109–12; planning and land use along, 5; population growth and proximity to, 102, 106; public access to, 10, 12, 89–91, 103, 107, 113; recreational use value of, 84, 103. *See also* San Francisco Bay
Cohen, Michael, 58, 123
Colorado River, 130–31
commissions, California state: Bay Conservation and Development Commission (BCDC), 18, 86, 98–101, 233; California Air Resources Board (CARB), 7, 16, 154–55; California Energy Commission (CEC), 16, 18, 191–96, 233; California Energy Resources Conservation and Development Commission, 191; California Public Utility Commission (CPUC), 191–94, 219; California State Lands Commission, 96; Coastal Commission, 16, 86, 104–12; Motor Vehicle Pollution Control Board (MVPCB), 173; Public Utilities Commission, 16, 220; San Francisco Bay Conservation and Development Commission, 98, 114; Smoke and Fumes Commission (LA), 153, 158–59; State Forestry Commission, 65–66; State Lands Commission, 86, 114; State Parks Commission, 73–75, 233
Communities United Against the Dirty Energy Proposition, 211–12
computers, energy efficiency of, 196–97
Conness, John, 52–53
conservation: of energy, 152–53; fuel economy standards and, 181, 205; industry opposition to, 219–20; and oil consumption reduction goals, 219–20; of water resources, 141–42, 152–53
Cook, James, 91
"cooperative federalism" and environmental regulations, 241–42
Corte Madera, 97
costs of environmental protection, 6, 149–50, 242–43; borne by industry, 237–38; citizen willingness to accept, 186; economic depression or recession and, 210–11, 216; for greenhouse gas reduction, 204; increased consumer prices, 217, 218; industry and responsibility for, 187;

"overregulation" and, 240–41; reduced productivity and employment, 43, 78, 80, 108
courts, judicial, and establishment of policy, 39–46

dams and reservoirs, 20, 118, 147–48; and damage claims, 29; diminishing returns for future construction of, 138; environmental damage caused by, 37; on Feather River (*see* State Water Project); flood control and, 41, 44, 130; Hetch Hetchy project (*see* Hetch Hetchy reservoir); and hydroelectric power generation, 120, 130; and irrigation for agriculture, 34, 44, 118, 127; Lake Mead, 130–31; map of, *116*; mining and construction of, 29, 30, 32–33, 44; and natural watersheds, 118; New Melones Reservoir, 136–38; public opposition to, 135–38; and recreational use, 121, 122, 132–33; Shasta Lake, 132–33; and urban demand for water, 118, 124
Dasmann, Raymond, 43–44
Davis, Gray, 203, 206
Death Valley, 3
decoupling and energy efficiency, 5, 193–94
de León, Kevin, 219–20
Del Norte Coast Redwoods State Park, 72
Department of Public Health, 173
deregulation, 8, 189
deserts, agriculture and irrigation of, 20, 33–34, 130–31
Deukmejian, George, 18, 110, 199
Dicapua, Michael, 216
Dickey Water Pollution Act, 16
Dingell, John, 177–78
Dos Rios Dam, 136
Dowd, A. T., 62
Drainage Act of 1880, 41
Drake, Sir Francis, 25
drought, 117, 144; artificial "water famine," 128; climate change and severity of, 152; and hydraulic management systems, 138
Duddleston, William, 108

earthquake of 1906: and construction of Hetch Hetchy reservoir, 122; demand for lumber following, 67, 70
Ecological Society of America, 200
economic development: and access to water resources, 133–34, 237; and California as market, 17; of coastlines, 84; and costs of environmental protection, 44–45, 210–11, 216; and environmental amenities, 102;

environmental quality as advantage to, 15, 154, 159–60, 208, 235, 242–44; environmental regulations and, 5–6, 235, 237, 243–44; as an environmental threat, 19–20; and greenhouse gases, 19; and Gross Domestic Product (GDP) of California, 3, 6, 17, 243; pollution as threat to, 15
Eel River, 135–36
Ekland, Sarah, 159–60
electricity, 210; demand for, 192, 198; energy efficiency and, 198 (*see also* appliances); and hydroelectric power generation, 120, 123, 130; net metering and residential production of, 199–200, 210, 218–19; rates to consumers for, 197–98, 220. *See also* utility companies
electric vehicles, 15, 183, 214–15, 220, 229
elites: as leaders in policy initiatives, 14, 48–49, 68, 72, 98; and mobilization, 58–59
Emerson, Ralph Waldo, 51
Emeryville, 97
energy crisis, 181, 189, 191, 201
energy efficiency, 5; appliance manufacturers and opposition to, 190–92, 195; and appliance standards, 195–97; building codes and, 5, 194–95, 198, 242–43; and conservation, 192–93, 195–96, 201; decoupling and, 5, 193–94; and electrical rates, 198; incentives and, 197, 205; projected energy needs and, 190–93; and reduced consumer costs, 197; and reduction of greenhouse gases, 189; research and development for, 195–96; uniform standards for, 239–40
energy resources, 130; and air pollution, 10; commercial and residential rates for, 6; conservation of, 152–53, 192–93, 195–96, 201; demand for, 10; electricity (*see* electricity); petroleum (*see* oil industry); and Public Utilities Commission, 16
Environmental Defense Fund, 193, 208, 222
Environmental Entrepreneurs, 202
Environmental Protection Agency, California, 207
Environmental Protection Agency (EPA, federal): and automotive emissions standards, 7–8, 181, 183; and California standards as benchmark, 8, 183; and Energy Star certification for appliances, 197; and waiver for more stringent standards in California, 176–79, 187, 205, 238, 240
environmental quality, as economic advantage, 15, 154, 159–60, 208, 235, 242–44

Environment California, 210
Erie, Steven, 127, 128, 148
Esty, Daniel, 233–34
Eureka Lake and Yuba Canal Company, 33

Farmer, Jared, 64, 67
Feather River, 134–35; Oroville dam on, 133; Sawyer decision and, 44
Federal Air Pollution Control Act, 172
federal government: and administrative capacity, 61, 62; air pollution regulation by, 158–59; and California, 5, 17, 26–28, 89, 154, 177–80; "California effect" and influence on, 7–9, 154–55, 187–89, 197, 204; and funding for parks and recreation, 75; and interstate commerce, 175; and Kyoto Protocol, 201; and navigable waterways, 42, 146; and offshore oil deposits, 92, 95–96, 114; and oil revenues, 93; as owner of public lands, 29–30, 46, 125–26; petroleum policy and, 89; and "sagebrush rebellion," 241–42; Sierra Club and, 78–79; and state leadership on regulations, 238–39; and states' rights, 177; and uniform standards, 196, 239–40; and water quality standards, 142
federalism: and "California Effect," 7–9, 187–88; cooperative, 239, 241; iterative, 154; and risk of regulatory lapses, 238–39; and state's rights arguments, 177–78, 242
Feinstein, Dianne, 179–80
Fish and Game Commission, 15–16
fisheries: habitat destruction and, 37–38, 94, 132; habitat restoration and, 144–45; Native Americans and, 24; Sacramento–San Joaquin Delta, 139–40; San Francisco Bay, 96; Sawyer decision and, 44; water resources and, 143
flooding, 35–36, 41, 45–46, 117, 131
Ford Motor Company, 177
forest resources, 3; administrative management of, 65–66; climate change and, 10, 228; competing demands for, 231; and creation of forest reserves, 55, 65–66, 238; and deforestation, 65–66; exhaustion of, 65–66, 236; and inland precipitation, 69; lumber industry and extraction of (see logging); Native Americans and, 24; New York and protection of, 55, 234, 238; private ownership of, 64, 67, 74; railroad ownership of, 64; and reforestation, 4, 80–81. See also coastal redwoods; sequoias
Freeway and Expressway Act, 171

freeways and highways, 19, 171
Friends of the Earth, 141–42, 146
Friends of the River, 141–42
fuel economy standards, 181, 205
funding for preservation and conservation: bond issues, 73–74, 75–76, 109; budget cuts and, 110; federal sources of, 64, 75; Land and Water Conservation Fund, 75–76; oil royalties as, 75; philanthropy and, 64, 68, 69–71, 72, 78–79, 81–83, 90
fur trapping, 25

Gaines, Ted, 224
Garcetti, Eric, 145
Gearhart, B. W., 132
General Grant National Park. See Kings Canyon National Park
geography of California, 1–4; and aesthetic value, 12; air pollution and smog linked to, 154, 156–57, 203; and California identity, 212; and competition for resources, 127; and environmental activism, 13–14, 21; environmental policies and, 9–11; hydraulic mining and, 46–47; and local politics, 233–34; map, 2, 3; and policy leadership, 17, 27–28, 154, 177–80; and water resources, 20
geothermal industry, 198, 224
Get Oil Out (GOO), 95
Gibbons v. Ogden, 42
Global Climate Leadership Memorandum of Understanding ("2 MOU"), 226
Global Warming Solutions Act, 5; CARB and implementation and enforcement of, 209–10
Golden, Kevin, 201
gold mining: economic power of, 41; employment in, 34; federal interest in, 29–30; and the Gold Rush, 26–27; hydraulic management systems and, 24; hydraulic mining (see hydraulic mining); and industrial air pollution, 44; map, 23; mercury and, 36–37; placer mining, 30–31; and population growth, 27; production and profitability statistics for, 29–30, 34; regulation of, 44–45; toxic wastes and, 44; and water rights, 28–30
Grant, Wyn, 170
grazing, 30, 52, 56, 58, 61, 63
Great Depression: and conservation efforts, 73–74; and public works projects, 132
Greeley, Horace, 48, 51, 52, 82
"Green Book" (climate change report), 200

greenhouse gases, 189–90; and Advanced
Clean Cars Program, 213–15; and business, 208–9, 216; and cap-and-trade system, 19, 189, 215–18, 221–24, 225, 240;
clean technology and, 15, 208–9; and
emissions baselines, 200; goals for reduction of, 5, 198, 205–6, 209–10, 219, 221,
225, 227; and Global Climate Leadership
Memorandum of Understanding, 226;
industrial facilities as source of, 221; international cooperation to control, 226–27;
Kyoto Protocol and, 201; Pavely bill and
limits on, 201–4; personal vehicle ownership and, 19; as public health issue, 203;
and Regional Greenhouse Gas Initiative,
216; restrictions on, 5
"green" identity, 4, 179, 209–10, 234
Gross Domestic Product (GDP) of California, 3, 6, 17, 243
Gulick, Esther, 98

Haagen-Smit, Arie Jan, 165, 176, 233
Hanak, Ellen, 147
Hanemann, W. Michael, 194
Harriman, Edward H., 61
Harris, Ellen Stern, 104
Harrison, Benjamin, 57–58, 64, 66
Harvey, Hal, 226
Hayes, Samuel, 236
hazardous wastes, 9, 36–37, 96, 239
Healy, Robert, 109
Hearst, George, 57
Hetch Hetchy reservoir, 71, 118, 148–49; and
competing public interests, 121–22, 123–
24; funding for, 122, 123; and hydroelec-
tric power, 123; national park status of,
120; opposition to, 120–23, 234; and rec-
reational use, 121; and San Francisco's
need for water, 119–24
Hickel, Walter, 95
Hittell, Henry, 27
Holdren, John, 243
"home rule," 99–100
Hoover Dam, 130–31
Humbolt Redwoods State Park, 72, 80
Hundley, Norris, 25, 131, 134
Huntington, Collis, 57
Hurst, James Willard, 236
Hutchings, James, 51, 55
hybrid vehicles, 8, 204, 214–15
Hydraulic Miners Association (HMA),
39–40
hydraulic mining, 9, 231; 1884 ban on,
22, 42–45; access to water for, 28–29;

agriculture and opposition to, 14–15, 22,
38–40, 42; citizen mobilization against,
12, 39, 42; debris from, 4, 12, 33–35, 39,
42; economic impact of, 43; effect on
Native Americans of, 37–38; employment in, 34; flooding linked to, 41, 117;
forests damaged by, 37; geography and,
46–47; and industrial air pollution, 38;
and large-scale environmental damage,
33–38; opposition to control of, 39–40;
responsibility for damages from, 39–41;
Sawyer decision on, 42–45; technology
for, 31–33; toxic waste from, 36
hydrogen fuel cell cars, 214–15

implementation of policy. See under administrative capacity
industrial pollution. See gold mining
infill and coastal degradation, 10
initiative process, 105–8, 113–14

Jackson, Lisa, 205
Jacobs, Chip, 176
Jedediah Smith Redwoods State Park, 72
J. G. Boswell land company, 143
Johnson, Lyndon, 75
Johnson, Robert, 56–57
Johnson, Stephen, 205
Jordan, David Starr, 58–59, 68
judicial decisions: on cap-and-trade, 217,
222; Gibbons v. Ogden, 42; and first environmental protections, 4, 22, 45–46;
against industry as a whole, 39; and legal
liability for environmental damages, 39–
44; Nollan v. California Coastal Commission, 111–12; and questions of jurisdiction,
39–40, 42, 92, 95–96, 114, 146, 175; Sawyer decision, 42–45; and Spring Valley
Mine suit, 38–39; and water rights, 28–
29; Woodruff v. North Bloomfield Mining
and Gravel Company, 42–44

Karapin, Roger, 203
Kearns, Faith, 152–53
Kelley, Robert, 32
Kelly, William, 176
Kenetech, 199
Kennedy, Robert, 177, 242
Kennedy, Robert, Jr., 206
Kent, William, 8, 69–71, 121–22
Kerr, Kay, 98
Ketcham, Hank, 107
Keyes, James, 39–40
Keyser, Phil, 39–40

King, Thomas Starr, 52
Kings Canyon National Park, 64, 65
Knight, Goodwin, 172
Konitsky, David, 239
Kotzebue, Otto von, 25
Kuchel, Thomas, 18, 172
Kyoto Protocol, 201–2

Lake Mead, 130–31
Lake Merritt, 96
Land and Water Conservation Fund, 75–76
Lands Commission, 88–89
Lane, Melvin, 107
Lawrence Berkeley National Laboratory,
    Energy and Environment Division, 194
leadership, environmental, 3–5, 162, 243–44;
    and air pollution research and control,
    163, 174, 176–80, 180–81, 183; and auto-
    motive emissions standards, 174–75, 188;
    and California as "superregulator," 188;
    "California Effect" and, 7–9, 155, 187–88,
    190, 197, 204, 227; and California's role as
    policy laboratory, 7, 27, 154–55, 183, 194,
    227, 240; in climate change research and
    regulation, 226–27 (see also greenhouse
    gas reductions under this heading); and
    "cooperative federalism," 241–42; and
    energy-efficient appliance standards, 196;
    federalism and, 238–39; on greenhouse
    gas reductions, 203–4, 209–10, 217–18,
    230; and international cooperation on cli-
    mate change, 8–9, 226–27; and renewable
    energy sources, 224–25
League of Conservation Voters, 202–3
Leavitt, Wendy, 7, 188
LeConte, Joseph, 58
Lehrer, Tom, 96
Leslie Salt Company, 99
levees, 36, 37, 41
Levinson, Mark, 198
Lincoln, Abraham, 54
Lloyd, Alan, 182
local interests: divergence between northern
    and Southern California of, 89–90, 113,
    142, 144; and environmental amenities, 13,
    81, 90, 102, 103, 113, 235; NIMBYism and,
    13–14, 46–47, 59, 124, 233–34; and sup-
    port for water projects, 134, 142, 144, 150
logging, 79; air pollution regulations opposed
    by, 162; clear-cutting, 79–80; and com-
    mercial management of forests, 80–81;
    and demand for lumber, 9, 65, 67, 70, 71;
    and exhaustion of forest resources, 65,
    236; "just compensation" in negotiations

with, 72, 79–80; and private ownership
    of forest lands, 67, 74; of redwoods, 9,
    66–68, 80, 237; of sequoias, 63, 66, 82;
    park expansions opposed by, 79; state
    regulation of, 4, 65–66, 80–81; in Yo-
    semite and the Sierras, 56, 82; Yosemite
    protections opposed by, 57–58, 61
Long, Russell, 204
Los Angeles: air pollution in, 5, 10, 12, 15,
    154–56, 174 (see also Los Angeles Air Pol-
    lution Control District); and beaches as
    public good, 89–91; forest watershed pro-
    tection and, 66; geographical vulnerabil-
    ity to air pollution of, 10, 19, 154, 156–57,
    185, 232; importance of environmental
    quality to, 15, 154, 159–60, 208; oil wells
    in, 10, 74, 86–88, 113; smoke abatement
    efforts in, 155–56; water resources for,
    115–16, 124–31
Los Angeles Air Pollution Control District:
    business opposition to, 162; creation of,
    161–62; and emissions standards, 173, 178;
    and evidence of link between auto emis-
    sions and smog, 164–65, 170–71; and first
    motor vehicle control laboratory, 172;
    funding of, 172; and improved air quality,
    163; and legal authority to regulate auto
    emissions, 164
Los Angeles Aqueduct, 125–29; dust pollu-
    tion linked to, 145–46
Los Angeles Department of Water and
    Power (LADWP), 126
Los Angeles River, 124–25
Lu, Sophie, 226
lumber. See logging

Marcus, Felicia, 152
marine sanctuaries, 92–93
Mariposa Battalion, 50
Mariposa sequoia grove, 4, 48–49, 52–55,
    63
Marysville, 36
Mather, Stephen, 8
Mathews, Joe, 118
Mathis, Devon, 223
Mayer, Louis B., 90
Mayes, Chad, 223
McCarthy, Kevin, 109
McDuffie, Duncan, 73
McKinley, William, 66
McLaughlin, Sylvia, 98
McWilliams, Carey, 27
Merced River, 57
mercury, 36–37, 44

Midwestern Greenhouse Gas Reduction Act, 218
mining. *See* gold mining
Mining Act (1866), 30
mobilization, by businesses, 39–40; against Proposition 20, 113
mobilization of public, 231; aesthetic value and, 59, 81–83, 103, 150, 232; against air pollution, 158–60, 178; artists and, 51, 107; climate change concerns and, 228; and coastline protection, 84–85, 104–12, 113; and court actions, 38–40; and grassroots support for regulation, 13–14; and "green" state identity, 14; and Hetch Hetchy project, 122; against hydraulic mining, 12, 38–40, 42; inspired by Muir, 56–57, 63; national awareness and, 82–83, 94–95; NIMBYism and, 12–14, 46–47, 59, 81, 233–34; against Proposition 23, 212–13; and redwood protection, 13–14, 68–69, 82; and San Francisco Bay protection efforts, 98, 100, 113; and Santa Barbara oil spill, 94–95; Sierra Club and, 59–60; and Stanislaus River, 136–37; against water projects, 120–23, 135–38; and Yosemite preservation, 48–49
Molina, Mario, 8
Mono Lake, 129–30, 145–46, 149
Motor Vehicle Pollution Control Act, 173, 175
Motor Vehicle Pollution Control Board (MVPCB), 173; and federal air pollution standards, 175–76
Mount Diablo State Park, 72–73, 74
Mount Whitney, 3, 125
Muir, John: death of, 123; and federal stewardship of wilderness, 60–61, 122; on gold mining, 34; and Hetch Hetchy water project, 120–23; political activism of, 56–58; as preservation advocate, 8, 48; as self-taught naturalist, 55; and sequoia preservation, 63–65; and Sierra Club, 58, 60–61; and Southern Pacific Railroad, 57; as "voice for wilderness," 56–57, 63; and Yosemite preservation efforts, 48, 55–58, 60–61
Muir Woods National Monument, 69–71
Mulholland, William, 125, 127, 128, 129
Mundo, Philip, 235
Murphy, George, 18, 176–77
Muskie, Edmund, 176

Nagourney, Adam, 110
Nash, Gerald, 3

National Audubon Society, 146
national parks, in California, 4
National Park Service, 62
National Park Service Act, 123
National Resource Defense Council, 202, 206
National Wild and Scenic Rivers Act, 135
National Wild and Scenic Rivers System, 138
Native Americans: coastal resources and, 24; and mining, 37–38; population in California of, 24, 38; relocation of, 50–51, 136
natural gas, 201; as by-product of oil extraction, 10, 87; rates for, 201
net metering, 199–200, 210, 218–19
New Melones Reservoir, 136–38
New York, 234; air pollution in, 163, 175; autonomy and environmental regulations of, 241–42; California as model for, 163, 205, 214; Central Park, 54, 121; forest protection in, 55, 234, 238; Hudson Valley, 234
Niagara Falls, 53–54
Nichols, Mary, 186, 214
NIMBYism, 13–14, 46–47, 59, 81, 233–34
Nixon, Richard, 95
Nollan v. California Coastal Commission, 111–12
Norman, Harry, 160
nuclear power, 110, 190, 195, 220, 225

Oakland, 97, 99
Obama, Barack, 205
Office of Research, California Assembly, 180
Office of State Engineer, 22–23, 233
oil drilling: coastal, 74; as environmental threat, 9–11 (*see also* oil spills); offshore, 10, 86–87, 112; proposed bans on, 88–89, 95–96; in residential LA neighborhoods, 86–88; slant drilling, 74–75, 87; State Parks Commission and, 74–75; as threat to tourism industry, 87, 92
oil industry: air pollution regulations opposed by, 162; and beach oil pollution, 88 (*see also* oil spills); and California regulations, 89; climate change legislation opposed by, 208–9; consumption reduction goals opposed by, 219–20; fracking, 237; greenhouse gas regulation opposed by, 202, 211, 216–17, 229; local opposition to, 86–88, 92–93; Pavley bill opposed by, 202; productivity and profitability of, 9–10, 86–87, 96, 229, 231; royalties from, 75, 88, 93; in San Joaquin Valley, 86, 96; Submerged Lands Act and, 92; and support for state parks, 74–75; tourism as economic competition for, 92

oil spills, 10; fisheries damaged by, 94; natural seepage, 91; at Santa Barbara, 12, 93–96, 104, 105, 106; wildlife harmed by, 94, 104

Olmsted, Frederick Law, 51, 54, 82

Olmsted, Frederick Law, Jr., 169

Olsen, Kristin, 219

Oroville, gold mining in, 33–34

Oroville dam, 133

Orsi, Jared, 103, 105–6

"overregulation," 240–41

Owens River and Owens Lake, 125; aqueduct project, 149; restoration of, 145

Pacific Electric Railway, 168

Pacific Gas & Electric, 199, 261

Pacific Legal Foundation, 111

Palomar Mountain, 74

Pardee, George, 60

Paris Climate Accord, 9, 222, 227

Parker, Doug, 152–53

Parsons, James, 9

partisan politics, 203; and cap-and-trade compromise, 223–24; and climate change legislation, 209; and support for environmental protections, 17–19, 113

Pataki, George, 205

Pavley, Fran, 201–4, 207, 221

Pavely bill (Assembly Bill 1493), 201–4, 206

Payson, Lewis, 63

Peripheral Canal: citizen opposition to, 141–42; Propositions 8 and 9 and, 142–45; and protection of Sacramento–San Joaquin Delta, 141–42

Perkins, George, 58–59

permitting systems, 109–11

petroleum industry. *See* oil industry

philanthropy and preservation, 69–71, 72, 78–79, 81–83, 90

Phillips, Sarah, 117, 233

Pickford, Mary, 90

Pinchot, Gifford, 122, 129

Planning and Conservation League, 141–42

policy implementation. *See under* administrative capacity

policy learning, 239–41

Polk, James, 26–27

population: and air pollution, 175; of California, 6; along coastline, 102; and consumption of natural resources, 103, 117, 119, 124, 129, 131, 149–50; and demand for recreational land use, 73, 76; environmental regulations and growth of, 5–6; and environmental threats, 11; of Los Angeles, 157; Native American, 24, 38

Prairie Creek Redwoods State Park, 72

precipitation: California's climate and, 20, 32, 69, 115–17; and droughts, 117, 138, 144, 152; global climate change and changes in, 228; and hydraulic management systems, 115, 125, 138, 139, 144

Progressive Era, 15–16, 119, 121–22, 129, 236

property rights, 24; environmental regulation and, 43–44; and just compensation, 72; regulatory takings and, 111–12; Sawyer decision and, 43–44; water rights and, 28–30, 126, 146

Proposition 8, 142–45

Proposition 9, 143

Proposition 20, 104–12, 113; business and opposition to, 107–8

Proposition 23, 228; defeat of, 212–13; citizen mobilization against, 211–13; and employment triggers, 210–11

Proterra, 214

public access: to California coast, 10, 12, 89–91, 103, 107, 113; as a right, 54–55; state park system and, 72–73. *See also* recreational value

public lands, map of, *49*

public transportation, 167–68; high-speed train, 217, 222, 224

public trust doctrine, 146

Public Utilities Commission, 16, 220

Pure Air Act, 180

Rabe, Barry, 7, 203, 209, 229–30, 235

railroads, 28; and air pollution regulations, 162; and environmental protection, 14–15, 57; and high-speed rail proposal, 217, 222, 224; as owners of forest lands, 64; and public transportation, 168–69; and tourism, 57

ranching, 25, 58, 209

Raymond, Israel Ward, 52

Reagan, Ronald, 18, 78, 101, 136, 142, 180, 191, 223, 233

real estate industry: environmental quality and, 15, 159, 160, 232; and infill of San Francisco Bay, 10, 96–98, 105–6; and local opposition to shoreline oil development, 15, 87–90; and suburban sprawl, 167; and support for government regulation, 159; and support of state parks, 73

recreational value: of coastlines, 84, 103; increased demand for, 73, 76; and reservoirs, 121, 132–33; of rivers, 150–51; of Sacramento–San Joaquin Delta, 139

Redwood Canyon, 64–65

Redwood Creek (Redwood National Park), 76–80
Redwood National Park, 76–80
redwoods. *See* coastal redwoods; sequoias
Regional Greenhouse Gas Initiative, 216
regulatory institutions (California political infrastructure). *See* administrative capacity; commissions, California state
Reilly, William, 1, 7–8, 205
Reisner, Marc, 144
renewable energy: battery energy storage facilities and, 221; California as leader in, 224–25; California targets for, 220–21; global warming as context for, 207–11, 213; industry as advocate for, 15; and renewable portfolio standard (RPS), 201–2, 220; and state-funded research subsidies and incentives, 192, 199–200; state mandates for, 5, 189, 199, 206
renewable portfolio standard (RPS), 201–2, 220
research: on air pollution, 5, 164–66, 171–72, 233; and California as policy laboratory, 7, 27, 154–55, 183, 194, 227, 240; California Energy Commission (CEC) and, 191–92, 194–95; in energy efficiency, 194–95; expertise and, 180; federal emphasis on, 172; funding for, 165, 172, 194; industry and, 165; at Lawrence Berkeley National Laboratory, 194; policy and, 200; universities as resource for, 165, 194, 233, 243
rice, 139
Richmond, 97
Righter, Robert, 121
rivers: inland shipping and, 37; jurisdiction over, 42–43, 44; lag in protection of, 149; as "mere plumbing," 118; National Wild and Scenic Rivers Act and protection of, 135, 138; recreational use and value of, 150–51. *See also specific rivers*
Rockefeller, John D., 74
Roosevelt, Franklin D., 132
Roosevelt, Theodore, 64, 66, 69, 128–29; and Yosemite conservation, 60
Rosenfeld, Art, 194–95
Round Valley, 135–36

Sabin, Paul, 89
Sacramento River, 138–39; hydraulic mining debris and, 35–37; Sawyer decision and, 44; Shasta Dam and, 132
Sacramento–San Joaquin Delta: agriculture and, 139; aqueduct project in, 133; ecological fragility of, 139–40, 144–45;

geography of, 138–40; Peripheral Canal and protection of, 140–41; as regional watershed, 139; salt-water incursion and salinity levels in, 139–40; water management and, 20; as wildlife habitat, 139
Sacramento Valley: agriculture and opposition to gold mining in, 14–15, 42; flood control in, 45–46, 131
Salton Sea, 146–47
Salton Sea Authority, 147
Salyer land company, 143
San Bernardino National Forest, 66
San Diego, 74, 115–16, 131, 167; and State Water Project, 133
San Diego Gas and Electric Company, 195
San Francisco: and earthquake of 1906, 67, 70, 122; Hetch Hetchy and water for, 119–24, 128–29, 151; and support for environmental legislation, 208
San Francisco Bay, 3; commercial development of, 102; Hudson Bay trading post located on, 25; hydraulic mining and sedimentation in, 35; industrial and municipal waste pollution in, 96; land "reclamation" in, 10, 96–97, 98, 102; and legislative and state protection efforts, 98, 100–102; local opposition to development along, 97–99; opposition to environmental protection of, 99–100, 113; and public access to shoreline, 101; salinity levels in, 140; and Save Our Bay Action Committee (SOBAC), 100; and Save San Francisco Bay Association, 98; Sempervirens Club and protection of, 113; shrinking size of, 97, 231; Sierra Club and, 59, 113; as wildlife and waterfowl habitat, 96, 101
San Francisco Bay Conservation and Development Commission (temporary), 98, 114
San Gabriel Forest Reserve, 66
San Joaquin River, 138–39
San Joaquin Valley, 133; and inland delta (*see* Sacramento–San Joaquin Delta)
San Pablo Bay, 35
San Rafael, 97
Santa Barbara: and beaches as public good, 90–91, 113; offshore oil extraction at, 10, 12, 86, 91–96; oil spill at, 12, 93–96, 104, 105, 106
Santa Monica Bay, 88
Sausalito, 97
Save Our Bay Action Committee (SOBAC), 100
Save San Francisco Bay Association, 98

Save-the-Redwoods League, 14, 71–72, 73; Sierra Club contrasted with, 78–79

Sawyer, Lorenzo (Sawyer decision), 42–45

Scalia, Antonin, 111

Schwarzenegger, Arnold, 8, 18, 179–80, 206, 207, 214, 221, 223–24

sea levels, climate change and, 10, 205, 228

Sears, John, 52

Sempervirens Club, 14, 48; and coastal redwood conservation, 68–69; and San Francisco Bay protection, 113

Senate Bill 350, 220

Senger, Henry, 58

Sequoia National Park, 64

sequoias: climate change as threat to, 228; and creation of National Parks, 63–64; General Sherman Tree, 62; legislative protections of, 63–64; logging and commercial value of, 63, 66, 82; and Mariposa grove preservation efforts, 4, 48–49, 52–55, 63; national pride in, 62–63; protection of, 80, 82–83, 113, 124, 232–33; tourism and, 63, 65; as unique natural wonder of California, 3, 62–63

Shaler, Robert, 25

Shasta Dam, 132

Shasta Lake, 132–33

Shoreline Planning Association, 90

Shultz, George, 223

Sierra Club, 14, 223; and coastline protections, 104, 106; as consumers of forest products, 67; and environmental ethos, 77; Hetch Hetchy water project supported by, 121–22; and Mono Lake, 146; as national environmental leader, 123; Pavley bill supported by, 202–3; Peripheral Canal opposed by, 142–43; and Redwood National Park, 76–80; and San Francisco Bay protection efforts, 100, 113; Save-the-Redwoods League contrasted with, 78–79; Yosemite and establishment of, 58–60

Sierra Forest Reserve, 64

Sierra Nevada Mountains, 3

Simon, Ted, 140

Smith River, 135

Smoke and Fumes Commission (LA), 153, 158–59

Snell, Bradford, 168

soil: hydraulic mining and erosion of, 35–36; and sedimentation, 35–36; toxic waste in, 36

solar power, 224; business opposition to, 210; incentives for investment in, 198–

200, 208, 210, 217, 218; net metering policy and, 199–200, 210, 218–19; residential, 199–200, 210, 218–19

Southern California Edison, 217

Southern California Gas Company, 158

Southern Pacific Railroad, 75, 82; and coastal redwood protection, 69; and sequoia protection, 64; and Yosemite, 61

Spanish Empire, 25

Spring Valley Water Company, 119, 120, 124

Stamp Out Smog (SOS), 166

Stanford, Leland, 35–36

Stanford Research Institute, 165

Stanislaus River, 136–37

Starr, Kevin, 3, 26, 51–52, 55, 62–63, 134

State Forestry Commission, 65–66, 233

State Lands Act, 74, 88–89, 92

State Lands Commission, 86, 114, 233

state parks, 48–49; Big Basin redwoods, 69; coastal redwoods protected in, 69–74; federal support and expansion of, 75–76; funding for, 61, 72–73, 88; land acquisition for, 72–78; and political controversies, 77–79; visitor statistics for, 74

State Parks Commission, 73–75, 233

State Water Pollution Control Board, 16

State Water Project, 133–34, 139–42, 149, 151

Stavins, Robert, 227

Stradling, David, 238

Strong, William, 162

Submerged Lands Act, 92

suburban sprawl, 19, 131

Suisan Bay, 35

Summerland Oil Field, 91–92

Sundesert nuclear power plant, 195

sustainability, 19–20

Sustainable Groundwater Management Act, 152

Sutro, Adolph, 39, 58–59

Swatt, Steve, 128

Swatt, Susie, 128

Tall Creek grove, 78

Tesla Motors, 15, 214–15, 229

tidelands: legal standards regarding use of, 104; oil development in, 92

Toulumne River, 57; Hetch Hetchy reservoir constructed on, 120

tourism, 3; and coastal redwoods, 80; Niagara Falls and, 53–54; and preservation of Yosemite, 52–54, 57; and railroads, 57; scenic attractions and, 3, 53–54, 69–70, 73, 82, 231, 243; sequoias and, 63, 65;

transportation and, 52–53; wilderness preservation and, 150–51; Yosemite and, 3, 51–52, 61
toxic wastes, 36–37
transportation: highways and freeways, 19, 76, 171; inland waterway, 37; railroads, 28; and tourism, 52–53. See also automobile industry
Treasure Island, 97
Treaty of Guadalupe Hidalgo, 26
Trump, Donald J., 8, 222, 224, 227, 239
Tucker, Robert, 161
Tulare Lake, 143
Twain, Mark, 34

Union of Concerned Scientists, 200, 202, 206
utility companies: CEC and regulation of, 191–93; CPUC and regulation of, 191–93; decoupling and, 5, 193; energy efficiency and conservation opposed by, 193; greenhouse gas emissions and, 213, 224–25; and growing demand for energy, 193, 197–98; and incentives for conservation, 197; and incentives for electric vehicles, 220; municipal water, 119–20; nuclear power, 110, 190, 195, 225; Pacific Gas & Electric, 199, 261; and power plant construction, 5, 10, 103, 153, 189, 190, 191, 193, 205, 228, 232; rates and cost to consumers of, 193, 198, 201, 210, 215–16, 220–21; and renewable energy sources, 5, 198–99, 207, 220–21, 224; San Diego Gas and Electric Company, 195

Vandever, William, 63
Vote Solar, 210

Walker, Richard, 13, 101
Warren, Charles, 192
Warren, Earl, 18, 162
Warren-Alquist Act of 1974, 191–92
water management systems: and aggressive management of water resources, 117–18, 232, 237; agricultural irrigation and, 10, 20, 33–34, 44, 130–36, 142, 148; aqueducts or ditches (see aqueducts); Boulder Canyon Project, 130–31; and construction costs, 126; dams and reservoirs (see dams and reservoirs); diminishing returns on investment in, 138; and drought, 138; federal support for, 130–31; and flood control, 41, 45–46, 131, 135–36; forest management and, 65; funding for, 128,

134, 138, 149; land acquisition for, 126–27; and location of water relative to demand, 115–17; opposition to, 120–23, 135–38, 140–42, 234; politics of, 148–51; and precipitation, 115, 125, 138, 139, 144; scope and impacts of, 147–49
water pollution, 16, 17, 39, 46, 96–102, 239, 241. See also oil spills
water resources: aggressive management of, 117–18, 232, 237; agriculture and, 10, 20, 33–34, 44, 115, 130–36, 142, 143, 148; aquifers/groundwater, 125, 126, 129, 131–32, 148, 152; climate change and, 10; competing demands for, 33, 141; and conservation measures, 152–53; demand for, 20–21, 32–34; economic growth and access to, 133–34, 237; gold mining and, 24; and hydropower generation, 120; infrastructure projects and management of (see water management systems); location of, 115–17; Native Americans and, 24; and pollution, 16, 17, 39, 46, 96–102, 239, 241 (see also oil spills); precipitation, 20, 32, 115–17, 125, 138, 139, 144, 152, 228; private users and, 152–53; regulation of, 152; rights to (see water rights); state management of (see water management systems); urban growth and, 70, 115, 118, 127, 128; watersheds, 57, 65, 149; wildlife and, 143
Water Resources Control Board, 16
water rights: California Doctrine and, 28–29; and doctrine of prior appropriation, 28; LA Aqueduct and, 125–26, 130; property rights and miner's control of, 28–30; and public trust value of resource, 146; and riparian law, 28, 40; state jurisdiction over, 46, 146, 152; State Water Project and, 141
watersheds: ecological protection and preservation of, 57; forest management and protection of, 65; lag in protection of, 149; "virtual," 148
weather. See climate, of California
Westbay Community Associates, 99
Western Climate Initiative, 261–62
Western Oil and Gas Association, 163, 165
Western States Petroleum Association, 208–9
wetlands: protection of, 103, 238; tidelands, 92, 104. See also Sacramento–San Joaquin Delta
wheat, 45

Wheeler, Benjamin, 60
wilderness: federal protection of, 75–80; as intrinsically valuable, 77, 103, 123, 137–38; Muir and value of, 57, 60, 81–82, 123; Progressive Era and utilitarian view of, 121; public opinion on, 123; Sierra Club and value of, 59, 76–77, 124; Theodore Roosevelt and conservation of, 60; tourism and, 150–51
Wilderness Act, 75
wildfires, 66; climate change and, 10, 200, 203, 205, 206, 228
wildlife: habitat restoration and, 144–45; hydraulic mining and destruction of, 37–38; Native Americans and, 24; oil spills and damage to, 94, 104; refuges for, 96, 101; and Sacramento–San Joaquin Delta, 139; and subsistence hunting, 38; water resources and, 143; wetland habitat destruction and, 103
Wild Rivers bill, 136
Wilson, Pete, 18, 112
Wilson, Richard, 136
Wilson, Woodrow, 122–23
wind energy, 198–99, 208, 224
"wise use" movement, 241–42

Woodruff, Edwards, 42–44
Woodruff v. North Bloomfield Mining and Gravel Company, 42–44
Worster, Donald, 56

Yellowstone National Park, 55, 56–57
Yosemite: business and preservation of, 52–53, 57; and early legislative protection efforts, 32–33; federal protection and stewardship of, 54–55, 60–61, 120; Mariposa sequoia grove in, 4, 48–49, 52–55, 63; Muir and, 48, 55–58; as national icon, 82; as National Park, 56–58, 60–61, 122; Native Americans of, 50–51; and preservation efforts, 48–49; as scenic wonder, 51–52; state control and protection of, 60–61; tourism and, 3, 51–52, 61. *See also* Hetch Hetchy reservoir
Young, C. C., 87
Yuba River, 35

zero-emissions vehicles (ZEVs), 182, 214–15, 225
Ziebarth, Marilyn, 43–44
Zond Corporation, 199
Zumwalt, Daniel, 64

Princeton Studies in American Politics:
Historical, International, and Comparative Perspectives
Ira Katznelson, Eric Schickler, Martin Shefter,
and Theda Skocpol, Series Editors

California Greenin': How the Golden State Became an Environmental Leader
by David Vogel

Building an American Empire: The Era of Territorial and Political Expansion
by Paul Frymer

Racial Realignment: The Transformation of American Liberalism, 1932–1965
by Eric Schickler

When Movements Anchor Parties: Electoral Alignments in American History
by Daniel Schlozman

Electing the Senate: Indirect Democracy before the Seventeenth Amendment
by Wendy J. Schiller and Charles Stewart III

The Substance of Representation: Congress, American Political Development, and
Lawmaking by John S. Lapinski

Looking for Rights in All the Wrong Places: Why State Constitutions Contain America's
Positive Rights by Emily Zackin

Paths Out of Dixie: The Democratization of Authoritarian Enclaves in America's Deep
South, 1944–1972 by Robert Mickey

Fighting for the Speakership: The House and the Rise of Party Government
by Jeffery A. Jenkins and Charles Stewart III

Three Worlds of Relief: Race, Immigration, and the American Welfare State from the
Progressive Era to the New Deal by Cybelle Fox

Building the Judiciary: Law, Courts, and the Politics of Institutional Development
by Justin Crowe

Still a House Divided: Race and Politics in Obama's America by Desmond S. King and
Rogers M. Smith

The Litigation State: Public Regulations and Private Lawsuits in the United States
  by Sean Farhang

*Reputation and Power: Organizational Image and Pharmaceutical Regulation
  at the FDA* by Daniel Carpenter

Presidential Party Building: Dwight D. Eisenhower to George W. Bush
  by Daniel J. Galvin

*Fighting for Democracy: Black Veterans and the Struggle against White Supremacy
  in the Postwar South* by Christopher S. Parker

The Fifth Freedom: Jobs, Politics, and Civil Rights in the United States, 1941–1972
  by Anthony Chen

Reforms at Risk: What Happens after Major Policy Changes Are Enacted
  by Eric Patashnik

The Rise of the Conservative Legal Movement: The Long Battle for Control of the Law
  by Steven M. Teles

Why Is There No Labor Party in the United States? by Robin Archer

*Black and Blue: African Americans, the Labor Movement, and the Decline
  of the Democratic Party* by Paul Frymer

*Political Foundations of Judicial Supremacy: The Presidency, the Supreme Court,
  and Constitutional Leadership in U.S. History* by Keith E. Whittington

*The Transformation of American Politics: Activist Government and the Rise
  of Conservatism* edited by Paul Pierson and Theda Skocpol

Disarmed: The Missing Movement for Gun Control in America
  by Kristin A. Goss

Filibuster: Obstruction and Lawmaking in the U.S. Senate
  by Gregory J. Wawro and Eric Schickler

Governing the American State: Congress and the New Federalism
  by Kimberley S. Johnson

*What a Mighty Power We Can Be: African American Fraternal Groups and the
  Struggle for Racial Equality* by Theda Skocpol, Ariane Liazos, and Marshall Ganz

When Movements Matter: The Townsend Plan and the Rise of Social Security
  by Edwin Amenta

Shaping Race Policy: The United States in Comparative Perspective
  by Robert C. Lieberman

How Policies Make Citizens: Senior Political Activism and the American Welfare State
  by Andrea Louise Campbell

Dividing Lines: The Politics of Immigration Control in America by Daniel J. Tichenor

*Managing the President's Program: Presidential Leadership and Legislative Policy
  Formulation* by Andrew Rudalevige

Shaped by War and Trade: International Influences on American Political Development
edited by Ira Katznelson and Martin Shefter

Dry Bones Rattling: Community Building to Revitalize American Democracy
by Mark R. Warren

Disjointed Pluralism: Institutional Innovation and the Development of the U.S. Congress
by Eric Schickler

*The Forging of Bureaucratic Autonomy: Reputations, Networks, and Policy Innovations
in Executive Agencies, 1862–1928* by Daniel P. Carpenter

*The Rise of the Agricultural Welfare State: Institutions and Interest Group Power
in the United States, France, and Japan* by Adam D. Sheingate

*In the Shadow of the Garrison State: America's Anti-Statism and Its Cold War Grand
Strategy* by Aaron L. Friedberg

Stuck in Neutral: Business and the Politics of Human Capital Investment Policy
by Cathie Jo Martin

Uneasy Alliances: Race and Party Competition in America by Paul Frymer

Faithful and Fearless: Moving Feminist Protest inside the Church and Military
by Mary Fainsod Katzenstein

*Forged Consensus: Science, Technology, and Economic Policy in the United States,
1921–1953* by David M. Hart

*Parting at the Crossroads: The Emergence of Health Insurance in the United States and
Canada* by Antonia Maioni

Bold Relief: Institutional Politics and the Origins of Modern American Social Policy
by Edwin Amenta

The Hidden Welfare State: Tax Expenditures and Social Policy in the United States
by Christopher Howard

Morning Glories: Municipal Reform in the Southwest by Amy Bridges

Imperiled Innocents: Anthony Comstock and Family Reproduction in Victorian America
by Nicola Beisel

The Road to Nowhere: The Genesis of President Clinton's Plan for Health Security
by Jacob Hacker

The Origins of the Urban Crisis: Race and Inequality in Postwar Detroit
by Thomas J. Sugrue

Party Decline in America: Policy, Politics, and the Fiscal State
by John J. Coleman

*The Power of Separation: American Constitutionalism and the Myth of the Legislative
Veto* by Jessica Korn

*Why Movements Succeed or Fail: Opportunity, Culture, and the Struggle for Woman
Suffrage* by Lee Ann Banaszak

Kindred Strangers: The Uneasy Relationship between Politics and Business in America
    by David Vogel

From the Outside In: World War II and the American State
    by Bartholomew H. Sparrow

Classifying by Race edited by Paul E. Peterson

Facing Up to the American Dream: Race, Class, and the Soul of the Nation
    by Jennifer L. Hochschild

Political Organizations by James Q. Wilson

Social Policy in the United States: Future Possibilities in Historical Perspective
    by Theda Skocpol

Experts and Politicians: Reform Challenges to Machine Politics in New York, Cleveland, and Chicago by Kenneth Finegold

Bound by Our Constitution: Women, Workers, and the Minimum Wage
    by Vivien Hart

Prisoners of Myth: The Leadership of the Tennessee Valley Authority, 1933–1990
    by Erwin C. Hargrove

Political Parties and the State: The American Historical Experience
    by Martin Shefter

Politics and Industrialization: Early Railroads in the United States and Prussia
    by Colleen A. Dunlavy

The Lincoln Persuasion: Remaking American Liberalism
    by J. David Greenstone

Labor Visions and State Power: The Origins of Business Unionism in the United States
    by Victoria C. Hattam

A NOTE ON THE TYPE

This book has been composed in Adobe Text and Gotham.
Adobe Text, designed by Robert Slimbach for Adobe,
bridges the gap between fifteenth- and sixteenth-century
calligraphic and eighteenth-century Modern styles.
Gotham, inspired by New York street signs, was designed
by Tobias Frere-Jones for Hoefler & Co.